Profile of
21st Century English Teachers' Association of Korea

I. A Brief History of 21st C.E.T.A.

21st Century English Teachers' Association of Korea (21st C.E.T.A.) was first promoted by 21 English teachers in high school at Seogang University in Korea on August 14, 1996.

Since March 1, 1997, whoever teaches English in elementary, middle school and high school, and universities in Korea could have joined our association.

At present, 189 English teachers in 148 elementary, middle, and high schools, and universities located in Seoul, Gyunggi province and Incheon Metropolitan city are working together for contributing to improve English education and educational realities in Korea.

Most of the members maintain a tradition of personal attention to students and devotion to research. Some eminent professors for our alma maters are giving advice and suggestion for our association.

II. Objective

The objective of our association is as follows :
(1) to help Korean students and Asian students expand their viewpoint internationally by extensive understanding of foreign culture and to cultivate their abilities to use foreign language
(2) to research into theories on general English education including English teaching methods and to develop English teaching materials
(3) to translate and to publish cultural books and English reference books for students
(4) to produce a bilingual edition of valuable Eastern and Western classics and English comic books as a guide to good and intellectual life
(5) to award scholarships to students
(6) to protect and advocate English teachers' right and interest
(7) to promote mutual friendship among English teachers

III. Association and Location

Our association holds regular general meetings every third Friday as well as project meetings as required. All members are encouraged to actively participate in discussions related to the association's activities. Membership into the 21st C.E.T.A is open to all English teachers in Korea and Asian countries, and those in the community who have a strong interest in improving English education in Korea and Asian countries. In regard to our objective related to procuring high quality material, we make ourselves open to receive suggestions, manuscripts, and research papers from the public. For those who send us manuscripts, we will review them and if we find them acceptable we will contact you to discuss payment. If you have any inquiries about our organization, please don't hesitate to contact us using the address below.

21ˢᵗ Century English Teachers' Association of Korea (21世紀 英語敎育硏究會)

Chairman Jeong Seung-Nam Ph. D. (English teacher, Daesung High School, Seoul, Korea)

Address: 2nd Floor, 444-57, Bulkwang 2-dong, Eunpyung-gu, Seoul, 122-863, KOREA.
Phone: 82-2-386-4802, 384-3348 / Mobile: 82-10-8357-2230
Fax: 82-2-384-3348
E-mail: ceta211@yahoo.com / ceta21@hanmail.net
Blog : http://blog.daum.net/ceta21
Web-site : www.ceta21.com / www.stamford.co.kr

As all of our members are involved in English education, we are confident that we can greatly contribute to English education in Korea. Our activities have received coverage in the Korean press, the Malaysian press, the Singaporean press, the Canadian press and the Australian press, etc.

IV. Association's Activities

Members of 21ˢᵗ C.E.T.A. are divided into subgroups to more effectively carry out the following activities:

(1) Development of grade-specific programs and teaching materials which will enhance student
    English conversation skill and listening ability.
(2) Research into English testing methods with emphasis on improvement, reliability, applicability, and relevance
(3) Research into utilization of the Internet as a viable English teaching tool inside the classroom.
(4) Development of various English reading materials, English reference books, English course books, English comic book series which will motivate and captivate students
(5) Due to lots of success of educational trip to overseas countries such as Malaysia, Canada, Singapore, Hongkong, Taiwan, Australia, America, the United Kingdom, Switzerland, Austria, and China, our association is committed to making it a tradition to regularly visit the Education Ministries of various countries. Our policy is to keep our minds open and to broaden our awareness of global education trends.

Each member will be put into the appropriate subgroup where his/her major and expertise may be best utilized.

V. Publishing Activities

Our association have been publishing over 410 volumes related to English education and general knowledge, etc. through more than 30 publishing companies in Korea and 13 publishing companies in the world. We have been publishing various *English Story Books* and *World's Greatest Works of Literature(Western Classics) Comic Book Series* (western classics), *World Famous Fairy Tales Comic Book Series*, *World Eminent People Comic Book Series* written in English. The collection includes the 'Treasure Island', 'Moby Dick', 'Gulliver's Travels', 'The Jungle Book', and 'Robinson Crusoe', 'Romeo and Juliet', 'The War of the Worlds', etc.

Our members are also actively working together to develop high quality English study material for primary, middle, and high school students.

VI. Privileges exclusive to members

Those who become 21st C.E.T.A.'s members will be have following privileges available to them.
(1) Full access to 21st C.E.T.A.'s collection of Graduate School test and essay materials
(2) Full access to 21st C.E.T.A.'s library of information and materials useful for English class preparation
(3) Free subscription to all 21st C.E.T.A. publications
(4) Be a recipient of 21st C.E.T.A.'s profit allocation programs
(5) Partial or full financial support for overseas training trips

The references owned by 21st C.E.T.A. are as follows:
(1) Over 1,000 English related research papers
(2) Summaries, abstracts, and tests related to education graduate schools
(3) Over 1,000 English related books including English literature, linguistics, grammar, teaching method, history, syntax, and theory
(4) Over 50,000 general books written in English including literature, science, philosophy, sociology, universe, education, environment, fairy tales, folk tales, world history, culture, general knowledge and common sense, etc.

VII. Our Vision

Our association will use our role as educators to encourage 'Korea's and Asian next generation' to pursue higher learning, to respect intellectual curiosity, to seek true courage and to be visionary leaders. We would also like to develop effective teaching methods, to make high quality study books, and to continue publishing entertaining and educational bilingual comic books.

We have a deep interest in your opinion and look forward to receiving your feedback. We will always strive to improve our personal qualities, to increase our capabilities, to produce world class teaching materials and to be the best teachers possible.

Special Guide

한 권으로 끝내는 초 중 고
필수 영문법(구문) 사전

영문법을 수학 공식처럼 체계적으로 공부한다!

21세기 영어교육연구회
(21st C.E.T.A.)

Essential
English Grammar

청어

한 권으로 끝내는 초·중·고등학교
필수 영문법(구문) 사전

21세기 영어교육연구회 지음

발행처 · 도서출판 **청어**
발행인 · 이영철
기   획 · 최윤영 | 김홍순
영   업 · 이동호
편   집 · 김영신 | 방세화
디자인 · 오주연
제작부장 · 공병한
인   쇄 · 두리터

등   록 · 1999년 5월 3일(제22-1541호)

1판 1쇄 인쇄 · 2010년 11월 10일
1판 1쇄 발행 · 2010년 11월 18일

주소 · 서울시 서초구 서초동 1588-1 신성빌딩 A동 412호
대표전화 · 586-0477
팩시밀리 · 586-0478

블로그 · http://blog.naver.com/ppi20
E-mail · ppi20@hanmail.net
ISBN · 978-89-94638-09-6 (93740)

Special Guide

한 권으로 끝내는 초 중 고
필수 영문법(구문) 사전

21세기 영어교육연구회
(21st C.E.T.A.)

머리말 ●

   영문법을 공부한다는 것은 매우 흥미롭고 재미있는 일이지만, 아차하면 자질 구레하고 재미없는 것만 따지거나 그저 문법 규칙을 외우다 보면 흥미를 잃고 싫증이 나고, 영문법 공부가 지루하고 따분해진다. 따라서, 영문법을 수학 공식 처럼 보다 체계적으로 정리한다면, 자연스럽게 영문법이 어떻게 형성되었으며 어떻게 변하였는지 이해하기 쉽게 된다. 특히 영어를 모국어로 사용하는 사람들 의 영어적 사고방식(English Mind)과 그들의 풍속과 언어적 습성을 자연스럽 게 이해할 수 있다. 실용적인 영문법을 익히고, 부끄럽지 않은 표준적인 영문법 을 익히기 위해서, 이 책은 필수 영어 문법과 구문의 내용을 그 각각의 용법과 더불어 유기적으로 학습하여, 영어 독해 및 표현 능력을 향상시킬 수 있도록 구 성했다.

   이 책은 초·중·고등학교 및 대학교 학생과 일반인이 쉽게 학습할 수 있도록 필수 영어 문법과 구문의 핵심 내용을 주제별로 24개 항목으로 망라했으며, 항 목별로 가능한 한 풍부한 예문과 해설을 체계적으로 제시함으로써 그 의미를 충 분히 이해할 수 있도록 구성했다.

   특히, 이 책은 21세기 영어교육연구회(21st C.E.T.A.) 선생님들이 영어를 공 부하고 학생들을 가르치면서 틈틈이 모아 두었던 영문법(English Grammar) 자료를 정리·요약하여 집필한 것이다. 한편으로는 감개무량한 보람과 긍지를 느끼면서 또 한편으로는 부족함으로 실망과 자괴심이 어우러진 힘든 작업이었 다. 이 책은 방대하고 난해한 영문법을 가능한 한 이해하기 쉽게 체계적이며, 압 축적으로 정리함으로써 학생들의 부담을 줄이고, 어떠한 영문독해도 학생 스스 로 공부하여 영어를 바르게 구사하고 이해하면서 쉽게 활용할 수 있도록 구성하 였다.

이 책의 특징을 요약해 보면 다음과 같다.

첫째, 학생들이 학습할 때 여러 영문법 책이나 구문집 및 참고서를 동시에 참조해야 하는 불편을 제거하고 쉽게 찾고 이해할 수 있도록 사전화(辭典化)했다. 즉 마치 수학 공식을 공부하듯이, 어느 한 문법상황이나 구문을 찾으면 그 문장의 변형과 자세한 예문이 그 밑에 상세한 설명과 함께 분석·비교되어 있다.

둘째, 출제 빈도가 높고 반드시 알아야 할 핵심 문법 사항과 구문을 24개 항목의 소제목(Sub-title)으로 나누어 한눈에 쉽게 들어오도록 체계적으로 시각화(Visualize)했다.

셋째, 수험생에게 과다한 부담을 주는 내용은 가능한 한 총 집약하여 쉽게 풀어 설명했다.

넷째, 초등학교, 중학교는 물론 고등학생들의 대학수학능력시험·학교내신·TOEFL·TOEIC·IELTS·'A' Level Test에 대한 대비와 더불어 영문법에 대한 확실한 이해와 자신감을 얻을 수 있도록 쉽게 설명했다.

다섯째, 영문법의 기본 문형을 제시하고 이에 대한 예제를 주·객관식으로 고루 섞어 다양하게 제시했으며, 〈종합 평가 문제〉를 실어 자신의 실력을 자가 진단하고 각종 시험에 대비할 수 있도록 구성했다.

21세기 영어교육연구회

회장 **정 승 남**

차례 contents

Chapter 1

문장의 구성요소(Sentence Structure)

01 영어 모음 도표(The Chart of English Vowel Phonemes) ·········· 18
02 영어 자음 도표(The Chart of English Consonant Phonemes) ······· 19
03 문장(Sentence)의 분류 ·········· 20
04 구조(構造:Structure)에 의한 분류 ·········· 21
05 문장의 구성요소와 5형식 ·········· 24
06 대표적 불완전 자동사 ·········· 25
07 유사보어(類似補語) : 추가보어(追加補語) ·········· 25
08 자동사로 혼동하기 쉬운 타동사(3형식 동사) ·········· 28
09 수여동사(4형식)로 혼동하기 쉬운 완전 타동사(3형식 동사) ···· 29
10 동족목적어(Cognate Object)의 표현 ·········· 30
11 3형식으로 혼동하기 쉬운 수여동사(4형식 동사) ·········· 31
12 ┌ S(주어) + 수여동사 + I.O.(간접 목적어) + D.O.(간접 목적어)[4형식]
　　└ S(주어) + 수여동사 + D.O.(간접 목적어) + 전치사 + I.O.(간접 목적어)[3형식]32
13 4형식과 5형식의 구별 방법 ·········· 33

Chapter 2

명사(Noun)와 대명사(Pronoun)

01 명사(名詞 : Noun) ·········· 35
02 명사의 성(性 : Gender) [국가를 나타낼 때] ·········· 38
03 명사의 성(性) ·········· 38
04 복합 명사(Compound Noun) ·········· 39
05 복합 명사의 복수 ·········· 40
06 단·복수 동형어(同形語) ·········· 41
07 절대 복수 ·········· 41
08 분화 복수(의미가 다른 단수와 복수) ·········· 42
09 외래어 복수 ·········· 43
10 물질 명사나 추상 명사의 단위 표시 ·········· 44
11 쌍을 이루는 물건을 나타내는 명사 ·········· 45
12 전치사(with, by, in, on. to to) + 추상 명사 = 부사 ·········· 45
13 of + 추상 명사 = 형용사 ·········· 46
14 all + 추상 명사 = very(extremely) + 형용사 (매우 ~한) ·········· 46
15 부정대명사(Indefinite Pronoun) ·········· 47
16 부정 대명사 one과 지시 대명사 It ·········· 48
17 부정 대명사 one을 사용하지 못하는 경우 ·········· 49
18 부정 대명사 one의 주의해야 할 용법 ·········· 49
19 the + 형용사 = 복수 보통 명사 ·········· 52

20 the + 형용사 = 추상 명사 ·························· 52
21 재귀 대명사 oneself의 용법 ·························· 53
22 It ·························· 55
23 이중 소유격(Double Genitive) ·························· 61
24 소유격 의미 ·························· 62
25 So와 Neither ·························· 62
26 To + one's + great + 감정을 나타내는 추상 명사(~하게도) ·························· 64
27 A of B = B like A (A와 같은 B) ·························· 65
28 Everything, Something, Nothing ·························· 65
29 S(주어) + V(동사) + a(n) + 형용사 + 명사(사람)~ ·························· 66

Chapter 3
동사(Verb)와 시제(Tense)

01 과거의 동작의 결과가 현재에 남아 있음을 나타내는 현재완료 (have + p.p.) ·· 69
02 S(주어) + have + P.P. + since + 주어 + P(과거동사) ·························· 69
03 become과 come to (~이 되다) ·························· 70
04 make it ·························· 70
05 read / go / run (~라고 쓰여 있다) ·························· 71
06 occur to / strike / hit upon (생각이 문득 떠오르다) ·························· 72
07 wear와 put on의 차이 ·························· 72
08 see와 look의 혼동 ·························· 73
09 remember와 remind의 혼동 ·························· 73
10 sleep과 go to bed의 혼동 ·························· 73
11 know와 learn의 혼동 ·························· 74
12 learn과 study의 혼동 ·························· 74
13 care for와 take care of의 혼동 ·························· 75
14 fall과 fell의 혼동 ·························· 75

Chapter 4
동명사(Gerund)

01 cannot help~ing (~ing 하지 않을 수 없다) ·························· 78
02 It is no use~ing (~ing 해 보아도 아무 소용없다) ·························· 78
03 There is no~ing (~ing 할 수 없다) ·························· 79
04 On~ing (~ing 하자마자 곧) ·························· 79
05 In~ing = When + S(주어) + V(동사) ·························· 80
06 of one's own ~ ing (자신이 손수 ~ing 한) ·························· 80

07 feel like ~ ing (~ing 하고 싶다 ; ~ing 할 마음이 생기다) 80
08 What do you say to ~ ing (~ing 하지 않으시렵니까?) 81
09 be worth ~ ing (~ing 할 가치가 있다) 82
10 It goes without saying that + S(주어) + V(동사) 82
11 come near ~ ing 83
12 be(get) used to ~ ing 84
13 be on the point of ~ ing 85
14 be far from ~ ing 85
15 S(주어) + cannot + V(동사) ⓐ without ⓑ + ing 86
16 There is no + N(명사) + but + V(동사) ~ 86
17 S + be busy (in) ~ ing (~ 하느라 바쁘다) 87
18 S(사물) + want / need + V(동사) + ing(능동대명사) 88
19 go ~ ing (~ing 하러 가다) 89
20 look forward to ~ ing (~ing를 갈망하다, 학수고대하다.) 89
21 S(주어) + have + a hard time + (in) ~ ing 90
22 S(주어) + lose no time + in ~ ing 90
23 S(주어) + kill time ~ ing (~하며 시간을 보내다) 90
24 S(무생물 주어) + prevent + ⓐ(목적어) from ~ ing 91
25 S(주어) + be opposed to ~ ing (~ing를 반대하다) 92
26 contribute to ~ ing (~ing에 공헌하다) 92
27 turn one' s attention to ~ ing (~ing에 주의를 돌리다, ~ing에 관심을 갖다) 92
28 with a view to ~ ing (~ing 하기 위하여) 92
29 for fear of ~ ing (~ing 하지 않기 위하여) 93
30 S(주어) + be equal to ~ ing (~ing 할 능력이 있다) 93
31 S(주어) + devote + ⓐ + to ~ ing (~ing에 열중하다) 94
32 take to ~ ing (~ing에 빠지다) 94
33 fall to ~ ing (~ing을 시작하다) 94
34 S(주어) + be + 형용사 + 전치사(of, for, at) ~ ing 95
35 동격명사절 : 추상명사 + that + S + V ~ = 추상명사 + of + ~ ing ~ 96
36 S(주어) + V(동사) + 목적어 + of + 명사(구) ~ 97
37 S(주어) + V(동사) + 전치사(of, on, at) ~ ing ~ 98
38 S(주어) + remember ~ ing 99
39 S(주어) + forget ~ ing 100
40 S(주어) + try ~ ing / S(주어) + try + to 부정사 100

부정사(Infinitive)

01 S(주어) + remember + to 부정사 ~ 102
02 S(주어) + forget + to 부정사 ~ 102
03 S(주어) + be sure to + V(동사) ~ 103

04 가주어(형식 주어)/진주어 (It ~ to + ⓥ) ································· 104
05 가목적어/진목적어 ··· 104
06 의문사 + to 부정사 [명사구] ··· 105
07 be + to 부정사 [예정] ·· 106
08 be + to 부정사 [의무, 당연] ··· 107
09 be + to 부정사 [가능] ·· 107
10 be + to 부정사 [운명] ·· 107
11 If + S(주어) + be + to 부정사 [의도, 소망] ······························· 107
12 be + to 부정사 [명령, 필연] ·· 108
13 부정사의 부사적 용법 ··· 108
14 so ~ as to + V(동사) / enough to + V(동사) ····························· 112
15 S(주어) + V(동사) + too ~ to 부정사 ······································· 112
16 S(주어) + V(동사) + too + 형용사/부사 + for + N(명사) ················· 113
17 S(주어) + V(동사) + too ~ not to 부정사 ·································· 114
18 S(주어) + V(동사) + not too ~ to 부정사 ·································· 114
19 부정주어(No,Not) + so ~ but that ·· 114
20 S(주어) + V(동사) + only too ~ to 부정사 ································· 115
21 Hope와 to 부정사와의 관계 ·· 115
22 문장의 일부를 대신 받는 〈so〉와 〈to〉 ····································· 116
23 S(주어) have only to + V(동사) ~ ··· 117
24 You do nothing but + V(동사원형) ~ ·· 119
25 It takes + 시간(기간) + to 부정사 ~ ·· 119
26 It costs + 돈(금액) + to 부정사 ~ ·· 119
27 S(주어) + have + the + 추상 명사 + to 부정사 ···························· 120
28 hope [want, wish, expect, intend, promise…]+단순 부정사=미래의 일 ······ 121
29 hoped/wanted + 완료형 부정사(to have + p.p.) ···························· 121
30 It + V(동사) + 형용사 + for + 목적격(사람) + to 부정사 ~ ··············· 123
31 It is + difficult / easy + for + 목적격(사람) + to 부정사 ~ ············· 124
32 It is + likely + that + S(주어) + V(동사) ~ ······························· 125
33 It is + good / bad / kind + of + 목적격(사람) + to 부정사 ~ ············· 126
34 You may come tomorrow if it is convenient to(for) you. ··············· 126
35 사역동사(使役動詞) ··· 127
36 have / get + 목적어(사물) + p.p.(과거분사) ································· 129
37 지각동사(知覺動詞) ··· 130
38 to 부정사만을 목적어로 받는 타동사 ·· 133
39 동명사만을 목적어로 받는 타동사 ··· 134
40 동명사 to 부정사 양쪽을 다 목적어로 받는 동사 ···························· 135

분사구문(Participial Construction)

01 분사구문(分詞構文 : Participial Construction) 137
02 (부사절을) 분사구문으로 고치는 방식(복문=>단문) 137
03 분사구문 작성상의 주의 사항 139
04 분사구문의 종류 140
05 분사구문의 강조 143
06 무인칭 독립분사 143
07 부대 상황을 나타내는 with 144
08 분사의 형용사화 146
09 의사분사(擬似 分詞) : 복합 형용사 148

조동사(Auxiliary Verb)

01 S(주어) + will + have + p.p 153
02 S(주어) + may + have + p.p 153
03 S(주어) + must + have + p.p 154
04 S(주어) + cannot + have + p.p 154
05 S(주어) + need not have + p.p 155
06 S(주어) + should + have + p.p 156
07 S(주어) + could have + p.p 157
08 S(주어) + may well + V(동사원형) ~ 157
09 S(주어) + may as well + V(동사원형) ~ 158
10 S(주어) + may as well A as B 158
11 would rather A than B 158
12 lest ~ should 159
13 can ~ / be able to + V 159
14 Used to 와 Would 160
15 S(주어) + cannot + V(동사) ~ too + 형용사/부사 162
16 미래시제 will, shall 의 용법 166

태(態:Voice => 수동태/능동태)

01 수동태의 형식과 시제 171
02 태(態)의 전환 173
03 부정문의 수동태 175
04 조동사가 있는 수동태 175
05 명령문의 수동태 176

06 의문문의 수동태 ──────────────────────── 176
07 목적어가 that절인 경우의 수동태 ───────────── 177
08 부정주어 능동태의 수동태로의 전환 ────────── 180
09 동작 수동태와 상태 수동태 ──────────────── 181
10 동사구의 수동태 ─────────────────────── 181
11 by ~의 생략 ───────────────────────── 182
12 by 이외의 전치사를 사용하는 경우 ─────────── 183
13 기타 문장 중의 수동태 ──────────────────── 184

Chapter 9
가정법(Subjunctive Mood)

01 현재시제의 미래시제 대용(代用:대신 쓰이는 경우) ──────── 187
02 명령문 + and / or ───────────────────── 188
03 otherwise + S + 가정법 과거 ───────────── 189
04 otherwise + S + 가정법 과거완료 ──────────── 189
05 But for / Without + N(명사), 가정법 과거 ─────── 190
06 But for / Without + N(명사), 가정법 과거 완료 ──── 191
07 It is (high/about) time + that + S(주어) + 과거동사 ── 191
08 I wish가 이끄는 가정법 문장 ───────────────── 192
09 as if + S(주어) + 과거동사 ~ (가정법 과거) ──────── 194
10 as if + S(주어) + had + p.p.~ (가정법 과거완료) ──── 194
11 In cause(that) + S(주어) + V(직설법 현재동사) ────── 195
12 Provide(that) + S(주어) + V(직설법 현재동사) ────── 196
13 S(주어) + V(제안/충고/주장/요구) + that + 주어 + (should) + 동사 ~ ── 197
14 조건절 대용어구(전치사일 때) ───────────────── 200
15 조건절 대용어구(단어:명사구일 때) ───────────── 201
16 조건절 대용어구(접속사 I) ─────────────────── 201
17 조건절 대용어구(접속사 II) ────────────────── 202
18 조건절 대용어구(부정사일 때) ──────────────── 203
19 조건절 대용어구(형용사절/분사구문) ─────────── 204
20 가정법의 관용어구 ───────────────────────── 204
21 Once(접속사) + S(주어)+ V(동사) ~ , S′ + V′ ⋯ ───── 205

Chapter 10
화법(話法:Narration)

01 전달동사 Say 와 Tell ───────────────────── 207
02 화법의 기본 형태와 종류 ────────────────────── 207
03 직접화법을 간접화법으로 전환할 때 변화하는 것 ──── 209

04 피전달문이 평서문(서술문)인 경우 ·· 211
05 단순 미래와 의지 미래의 화법 ·· 211
06 피전달문이 의문문인 경우의 간접화법 ·· 214
07 피전달문이 기원문인 경우의 간접화법 ·· 215
08 피전달문이 명령문인 경우의 간접화법 ·· 216
09 피전달문이 감탄문인 경우의 간접화법 ·· 217
10 관용적 용법의 화법 ·· 218
11 특수한 경우의 화법 ·· 219
12 피전달문이 and, but, or 등으로 연결된 중문(重文)인 경우의 화법 ··· 220
13 접속사가 for, as인 경우의 화법 ·· 221
14 「명령문, and(or) + S(주어)+ V(동사)…」의 경우의 화법 ·············· 221
15 피전달문이 접속사 없이 여러 개의 문장으로 연결되어 있는 화법 ··· 222
16 묘출화법과 혼합화법 ·· 222

Chapter 11 관계 대명사(Relative Pronoun)

01 관계 대명사 ··· 226
02 관계 대명사의 종류 ·· 227
03 소유격 관계 대명사 ·· 228
04 선행사 + 관계 대명사 ·· 229
05 선행사 + to 부정사 ··· 229
06 N(명사) + to 부정사 ·· 230
07 관계 대명사 + to 부정사 ··· 231
08 관계 대명사와 전치사의 위치 ··· 233
09 의사 관계 대명사(as / but) ··· 233
10 관계 형용사 What ··· 235
11 복합 관계 형용사 ··· 236
12 복합 관계사 ··· 236
13 관계 대명사 what ·· 238
14 what he is (his character) / what he has (his wealth) ················· 239
15 A is to B what (as) C is to D ·· 240
16 what we call ··· 241
17 what with A and what with B ·· 241

Chapter 12 관계 부사(Relative Adverbs)

01 관계 부사 ··· 243
02 관계 부사의 종류 ··· 244

접속사(Conjunction)와 절(節:Clause)

01 and의 주의할 용법 248
02 neither A nor B 248
03 nor와 neither의 구별 249
04 상관접속사의 인칭과 수(단수/복수)의 일치 250
05 now that/Seeing that/In that/On the ground that 250
06 at once A and B 252
07 not A until B 253
08 양보 부사절의 접속사 254
09 양보 부사절 255
10 부사절·부사구의 여러 형태 256
11 owing partly to A and partly to B 256
12 as it is 257
13 As(so) long as 와 As(so) far as 257
14 명령문형의 양보부사절 261
15 부정(否定)의 전이(轉移) (Transferred Negation) 264

형용사(Adjective)

01 be similar to ~ 266
02 나이(연령) 표현 방법 266
03 S(주어) + V(동사) + 배수사(N times) + 비교급 + 도량형 형용사
    + than + 명사 267
04 prefer A(동명사) to B(동명사) 269
05 비교급 + than ~ (우등비교) 270
06 less + 원급 + than ~ (열등비교) 270
07 비례 비교급[the(관계 부사) + 비교급 ~ the(지시부사) + 비교급…] ... 270
08 양보(even)의 뜻을 가진 최상급 271
09 no more than / not more than 272
10 no less than / not less than 273
11 no more A than B 273
12 no less ~ than / not less ~ than 274
13 원급으로 사용되는 관용어구 274
14 동일인, 동일물의 비교 275
15 최상급을 표시하는 원급·비교급 276
16 S(주어) + V(동사) + as + 형용사 원급 + as + any + 단수 명사 ... 277
17 S(주어) + know better than to 부정사 ~ 278
18 much(still) more / much(still) less 279
19 the + 비교급 + of the two + (명사) 279
20 형용사의 직유적 비유 표현[as ~ as 비유법(Simile)] 280

21 고유 형용사 ·· 282
22 한정사(限定詞 : Determiner) ···································· 283
23 전치한정(前置限定) 형용사가 두 개 이상일 때의 어순 ·········· 284

Chapter 15 부사(Adverb)

01 뜻을 구별해야 할 주요 부사 ······································ 286
02 부사 already, yet, still ··· 287
03 on earth / in the world ·· 288
04 Here you are 와 Here it is ···································· 290

Chapter 16 관사(Article)

01 관사의 생략 ··· 292
02 관사의 유무에 따라 달라지는 표현 ····························· 294
03 관사의 위치 ··· 295

Chapter 17 의문 대명사(Interrogative Pronoun)

01 Who와 Whom ·· 298
02 Whoever와 Whomever의 구별 ······························· 301
03 What과 How의 선택 ·· 302
04 What과 Which의 선택 ··· 304
05 수사(修辭) 의문문 ··· 304
06 간접 의문문 ·· 306

Chapter 18 전치사(Preposition)

01 장소를 나타내는 전치사 ·· 309
02 제공·위탁·선사·부여를 나타내는 with ······················· 310
03 유도·행동의 방향을 나타내는 into, out of ················· 312
04 제거를 나타내는 of ··· 314
05 수단을 나타내는 by와 with ······································ 317
06 교통 수단을 나타내는 by ··· 317

07 통신수단을 나타내는 by ⋯⋯⋯⋯⋯⋯⋯⋯⋯⋯⋯⋯⋯⋯⋯⋯ 318
08 차이를 나타내는 by ⋯⋯⋯⋯⋯⋯⋯⋯⋯⋯⋯⋯⋯⋯⋯⋯⋯⋯ 318
09 계량의 단위를 나타내는 by ⋯⋯⋯⋯⋯⋯⋯⋯⋯⋯⋯⋯⋯⋯ 319
10 주어가 바뀔때 주의해야 할 표현 ⋯⋯⋯⋯⋯⋯⋯⋯⋯⋯ 319
11 결과의 전치사 to ⋯⋯⋯⋯⋯⋯⋯⋯⋯⋯⋯⋯⋯⋯⋯⋯⋯⋯⋯ 320
12 타동사 + 목적어 + 전치사 + the + 신체의 일부 ⋯ 322
13 but/except/save + to 부정사 ⋯⋯⋯⋯⋯⋯⋯⋯⋯⋯⋯⋯ 323
14 to the north와 in the north ⋯⋯⋯⋯⋯⋯⋯⋯⋯⋯⋯⋯ 325
15 접촉의 전치사 on ⋯⋯⋯⋯⋯⋯⋯⋯⋯⋯⋯⋯⋯⋯⋯⋯⋯⋯ 326
16 beyond를 이용한 관용어구 ⋯⋯⋯⋯⋯⋯⋯⋯⋯⋯⋯⋯⋯ 327
17 전치사 with ⋯⋯⋯⋯⋯⋯⋯⋯⋯⋯⋯⋯⋯⋯⋯⋯⋯⋯⋯⋯⋯ 328

Chapter
19
특수 구문(삽입 · 공통관계 · 부정 · 도치 · 강조 · 생략)

01 삽입절 ⋯⋯⋯⋯⋯⋯⋯⋯⋯⋯⋯⋯⋯⋯⋯⋯⋯⋯⋯⋯⋯⋯⋯⋯ 333
02 공통 관계 ⋯⋯⋯⋯⋯⋯⋯⋯⋯⋯⋯⋯⋯⋯⋯⋯⋯⋯⋯⋯⋯⋯ 333
03 부분 부정과 전체 부정 ⋯⋯⋯⋯⋯⋯⋯⋯⋯⋯⋯⋯⋯⋯⋯ 334
04 부정어구의 도치 ⋯⋯⋯⋯⋯⋯⋯⋯⋯⋯⋯⋯⋯⋯⋯⋯⋯⋯ 336
05 부사(구)의 도치 ⋯⋯⋯⋯⋯⋯⋯⋯⋯⋯⋯⋯⋯⋯⋯⋯⋯⋯ 337
06 강조의 조동사 ⋯⋯⋯⋯⋯⋯⋯⋯⋯⋯⋯⋯⋯⋯⋯⋯⋯⋯⋯ 338
07 very에 의한 강조 (명사 강조) ⋯⋯⋯⋯⋯⋯⋯⋯⋯⋯⋯ 338
08 의문사가 있는 의문문의 it ~ that 강조구문 ⋯⋯⋯⋯ 339
09 생략 (격언, 계시, 광고, 관용적 표현) ⋯⋯⋯⋯⋯⋯⋯ 339
10 게시문구(揭示文句:Notices) ⋯⋯⋯⋯⋯⋯⋯⋯⋯⋯⋯ 340

Chapter
20
무생물 주어(物主 構文)

01 생물 주어(人主 構文)와 무생물 주어(物主 構文) ⋯ 343

Chapter
21
병렬(평행) 구조(Parallel Structure or Parallelism)

01 병렬(평행) 구조 ⋯⋯⋯⋯⋯⋯⋯⋯⋯⋯⋯⋯⋯⋯⋯⋯⋯⋯⋯ 350

Chapter 22

기타(Miscellany) - (1)

01 방향 표시법 356
02 인칭 대명사의 배열법 356
03 Story와 Floor 357
04 means를 포함한 관용어구 358
05 Yes, No의 응답에서 주의할 사항 359
06 실수하기 쉬운 표현 361
07 수사(數詞)와 관련된 but 362
08 숫자가 들어가는 관용 표현 364
09 미국의 돈(American Money) 365
10 시간을 묻는 표현 366
11 돈을 세는 법 371
12 규격을 말하는 법 371
13 소수(Decimal) 읽는 법 372
14 분수(Fraction) 읽는 법 373
15 가감승제(加減乘除) 373
16 비율(Ratio) 374
17 온도 읽는 법 374
18 번지수, 빌딩번호, 호실번호 읽는 법 375
19 전화번호 읽는 법 376
20 전화와 관련된 표현 377

기타(Miscellany) - (2)

01 기식군(氣息群:Breath-Group) 382
02 구두점 (Punctuation) 383
03 부가의문문(Tag-question) 390
04 부가의문문에 대한 응답으로 안성맞춤인 「That's right」 ... 395
05 cloth / clothe / clothes / clothing 396
06 Word Stress(어강세) 396
07 Phrase Stress(구강세) 399
08 Sentence Stress(문장 강세) 400
09 주의해야 할 강세(Stress) 401
10 그리스·로마 신과 그 지위 402
11 Western Superstition(서양의 미신) 403

종합 평가 문제

407

제1장
Essential English Grammar

문장의 구성요소
(Sentence Structure)

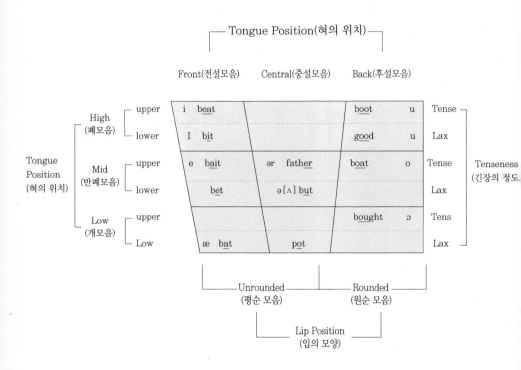

Tense Vowel (긴장 모음:장모음) : i, u, e, ər, o, ɔ

Lax　Vowel (이완 모음:단모음) : I, u, ɛ, ə, æ, α

Unrounded Vowel (평순 모음: 平脣 母音) : i, I, e, ɛ, æ, ər, ə[ʌ], α

Rounded Vowel　(원순 모음: 圓脣 母音) : u, U, o, ɔ

영어 자음 도표
(The Chart of English Consonant Phonemes)

Manner of articulation 조음 방법:음의 종류) ╲ Position of articulation (조음 장소)		Voicing (소리:聲)	Bilabial (양순음)	Labio dental (순치음)	Inter dental (치간음)	Alveolar (치조음)	Alveo Palatal (치조 구개음)	Velar (연구개음)	Glottal (성문음)
Obstruents 《장애음 :안울림 소리)	Stops (파열〈폐쇄〉음)	Voiceless	P(ㅍ)			t (ㅌ)		k(ㅊ)	ʔ
		Voiced	b(ㅂ)			d (ㄷ)		g(ㄱ)	
	Fricatives (마찰음)	Vl(무성음)	Φ	f	θ	s (ㅅ)	ʃ		h (ㅎ)
		Vd(유성음)	β	v	ð	z (ㅈ)	ʒ		
	Affricatives (파찰음)	Vl(무성음)						tʃ	
		Vd(유성음)						dʒ	
Resonants (= Sonorants) 《공명음 :울림 소리)	Nasals (비음:鼻音)	Vd (유성음)	m(ㅁ)			n(ㄴ)		ŋ(ㅇ)	
	Lateral (설측음)	Vd (유성음)				r,l(ㄹ)			
	Glides (반모음:활음)	Vd (유성음)	w(ㅗ/ㅜ)			ər	y[j]	w(ㅗ/ㅜ)	

03 문장(sentence)의 분류

I. 형식(形式)에 의한 분류(Onions에 의한 분류)

[1] 제1형식 : S + V　　　　Ex) Snow falls. (완전 자동사)

[2] 제2형식 : S + V + S.C.　Ex) I am a boy. (불완전 자동사)

[3] 제3형식 : S + V + O　　Ex) The boy caught the ball. (완전 타동사)

[4] 제4형식 :　S + V + I.O. + D.O. (수여동사)

　　　　　　　　S + V + D.O. + 전치사 + I.O. (3형식 문장으로 전환 가능)

Ex) ┌ My mother gave me the money. (4형식)
　　└ My mother gave the money to me. (3형식)

[5] 제5형식 : S + V + O + O.C. (불완전 타동사)

Ex) <u>Many people</u> <u>think</u> <u>her</u> <u>happy</u>.　<u>I</u> <u>believe</u> <u>him</u> to be honest.
　　　　S　　　　V　　O　O.C.　　S　　V　　O　　O.C.

II. 의미(意味)에 의한 분류

[1] 평서문(Declarative Sentence) : I think that you're wrong.

[2] 의문문(Interrogative Sentence) : Will you come with me this evening?

[3] 명령문(Imperative Sentence) : Work hard, and you will succeed.

[4] 감탄문(Exclamatory Sentence) : How beautiful she looks !

III. 구조(構造:Structure)에 의한 분류

[1] 단문(短文:Simple Sentence) : S + V

[2] 중문(重文:Compound Sentence) : S + V and S + V

[3] 복문(複文:Complex Sentence) : 주절 + 종속절

[4] 혼합문(混合文:Mixed Sentence) : 중문 + 복문

제1장 **문장의 구성요소 (Sentence Structure)**

04 구조(構造:Structure)에 의한 분류

I. 단문(短文 : Simple Sentence)

☞ 주부(主部), 술부(述部)(S+V)관계가 1번밖에 없는 것. 즉 절(節)이 없는 것으로, 구(句)는
있어도 좋다.

Ex) <u>He</u> <u>drinks</u> <u>a glass of water.</u>
      S   V   명사구

 <u>Being a poor girl,</u> <u>she</u> <u>could</u> do nothing.
    분사구문(부사구)   S   V

 <u>Trial and error</u> <u>is</u> the source of our knowledge. (시행착오가 지식의 근원이다.)
   S(2개의 주어)   V

=> 단문이라 해서 반드시 짧은 것은 아니다. 수식어가 붙을 수 있기 때문이다.

II. 중문(重文 : Compound Sentence)

☞ 2개 이상의 단문이 대등한 문법적 관계로 묶는 and, but, or, for, either ~ or 등
등위 접속사, 또는 therefore, moreover, however, consequently 등 접속부사
로 연결된 것으로, 이 절을 각각 「독립절」 또는 「등위절」이라 부른다.

Ex) A cat and a dog had a fight <u>and</u> they got hurt.
 He felt no fear, <u>for</u> he was brave.
 There was not one there, <u>so</u> he went away.
 <u>Either</u> the mail-carrier hasn't come yet <u>or</u> there aren't any
 letters for me this morning.
 (오늘 아침엔 우체부 아저씨가 아직 오지 않았던지, 아니면 편지가 없나 보다.)
 I think; <u>therefore</u> I am.
 A man dies, his name remains.

III. 복문(複文 : Complex Sentence) [복문 = 주절 + 종속절]

☞ 한 개의 주절(主節)에 한 개 이상의 종속절이 붙어 있는 것으로, 이때 2개의 절(節)을
연결하는 것은 종속 접속사·관계사 등이다. 종속절에는 ①명사절 ②형용사절 ③부
사절의 3종류가 있다.

cf) 종속절이란 복문에서 접속사나 관계사(관계 대명사, 관계 부사)가 있는 문
장을 말하며, 단문은 곧 접속사나 관계사를 없애는 것을 말한다.

① 명사절

I believe (that) he is right.
  (주절)   (종속절:명사절)

② 형용사절

I know the man who is standing there.
     (주절)   (종속절)
       ┗━━━━━━━━━┛
     명사수식(형용사절)

The man whose ladder we borrowed lived at the corner.
   S   (종속절)   (주절)
   ┗━━━━━━━━━━┛
(우리에게 그 사다리를 빌려준 사람은 저 모퉁이에 산다.)

③ 부사절

She could not come because she was ill.

If you had seen it, you should have shuddered.
(그것을 보았더라면, 당신은 몸서리 쳤을거요.)

Ⅳ. 혼합문(混合文 : Mixed Sentence) : 「중문(重文) + 복문(複文)」

☞ 중문(重文)을 구성하는 등위절(coordinate clause)이 그 안에 종속절(subordinate
clause)을 가지고 있는 것을 말한다. 즉 「중문(重文) + 복문(複文)」을 말한다.

Ex) The earth is a globe that always turns (a)round, and at the
       (주절)   (종속절:형용사절)   〈등위절〉
         ┗━━━━━━━━━━┛

same time it moves round the sun.
           S V
(지구는 언제나 돌고 있는 구체(球體)이고, 동시에 그것은 태양 주위를 돌고 있다.)

* 다음의 단문(短文)을 복문(複文)으로 바꾸시오.

1. He seems to be ill.

   _____.

2. He was too young to be trusted with the work.

   _____.

3. I got up early so as to catch the train.

   _____.

4. I never see you without thinking of my brother.

   _____.

(정답) 1. It seems that he is ill.

     2. He was so young that he could not be trusted the work.

     3. I got up early so that I might catch the train.

     4. When I see you, I always think of my brother.

문장요소 주요소

주 어
- ① 명 사   The pretty <u>birds</u> in our garden sing merrily.
- ② 대명사   <u>We</u> choose him our leader.
- ③ 부정사   <u>To see</u> is to believe.
- ④ 동명사   <u>Seeing</u> is believing.
- ⑤ 명사구   <u>To tell a lie</u> is wrong.
- ⑥ 명사절   <u>That he is honest</u> is clear.

동 사
- 자동사
  - 완전 자동사   Birds <u>fly</u>.
  - 불완전 자동사   Flowers <u>are</u> beautiful.
- 타동사
  - 완전 타동사   I <u>like</u> dog.
  - 수여동사   I <u>gave</u> him a dictionary.
  - 불완전 타동사   I <u>made</u> him happy.

목적어
- ① 명 사   He practiced <u>tennis</u> regularly.
- ② 대명사   I gave <u>him</u> up for dead.
- ③ 동명사   I enjoy <u>reading</u> a novel.
- ④ 부정사   He wanted <u>to go</u> there.
- ⑤ 명사구   I don't know <u>how to swim</u>.
- ⑥ 명사절   No one understand <u>why he had killed himself</u>.

보 어
- ① 명 사   He is a <u>boy</u>.
- ② 대명사   <u>What</u> are you?
- ③ 동명사   It is <u>throwing</u> your money away.
- ④ 부정사   To see is <u>to believe</u>.
- ⑤ 형용사구   His life is <u>in danger</u>.
- ⑥ 명사절   The trouble is <u>that he is apt to get angry</u>.
- ⑦ 형용사   He looks <u>old</u> for his age.
- ⑧ 분 사   He kept <u>standing</u> outside.
- ⑨ 부 사   The storm will be <u>over</u>.

종속요소
수식어
- ① 형용사   The pretty <u>little</u> birds in the cage sing.
- ② 형용사구   The girl <u>with black eyes</u> is his sister.
- ③ 형용사절   This is the book <u>which I am looking for</u>.
- ④ 부 사   This little pretty bird <u>always</u> sings <u>merrily</u>.
- ⑤ 부사구   We treated the boy <u>with kindness</u>.
- ⑥ 부사절   We go to beach <u>when it is hot</u>.
        <u>If I am wrong</u>, you are not right.

연결어
- 전치사 : I go <u>to</u> school <u>with</u> him <u>by</u> bus.
- 접속사 : She is old <u>but</u> she is still beautiful.

독립요소
- 호 격 : <u>Mary</u>, open the door.
- 감탄사 : <u>Hurrah</u>! We have no lesson today.

동 사

자동사 (vi)	완전 자동사 ------------- (S + V)	제1형식
	불완전 자동사 ----------- (S + V + S.C.)	제2형식
타동사 (vt)	완전 타동사 -------------(S + V + O)	제3형식
	수여동사 ---------------(S + V + I.O + D.O.)	제4형식
	불완전 타동사 ----------- (S + V + O + O.C.)	제5형식

대표적 불완전 자동사

[1] be 동사 group => (어떤 성질, 상태가) ~이다, ~에 머물러
    있다.
　◆ look ~같이 보이다 : He <u>looks</u> happy.
　◆ taste ~맛이 나다 : This milk <u>tastes</u> sour.
　◆ smell ~냄새가 나다 : Roses <u>smell</u> sweet.
　◆ sound ~으로 들리다 : This <u>sounds</u> strange.
　◆ keep ~로 유지하다 : She <u>kept</u> silent.
　◆ remain ~상태에 있다 : He <u>remains</u> a bachelor.

[2] become 동사 group => ~로 되다.(상태의 변화를 나타낸다)
　◆ get ~이 되다 : He <u>got</u> angry all of a sudden. (그는 갑자기 화가 났다.)
　◆ turn ~로(이) 되다 : She <u>turned</u> pale. (그녀는 얼굴이 창백해졌다.)
　◆ grow ~이 되다 : He <u>grew</u> old. (그는 늙었다.)
　◆ fall ~이 되다 : His brother <u>fell</u> ill. (병이 났다.)
　◆ go ~이 되다 : He <u>went</u> mad. (미쳐 버렸다.)
　◆ run ~이 되다 : The river <u>ran</u> dry. (그 강은 말라붙었다.)

07 유사보어(類似補語) : 추가보어(追加補語)

☞ 「유사(추가)보어」란 일상적으로는 보어없이 완전 자동사로만 쓰이던 동사 뒤에서 보
   어 역할을 하기 위해 첨가된 보어를 말한다. 원래는 보어가 아니지만 보어와 유사한
   기능을 하므로 「유사보어」란 이름이 붙었다. 해석은 「~의 상태로」이다. 주로 주어
   의 상태를 추가적으로 서술하는 보어의 관계에 있기 때문에 「추가보어」라고도 한다.
   즉, 보어를 취할 수 없는 완전 자동사가 문장을 간결하게 표현하기 위해 보어를 취
   하는 것을 말한다.
   유사보어[類似補語: 추가보어(追加補語)]를 취하는 동사에는 「die, go, meet, part(헤
   어지다), marry, live」 등이 있다.

| Essential English Grammar | 25

Ex) She lived and died a virgin.
(그녀는 처녀로 살다가 죽었다.)

⌈ She sat at the window sewing.
⌊ She was sewing when she sat at the window.
(그녀는 바느질을 하며 창가에 앉아 있었다.)

⌈ They came running.
⌊ They were running when they came.
(그들은 뛰어서 왔다.)

⌈ He came home very much depressed.
⌊ He was very much depressed when he came home.
(그는 아주 울적한 기분으로 집으로 왔다.)

⌈ She asked him in tears to come again.
⌊ She was in tears when she asked him to come again.
(그녀는 눈물을 흘리며 그에게 다시 와달라고 했다.)

⌈ Tired and sleepy, I went to bed.
⌊ I was tired and sleepy when I went to bed.
(지치고 졸리어서 나는 잠자리에 들었다.)

⌈ A genius dies young.
⌊ A genius dies when he is young.
(천재는 젊어서 죽는다.)

⌈ He is at home sick.
⌊ He is sick when he is at home.
(그는 병들어 집에 있다.)

⌈ We parted the best of friends.
⌊ We were the best of friends when we parted.
(우리는 가장 절친한 친구로서 헤어졌다.)

⌈ He died the richest man in the state.
⌊ He was the richest in the state when he died.
(그는 그 주(州)에서 가장 부유한 사람이 되어서 죽었다.)

⌈ She left them a merry, kittenish child. She returned a full
grown woman.
⌊ She was a merry, kittenish child when she left them. She was a
full grown woman when she returned.
(그녀는 그들에게서 떠나갔을 때에는 쾌활한 꼬마 말괄량이였다. 그러나
완전히 성장한 여인이 되어 돌아왔다.)

1 다음을 단문으로 고치시오.

1. Carnegie was not rich when he died.　(정답)
　_____.　　=〉Carnegie did not die <u>rich.</u>

2. John was an enemy when he left.
　_____.　　=〉John left an <u>enemy.</u>

3. He was disgraced when he died.
　_____.　　=〉He died <u>disgraced.</u>

4. Everybody is equal when he is created.
　_____.　=〉Everybody is created <u>equal.</u>

5. He was exhausted when he returned home.
　_____. =〉He returned home <u>exhausted.</u>

2 (　　)안의 동사를 적당한 형태로 고치시오.

1. He went home (<u>satisfy</u>) with my explanation.　(정답)
　　　　　(　　　　　)　　　　　=〉satisfied

2. He went out (<u>surprise</u>) at the news.
　　　　　(　　　　　)　　　　　=〉surprised

3. With an eye (<u>bandage</u>) I could not write properly.
　　　　　(　　　　　)　　　　　=〉bandaged

4. He sank down on his bed (<u>exhaust</u>).
　　　　　　　(　　　　　)　　　　=〉exhausted

3 다음을 해석하고 밑줄 친 부분을 복문으로 전환하시오.

After three months spent in a sweet seaside resort, where unoccupied men and ladies happily congregate, <u>I returned to Paris refreshed.</u>

(정답) I was refreshed wen I returned to Paris.

08 자동사로 혼동하기 쉬운 타동사 (3형식 동사)

- ◆ attend ~에 참석하다   Ex) He <u>attended</u> the party.
- ◆ address ~에게 말을 걸다 Ex) She <u>addressed</u> me in English.
- ◆ approach ~에 접근하다   Ex) He <u>approached</u> the window.
- ◆ await ~을 기다리다   Ex) Death <u>awaits</u> all men.
- ◆ discuss ~을 토의하다   Ex) We <u>discuss</u> the problem.
- ◆ enter ~에 들어가다   Ex) He <u>entered</u> the room.
- ◆ follow ~을 따르다   Ex) I will <u>follow</u> you.
- ◆ inhabit ~에 거주하다   Ex) Nobody <u>inhabits</u> the island.
- ◆ join ~와 함께 하다   Ex) <u>Join</u> us in a short stroll.
- ◆ marry ~와 결혼하다   Ex) I want to <u>marry</u> her.
- ◆ mention 언급하다   Ex) If you <u>mention</u> me, he will let you in.
- ◆ leave ~을 떠나다   Ex) He <u>left</u> Seoul for England.
- ◆ reach ~에 도달하다   Ex) I <u>reached</u> the station on time.
- ◆ resemble ~를 닮다   Ex) She <u>resembles</u> her mother.

TEST

* 다음의 문장을 읽고 어법상 옳으면 O 틀리면 X표를 하시오.

1. She <u>awaited</u> her daughter.(O)

  => await = wait for [타동사 = 자동사 + 전치사]

2. She <u>awaited</u> for her daughter.(X)

3. We <u>discussed</u> the matter.(O)

4. We <u>discussed</u> about the matter.(X)

5. We <u>talked</u> over the matter.(O)

6. He <u>entered</u> the house.(O)

7. He <u>entered</u> into the house.(X)

☞ enter into + 추상명사 = begin, start (~을 시작하다)

  Ex) Both of the countries entered into the war.

    (그 두 나라는 전쟁을 시작했다.)

He entered into conversation with Jennifer.
(그는 제니퍼와 이야기를 시작했다.)

8. Some foxes <u>inhabited</u> the den.(O)

9. Some foxes <u>inhabited</u> in the den.(X)

10. She <u>mentioned</u> it briefly.(O)

11. She <u>mentioned</u> of it briefly.(X)

12. She <u>spoke of</u> it briefly.(O)

13. She <u>married</u> an American.(O)

14. She <u>married</u> with an American.(X)

15. An American <u>was married to</u> her.(O)

16. Many students <u>attended</u> the class. (O)

17. Many students <u>attended</u> to the class. (X)

cf) attend on ~에 시중들다

Ex) She <u>attended on</u> her sick grandfather.(=serve)

(그녀는 병환중인 할아버지를 돌봐 드렸다.)

attend to ~에 유의하다

Ex) They <u>attended to</u> strictly national interests.

(그들은 나라의 이익에 관계되는 점에만 주의를 기울였다.)

09 수여동사(4형식)로 혼동하기 쉬운 완전 타동사(3형식 동사)

☞ 「~에게」 해당되는 부분은 「to+(대)명사(부사구)」로 처리한다.

◆ announce 알리다 : He <u>announced</u> his plan <u>to us.</u>

◆ describe 기술하다 : He <u>described</u> it <u>to me.</u>

◆ explain 설명하다 : He <u>explained</u> this phenomenon <u>to me.</u>

◆ introduce 소개하다 : She <u>introduced</u> her father <u>to him.</u>

◆ propose 제의하다 : I <u>proposed to him</u> that we should go there.

◆ prove 증명하다 : She <u>proved to me</u> that he was right.

◆ confess 고백(자백)하다 : She <u>confessed</u> her secret <u>to her friends.</u>

※ 위의 것과 유사한 것 중에 <u>ask, tell</u>은 수여동사가 가능하다.

TEST

* 다음의 문장을 읽고 어법상 옳으면 O 틀리면 X표를 하시오.

- I will <u>explain</u> <u>to you</u> what this means. (O)
- I will <u>explain</u> what this means <u>to you.</u> (O)
- I will <u>explain</u> you what this means. (X)

- She <u>introduced</u> <u>to me</u> her sister. (O)
- She <u>introduced</u> her sister <u>to me</u>. (O)
- She <u>introduced</u> me her sister. (X)

- He <u>announced</u> to <u>his friends</u> his plan. (O)
- He <u>announced</u> his plan <u>to his friends.</u> (O)
- He <u>announced</u> his friends his plan. (X)

- He <u>confessed</u> <u>to his teacher</u> the fact. (O)
- He <u>confessed</u> the fact <u>to his teacher.</u> (O)
- He <u>confessed</u> his teacher the fact. (X)

 10 동족 목적어(Cognate Object)의 표현

- S(주어) + V(동사) + 관사 + 형용사 + 동족 목적어
- S(주어) + V(동사) + 부사

☞ 본래 자동사가 동사와 어원이 같거나 유사한 뜻의 명사를 목적어로 취하여 타동사 화 하는 경우를 말한다.

Ex) She <u>dreamed</u> a strange <u>dream</u> last night.

- He <u>lived a happy life.</u>
- He <u>lived happily.</u>

- He <u>slept a sound sleep</u> after a long day's work.
- He <u>slept soundly</u> after a long day's work.

- On hearing my joke, he <u>laughed a hearty laughter.</u>
- On hearing my joke, he <u>laughed heartily.</u>

30   제1장 문장의 구성요소 (Sentence Structure)

      [Rich as he was, he <u>lived a simple life.</u>
      [Rich as he was, he <u>lived simply.</u>

      [He <u>died a natural death</u> at the age of ninety.
      [He <u>died naturally</u> at the age of ninety.

      [Nobel made a fortune but <u>lived a simple life.</u>
      [Nobel made a fortune but <u>lived simply.</u>

3형식으로 혼동하기 쉬운 수여동사 (4형식 동사)

☞ 다음의 동사는 간접 목적어와 직접 목적어의 순서를 바꾸지 못한다.
　 즉, 3형식의 문장으로 쓰면 틀린 문장이 된다.

◆ cost (비용이) 들다 : That watch <u>cost</u> me $50.

◆ envy 질투 (시기)하다 : I <u>envy</u> you your success.

◆ forgive ~를 용서하다 : They <u>forgave</u> him his offences.

◆ pardon ~를 용서하다 : Please <u>pardon</u> me my mistakes.

◆ save ~를 구하다(절약하다) : It <u>saved</u> her much time.

◆ spare 떼어놓다 : Can you <u>spare</u> me a minute?

* 다음의 문장을 읽고 어법상 옳으면 O 틀리면 X표를 하시오.

  [I envy him his patience.(O)
  [I envy his patience of him.(X)
  [I envy him for his patience.(O)

  [Please spare him the trouble.(O)
  [Please spare the trouble from him.(X)
  [Please spare him from the trouble.(O)

  [Please pardon me my misbehavior from me at the party.(O)
  [Please pardon my misbehavior from me at the party.(X)
  [Please pardon me for my misbehavior at the party.(O)

┌ That will save me a lot of trouble.(O)
├ That will save a lot of trouble from me.(X)
└ That will save me from having to do a lot of trouble.(O)
┌ The work cost her health.(O)
└ The work cost her health from her.(X)
┌ God will forgive you your sin.(O)
└ God will forgive your sin from you.(X)

┌ S(주어) + 수여동사 + I.O.(간접 목적어) + D.O.(간접 목적어) [4형식]
└ S(주어) + 수여동사 + D.O.(간접 목적어) + 전치사 + I.O.(간접 목적어) [3형식]

☞ 4형식 동사의 간접 목적어(I.O)와 직접 목적어(D.O)의 순서를 바꿀 때
  간접 목적어에 전치사(to, for, of, on, against)를 붙여 바꾼다.

[1] 전치사 to를 받는 경우

☞ pay, bring, hand, deny, sell, send, lend, give, owe, return, offer, etc.

┌ I paid him the money.(4형식)
└ I paid the money to him.(3형식)
┌ I gave him the book.(4형식)
└ I gave the book to him.(3형식)
┌ The philosopher gave them all his knowledge.(4형식)
└ The philosopher imparted all his knowledge to them.(3형식)

[2] 전치사 for를 받는 경우

☞ buy, build, make, get, order, choose, cook, leave, do, etc.

┌ I will buy you a watch.(4형식)
└ I will buy a watch for you.(3형식)
┌ I will make you a new suit.(4형식)
└ I will make a new suit for you.(3형식)
┌ He is building me a garage.(4형식)
└ He is building a garage for me.(3형식)

　　　　　　　　　　제1장 **문장의 구성요소** (Sentence Structure)

Father left me little money.(4형식)
Father left little money for me.(3형식)

[3] 전치사 of를 받는 경우

☞ ask, beg, require, inquire, demand, etc.

I asked him a question.(4형식)
I asked a question of him.(3형식)

May I ask you a favor?(4형식)
May I ask a favor of you?(3형식)
Will you do me a favor?(4형식)

[4] 전치사 on를 받는 경우

☞ play, impose, bestow, confer, etc,

He played me a trick.(4형식)
He played a trick on me.(3형식)

Tom played Mary a joke.(4형식)
Tom played a joke on Mary.(3형식)

They imposed me a tax of 100 dollars.(4형식)
They imposed a tax of 100 dollars on me.(3형식)

He bestowed me many kindness.(4형식)
He bestowed many kindness on me.(3형식)

13 4형식과 5형식의 구별 방법

[1] 타동사 + 목적어 + 명사에서　　목적어 = 명사 : (5형식)
　　　　　　　　　　　　　　　　　　　목적어 ≠ 명사 : (4형식)
[2] 타동사 + 목적어 + 형용사 ‥‥‥‥‥‥‥‥‥‥‥ (5형식)

Ex) He made his son a soldier. (son = soldier) (5형식)
　　 He made his son a toy. (son ≠ toy) (4형식)
　　 I think her happy. (5형식)

제2장
Essential English Grammar

명사(Noun)와
대명사(Pronoun)

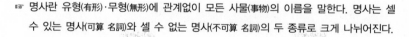

01 명사(名詞 : Noun)

☞ 명사란 유형(有形)·무형(無形)에 관계없이 모든 사물(事物)의 이름을 말한다. 명사는 셀 수 있는 명사(可算 名詞)와 셀 수 없는 명사(不可算 名詞)의 두 종류로 크게 나뉘어진다.

[1] 가산 명사(可算 名詞 : Countable Noun)
　① 보통명사(common noun)
　② 집합명사(collective noun)

[2] 불가산 명사(不可算 名詞 : Uncountable Noun)
　① 물질명사(material noun)
　② 추상명사(abstract noun)
　③ 고유명사(proper noun)
☞ 불가산 명사는 a, an을 사용할 수 없고, 복수형도 안된다.

[3] 명사의 변화
① 가산 명사를 불가산 명사로 쓸 수 있다. Ex) 보통명사 => 추상명사
　Ex) The pen is mightier than the sword.
　　　(文)　　　　　　　　　　(式)
　　　She felt the mother rise in her heart.
　　　　　　(모성애)

② 불가산 명사를 가산 명사로 쓰는 경우도 있다.

　Ex)　┌ 고유명사 ┐
　　　　├ 추상명사 ┤ => 보통명사
　　　　└ 물질명사 ┘

　Ex) This is a very good wine.
　　☞ 물질명사 wine이 보통 명사로 전용되어 「종류」를 나타냄.
　　　She must have been a beauty in her day.
　　☞ 추상명사 beauty가 보통명사로 전용되어 「미인(美人)」이 됨.
　　　He is a Don Quixote.
　　☞ 고유명사 돈키호테가 보통명사로 전용되어 「돈키호테 같은 사람」이 됨.
　　　There is a Mr. Brown wants to see you.

☞ 고유명사 Mr. Brown이 보통명사로 전용되어 「Brown씨라는 사람」이 됨.

We take several papers.

☞ 물질명사 「종이」가 보통명사로 전용되어 「신문, 논문, 서류」가 됨.

[4] 고유명사(固有名詞 : Proper Noun)

☞ 한 사람, 한 사물에만 쓸 수 있는 고유의 이름이다. (대문자로 쓰기 시작함)

Ex) Seoul, Mary, February, Venus, Korea, Newton, The Han river, etc.

[5] 보통명사(普通名詞 : Common Noun)

☞ 같은 형태를 가진 사람 . 사물에 공통적으로 쓰인 이름이다.

Ex) dog, desk, tree, river, day, school, hospital, home, etc.

[6] 물질명사(物質名詞 : Material Noun)

☞ 물질이라고 생각되는 일정한 형태가 없는 물건의 이름이다.

Ex) water, air, wood, gold, beer, smoke, bread, etc.

[7] 추상명사(抽象名詞 : Abstract Noun)

☞ 성질·동작·상태 또는 일정한(생각)을 나타내는 이름이다.

즉 추상명사란 상태·사건·감정 등 추상적인 것을 나타낸다.

Ex) peace, truth, beauty, friendship, love, etc.

[8] 집합명사(集合名詞 : Collective Noun)

☞ 개체가 모인 집합체에 붙여진 이름이다.

즉, 여러 개체가 모여 하나의 집단을 형성하는 것으로 집합명사가 하나의 단위로서
단일성(oneness)을 나타내면 단수 취급한다.

Ex) family, people, committee, cattle, furniture, audience, etc.

[9] 군집명사(群集名詞 : Noun of Multitude)

☞ 집합명사가 그 구성원(개별성)을 나타낼 때에는 복수 취급한다.

즉, 집합명사가 그 구성원이나 개체의 하나 하나의 성질을 강조할 때 복수 취급한다.
The police(경찰), the crew(승무원) 등은 항상 복수 취급을 하는 군집명사이다.

집합명사와 군집명사

구분＼내용	내 용	형 태	동 사
집합명사	전체중심	단수·복수	단수·복수
군집명사	개체중심	단 수	복 수

Ex) <u>My family</u> is a large one. (집합명사)
　　　(단수형태)

There <u>are</u> three <u>families</u> in my house. (집합명사)
　　　　　　(복수형태)

My family <u>are</u> all early risers, (군집명사)

My family <u>is</u> a large one, and <u>are</u> all well.
(나의 가족은 대가족이고, 모두 건강하다.)

cf)

보통명사 〈———→〉 집합명사

machine　　－ machinery　jewel － jewelry
poem　　　　－ poetry　　　scene － scenery
policeman　－ police

[10] 중요한 군집명사 / 집합명사

① people(국민.민족 / 사람들)　② committee(위원회 / 위원들)
③ class(계급.학급 / 학급.학생들)　④ audience(청중 / 청중들)
⑤ jury(배심원 / 배심원들)　　⑥ crowd(군중 / 군중들)

TEST

* 다음의 문장에서 알맞은 것을 고르시오.

1. The audience (run/runs) to nearly 5,000.

2. His class (is/are) composed of sixty boys and girls.

3. The committee (has/have) prepared a report.

4. The committee (is/are) divided on their opinions.

(정답) 1. runs　2. is　3. has　4. are

명사의 성(性 : Gender) [國家를 나타낼 때]

[1] 지리적 측면에서(국토를 나타낼 때) => 중성(it)

Ex) Looking at the map, we see France here.

It is one of the largest countries of Europe.

France is smaller than spain, but it is much more fertile.

America is rich in its natural resources.

[2] 정치, 경제, 문화적 측면에서 => 여성(she)

Ex) France has been able to increase her exports by 10 percent over the
last six months.

India has to solve her food problem,.

England is justly proud of her poets.

[3] 운동 경기 면에서 => 복수(they)

Ex) France have improved their chance of winning the world Cup.

 명사의 성(性)

① 남성 명사의 어미에 −ess 등을 붙이는 경우

prince 황태자	tiger 호랑이(수컷)	waiter 남자 급사
princess 공주	tigress 호랑이(암컷)	waitress 여자 급사
lion 사자(수컷)	god 신	emperor 황제
lioness 사자(암컷)	goddess 여신	empress 황후
heir 남자 상속인	steward 남자 안내원	author 저자
heiress 여자 상속인	stewardess 여자 안내원	authoress 여류작가
host 남자주인	master 주인, 소유자	millionaire 백만장자
hostess 여자주인	mistress 여주인, 주부	millionairess 여자백만장자

② 별개의 낱말을 사용하는 경우

⌈ nephew	남자조카	⌈ monk	남자 수도승
⌊ niece	여자조카	⌊ nun	수녀, 비구니
⌈ husband	남편	⌈ bull	황소
⌊ wife	아내	⌊ cow	암소

04 복합 명사(Compound Noun)

[1] 명사 + 동사 =〉 파생 명사
(1) sunrise(일출) =〉 the sun rise 「주어 + 동사」
   heartbeat(심장 박동), bus stop(버스 정류장), bullfight(투우)
(2) bloodtest(혈액검사) =〉 X tests blood 「목적어 + 동사」
   book cover(표지), finger print(지문), landmark(표지물)
(3) homework(숙제) =〉 X works at home 「부사적 요소의 명사 + 동사」
   sidewalk(보도:步道), eyesight(시력), sunbath(일광욕)

[2] 동사 + 명사
(1) rattlesnake(방울뱀) =〉 the snake rattles 「동사 + 주어」
   whirlpool(소용돌이), popcorn(팝콘), helpmate(원조자)
(2) rowboat(젓는 배) =〉 X rows the boat 「동사 + 목적어」
   pushcart(손수레), breakwater(방파제), pickpocket(소매치기)
(3) searchlight(탐조등) =〉 X searches with a light 「동사 + 부사적
   요소의 명사」
   showroom(전시장) washbowl(세면기) standpoint(관점)

[3] 명사 + 동사 + er
(1) taxpayer(납세자) =〉 X pays tax 「목적어 + 동사」
   flag-bearer(기수), record holder(기록 보유자), copywriter(광고
   문안자)
(2) baby sitter(아기 보아주는 사람) =〉 X sits with the baby

[4] 동명사 + 명사 / 명사 + 동명사

dancing girl(무용수), performing arts(무대 예술), drinking
water(음료수), chewing gum(츄잉껌), parking lot(주차장),
magnifying glass(확대경), swimming pool(수영장),
foodpoisoning(식중독), fish-farming(양어), sightseeing(관광),
daydreaming(몽상), homecoming(귀향).

[5] 명사 + 명사

windmill(풍차), gas stove(가스 난로), motorcar(자동차),
bloodstain(핏자국), windstorm(폭풍), doorknob(문의 손잡이),
sound waves(음파), eggshell(달걀껍질), watercourse(하천),
music box(뮤직 박스), power plant(발전소), oil field(유전),
girl friend(여자 친구), boy scout(보이 스카웃), pine tree(소나무),
frogman(잠수공작원), stone coal(무연탄), snowflake(눈송이).

[6] 형용사 + 명사

darkroom(암실), fine art(미술), goodwill(호의),
freeway(고속도로), strong arm(폭력), shorthand(속기),
white book(백서), highbrow(지식인), plain clothes(사복),
martial law(계엄령), high fashion(최첨단 유행).
martial art(무술, 무예)

05 복합 명사의 복수

[1] 원칙적으로 맨 마지막 말을 복수로 한다.

Ex) breakfasts(아침 식사), girlfriends(여자 친구), maidservants(하녀),
postmen(우체부), good-for-nothings(쓸모 없는 것(사람)), go-
betweens(중매인), forget-me-nots(물망초), touch-me-nots(봉숭아),
etc.

[2] 「man- + 명사」의 형은 양쪽 말을 다 복수로 한다.

Ex) manservant : menservants(하인), woman writer : women writers(여류 작가), woman-doctor : women-doctors(여의사), etc.

[3] 주요한 말을 복수로 하는 것.

Ex) passer-by : passers-by(통행인), looker-on : lookers-on(구경꾼), father-in-law : fathers-in-law(장인), man-of-war : men-of-war(군함), commander-in-chief : commanders-in-chief(사령관), etc.

06 단·복수 동형어(同形語)

Ex) deer(사슴), reindeer(순록), sheep(羊), swine(돼지), carp(잉어), cod(대구), mackerel(고등어), pike(강꼬치고기), salmon(연어), trout(송어), snipe(도요새), fish(물고기:fishes라고도 함), cannon(대포), craft(선박), yoke(멍에), corps(군단), dozen(12), score(20), hundred(100), thousand(1000), Chinese, Japanese, Portuguese, Swiss, means(수단), series(일련의), species(種), etc.

07 절대 복수

☞ 항상 복수형으로 쓰이는 명사로서 다음과 같은 것이 있다.

① 둘 이상의 부분으로 된 의류나 부속물

Ex) suspenders(바지의 멜빵), breeches(반바지), clothes(옷,의복), drawers(속바지,팬츠), pants(美:바지, 英:속바지), tights(타이츠,팬티 스타킹), trousers(바지), weeds(상복:喪服), etc.

② 둘 이상의 부분으로 된 기구

Ex) arms(무기), bellows(풀무), compasses(나침판), fetters(차꼬,족쇄), gallows(교수대), gyves(차꼬, 족쇄), nippers(집게), pincers(뻰지), scales(저울), scissors(가위), shackles(수갑) shears(절단기, 큰가위),

spectacles(안경), tongs(집게), tweezers(족집게, 핀세트), etc.

☞ 이러한 것을 셀 때에는 보통 단위어(a pair of, two pairs of)와 같이 쓴다.

③ 여러 개로 이루어진 신체의 부분

Ex) bowels(창자), entrails(동물의 내장), loins(허리), sinews(힘줄:tendon), brain(s)(뇌), giblets(닭의내장), gut(s)(창자, 내장), whisker(s)(구렛나루), etc.

④ 유희(놀이)의 명칭

Ex) all-fours(카드 놀이), billiards(당구), cards(카드 놀이), checkers(체커: 체스판에서 12개의 말을 써서 함), marbles(공기 놀이), ninepins(9주희: 현대 볼링의 시초), etc.

⑤ 학문에 관한 것

Ex) economics(경제학), ethics(윤리학), politics(정치학), mathematics(수학), etc.

⑥ 병명(病名)에 관한 것

Ex) measles(홍역), rabies(공수병, 광견병), etc.

⑦ 기타

Ex) amends(보상), assets(자산), belongings(소유물), chemicals(화학약품), eatables(식료품), limits(한계점), remains(유물, 유적), ruins(폐허), savings(저축), wages(임금), thanks(감사), etc.

08 분화 복수 (의미가 다른 단수와 복수)

advice(충고)	content(만족)	etter(문자)	paper(종이)
advices(통지)	contents(내용,목차)	letters(문학)	papers(서류)
air(공기)	custom(습관)	manner(방법)	quarter(1/4)
airs(뽐내는 태도)	customs(관세)	manners(예절)	quarters(숙소)
arm(팔)	effect(효과)	mean(중간, 평균)	return(돌아옴)
arms(무기)	effects(동산:動産)	means(수단)	returns(통계표)
ash(재)	force(힘)	number(수)	service(봉사)
ashes(유골)	forces(군대)	numbers(운율:산술)	services(직무)

authority(권한)	glass(유리)	pain(고통)	spectacle(광경)
authorities(당국)	glasses(안경)	pains(수고)	spectacles(안경)
color(색깔)	good(이익)	part(부분)	water(물)
colors(군기)	goods(상품)	parts(재능)	waters(강, 바다)
work(일)	writing(쓰기)		
works(공장)	writings(저작)		

09 외래어 복수

① us => i

- focus(촛점)
- foci
- focuses
- stimulus(자극)
- stimuli
- genius(수호신, 천재)
- genii(수호신)
- geniuses(천재)

② on => a

- phenomenon(현상)
- phenomena
- criterion(기준)
- criteria

③ um => a

- datum(자료)
- data
- medium(매개, 매체)
- media
- bacterium(박테리아)
- bacteria
- agendum(비망록)
- agenda

④ a => ae

- formula(공식)
- formulae/formulas
- larva(애벌레)
- larvae
- alumna(동창생)
- alumnae

⑤ is => es

- oasis(오아시스)
- oases
- crisis(위기)
- crises
- basis(기초)
- bases

⑥ ma => mata

- stigma(치욕)
- stigmata
- stigmas

⑦ eau => eaux

- bureau(국:局)
- bureaux
- bureaus

⑧ ex.ix => ices

- index(지수, 색인)
- indices(지수)
- indexes(색인)

⑨ 기타

- madam(부인)
- mesdames
- monsieur(~씨)
- messieurs

```
┌ plateau(고원)        ┌ vortex(소용돌이)
├ plateaux            ├ vortices
└ plateaus            └ vortexes
```

10 물질 명사나 추상 명사의 단위 표시

a piece of chalk, a piece of news, a piece of information,
a piece of music, a piece of furniture, a piece of land,
a piece of meat, a piece of poetry, a piece of machinery,
a piece(word) of advice, a bunch(cluster) of flowers,
a bunch of bananas, a cluster of grapes, a shower of rain,
a flash of lightning, a bolt of thunder, a cup of coffee,
a cup of tea, a glass of water, a glass of milk,
a handful of rice, a handful of straw, a handful of soil,
a handful of sand, a bar of chocolate, a bar(cake) of soap,
a pack of cigarettes, an article of furniture,
a sheet(piece) of paper, a group of islands, a ball of thread
a galaxy of stars, a spoonful(lump, pound) of sugar,
a loaf(slice) of bread, a stroke of luck, a stroke of fortune,
a school(shoal) of fish, a school of whales, a flock of sheep,
a flock of birds, a head(herd) of ox, a swarm of bees,
a swarm of ants, a swarm of locusts, a pair of scissors,
a pair of shoes. a pair of glasses, a pair of socks,
a pair of trousers, a pair of gloves, etc.

11 쌍을 이루는 물건을 나타내는 명사가 단위어(a pair of)와 함께 쓰이면 「단수 취급」하고, 단위어 없이 직접 쓰이면 「복수 취급」한다.

Ex) There <u>was</u> a pair of trousers on the table.
(테이블 위에 바지 한 벌이 있었다.)

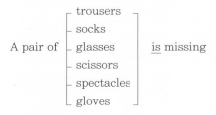

A pair of
- trousers
- socks
- glasses   is missing
- scissors
- spectacles
- gloves

Two pairs of gloves <u>are</u> missing. (장갑 두 켤레가 없어졌다.)
My socks <u>are</u> worn out. (양말이 다 닳아 헤어졌다.)

12 전치사(with, by, in, on) + 추상 명사 = 부사

with care = carefully.   with no care = carelessly.
with charm = charmingly.   with confidence = confidently.
with diligence = diligently.   with delight = delightfully.
with emotion = emotionally.   with easy = easily.
with energy = energetically.   with interest =interestedly.
with happiness = happily.   with rapidity = rapidly.
in silence = silently.   in abundance = abundantly.
in earnest = earnestly.   in haste = hastily.
in private = privately.   in safety = safely.
in particular = particularly.   by accident = accidentally.
on purpose = purposely.   by design = intentionally.

of + 추상 명사 = 형용사

of ability = able.   of beauty = beautiful.
of significance = significant   of use = useful.
of no use = useless.   of value = valuable.
of no value = valueless.   of wealth = wealthy.
of sense = sensible.   of interest = interesting.
of help = helpful.   of service = serviceable.
of importance = important   of no importance = unimportant

TEST

* 두 문장의 의미가 같아지도록 빈 칸에 적당한 말을 쓰시오.

Iron is of great use
Iron is _____ _____

(정답) very useful.

14

all + 추상 명사
추상 명사 + itself
very(extremely) + 형용사 (매우 ~한)
* all + 복수 보통 명사 (매우 ~한)

She is all kindness.   The girl is all smiles.
She is kindness itself.   She looks very pleased.
She is very (extremely) kind.   (그 여자는 희색이 만연하다.)
(그 여자는 매우 친절하다.)

The boys are <u>all eyes and ears</u>.
The boys are <u>all attention</u>.
The boys are <u>attention itself</u>.
The boys are <u>very attentive</u>.
(그 소년들은 매우 주의 깊다.)
Attending the last lesson, Tom was <u>conscience itself</u>.
Attending the last lesson, Tom was <u>all conscience</u>.
Attending the last lesson, Tom was <u>very conscientious</u>.
(Tom은 마지막 수업에 참석했을 때, 대단히 열성적이었다.)

15 부정 대명사(Indefinite Pronoun)

☞ 「부정 대명사(不定 代名詞)」란 어떤 특정의 것을 가리키는 대명사가 아니라, 아무 것
도 정해진 것이 없는 막연한 것을 표시하는 대명사로, one, each, every, any,
some, all, both, none 등이 있다.

[1] 형용사적으로 쓰일 때

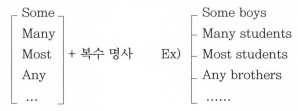

[2] 부정 대명사로 쓰일 때

☞ 「일부 + of + 전체」로 나타낸다. 즉, 여럿 중에서 일부를 가리키고자 할 때의 부정
대명사다.

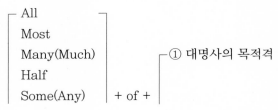

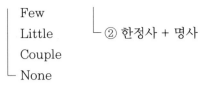

```
┌ Few
│ Little    ┐── ② 한정사 + 명사
│ Couple    ┘
└ None
```

☞ 한정사(限定詞)란 명사 앞에 놓이는 지시 관사(a,an,the), 형용사(this,that, these, etc.) 대명사의 소유격(my, your, his, etc.)를 말한다.

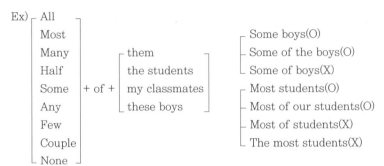

```
Ex) ┌ All
    │ Most
    │ Many                ┌ them          ┌ Some boys(O)
    │ Half                │ the students  ├ Some of the boys(O)
    │ Some   + of +  │ my classmates └ Some of boys(X)
    │ Any                 └ these boys    ┌ Most students(O)
    │ Few                                 ├ Most of our students(O)
    │ Couple                              ├ Most of students(X)
    └ None                                └ The most students(X)
```

16 부정 대명사 One과 지시 대명사 It

☞ 부정 대명사란 특정한 사람이나 물건 또는 확실한 수량 등을 가리키지 않는 대명사를 말한다.

① 부정 대명사 one = a + 단수명사

Ex) ┌ Have you ever seen a lion?
　　└ Yes, I have seen one in the zoo.

② 지시 대명사 It = the + 단수명사

Ex) ┌ Have you ever seen the lion?
　　└ Yes, I have seen it once.

부정 대명사 one을 사용하지 못하는 경우

[1] 셀 수 없는 명사(물질 명사·추상명사) 대신 one을 사용할 수 없다.

> I like red <u>wine</u> better than white <u>one</u>. (X)
> I like red <u>wine</u> better than white. (0)

[2] 소유격 + own 뒤에 one을 사용할 수 없다.

> This <u>bed</u> is my own <u>one</u>. (X)
> This <u>bed</u> is my own. (0)

[3] 수사(數詞) 다음에 one을 사용할 수 없다.

> He had three <u>brothers,</u> and I have two <u>ones</u>. (X)
> He had three <u>brothers,</u> and I have two. (0)

[4] 최상급 형용사 및 the + 비교급 뒤에 one을 사용할 수 없다.

> He has two <u>sisters;</u> the elder is more beautiful than the younger <u>one</u>. (X)
> He has two <u>sisters;</u> the elder is more beautiful than the younger. (0)

부정 대명사 one의 주의해야 할 용법

[1] one~the other 「(둘 중) 하나~다른 하나」

☞ 둘 중에서 하나를 취한 나머지 하나를 나타낼 때 쓴다.

　Ex) I have two dogs ; <u>one</u> is white, and <u>the other</u> (is) black.
　　(나는 두 마리의 개를 갖고 있는 데, 하나는 희고, 다른 하나는 검다.)

[2] one~another(또는 a second) …a third …a fourth (a + 서수로 표시)

☞ 많은 것을 하나하나 열거할 때 쓴다.

「(여러 개 중에서) 하나 …또 하나 …또 하나 …또 하나」

Ex) <u>One</u> is red, <u>another</u> is white, and <u>a third</u> is green.
　　(하나는 붉고, 또 하나는 희고, 또 하나는 녹색이다.)

[3] <u>still(yet) another</u> ; 하나, 또 하나, 또 하나, …' 라는 식으로 세어 나갈 때 처음 하나는 one, 다음 하나는 another, 세 번째 이상에서의 또 하나는 「still another」 또는 「yet another」이라고 한다.

Ex) …And his extraordinary coolness gave him <u>yet another</u> distinction in the society.
　　(…그리고 그의 비범한 침착성은 이 사교계에서 그에게 <u>또 다른</u> 명성을 가져다주었다.)

[4] The first … the second …. the third …. the fourth ….
☞ 명확한 서수를 나타낼 때 쓴다.

[5] one ~ the others 「(여러 개 중에서)하나~나머지 전부」
☞ 여러 개 중에서 하나를 취한 나머지 전부를 나타낼 때 쓴다.

Ex) I have three brothers ; <u>one</u> is in Seoul, and the <u>others</u>(the rest) (are) in Busan.
　　(나는 세 형제가 있는 데, 한 사람은 서울에 있고, 나머지는 부산에 있다.)

[6] some ~ others 「어떤 것들은~또 어떤 것들은」
☞ 여러 개 중에서 일부를 취한 나머지 일부를 나타낼 때 쓴다.

Ex) <u>Some</u> say "yes", and <u>others</u> say "no".
　　(일부는 "네"라고, 또 일부는 "아니오"라고 말했다.)
=〉 즉 "yes"도 "no"도 대답하지 않은 사람이 있음을 나타낸다.

[7] some ~ the others 「일부는~나머지 전부」
☞ 여러 개 중에서 일부를 취한 나머지 전부를 나타낼 때 쓴다.

Ex) <u>Some</u> are my books, <u>the others</u> are hers.
　　(일부는 내 책이고, 나머지는 모두 그녀의 책이다.)

TEST ⚞⚞⚞⚞⚞⚞⚞⚞⚞⚞⚞⚞⚞⚞⚞⚞⚞⚞⚞⚞⚞⚞⚞⚞

* 다음 글을 읽고 _____에 알맞은 것을 고르시오.

1. In summer, Some people go to the seaside, and _____ to the mountains.

① another　② others　③ the others　④ ones　⑤ the other

(정답) ②

2. Here are four suitcases, but I can carry only two.

　 Please bring _____.

① another　② others　③ the others　④ ones　⑤ the other

(정답) ③

[8] ┌ the one　　 ~　 the other　　┐　「前者 ~ 後者」
　　├ that(those) ~　 his(these)　 │
　　├ the former ~　 the latter　 │
　　└ the first　　 ~　 the second ┘

Ex) I studied English and French, and found <u>the one</u> easier than <u>the other</u>.
　　　　　　　　　　　　　　　　　(=English)　　　　　(=French)
Alcohol and tobacco are both injurious ; <u>this(the latter)</u> , however,
less than <u>that(the former)</u>.　　　　　　(=tobacco)
　　　　　(=Alcohol)
(술과 담배는 둘다 해롭지만, 후자(담배)는 전자(술)보다는 덜 해롭다.)
Dogs are more faithful than cats ; <u>these</u> attach themselves to places
and <u>those</u> to persons.　　　　　　(=cats)
　　(=dogs)
(개는 고양이보다 더 충성스럽다; 고양이는 장소에 집착하는데, 개는 사람에
집착하기 때문이다.)

[9] ┌ A is <u>one thing</u> and B (is) <u>another (thing)</u> ┐ (A와 B는 서로 별개의
　　└ A is quite different from B 　　　　　　　　　│ 것이다,A와 B는 다르다)

Ex) To know is <u>one thing</u> and to teach is <u>another</u>.
　　(아는 것과 가르치는 것은 서로 별개의 것이다.)
　　Saying is <u>one thing</u> and doing is <u>another.</u>
　　(말하는 것과 행하는 것은 서로 별개의 것이다.)

It is one thing to own a library ; it is quite another to use it wisely.
(장서를 갖는 것과 그것을 현명하게 이용하는 것은 아주 다른 것이다.)

19 the + 형용사 = 복수 보통 명사 (복수 취급한다)

Ex) The happy are apt to look down (up)on the unhappy.
    (= Happy people)   (= unhappy people)
    (행복한 사람들은 불행한 사람들을 업신여기는 경향이 있다.)
    In some countries the many have to labour for the few.
                (= many people)   (= few people)
    (어떤 나라에서는 다수가 소수를 위해 일해야 한다.)

☞ the rich = rich people,   the poor = poor people

  the sick = sick people,   the absent = absent people

  the brave = brave people,   the old   = old people

  the disabled = disabled people, the handicapped = handicapped people(장애인)

20 the + 형용사 = 추상 명사 (단수 취급한다)

Ex) She has an eye for the beautiful.
              (= beauty)
    (그녀는 美를 보는 눈이 있다.)
    A youth strives for the impossible.
             (= impossibility)
    (젊은이는 불가능한 것을 얻으려고 노력한다.)

☞ the true = truth(眞),   the good = goodness(善)

  the wrong = wrongness(잘못),   the right = rightness(정의)

  the graceful = gracefulness(우아), the sublime = sublimity(숭고)

21 재귀 대명사 oneself의 용법

[1] for oneself = without other's help = independently (자기
    힘으로, 스스로)
  Ex) A baby cannot stand <u>for itself.</u>
      He has done the work <u>for himself.</u>

[2] of oneself = naturally = spontaneously (저절로)
  Ex) The door opened <u>of itself.</u>

[3] by oneself = alone (혼자서, 홀로)
  Ex) He came to live <u>by himself.</u>(그는 혼자 살게 되었다.)
      The woman lives <u>by herself</u> in the hut by the sea.

[4] to oneself (자기에게만, 혼자서만)
(1) have ~ to oneself (독점하다)
  Ex) He has the large room <u>to himself.</u>
(2) keep ~ to oneself (비밀로 하다)
  Ex) She <u>kept</u> the plan <u>to herself.</u>
      Let's keep this matter secret from others.
      Let's <u>keep</u> this matter to <u>ourselves.</u>
(3) keep (oneself) to oneself (남들과 어울리지 않는다)
  Ex) Some people are gregarious, others keep to themselves.
      (어떤 사람들은 사교적이지만, 또 어떤 사람들은 남들과 어울리지 않는다.)
(4) read ~ to oneself (묵독하다)
  Ex) She <u>read</u> the letter <u>to herself.</u>

[5] beside oneself = out of one's sense = insane = mad
    (제정신을 잃고, 흥분하여, 제정신이 아닌, 미친)
  Ex) They were <u>beside themselves</u> with joy.

[6] in spite of oneself = unconsciously
    = without consciousness (자기도 모르게)
  Ex) He yawned again and again <u>in spite of himself.</u>

[7] in itself = naturally = by nature = in its own nature
　　(본래, 본질적으로, 그 자체)
　Ex) Advertising in modern times has become a business in itself.
　　　(현대의 광고는 그 자체로 하나의 기업이 되었다.)

[8] pride oneself on = take pride in = be proud of
　　= boast of = make a boast of (~ 을 자랑스럽게 여기다)
　Ex) ┌ He prides himself on his wealth.
　　　├ He takes prides in his wealth.
　　　├ He is proud of his wealth.
　　　├ He boasts of his wealth.
　　　└ He makes boasts of his wealth.

[9] oversleep oneself (늦잠 자다, 너무 자다)
　Ex) He overslept himself this morning and was late for school.

[10] overeat oneself (과식하다)
　Ex) I overate myself this morning.

[11] overwork oneself (과로하다)
　Ex) Don't overwork yourself.

[12] 재귀 대명사의 재귀용법과 강조용법
(1) 재귀용법 : 이때의 재귀 대명사는 생략할 수 없다.
　Ex) Heaven helps those who help themselves.
　　　(하늘은 스스로 돕는 자를 돕는다.)
　　　He absorbed himself in reading.
　　　(그는 독서에 열중하고 있다.)
(2) 강조용법 : 이때는 생략해도 문장이 성립된다.
　Ex) He painted this picture himself.
　　　(그가 이 그림을 자신이 그렸다.)
　　　I myself made mistakes.
　　　(내 자신도 실수를 저질렀다.)

[13] S(주어) + V(동사) + 재귀 대명사 = S(주어) + be + P.P(과거분사)

(1) ┌ Everyone knew you would <u>distinguish yourself</u> at college.
    └ Everyone knew you would <u>be distinguished</u> at college.
    (모든 사람들이 네가 대학에서 <u>뛰어나리(두각을 나타내리)</u>라는 것을 알았다.)

(2) ┌ He <u>engaged himself</u> in a trade.
    └ He <u>was engaged</u> in a trade.
    (그는 장사에 종사했다.)

(3) ┌ We <u>devoted ourselves to</u> studying.
    └ We <u>were devoted to</u> studying.
    (우리는 연구에 몰두했다.)

(4) ┌ We <u>applied ourselves</u> to studying English.
    └ We <u>were applied to</u> studying English.
    (우리는 영어 공부에 몰두했다.)

(5) ┌ She <u>absented herself from</u> school.
    └ She <u>was absent from</u> school.
    (그녀는 학교를 결석했다.)

(6) ┌ The boy <u>lost himself</u> in the wood.
    └ The boy <u>was lost in</u> the wood.
    (그 소년은 숲에서 길을 잃었다.)

* lose oneself = lose one's way = get(be) lost = go astray (길을 잃다)

(7) ┌ He <u>presented himself at</u> the meeting.
    └ He <u>was present at</u> the meeting.
    (그는 그 모임에 참석했다.)

 22 It

[1] 지시대명사
☞ 앞에 나온 내용을 가리킬 때

Ex) ┌ Have you ever seen the lion?
    └ Yes, I have seen it once.

[2] 가주어(假主語 : 형식주어) It가 사용되는 구문

☞ 아래와 같은 구문속의 It는 가주어(형식주어)이므로 진주어를 찾아 가주어(假主語)자리에 넣고 해석한다.

Ex) It won't do to be rude to strangers.
    It matters little whether he agrees with us or not.
    It happened that I was out that day.
    It seems that she knows nothing of it.
    It is worth while to read(or reading) this book.
    It doesn't make any difference whose fault it is.
    (= It's all the same whose fault it is.)

[3] 가목적어(형식 목적어) It가 사용되는 구문

☞ 동사 바로 뒤에 it가 오고 그 뒤에 ① to do ~ ② doing ~ ③ S+V(절) ~ 이 오면 it
는 가목적어, 그리고 뒤따르는 to do ~ , doing ~ , S+V(절) ~ 은 진목적어가 된다.
이때는 진목적어 ①, ②, ③을 가목적어 it 자리에 놓고 해석을 하는 것이 요령이다.

Ex) I make it a rule to go to bed at ten.
    We found it difficult rowing across the river.
    I think it natural that she should decline your offer.
    I took it for granted that you would want to see the play.

TEST

* 다음을 복문은 단문으로, 단문은 복문으로 전환하시오.

1. He thinks it impossible to master English in a few days.
   (=>   )

2. You will find that it is difficult to solve the problem.
   (=>   )

3. He thinks it a pity that John left school.
   (=>   )

4. I found that it was difficult to write English well.
   (=>   )

5. People will find it easier to learn another language of the same
   family.
   (=>   )
(정답)

1. He thinks that it is impossible to master.
2. You will find it difficult to solve the problem.
3. He thinks that it is a pity that John left school.
4. I found it difficult to write English well.
5. People will find that it is easier to learn another language
   of the same family.

[4] depend upon(on) it

☞ 「문장의 앞이나 뒤에 쓰여」 확실히, 틀림없이」라는 부사 요소로 depend upon it that
   ~의 구문에서 생겨난 것이다. 즉,「(文頭 또는 文尾에서)틀림없다」로 해석한다. it은 느닷
   없이 that ~가 on의 목적어가 될 수 없으므로 넣은 이것과 동격의 형식 목적어 it이다.
   Ex) You may <u>depend upon it that</u> it won't happen again.
       (그러한 것은 두번 다시 일어나지 않습니다.)
       The strike will ruin the country, <u>depend upon it.</u>
       (틀림없이 그 파업은 나라를 망칠 것이다.)

[5] See (to it) that

☞ 「See to it that ~ 」에서 it은 전치사 to가 that절을 목적어로 취할 수 없으므로, 이
   두 요소의 충돌을 피하기 위한 일종의 장치(가목적어)이다. 흔히 (to it)를 생략하고
   「See that~ 」으로 많이 쓴다.

① ~하도록 주선하다.
   Ex) She is the one who <u>sees to it that</u> a service man repairs it.
       (그녀가 수리공에게 그것을 고치도록 주선한 바로 그 사람이다.)

② ~에 주의하다. ~을 돌보다. (= attend to. look after, take care of)
   Ex) <u>See to it that</u> you do not fall.
       (넘어지지 않게 조심하라.)
       <u>See to it that</u> it never happens again.
       (다시는 그러한 일이 일어나지 않도록 주의하라.)
       The young must <u>see to it that</u> the old should not feel lonely.
       (노인네들이 고독하지 않도록 보살펴 드려라.)

I' ll <u>see to</u> the patient.
(제가 그 환자를 돌보겠습니다.)

③ 꼭(반드시, 틀림없이) ~시키다. (be sure to, make sure that)

    Ex) <u>See to it that</u> the door is closed.

       (틀림없이(꼭/반드시) 문을 닫아라.)

       <u>See (to it) that</u> the door locked before you leave.

       (나갈 때 문이 잠겼나 꼭 확인하라.)

④ 일(따위를) 맡아 처리하다.

    Ex) I' ll <u>see to that.</u>

       (내가 맡아 처리하겠다.)

[6] take it for granted that S+V ~ (~을 당연한 것으로 생각하다.)

☞ 「~을 당연하거나(사실이거나) 이미 해결된 것으로 여기다.」(= consider ~as true or already settled)의 뜻이다. 「take it for granted that S+V~ 」에서 it은 take란 동사가 that절(節)을 목적어로 취할 수 없기 때문에 생겨난 일종의 완충장치이다.

    Ex) We tend to <u>take</u> our liberties <u>for granted.</u>

       (우리의 자유를 당연한 것으로 생각하는 경향이 있다.)

       I <u>take it for granted that</u> all human beings must die.

       (모든 인간은 반드시 죽는다는 것을 당연하게 여긴다.)

       In the past we <u>took</u> the survival of the human race <u>for granted.</u>

       (과거에 우리는 인류가 살아 남는다는 것은 당연한 것으로 여겼다.)

TEST

* 다음을 영작하시오.

    그들은 그들의 권리를 당연한 것으로 생각한다.

(=>   )

(정답) They take their rights for granted.

[7] It ~ that 강조 구문

☞ 독해지문 중「It is [was] A that~ 」와 같은 구문이 나오면 다음과 같은 요령으로 해석한다.

① A가 「(대)명사」이고 「~부분」이 「불완전한」문장이면 「It ~ that ~」
강조구문이고 「 ~한 것은 A 이다[였다]」로 해석한다.

Ex) It's John that[who] said so (that절에 said의 목적어가 없음)

It's Spain that they're going to on holiday.

What was it that he found in the forest?

Who was it that said so?

What is it you are looking for? (당신이 찾고 있는 것이 무엇입니까?)

☞ What is it [that] you are looking for의 that을 생략한 것으로 「it=that you looking for (강조주어)」이며, 이 경우의 that은 관계대명사다.

② A가 「부사」이고 「 ~부분」이 「완전한 문장」이면 「It ~ that ~」은 강조구문이고 「 ~한 것은 A 이다[였다]」로 해석한다.

Ex) It was three weeks later that Mr. Baker heard the news.

It was because his mother was ill that he was absent.

③ A가 「형용사」이면 「It」는 「가주어」, 「that~ 」는 「진주어」를 나타내는 문장이 된다.

Is it true (that) you're getting married?

④ 「There is ~」, 「It is ~」의 강조 구문에서는 「주격 관계 대명사」를 생략할 수 있다.

Ex) There is a lady (who) wants to see you.

It was Wilson (that) told me this.

⑤ 강조하는 말에 따라 that 대신 who, which, where, when 따위를 쓰는 경우가 있다.

Ex) It was Mary that[who] won the first prize at the flower show.

It was the first prize that[which] Mary won at the flower show.

It was at the flower show that[where] Mary won the first prize.

[8] 강조 구문 It과 가주어(형식 주어) It 구문의 구별

☞ It is(was)와 that 사이의 말이 명사. 대명사인 경우 강조 구문인지 형식주어 구문인지 혼동이 될 때가 있다.

다음 두 문장을 비교하자.

Ex) It is you that are wrong. [강조 구문]

(잘못된 것은 너다.)

It is a pity that you lost such a chance. [형식주어 구문]

(네가 그런 기회를 잃은 것은 유감이다.)

=> It is[was]와 that을 제거해서, 그 명사·대명사가 주어 또는 술어동사의 목적어이면
   강조 구문, 그렇지 않으면 형식주어 구문이다.

[9] 비인칭 주어 It

☞ It이 문장의 주어로 쓰여 「날씨, 시간, 거리, 가격, 명암」 따위를 나타내는 용법이다.

Ex) What time is it now? – It's ten o'clock. ------------------- (시간)

┌ It is three years since I last met you.
├ How long does it take you to go to Seoul by bus.
└ It takes two hours for me to go to Seoul by bus.
It takes me two hours to go to Seoul by bus.
It was raining / snowing. ------------------------- (날씨)
It is warm / cold / windy.
How far is it from here to the station? ------------- (거리)
It is two miles.
How much does it cost you to buy that book. ----------(가격)
It costs five dollars for me to buy that book.
It costs me five dollars to buy that book.
It was quite dark when I got home. -----------------(명암)
How it is dark !

[10] 막연한 상황(狀況)을 나타내는 It

☞ 주위의 상태나 사정·상황을 막연하게 나타내는 용법이다. 또는 전후문맥으로 알 수
   있는 것을 가리킨다.

Ex) How is it going with you? (당신은 어떻게 지내십니까?)
    Whose turn is it next? (다음 차례는 누구냐?)
    That's the best(worst) of it. (최고다 / 최악이다.)
    As it happened, ~ (때마침~ , 공교롭게~)
    If it had not been for your help ~ (너의 도움이 없었다면~)
    = But for〈Without〉 your help ~

TEST

* 다음 글을 읽고 주어 It가 무엇을 가리키는가를 정확히 파악하고 우리말로 옮
  기시오.

   In the modern, it is almost as if the only reality is that recorded by
the television cameras.

23 이중 소유격(Double Genitive) : A(this, that) + 명사 + of + 속격(소유대명사)

☞ 이중 소유격이란 of와 's의 두가지를 함께 표시할 때 쓰는 말이다.

a, an, one, two, some, any, no, this, that, these, those 등은 소유격과 나란
히 쓸 수 없고 이중 소유격을 쓴다. 즉 이러한 낱말은 my, his, her, your, their
따위의 인칭 대명사 앞, 또는 뒤에 바로 쓸 수 없으며, 반드시 「a(an, this, that 등)
+ 명사 + of + 소유 대명사」꼴로만 쓴다.

$$\begin{bmatrix} a \\ this \\ that \end{bmatrix} \text{friend of mine} \qquad \begin{bmatrix} a \\ this \\ that \end{bmatrix} \text{hat of hers}$$

$\begin{bmatrix} \text{Mr. Ford's this house. (X)} \\ \text{This house of Mr ford's (O)} \end{bmatrix}$ $\begin{bmatrix} \text{My father's friend's that car (X)} \\ \text{That car of my father's friend (O)} \end{bmatrix}$

$\begin{bmatrix} \text{Henry's that new hat (X)} \\ \text{That new hat of Henry's (O)} \end{bmatrix}$

☞ 이 때 of 아래 속격(소유대명사)은 언제나 「사람」을 뜻하는 말이다.

Ex) $\begin{bmatrix} \text{This handle of knife's is no good. (X)} \\ \text{This knife's handle is no good. (O)} \end{bmatrix}$

cf) $\begin{bmatrix} \text{A friend of mine} \\ \text{My friend} \end{bmatrix}$

☞ 「A friend of mine」은 「불특정(不特定)」한 친구를 가리키고, 「My friend」는 상대방
이 어떤 의미를 알고 있는 「특정(特定)」의 친구를 뜻한다. 따라서 막연하게 「My
friend came to see me」라 할 수 없고, 「A friend of mine(또는 One of my
friends) came to see me」가 된다. 그러나 「my friend」는 사람의 이름과 함께
사용할 수는 있다.

Ex) <u>My friend Smith</u> came to see me.
   This is <u>my friend Johnson.</u>

⟨소유격의 의미⟩
[Shakespeare's works = the works written by Shakespeare]
(셰익스피어가 쓴 작품)

Ex) This is ┌ my brother's house.(소유자 : 내 형의 집)
             ├ the house of my brother.
             └ the house which belongs to my brother.
   That is ┌ Edison's gramophone.(발명자 : 에디슨이 발명한 축음기)
           └ the gramophone invented by Edison.
   This is ┌ children's clothing.(대상 : 아동복)
           └ lothing for children.
   Tell me ┌ the time of the party's arrival.
           │ (주격 관계 : 그 파티가 돌아옴)
           └ when the party will arrive.
   I heard ┌ my son's praises.(목적격 관계 : 아들을 칭찬함)
           └ them praise my son.

So와 Neither

[1] 긍정일 때 : So + 조동사 (be동사, do동사 등) + S(주어)
   (S 또한 그렇다)

① 앞에 나온 문장의 조동사와 동사에 따라 그 조동사, 동사가 be 동사인 경우-
   S에 맞는 be 동사를, 기타 동사인 경우는 do(does, did)를, 완료 시제의 경-
   는 have(has, had)등을 사용한다.
② S(주어)에 강세(Stress)가 있다.
③ 이 구문의 부정은 <u>neither + 조동사 + S</u>이다.

④ 이때의 So는 also, too(~도 또한)의 의미이다.

Ex) ⌈ A : I want to have a rest.
    ⌊ B : So do I. (= I want to have a rest, too)
    He <u>can</u> speak English, and so <u>can</u> I (= I <u>can</u> speak English, <u>too</u>)
    He <u>is</u> rich . So <u>am</u> I(= I <u>am</u> rich, <u>too</u>)
    He <u>saw</u> her. So <u>did</u> I (= I <u>saw</u> her, <u>too</u>)
    He <u>has been</u> abroad. So <u>have</u> I (= I <u>have been</u> abroad, <u>too</u>)

[2] 부정일 때 : <u>Neither + 조동사(be 동사, do 동사 등)</u> +S(주어)
(S 또한 아니다)

EX) ⌈ A : He doesn't like Jim.
    ⌊ B : Neither do I (= I <u>don't</u> like him, <u>either</u>)
    If you do not go, neither <u>will</u> I (= I <u>will not</u> go, <u>either</u>)
    He <u>can't</u> speak English. Neither <u>can</u> I
    (= I <u>can't</u> speak English, <u>either</u>)
    He <u>is not</u> rich. Neither <u>am</u> I (= I <u>am not</u> rich, <u>either</u>)
    He <u>did not</u> see her. Neither <u>did</u> I (= I <u>didn't</u> see her, <u>either</u>)
    He <u>has not</u> been abroad. Neither <u>have</u> I
    (= I <u>have not</u> been abroad, <u>either</u>)

[3] So + S(주어) + 조동사 (사실 S(주어)는 그렇다)
☞ 이때의 「So」는 「yes, really(사실)」의 의미이다.

Ex) ⌈ A : You look tired
    ⌊ B : So I am (=<u>Yes,</u> I am tired)
    Mr. Smith <u>can</u> speak French. So he <u>can</u>
    (= <u>Yes,</u> he <u>can</u> speak French)
    He <u>is</u> a millionaire. So he <u>is</u> (= <u>Yes,</u> he <u>is</u> a millionaire)
    He <u>married</u> her. So he <u>did</u> (= <u>Yes,</u> he <u>married</u> her)
    He <u>has been</u> to Africa. So he <u>has</u> (= <u>Yes,</u> he <u>has been</u> to Africa)

* 다음의 대화에서 빈 칸에 가장 알맞은 것을 고르시오.

A : I went to see the football game yesterday.

B : _____. It was quite exciting.

① So I went   ② So did I   ③ I'd like to
④ All right   ⑤ Neither did I

(정답) ②

---

26 ┌ To + one's + great + 감정을 나타내는 추상 명사(~하게도)
     └ S(주어) + be + much/greatly + 감정을 나타내는 형용사 + to 부정사

┌ I was surprised to find her gone.
└ To my surprise, I found her gone.
 (내가 놀랍게도 그녀는 가버렸다.)

┌ I was greatly astonished to find him dead.
└ To my great astonishment, I found him dead.
 (나는 그가 죽은 것을 알고서 깜짝 놀랐다.)

┌ To my great surprise, I found the classroom empty.
└ I was much surprised to find the classroom empty.
 (놀랍게도 교실은 텅 비어 있었다.)

┌ He has done it well, so we are satisfied with him.
├ He has done it well enough to satisfy us.
└ He has done it well to our satisfaction.
 (그가 그것을 매우 잘 하였으므로, 우리들은 그에게 만족하였다.)

┌ He kept the church clean, so the vicar was satisfied with him.
├ He kept the church clean enough to satisfy the vicar.
└ He cleaned the church to the satisfaction of the vicar.
 (그는 교회를 깨끗하게 관리했기 때문에 목사는 그를 흡족하게 생각했다.)

to	my delight	(내가 즐겁게도)
	my disappointment	(내가 낙심천만하게도)
	my sorrow	(내가 슬프게도)
	my relief	(내가 안심하게도)
to	her shame	(그녀가 부끄럽게도)
	her grief	(그녀가 비통하게도)
	his regret	(그가 유감스럽게도)
	his distress	(그가 괴롭게도)

27 a(n) + 단수 보통 명사 + of + a(n) + 단수 보통 명사
(A) (B)
A of B = B like A (A 와 같은 B)

Ex) ┌ She was an angel of a wife.
    ├ She was a wife like an angel.
    └ She was an angelic wife.
    (그녀는 천사같은 부인이다.)
    He is an oyster of a man. (그는 과묵한 사람이다.)
    a brute of a husband = a husband like a brute (짐승 같은 남편)
    a pig of a fellow = a fellow like a pig (돼지 같은 녀석)
    a palace of a house = a house like a palace (궁전 같은 집)

28 Everything, Something, Nothing

[1] Everything : (서술적으로 쓰여) 가장 중요(소중)한 것.
              (=thing of the greatest importance)
Ex) Money is everything to him.
    (돈이 그에게는 가장 소중한 것이다.)
    She's beautiful, I agree, but beauty is not everything.
    (그녀가 아름답다는 것은 수긍이 가지만 아름다움이 가장 중요한 것은 아니다.)
    You mean everything to me.
    (너는 나에게 가장 소중한 사람이다.)

[2] Something : 「상당한 것」「대단한 사람」「뛰어난 인물」「중요한 사람(것)」

    Ex) He thinks <u>something</u> of himself.
        (그는 자기 자신을 <u>대단한 인물</u>로 여기고 있다.)
        He is <u>something</u> in the department.
        (그는 부내(部內)에서 <u>중요인물</u>이다.)

[3] Nothing : 「하찮은 것」「무가치한 것」「보잘것없는 사람」

    Ex) He is <u>nothing</u> to me.
        (그는 내게 <u>무가치한 인간</u>이다.)
        She was a humble <u>nobody</u> a few years ago.
        (그녀는 몇 년 전 만해도 아주 <u>하찮은 사람</u>이었다.)
        He is just a <u>nobody.</u>
        (그는 정말 <u>하찮은 사람</u>이다.)
        She is <u>nothing,</u> if not pretty.
        (미인이라는 것이 단 하나의 장점이다.)
           He is nobody.(X)
           He is a nobody.(O)

29
  S(주어) + V(동사)+ 부사~
  S(주어) + V(동사) + a(n) + 형용사 + 명사(사람)~

☞ 어떤 동사를 그 동사의 명사형 (change = make a change)과 다른 동사 (여기서 make)를 이용해서 표현하는 방법으로 영어에는 매우 발달되어 있다. 이때 부정관사와 전치사는 필요한 경우에만 붙인다.
추상명사라도 그 앞에 형용사가 오면 대개 부정관사(a, an)를 사용한다. 이렇게 만들어진 말은 마치 한 단어인 것처럼 기억해 두어야 한다.

    Ex) ┌ She cooks well.
        └ She is <u>a good cook.</u>
       ┌ He works hard.
       └ He is <u>a hard worker.</u>
       ┌ She speaks English well
       └ She is <u>a good speaker of English.</u>

$$\begin{bmatrix} \text{She swims well.} \\ \text{She is } \underline{\text{a good swimmer}}. \end{bmatrix}$$

$$\begin{bmatrix} \text{She rises early.} \\ \text{She is } \underline{\text{an early riser}}. \end{bmatrix}$$

$$\begin{bmatrix} \text{She plays tennis well.} \\ \text{She is } \underline{\text{a good player of tennis}}. \end{bmatrix}$$

$$\begin{bmatrix} \text{She has } \underline{\text{progressed remarkably}} \text{ in learning.} \\ \text{She has } \underline{\text{made a remarkable progress}} \text{ in learning.} \end{bmatrix}$$

$$\begin{bmatrix} \text{They } \underline{\text{started early}} \text{ the next morning.} \\ \text{They } \underline{\text{made an early start}} \text{ the next morning.} \end{bmatrix}$$

$$\begin{bmatrix} \text{They } \underline{\text{studied}} \text{ the problem } \underline{\text{carefully}}. \\ \text{They } \underline{\text{made a careful study}} \text{ of the problem.} \end{bmatrix}$$

$$\begin{bmatrix} \text{She knows some Spanish.} \\ \text{She } \underline{\text{has some knowledge of Spanish}}. \end{bmatrix}$$

$$\begin{bmatrix} \text{He understands the issue well.} \\ \text{He } \underline{\text{has a good understanding of the issue}}. \end{bmatrix}$$

TEST

* 다음의 밑줄 친 부분을 괄호 안에 지시한 품사로 바꿔 두 문장의 의미가 같게 하시오.

1. ┌ John was much <u>pleased</u> with your kind invitation.(명사로)
   └ Your kind invitation was _____ _____ _____ John.

2. ┌ Betty <u>responded</u> briefly to the question. (명사로)
   └ Betty gave _____ _____ _____ to the question.

3. ┌ They <u>concluded</u> hastily about the matter. (명사로)
   └ They reached _____ _____ _____ about the matter.

4. ┌ Ned had a most hearty <u>reception</u>.(동사로)
   └ Ned was _____ _____ _____ .

5. ┌ The scene <u>impressed</u> me very much. (형용사로)
   └ The scene _____ very _____ me.

(정답) 1. a great pleasure 2. a brief response 3. a hasty conclusion
    4. received very heartily 5. was, impressive to.

제3장
Essential English Grammar

동사(Verb)와 시제(Tense)

01 과거의 동작의 결과가 현재에 남아 있음을 나타내는 현재완료 (have + p.p.)

I <u>have bought</u> a dictionary.

I bought a dictionary, and I have it now.

(나는 사전 한 권을 샀다. – 그래서 지금 갖고 있다.)

He <u>has returned</u> home.

He returned home, and is now at home.

(그는 집에 돌아왔다. – 그래서 지금 집에 있다.)

Spring has come. = Spring came and is here now.

    (봄이 왔다.)   (동작의 완료)

  cf) Spring is come. = It is spring now.

      (봄이로군.)   (현재의 상태)

He <u>has gone</u> to America.

He went to America, and is now in America.

(그는 미국에 갔다. – 그래서 지금 여기에 없다.)

02 S(주어) + have + P.P. + since + 주어 + P(과거동사)

Ten years <u>have passed</u> since he <u>died</u>.

It <u>is</u> ten years since he <u>died</u>.

He <u>died</u> ten years ago.

He <u>has been dead</u> for ten years.

He <u>has been dead</u> these ten years.

(그가 죽은지 10년이다.)

03 become과 come to (~이 되다)

☞ become 뒤에는 형용사, 명사가 보어로 오고, 부정사는 보어로 오지 못한다. 따라
서 to 부정사가 보어로 올 때는 come to + ⓥ[= learn to + ⓥ]로 쓴다.

Ex) He will become a teacher.(그는 선생님이 될 것이다.)
   You will come to appreciate my kindness. (당신은 나의 친절에 감
   사하게 될 것입니다.)

cf) come to + ⓝ 「의식을 되찾다, 되살아나다」(=recover consciousness)

Ex) She fainted but came to in a few minutes. (그녀는 기절했지만, 잠
   시 후 의식을 되찾았다.)

04 make it

☞ 「make it」은 「시간 약속을 하다, (기차, 모임 등의)시간에 대다, 잘 처리하다, 성공
하다, (~에)용케 도달하다」의 여러 가지 의미를 갖고 있다.

Ex) ┌ What time shall we make it?
    └ What time shall we meet?
      (우리 몇 시에 만날까요?)
    ┌ Let's make it at ten.
    └ Let's meet at ten.
      (10시에 만납시다.)
      We've just made it.
      (그럭저럭 시간에 댔다.)
      Let's make it some other time.
      (다음 기회에 합시다.)
      Please, make it quick.
      (빨리 서두르시오.)
      Did you make it to the theater on time?
      (극장에 정각에 닿았습니까?)

제3장 동사(Verb)와 시제(Tense)

Read / Go / Run (~라고 쓰여 있다)

[1] Read (~이라고 쓰여 있다)

Ex) The message <u>reads</u> as follows.
(傳言에는 다음과 같이 쓰여 있다.)

My reports generally <u>reads</u> "Has little ability but does his best."
(내 통지표는 대개 「능력은 별로 없으나 노력은 하고 있음」이라고 쓰여 있었다.)

[2] So goes (그렇게 쓰여 있다 / 그렇게 말한다)

☞ So는 앞문장 전체를 받는 부사로 Thus로 대신 쓸 수 있다.
go는 「~라고 쓰여 있다, ~라고 되어 있다」의 의미이다.

Ex)
  ┌ "Love your neighbor as yourself."
  └ So <u>goes</u> the bible. (성경에 그렇게 쓰여 있다.)
  ┌ They lived happily from that time on.
  └ So <u>goes</u> the story. (그 이야기는 그렇게 쓰여 있다.)
  ┌ "When in Rome, do as the Romans do."
  └ So <u>goes</u> a proverb. (속담에 그렇게 말하고 있다.)

[3] Run (~라고 쓰여 있다, ~라고 전해지다 = be told or written)

Ex) His statement <u>runs</u> as follows.
(그의 성명서는 다음과 같다.)

How does the first verse <u>run?</u>
(처음 1절은 무어라고 되어 있느냐?)

So the story <u>ran.</u>(= That is what was told or said)
(이야기는 그렇다.)

The story <u>runs</u> that… (It is said that…)
(…하다는 소문이다.)

The agreement <u>runs</u> in these words.
(협정은 이런 문구로 쓰여 있다.)

06 occur to/strike/hit upon
(생각이 문득 떠오르다)

사물 주어 + occur to + 사람
사람 주어 + hit upon + 사물

A happy thought <u>occurred to</u> me.
A happy thought <u>struck</u> me.
A happy thought <u>dawned on</u> me.
A happy thought <u>flashed on</u> me.
A happy thought <u>came upon</u> me.
A happy thought <u>came across</u> my mind.
I <u>hit upon</u> a happy thought.
(나는 즐거운 생각이 문득 떠올랐다.)

07 wear 와 put on의 차이

☞ 「wear」는 옷이나 장신구를 몸에 걸치고 있는 「상태」를 말하며("Wear" means to have upon the body as a garment or as an ornament.), 「put on」은 그것을 몸에 걸치는 「동작」을 말한다("To put on" denotes a simple act).

Ex) This man always <u>wears</u> black shoes.(O)
This man always <u>put on</u> black shoes.(X)
(이 남자는 항상 검은 구두를 신고 있다. – 상태)

I <u>put on</u> my clothes in the morning.(O)
I <u>wear</u> my clothes in the morning.(X)
(나는 아침에 옷을 입습니다. – 동작)

☞ 동사 「dress」는 「put on」과 거의 비슷한 의미이지만, 「dress」의 목적어는 「사물」이 아니고 「사람」이다.

Ex) He <u>dressed</u> <u>himself</u> and went out.
(그는 옷을 입고 나갔다.)
The mother <u>dressed</u> her <u>baby.</u>
(어머니는 아기에게 옷을 입혔다.)

08 see와 look의 혼동

┌ He <u>was looking</u> out of the window. (O)
└ He <u>was seeing</u> out of the window. (X)
(그는 창 밖을 보고 있었다.)

☞ 「see」는 「눈으로 바라보다」의 의미이지만,
　「look」은 보기 위해서 시선을 돌리는 동작을 말해준다.

　Ex) I <u>looked</u> up and <u>saw</u> the airplane.
　　　(올려다보니 비행기가 보였다.)

09 remember와 remind의 혼동

┌ Please <u>remind</u> me to give it back. (O)
└ Please <u>remember</u> me to give it back. (X)
(그것을 돌려주는 일을 나에게 상기시켜 주십시오.)

☞ 「remember」는 「기억하다」라는 의미. 「remind」는 다른 사람에게 「상기시키다」라
　는 의미다.

　Ex) I <u>remember</u> what you told me.
　　　(나는 당신에게 들은 것을 기억하고 있다.)

10 sleep과 go to bed의 혼동

┌ I shall go to bed early tonight. (O)
└ I shall sleep early tonight. (X)
(오늘밤은 일찍 잠자리에 들겠다.)

☞ 「go to bed」는 「잠자기 위하여 침대에 눕다」라는 동작을 나타낸다.

Ex) He <u>went to</u> bed at nine o'clock, but he did not <u>sleep</u> until eleven o'clock.

(그는 9시에 누웠지만 11시까지 잠자지 않았다.)

☞ 「go to sleep」는 「잠에 빠지다」라는 의미다.

Ex) He <u>went to sleep</u> while he was in the cinema.

(그는 영화관에서 잠을 자 버렸다.)

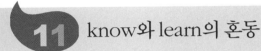

11 know와 learn의 혼동

He went to school to <u>learn</u> English.(O)
He went to school to <u>know</u> English.(X)

(그는 영어를 배우기 위해 학교에 갔다.)

☞ 「know」는 「learning」이 끝난 상태를 말하는 데 사용한다.

Ex) He <u>knows</u> how to swim.

(그는 수영하는 방법을 안다.)

또, 「know」를 「find out(발견하다)」, 「realize(깨닫다)」 대신에 사용해서는 안된다.

12 learn과 study의 혼동

He is <u>studying</u> at Gordon college.(O)
He is <u>learning</u> at Gordon college.(X)

(그는 골든 대학에서 공부하고 있다.)

☞ 「(어느 학교에서) 배우다」라는 의미로 「I learn at…」라고 하는 것은 틀리다. 「I study at…」, 또는 「I am a student of…」가 바르다. 즉 「study」가 적극적 노력을 수반하는데 비해 「learn」은 연습이나 수업으로 배우는 수동적인 과정을 나타낸다.

care for와 take care of의 혼동

He doesn't <u>take care of</u> his money.(O)
He doesn't <u>care for</u> his money.(X)
(그는 자신의 돈을 소중하게 여기지 않는다.)

☞ 「take care of」는 「~을 돌보다(=look after)」의 의미이며,
「care for」는 「~을 좋아하다(=like)」의 의미다.

Ex) I don't <u>care for</u> the book.
(나는 그 책을 좋아하지 않는다.)

(1) He <u>pays no attention to</u> my advice.(O)
He does not <u>care for</u> my advice.(X)
(그는 나의 충고를 들으려고 하지 않는다.)

(2) He <u>takes no care over</u> his work.(O)
He does not <u>care for</u> his work.(X)
(그는 일을 하는 데 주의가 부족하다.)

(3) He <u>took no notice of</u> him.(O)
He <u>took no care of</u> him.(X)
(그는 자신을 돌아보지 않았다.)

(4) No one <u>took care of</u> him during his illness.(O)
No one <u>cared for</u> him during his illness.(X)
(그가 아픈 동안 아무도 그를 돌보아 주지 않았다.)

fall과 fell의 혼동

John <u>fell</u> down and broke his leg.(O)
John <u>fall</u> down and broke his leg.(X)
(존은 넘어져서 다리가 부러졌다.)

☞ 「fall」의 동사변화는 「fall – fell – fallen」이다.
「fell」은 「베어 쓰러뜨리다」라는 의미고, 동사변화는
「fell – felled – felled」이다.

Ex) The wood-cutter <u>felled</u> a large tree.
(그 나무꾼은 큰 나무를 베어 쓰러뜨렸다.)

제4장

Essential English Grammar

동명사(Gerund)

01 cannot help ~ing
(~ing하지 않을 수 없다)

I cannot help laughing at the sight.

I cannot
- avoid laughing ——————————— at the sight.
- keep
- refrain ⎱ from laughing
- abstain
- but
- help but ⎱ laugh at the sight.
- choose but

I
- have no choice but to ⎱ laugh at the sight.
- can not do nothing but

(나는 이 광경을 보고 웃지 않을 수 없다.)

02 It is no [use / good] ~ing
(~ing 해 보아도 아무 소용없다)

It is no [use / good] crying over spilt milk.

It is [of no use / useless] to cry over spilt milk.

There is no use (in) crying over spilt milk.

What is the [use of / point] crying over spilt milk. [수사(修辭)의문문]

(엎질러진 우유를 놓고 울어도 아무 소용없다.)

It is no use my going to see her.

what is the use of my going to see her.

(내가 그녀를 만나러 가 본들 무슨 소용이었어.)

03　There is no ~ing (~ing할 수 없다)

┌ <u>There is no</u> denying the fact.
├ It is impossible to deny ┐
├ We can not deny ──────┤ the fact.
└ No one deny ──────────┘
(그 사실을 부인할 수 없다.)

04　┌ on ┐ ~ing (~ing 하자마자 곧)
　　└ upon ┘

┌ <u>On seeing</u> me,
├ As soon as he saw me,
├ The moment ┐
├ The instant ┤ he saw me,　　he ran away.
├ Immediately ┘
├ Directly
├ When he saw me,
├ No sooner had he seen me ┐ than he ran away.
├ He had no sooner seen me ┘
├ Scarcely ┐ had he seen me ┌ when ┐ he ran away.
├ Hardly ──┘　　　　　　　 └ before ┘
├ He had ┌ scarcely ┐ seen me ┌ when ┐ he ran away.
│　　　　└ hardly ──┘　　　　 └ before ┘
└ <u>At the sight of</u> me, he ran away.
(그는 나를 보자마자 곧 달아났다.)

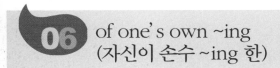

05 In ~ ing = When + S(주어) + V(동사)

> Be polite <u>in speaking</u> to others.
> Be polite <u>when you speak</u> to others.
> (다른 사람과 말할 때는 공손하라.)

06 of one's own ~ing
(자신이 손수 ~ing 한)

> S(주어) + V(동사) ~ of one's own ~ ing
> S(주어) + V(동사) ~ that(which) + S(주어) + oneself + P(과거동사)
> S(주어) + V(동사) ~ that(which) + S(주어) + have + P.P.(과거완료) + oneself
> S(주어) + V(동사) ~ (which is) + P.P.(과거완료) + by oneself (수동태일 때)

> This is a picture <u>of my own painting</u>.
> This is a picture <u>which I have painted myself</u>.
> This is a picture <u>which I myself painted</u>.
> This is a picture <u>(which is) painted by myself</u>.
> (이것은 내 자신이 손수 그린 그림이다.)

07 feel like ~ing (~ing 하고 싶다)
(~ing 할 마음이 생기다)

> S(주어) + feel like + ~ ing
> S(주어) + feel(be) inclined to + V(동사)
> S(주어) + have a mind(wish) to + V(동사)
> S(주어) + be disposed to + V(동사)
> S(주어) + would like to + V(동사)

$\begin{cases} S(주어) + be\ in\ a\ good\ mood\ to + V(동사) \\ S(주어) + be\ in\ a\ good\ mood\ for + N(명사) \end{cases}$

Ex)
- I feel like going home now.
- I feel(am) inclined to go home now.
- I have a mind(wish) to go home now.
- I am disposed to go home now.
- I would like to go home now.
- I am in a good mood to go home now.
- I am in a good mood for going home now.

(나는 지금 집에 가고 싶다.)

TEST

* 다음에 _____ 에 적당한 말을 써 넣으시오.

She felt like taking a nap.
She was in a good _____ for a nap. (정답) mood

08 What do you say to ~ing
(~ing 하지 않으시렵니까?, ~ing 하는 게 어때?)

- What do you say to ~ ing
- What do you think of(about) ~ ing?
- What about ~ ing?
- How about ~ ing?
- How do you like ~ ing?
- Let's + V(동사) ~, shall we?
- Why don't you + V(동사) ~?

Ex)
- What do you say to going to the movies?
- What do you think of(about) going to the movies?
- What about going to the movies?
- How about going to the movies?

How do you like going to the movies?

Let's go to the movies, shall we?

Why don't you go to the movies?

(영화 보러 가지 않겠습니까?)

09 be worth ~ing (~ing할 가치가 있다)

S(주어) + be worth ~ ing

S(주어) + be worthy of ~ ing

S(주어) + be worthy to be + P.P(과거분사)

It is worth while to + V(동사) ~

It is worth while ~ ing(동명사)

(동명사나 to부정사의 목적어가 주어로 올 때)

Ex)

This novel is worth reading.

This novel is worthy of reading.

This novel is worthy to be read.

It is worth while to read this novel.

It is worth while reading this novel.

This novel is worth while reading(or to read)

(이 소설은 읽을 만한 가치가 있다.)

☞ worth while은 반드시 가주어(It), 진주어(to부정사 또는 동명사)를 받는다.

10 It goes without saying that + S(주어) + V(동사) (that 이하는 말할 필요도 없다)

It goes without saying that + S(주어) + V(동사)

It is needless to say that + S(주어) + V(동사)

It is of no need to say that + S(주어) + V(동사)

It is not too much to say that + S(주어) + V(동사)

제4장 동명사(Gerund)

┌ It is a matter of course that + S(주어) + V(동사)
└ It is quite obvious that + S(주어) + V(동사)

    Ex) ┌ It goes without saying that man is mortal.
        ├ It is needless to say that man is mortal.
        ├ It is of no need to say that man is mortal.
        ├ It is not too much to say that man is mortal.
        ├ It is a matter of course that man is mortal.
        └ It is quite obvious that man is mortal.
        (인간이 반드시 죽는다는 것은 말할 필요도 없다.)

11 ┌ come ┐ near (to) ~ing (가까스로 ~ing를 벗어나다)
     └ go ┘ (거의 〈하마터면〉~ing 할 뻔하다)

┌ S(주어) + come near (to) ~ ing
├ S(주어) + go near (to) ~ ing
├ S(주어) + nearly escape (from) ~ ing
├ S(주어) + barely escape (from) ~ ing
├ S(주어) + narrowly escape (from) ~ ing
└ S(주어) + have a narrow escape from ~ ing

    Ex) ┌ She came near (to) being drowned.
        ├ She went near (to) being drowned.
        ├ She nearly escaped (from) being drowned.
        ├ She barely escaped (from) being drowned.
        ├ She narrowly escaped (from) being drowned.
        └ She has a narrow escape from being drowned.
        (그녀는 가까스로 익사를 모면하였다.)

    cf) ┌ He had a narrow escape from death.
        ├ He escaped death by a hair's breadth.
        ├ He escaped death by(with) the skin of my teeth.
        └ He escaped death by the(a) turn of a hair.
        (그는 구사일생으로 살아났다.)

12 be(get) used to ~ ing (~ing하는 것을 규칙(습관)으로 하고 있다, ~에 익숙하다)

- be used to ~ ing
- be accustomed to ~ ing(or to + V)
- make a point of ~ ing
- be in the habit of ~ ing
- have a habit of ~ ing
- make it a rule(point) to + V(동사)
- It is one's rule to V(동사)

Ex)
- I am used to taking a short walk before breakfast.
- I am accustomed to taking(take) a short walk beforebreakfast.
- He makes a point of taking a short walk before breakfast.
- He is in the habit of taking a short walk before breakfast.
- He has a habit of taking a short walk before breakfast.
- He makes it a rule(point) to take a short walk before breakfast.
- It is his rule to take a short walk before breakfast.

(그는 늘 아침 식사 전에 가벼운 산보를 규칙적으로 하고 있다.)

[과거 시제일 때]
- He was accustomed to taking(take) a walk in the morning.
- He made a point of taking a walk in the morning.
- He was in the habit of taking a walk in the morning.
- He made it a rule to take a walk in the morning..
- He used to take a walk in the morning.(이때의 used to는 과거의 규칙적인 습관을 나타낸다.)

(그는 아침에 늘 산보를 하곤 했다.)

13 be ┌ on ┐ the point of ~ing (~ing 하려고 하다)
         └ upon ┘   (~ing 하려는 찰나다)

He was on the ┌ point ┐
              │ verge │ of being drowned.
              │ brink │
              └ edge ┘
He was about to be drowned.
(그는 막 익사하려는 찰나였다.)

14 ┌ be far from ~ing   (결코 ~ing 하지 못하다)
       └ be about from~ing (결코 ~ing 아니다)

She <u>was far from telling</u> a lie.
She <u>was above telling</u> a lie.
She <u>didn't tell</u> a lie ┌ at all.
                             └ in the least.

          ┌ never   ┐
          │ by no means   │
She   │ anything but │ told a lie.
          │ on no account │
          └ on no occasion ┘
She was <u>the last</u> woman <u>to tell</u> a lie.
(그녀는 결코 거짓말을 하지 않았다.)

15

$$S(주어) + \begin{bmatrix} 부정어 \\ never \\ cannot \\ hardly \\ scarcely \end{bmatrix} + V(동사) \ⓐ \quad \begin{bmatrix} without \ ⓑ + ing \\ (ⓐ하면 반드시 ⓑ하다) \\ but \ S(주어) + V(동사) \ⓑ \\ (ⓑ하지 않은 채 ⓐ하는 일은 없다) \end{bmatrix}$$

It <u>never</u> rains <u>without</u> pouring.
It <u>never</u> rains <u>but</u> it pours.
<u>Whenever</u> it rains, it pours.
<u>Everytime</u> it rains, it pours.
<u>Eachtime</u> it rains, it pours.
<u>When</u> it rains, it <u>always</u> pours.
<u>At any time</u> it rains, it pours.
(비가 오면 억수같이 퍼붓는다. – 禍不單行 = Misfortunes never come singly alone.)

I <u>cannot</u> see this watch <u>without</u> thinking of you.
I <u>cannot</u> see this watch <u>but</u> I think of you.
<u>Whenever</u> I see this watch, I think of you.
<u>Everytime</u> I see this watch, I think of you.
<u>Eachtime</u> I see this watch, I think of you.
<u>When</u> I see this watch, I always think of you.
This watch <u>reminds</u> me <u>of</u> you.
(이 시계를 볼 때마다 네가 생각난다.)

16 There is no + N(명사) + but + V(동사)~

☞ 부정어(no, not)뒤에 나오는 「but」은 「that ~ not」의 의미를 지닌다. 이때의 but은 유사(의사) 관계 대명사이다.

There is <u>no</u> rule <u>but</u> has some exceptions.
There is <u>no</u> rule <u>that</u> does not have some exceptions.

There is <u>no</u> rule <u>without</u> some exceptions.
Every <u>rule</u> has some exceptions.
(예외 없는 규칙은 없다.)

There is <u>no</u> parents <u>but</u> love their son.
There is <u>no</u> parents <u>who(that)</u> do <u>not</u> love their son.
<u>All parents</u> love their son.
(자기 자식을 사랑하지 않는 부모는 없다.)

There is <u>scarcely</u> a man <u>but</u> speaks well of Tom.
There is <u>scarcely</u> a man <u>that(who) doesn't</u> speak well of Tom.
<u>Everybody</u> speaks well of Tom.
(Tom을 칭찬하지 않는 사람은 거의 없다.)

17
S + be busy with + N(명사)
S + be busy (in) ~ing (~하느라 바쁘다)

Ex)
I am <u>busy with my homework.</u>
I am <u>busy (in) doing my homework.</u>
(나는 숙제를 하기에 바쁘다.)

My mother has been <u>busy with house cleaning.</u>
My mother had been <u>busy cleaning the house.</u>
(나의 어머니는 집안 청소를 하느라 분주했다.)

My father was <u>busy with his office work.</u>
My father was <u>busy doing his office work.</u>
(나의 아버지는 회사 일에 바쁘셨다.)

The children are <u>busy with their toys.</u>
The children are <u>busy playing with their toys.</u>
(그 아이들은 장난감을 가지고 노느라 정신이 없다.)

He is <u>busy with the study of English.</u>
He is <u>busy studying English.</u>
(그는 영어 공부를 하느라 바쁘다.)

The host is <u>busy with arriving guests.</u>
The host is <u>busy meeting (receiving) arriving guests.</u>
(그 주인은 도착하는 손님을 맞이하기에 분주하다.)

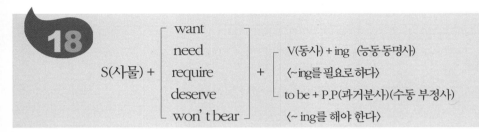

18

S(사물) + want / need / require / deserve / won't bear + V(동사) + ing (능동 동명사)
〈~ing를 필요로 하다〉
to be + P.P(과거분사)(수동 부정사)
〈~ing를 해야 한다〉

My watch <u>wants</u> <u>repairing.</u>(O)
My watch <u>wants</u> <u>to be repaired.</u>(X)
My watch <u>needs</u> <u>to be repaired.</u>(O)
I should <u>have</u> my watch <u>repaired.</u>(O)
(나의 시계를 고쳐야 한다.)

The garden <u>needs</u> <u>watering.</u>
The garden <u>needs</u> <u>to be watered.</u>
(정원에 물을 주어야겠다.)

He will <u>need</u> <u>looking</u> after.
He will <u>need</u> <u>to be looked</u> after.
(그는 누군가가 돌봐주어야 한다.)

My shoes <u>want</u> <u>mending.</u>
My shoes <u>need</u> to be <u>mended.</u>
(내 신은 수선이 필요하다.)

It <u>won't bear</u> <u>thinking</u> of.
It <u>won't bear</u> <u>to be thought</u> of.
(그 일은 생각하기도 지겹다.)

His language <u>wouldn't</u> <u>bear</u> <u>repeating.</u>
His language <u>was too bad to be repeated.</u>

제4장 동명사(Gerund)

(그의 말은 도저히 되풀이 할 것이 못된다.)

He <u>needs</u> <u>talking</u> to.
He <u>needs</u> <u>to be talked</u> to.
(〈이쪽에서〉 그에게 말을 붙일 필요가 있다.)

He <u>deserves</u> <u>helping.</u>
He <u>deserves</u> <u>to be helped.</u>
He <u>deserves</u> <u>to have</u> us <u>help</u> him.
(그는 도움을 받을 자격이 있다.)

19   go ~ing （~ing 하러 가다）

Ex) He will go ┌ swimming, climbing ┐
              ├ fishing, shopping ├
              └ hunting, skiing ┘
[그는 (수영, 등산, 낚시, 장보러, 사냥, 스키)하러 갈 것이다.)

20   look forward to ~ing
（~ing를 갈망하다, 학수고대하다）

He <u>looks forward to seeing</u> her
He <u>expects to see</u> her
He <u>anticipates seeing</u> her
He <u>is anxious to see</u> her.
(그는 그 여자를 몹시 만나보고 싶어 한다.)

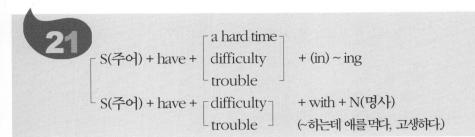

21

$$S(주어) + have + \begin{bmatrix} a\ hard\ time \\ difficulty \\ trouble \end{bmatrix} + (in) \sim ing$$

$$S(주어) + have + \begin{bmatrix} difficulty \\ trouble \end{bmatrix} + with + N(명사)$$
(~하는데 애를 먹다, 고생하다)

Ex) Does he <u>have a hard time speaking</u> English?
　　Did you <u>have any trouble driving</u> through the snow?
　　We <u>had no trouble (in) finding</u> his house.
　　Are you still <u>having difficulty with</u> mathematics?
　　We <u>had difficulty with</u> the obscure path through the forest.

He <u>has difficulty in hearing.</u>
He is <u>hard of hearing.</u>
(그는 귀가 멀었다.)
cf) hard of hearing 귀가 먼, 귀가 어두운

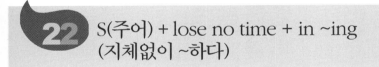

22 S(주어) + lose no time + in ~ing
(지체없이 ~하다)

Ex) We <u>lost no time in hurrying</u> to the station.
　　(우리는 즉시 정거장으로 서둘러 갔다.)

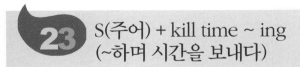

23 S(주어) + kill time ~ ing
(~하며 시간을 보내다)

Ex) He <u>killed time reading</u> a magazine while he waited.
　　(그는 기다리는 동안 잡지를 읽으면서 시간을 보냈다.)

　　　　　　　　　　　　　　　　　제4장 동명사(Gerund)

S(사람 주어) + cannot + V(동사) ~ 부사구(또는 부사절)

S(무생물 주어) ┌ prevent ┐
              │ keep   │
              │ disable │
              │ hinder │ ⓐ(목적어) from ~ ing
              │ prohibit│ (S는 ⓐ가 ~ ing하지 못하게 하다)
              │ stop   │
              └ restrain┘

S(무생물 주어) + make it possible for + 목적어 + to 부정사 ~

S(무생물주어) + forbid + 목적어 + to부정사 ~

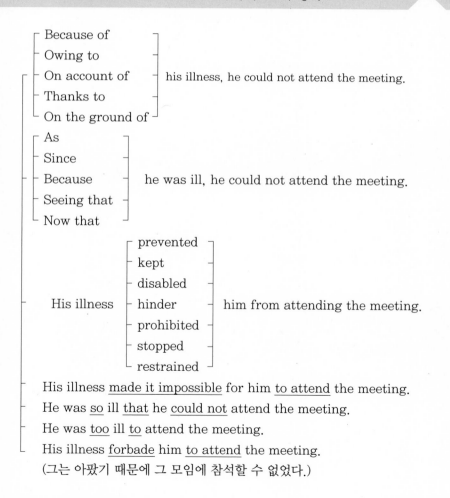

┌ Because of   ┐
├ Owing to   │
├ On account of   ┤ his illness, he could not attend the meeting.
├ Thanks to   │
└ On the ground of┘

┌ As   ┐
├ Since   │
├ Because   ┤ he was ill, he could not attend the meeting.
├ Seeing that │
└ Now that   ┘

              ┌ prevented ┐
              ├ kept   │
              ├ disabled │
His illness   ├ hinder   ┤ him from attending the meeting.
              ├ prohibited│
              ├ stopped   │
              └ restrained┘

His illness <u>made it impossible</u> for him <u>to attend</u> the meeting.

He was <u>so</u> ill <u>that</u> he <u>could not</u> attend the meeting.

He was <u>too</u> ill <u>to</u> attend the meeting.

His illness <u>forbade</u> him <u>to attend</u> the meeting.

(그는 아팠기 때문에 그 모임에 참석할 수 없었다.)

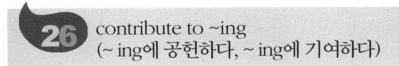

25 S(주어) + be opposed to ~ ing
(~ ing를 반대하다)

I am very much opposed to going there.
I object to going there.
I have an objection to going there.
(나는 거기 가는 것을 반대한다.)

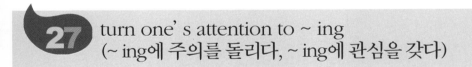

26 contribute to ~ing
(~ ing에 공헌하다, ~ ing에 기여하다)

Ex) He contributed to promoting the welfare of our society.
   (그는 사회복지 증진에 공헌했다.)

27 turn one's attention to ~ ing
(~ ing에 주의를 돌리다, ~ ing에 관심을 갖다)

Ex) He did not turn his attention to making a fortune until he was
   forty.
   (그는 40세가 될 때까지는 치부하는데 관심을 갖지 않았다.)

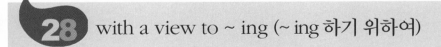

28 with a view to ~ ing (~ ing 하기 위하여)

Ex) I works hard
   with a view to succeeding.
   to succeed.
   in order to succeed.
   so as to succeed.

$\qquad$ for the purpose of succeeding.

$\qquad$ hat he may(can) succeed.

$\qquad$ so that he may(can) succeed.

$\qquad$ in order that may succeed.

(나는 성공하기 위해서 열심히 공부한다.)

29 for fear of ~ ing (~ ing 하지 않기 위하여)

Ex) He works hard
$\qquad$ for fear of failing.
$\qquad$ for fear that he should fail.
$\qquad$ lest he should fail.
$\qquad$ not to fail.
$\qquad$ so as not to fail.
$\qquad$ in order not to fail.
$\qquad$ that he may not fail.
$\qquad$ so that he may not fail.
$\qquad$ in order that he may not fail.

(그는 떨어지지 않기 위해서 열심히 공부한다.)

30 S(주어) + be equal to ~ ing / ⓝ (~ ing 할 능력이 있다, ~ing를 감당할 수 있다, (임무 등에) 적합하다)

Ex) I don't think you <u>are equal to</u> the task.
(나는 당신이 그 일을 충분히 할 수 있으리라 생각하지 않는다.)

He <u>is equal to</u> the task. (그는 그 일에 적격입니다.)

$\qquad$ He <u>was not equal to</u> doing the task.
$\qquad$ He <u>was unable to do</u> the task.
(그는 그 일을 할 능력이 없었다.)

31 S(주어) + [devote / apply] oneself to ~ing
(@를 ~ ing에 바치다, 열중하다, 전념하다, 몰두하다)

Ex) He <u>devoted all his time to</u> studying history.
　　(그는 그의 모든 시간을 역사 연구에 바쳤다.)

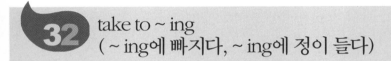

- I <u>apply myself to learning</u> German.
- I <u>give myself to learning</u> German.
- I <u>devote myself to learning</u> German.
- I <u>am applied to learning</u> German.
- I <u>am devoted to learning</u> German.
- I <u>am indulged in learning</u> German.
- I <u>am lost in learning</u> German.
- I <u>am absorbed in learning</u> German.
- I <u>am (pre)occupied with learning</u> German.
- I <u>am nuts on learning</u> German.

　(나는 독일어 공부에 열중하고 있다.)

32 take to ~ ing
(~ ing에 빠지다, ~ ing에 정이 들다)

Ex) He <u>took to</u> writing after he retired from the college.
　　(그는 대학을 은퇴한 후 글 쓰는데 정이 들었다.)

33 fall to ~ ing (~ 을 시작하다)

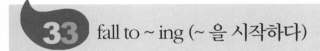

- They <u>fell to discussing</u> the serious problem.
- They <u>began to discuss</u> the serious problem.

(그들은 그 심각하게 문제를 토론하기 시작했다.)

　　　　　　　　　　　　　　　　　　제4장 동명사(Gerund)

> S(주어) + be + 형용사 + that + 주어 + 동사
> S(주어) + be + 형용사 + 전치사(of, for, at) ~ing

I am afraid <u>that I will hurt</u> your feelings.
I am afraid <u>of hurting</u> your feelings.

We are sure <u>that he will succeed.</u>
We are sure <u>of his succeeding.</u>

I am sure <u>that he will pass</u> the examination.
I am sure <u>of his passing</u> the examination.

I was sure <u>that she would come.</u>
I was sure <u>of her coming.</u>

He is confident <u>that he will win</u> the two-mile race.
He is confident <u>of winning</u> the two-mile race.

He was proud <u>that he was</u> rich.
He was proud <u>of being</u> rich.

He is proud <u>that he is</u> rich.
He is proud <u>of being</u> rich.
He <u>prides himself on</u> his riches.
He <u>takes pride in</u> his riches.

He is ashamed <u>that he made</u> such a mistake.
He is ashamed <u>of having made</u> such a mistake.

She was pleased <u>when he answered</u> in the affirmative.
She was pleased <u>at his answering</u> in the affirmative.

I am sorry <u>that I have made</u> a mistake.
I am sorry <u>for having made</u> a mistake.

He is sorry <u>that he did(has done)</u> so.
He is sorry <u>for his having done</u> so.

I am sorry <u>that I have caused</u> all this trouble.
I am sorry <u>to have caused</u> all this trouble.
I am sorry <u>for having caused</u> all this trouble.

cf) I regretted <u>that I had done</u> such a thing.
I regretted <u>to have done</u> such a thing.
I regretted <u>(of) having done</u> such a thing.

35 동격명사절 : 추상 명사 + that + S + V ~ = 추상 명사 + of + ~ing ~

[추상명사]

fact	possibility	report
chance	probability	hope
proof	likelihood	suggestion
certainty	doubt	evidence
idea	conclusion	rumor
news	opportunity	dream

☞ 추상 명사 뒤에 나오는 that절은 동격의 명사절이다.

There is no doubt <u>that he is</u> guilty.
There is no doubt <u>of his being</u> guilty.
(그는 유죄라는 데에 의심할 여지가 없다.)

제4장 동명사(Gerund)

There is no possibility <u>that he will win</u> the prize.
There is no possibility <u>of his winning</u> the prize.
(그가 상을 탈 가능성은 전혀 없다.)

There is little hope <u>that he will succeed.</u>
There is little hope <u>of his succeeding(success).</u>
(그가 성공하리라는 희망은 거의 없다.)

There can be no doubt <u>that he is</u> the best man for the job.
There can be no doubt <u>of his being</u> the best man for the job.
(그가 그 직에 가장 적합한 사람이라는 사실은 의심의 여지가 있을 수 없다.)

The fact <u>that he is honest</u> is known to everybody.
The fact <u>of his being honest</u> is known to everybody.
The fact <u>of his honesty</u> is known to everybody.
(그가 정직하다는 사실은 모든 사람에게 알려져 있다.)

The fact <u>that he is kind</u> is known to everybody.
The fact <u>of his being kind</u> is known to everybody
The fact <u>of his kindness</u> is known to everybody.
(그가 친절하다는 사실은 모든 사람에게 알려져 있다.)

36
S(주어) + V(동사) + 목적어 + that + 주어 + 동사 ~
S(주어) + V(동사) + 목적어 + of + 명사(구) ~

☞ 이러한 동사에는 advise, warn, convince, assure, tell 등이 있다.

The report advised him <u>that they had attacked the South.</u>
The report advised him <u>of their attack of the South.</u>

We warned them <u>that the roads were icy.</u>
We warned them <u>of the icy (condition of the) road.</u>

They warned us <u>that the task would be difficult.</u>
They warned us <u>of the difficulty of the task.</u>

He tried to convince the judge <u>that he was innocent.</u>
He tried to convince the judge <u>of his innocence.</u>

What I heard convinced me <u>that he was honest.</u>
What I heard convinced me <u>of his honesty.</u>

The teacher convinced me <u>that I was successful in the examination.</u>
The teacher convinced me <u>of my success in the examination.</u>

They assured the travels <u>that flying was safe.</u>
They assured the travels <u>of the safety of flying.</u>

She assured me <u>that she decided to join the club.</u>
She assured me <u>of her decision to join the club.</u>

He told his employer <u>that he wanted a pay raise.</u>
He told his employer <u>of his wish for a pay raise.</u>

He told me <u>that he planned to go abroad.</u>
He told me <u>of his plan to go abroad.</u>

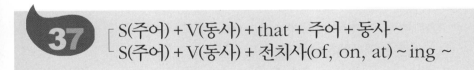

37 S(주어) + V(동사) + that + 주어 + 동사 ~
S(주어) + V(동사) + 전치사(of, on, at) ~ ing ~

☞ admit, complain, think, hear, repent, etc.

He admitted <u>that he was</u> in the wrong.
He admitted <u>of being</u> in the wrong.

He repented <u>that he had been</u> idle.
He repented <u>(of) having been</u> idle.

He repents <u>that he was</u> idle his youth.
He repents <u>(of) having been</u> idle in his youth.

I am glad to hear <u>that you have succeeded.</u>
I am glad to hear <u>of your having succeeded.</u>

They insisted <u>that I should go alone.</u>
They insisted <u>on my going alone.</u>

He insisted <u>that he would keep house.</u>
He insisted <u>on keeping house.</u>

I didn't much wonder <u>that he had gone away.</u>
I didn't much wonder <u>at his having gone away.</u>

38

S(주어) + remember ~ ing (과거의 뜻 : ~ 한 것을 기억하고 있다)
S(주어) + remember + that + 주어 + 과거동사 ~

I remember <u>seeing</u> him.
I remember <u>that I saw</u> him.
I remember <u>posting</u> the letter.
I remember <u>that I posted</u> the letter.
I remember <u>having seen</u> her before.
I remember <u>that I have seen</u> her before.

I remembered <u>having seen</u> her before.
I remembered <u>that I had seen</u> her before.

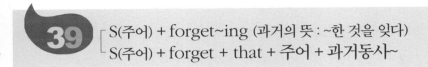

39 ⎡ S(주어) + forget~ing (과거의 뜻 : ~한 것을 잊다)
⎣ S(주어) + forget + that + 주어 + 과거동사~

⎡ I forget <u>going</u> there.
⎣ I forget <u>that I went</u> there.

⎡ I forget <u>posting</u> the letter.
⎣ I forget <u>that I posted</u> the letter.

⎡ I forgot <u>having posted</u> the letter.
⎣ I forgot <u>that I had posted</u> the letter.

40 ⎡ S(주어) + try ~ ing (한번 시험 삼아 ~ 해보다)
⎣ S(주어) + try + to부정사 (~하려고 애쓰다, 노력하다)

⎡ I tried <u>growing</u> potatoes here.
⎣ I actually grew some, to see if they would be successful crop.
(나는 시험 삼아 이곳에 감자를 재배했다.)

⎡ I tried <u>to grow</u> potatoes here.
⎣ I did my best to grow potatoes here.
(감자를 재배해 보려고 애써 봤다.)

제5장
Essential English Grammar

부정사(Infinitive)

S(주어) + remember + to 부정사~ (미래의 뜻 : ~할 것을 잊지않고 있다)
S(주어) + remember + that + 주어 + will(must, have to, should) + V(동사)~
S(주어) + don't forget to + V(동사)~

Please remember <u>to post</u> the letter.
Please remember <u>that you must post</u> the letter.
Please remember <u>that you have to post</u> the letter.
Please remember <u>that you should(will) post</u> the letter.
Please <u>don't forget to post</u> the letter.

He remembered <u>to post</u> the letter.
He remembered <u>that he had to post</u> the letter.
He remembered <u>that he would post</u> the letter.

I remember <u>to post</u> the letter.
I remember <u>that I will post</u> the letter.

I must remember <u>to ask</u> him.
I must remember <u>I will ask</u> him.

I will remember <u>to see</u> him.
I will remember <u>that I have to see</u> him.
I wiil remember <u>that I must see</u> him.
I will remember <u>that I shall see</u> him.

S(주어) + forget + to 부정사 ~ (미래의 뜻 : ~할 것을 잊다)
S(주어) + forget + that + 주어 + will(must, have to, should) + 동사 ~

Don't forget <u>to post</u> the letter.
Don't forget <u>that you must post</u> the letter.

제5장 부정사(Infinitive)

Don't forget <u>that you have to</u> post the letter.
Don't forget <u>that you should post</u> the letter.

I forget <u>to post</u> the letter.
I forget <u>that I must post</u> the letter.
I forget <u>that I had to post</u> the letter.
I forget <u>that I will post</u> the letter.

03

S(주어) + be sure to + V(동사)~(틀림없이(반드시)~ 할 것이다)
It is certain that + S(주어) + V(동사) ~
I am sure that + S(주어) + V(동사) ~

He <u>is sure to</u> turn up.
He will <u>surely</u> turn up.
<u>It is certain that</u> he will turn up.
I am sure <u>that he will turn up.</u>
I am sure <u>of his turning up.</u>
   ☞ 동명사의 의미상의 주어는 소유격이다.

She is sure to succeed.
She will surely succeed.

It is certain that she will succeed.
I am sure that she will succeed.
I am sure of her succeeding(success).

He is sure to come soon.
I am sure that he will come soon.

He is sure to live to eighty.
I am sure that he will live to eighty.

She was sure to be accepted as a tourist guide.
I was sure that she would be accepted as a tourist guide.

 ## 가주어(형식주어) / 진주어 (It ~ to + ⓥ)

☞ 주어가 부정사이고 복잡하거나 길어질 때는 대개 가주어(형식주어) 「it」를 쓴다.

Ex)
To get up early in the morning is good for health.
It is good for health to get up early in the morning.

To know oneself is difficult.
It is difficult to know oneself.

cf) It is not easy to speak English well.

 ## 가목적어(형식 목적어) / 진목적어

☞ 다음과 같이 불완전 타동사 make, find, think, believe 등의 목적어가 부정사일 때는 「It ~ to + ⓥ(가목적어 ~ 진목적어)형식」을 취한다.

Ex) I found it hard to master English.
　　　 (가목) O.C.　 (진목적어)

　　 => I found it was hard to master English.

I make it a rule to take breakfast at seven.
　　 (가목) O.C.　　　 (진목)

I found it easy to read this book.
　　 (가목)O.C.　 (진목)

I think it foolish to do so.
I think that it is foolish to do so.

TEST

다음의 두 문장을 한 문장으로 바꾸시오.(가목적어 it를 써서)

1. ⌈ It is wrong to tell a lie.
   ⌊ I think so.

   (   )

2. ⌈ It was difficult to learn English.
   ⌊ I found.

   (   )

3. ⌈ I study for two hours in the evening.
   ⌊ I make it a rule.

   (   )

(정답) 1. I think it wrong to tell a lie.

2. I found it difficult to learn English.

3. I make it a rule to study for two hours in the evening.

---

06 ⌈ 의문사 + to 부정사 [명사구]
⌊ 의문사 + S(주어) + ⌈ should ⌉ + V(동사) [명사절]
              ⌊ ought to ⌋
              ⌊ can   ⌋

⌈ I don't know where to go now.
⌊ I don't know where I should go now.

☞ know는 직접 to 부정사를 목적어로 취할 수 없고, 『의문사 + to 부정사』의 형태를 취한다.

⌈ I don't know what to do next.
⌊ I don't know what I should do next.

⌈ I can't decide which to buy.
⌊ I can't decide which I should buy.

There was no questions as to <u>whom to send.</u>
There was no questions as to <u>whom you should send.</u>

Please tell me <u>when to start.</u>
Please tell me <u>when I should start.</u>

He taught us <u>how to live</u> and <u>how to die.</u>
He taught us <u>how we should live</u> and <u>how we should die.</u>

"Where shall I go?" said Teresa.
Teresa did not know <u>where to go.</u>
                    (= where she should go)

"When shall I leave?" said Teresa.
Teresa did not know <u>when to leave.</u>
                    (= when she should leave)

I did not know <u>what to do.</u>
I did not know <u>what I ought to do.</u>
                    (=what I should do)

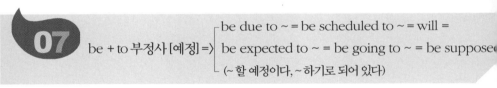

07 be + to 부정사 [예정] => be due to ~ = be scheduled to ~ = will =
be expected to ~ = be going to ~ = be suppose
(~ 할 예정이다, ~ 하기로 되어 있다)

We <u>are to meet</u> at the post office.

We
  are due to
  are scheduled to   meet at the post office.
  are going to
  are supposed to
  are expected to
  re slated to
  shall

(우리는 우체국에서 만나기로 되어 있다.)

08 be + to 부정사 [의무, 당연] =〉 must, should, ought to = have to (~해야 한다)

We <u>are to</u> obey the national law.
We <u>must</u> obey the national law.
(우리는 국법을 준수해야 한다.)

09 be + to 부정사 [가능] =〉 can, be able to (~할 수 있다)

Not a star <u>was to be</u> seen.
Not a star <u>could</u> be seen.
We <u>could</u> see no star.
We <u>could</u> not see a star.
(별을 한개도 볼 수가 없었다.)

10 be + to 부정사 [운명] =〉 ┌ be destined to ~ (~할 운명이다)
└ be doomed to ~

He <u>was never to see</u> his wife again.
He <u>was destined never to see</u> his wife again.
he <u>was doomed never to see</u> his wife again.
(그는 그의 처를 다시는 볼 수 없는 운명이었다.)

11 If + be + to 부정사 [의도, 소망] =〉 ┌ intend to ~ (~을 바란다면)
├ want to ~
└ wish to ~

Work hard if you <u>are to succeed.</u>
Work hard if you <u>want to succeed.</u>

(성공을 바란다면 열심히 공부하라.)

⌈ If you <u>are to succeed,</u> you must be diligent.
⌊ If you <u>wish to succeed,</u> you must be diligent.
(성공하고 싶으면, 부지런해야 한다.)

 ## be + to 부정사 [명령, 필연]
=〉 must, have to (~ 해야만 한다)

⌈ He <u>is to blame.</u>
⌊ He <u>must be blamed.</u>
(그는 비난 받아야 한다.)

⌈ You <u>are to do</u> as you are told.
⌊ You <u>must do</u> as you are told.
(들은 대로 행해야 한다.)

 ## 부정사의 부사적 용법 =〉 「부부동형」으로 암기

☞ 동사, 형용사, 다른 부사, 문장 전체를 수식한다.

[1] 목적 : ~ 하기 위하여, ~ 할 목적으로
    to + V = ⌈ so as to + V
           ⌊ in order to + V

☞ 부정사의 목적이나 뜻을 명확히 하기 위해 부정사 앞에 in order, so as를 첨가한다.

⌈ He works hard <u>to succeed.</u>
⌊ He works hard <u>in order to</u> succeed.
⌈ He works hard <u>so as to</u> succeed.
⌊ He works hard <u>for the purpose of</u> succeeding.

He works hard <u>with a view to</u> succeeding.

He works hard <u>that he may(can) succeed.</u>

He works hard <u>so that he may(can) succeed.</u>

He works hard <u>in order that he may succeed.</u>

He works hard <u>not to fail.</u>

He works hard <u>lest he should fail.</u>

He works hard <u>for fear of failing.</u>

He works hard <u>for fear that he should fail.</u>

He works hard <u>so as not to fail.</u>

He works hard <u>in order not to fail.</u>

He works hard <u>that he may(can) not fail.</u>

He works hard <u>so that he may(can) not fail.</u>

He works hard <u>in order that he may not fail.</u>

[2] 결과 : ～ 해서 ~하다, ~해보니 ~하였다.

(1) 無意志動詞(live, succeed, grow up, awake 등) + to부정사
☞ 이때의 부정사는 대개「결과」의 뜻이다.

(2) never + to 부정사 = and + S never + V
(～ 하여 결코 ~ 하지 못했다)

(3) only + to 부정사 = but + S + V(~ 했으나 ~ 했다)

He grew up <u>to be</u> a statesman.

He grew up <u>and became</u> a statesman.

(그는 자라서 정치가가 되었다.)

He left home <u>never to return.</u>

He left home <u>and (he) never returned.</u>

(집을 떠난 뒤 결코 돌아오지 못했다.)

He tried hard <u>only to fail.</u>

He tried hard <u>but (he) failed.</u>

(그는 열심히 했지만 그러나 실패했다.)

He <u>awoke</u> early <u>to study.</u>

He <u>awoke</u> early (in the morning) <u>and studied.</u>

(그는 일찍 (아침) 일찍 일어나서 공부했다.)

He didn't <u>live</u> <u>to see</u> his son a great man.

He <u>didn't see</u> his son a great man <u>when he lived.</u>

(그는 아들이 출세하는 것을 보지 못하고 죽었다.)

I <u>awoke</u> one morning <u>to find</u> myself famous.

(어느 날 아침 눈을 떠 보니 나는 유명한 사람이 되어 있었다.)

She didn't <u>live</u> <u>to see</u> her daughter become 20 years old.

(그녀는 자기 딸이 20세가 되는 것을 보지 못하고 죽었다.)

[3] 원인: ~해서 ~(하기)때문에)

주로 ┌ 감정의 형용사 + to부정사

└ 감정의 형용사 + that(because) + S + V ┘ 로 전환가능

┌ I'm glad <u>to see</u> you here.

└ I'm glad <u>that I see</u> you here.

┌ I'm sorry <u>that I hear</u> that.

└ I'm sorry <u>to hear</u> that.

☞ must be에 연결되는 부정사

He <u>must</u> be a fool <u>to do</u> such a thing.

(그런 말을 하다니, 그는 바보임에 틀림없다.)

☞ 의문사…?에서 사용된 부정사

┌ Who are you <u>to say</u> such a thing?

└ Who are you t<u>hat you should say</u> such a thing?

[4] 이유·판단의 근거 : ~하다니, ~하는 것을 보니

☞ 주로「단정적인 내용(must can't등) + to 부정사」의 형태를 취한다.

He <u>must be</u> mad to say so.

(그가 그렇게 말하는 것을 보니 미쳤음에 틀림없다.)

He <u>must be</u> foolish to do so.

(그가 그렇게 하다니 어리석은게 틀림없다.)

He <u>cannot be</u> mad to say so.

(그가 그렇게 말하는 것을 보니 미쳤을리가 없다.)

제5장 부정사(Infinitive)

[5] 조건 : ~하다면, ~하면, ~했다면, ~할 수 있다면

> to + V = it + S + could + V

I should be glad <u>to go</u> with you.
I should be glad <u>it I could go</u> with you.
(당신과 함께 갈 수 있다면 좋겠습니다.)

<u>To hear him talk,</u> you <u>would</u> take him for an American.
<u>If you heard him talk,</u> you <u>would</u> take him for an American.
(그가 말하는 것을 들으면, 너는 그를 미국 사람으로 생각할 것이다.)

<u>To hear him speak English,</u> you <u>would have taken</u> him for an American.
<u>To have heard him speak English,</u> you <u>would have taken</u> him for an American.
<u>If you had heard him speak English,</u> you <u>would have taken</u> him for an American.
(그가 말하는 것을 들었다면, 너는 그를 미국인으로 착각했을 것이다.)

[6] 정도 · 관점 · 범위 : 부사 too, enough, so등을 수식

He is <u>too</u> weak <u>to</u> do it.
He is <u>so</u> weak <u>that</u> he <u>can' t</u> do it.

She is wise <u>enough to</u> know it.
She is <u>so</u> wise <u>that</u> she <u>can</u> know it.

He was <u>so</u> foolish <u>as to</u> do so.
He was <u>so</u> foolish <u>that</u> he did so.

14 so ~ as to + V(동사)
       enough to + V(동사) => so ~ that + S(주어) + can + V(동사)

(너무 ~해서 그 결과 V(동사)하다)

He got up <u>so</u> early <u>as to be</u> in time for the train.
He got up early <u>enough to be</u> in time for the train.
He got up <u>so</u> early <u>that</u> he <u>could be</u> in time for the train.
(그는 매우 일찍 일어나서 기차시간에 댈 수 있었다.)

15 S(주어) + V(동사) + too ~ to 부정사
       S(주어) + V(동사) + so ~ that + 주어 + can't + 동사

(너무 ~ 해서 ~할 수 없다)

She is <u>too</u> obstinate for me <u>to</u> persuade.
She is <u>so</u> obstinate <u>that</u> I <u>can't</u> persuade her.
(그녀가 너무 완고해서 설득시킬 수 없었다.)

He is <u>too</u> weak <u>to</u> do it.
He is <u>so</u> weak <u>that</u> he <u>can't</u> do it.
(그는 너무 약해서 그 일을 할 수 없다.)

(주의)

S(사물 주어) + V(동사) + too~ to 부정사 + [사물 주어 받는 대명사]
                                    (쓰지 않는다)
S(사물 주어) + V(동사) + so~that + 주어 + can't + 동사 + [사물 주어 받는 대명사]

Ex) This book is <u>too</u> difficult for me <u>to read.</u>
     This book is <u>so</u> difficult <u>that</u> I <u>can't</u> read it.
     This stone is <u>too</u> heavy for me <u>to lift.</u>
     This stone is <u>so</u> heavy <u>that</u> I <u>can't</u> lift it.

16 S(사물 주어) + V(동사) + too + 형용사/부사 + for + N(명사) (N에게는 너무 ~ 하다)

☞ too ~ to 의 변형으로 볼 수 있다.

These shoes are <u>too</u> small <u>for me.</u>
These shoes are <u>too</u> small <u>for</u> me to put on.
These shoes are <u>so</u> small <u>that</u> I can't put them on.
(이 신발은 너무 작아서 신을 수가 없다.)

The scenery was <u>too</u> beautiful <u>for</u> words.
The scenery was <u>too</u> beautiful <u>to</u> describe.
The scenery was <u>so</u> beautiful <u>that</u> no words <u>could</u> describe it.
The scenery was beautiful <u>beyond describing(description).</u>
(그 경치는 말로써 표현할 수 없을 만큼 아름다웠다.)

The setting sun is <u>too</u> beautiful <u>for</u> words.
The setting sun is beautiful <u>beyond describing(description).</u>
(그 석양은 말로써 표현할 수 없을 만큼 아름다웠다.)

These apples are <u>too</u> ripe <u>for</u> cooking.
These apples are <u>so</u> ripe <u>that</u> they <u>are not</u> good for cooking.
(이 사과들은 요리하기에는 너무 익었다.)

The scenery was <u>too</u> miserable <u>for</u> words.
The scenery was <u>too</u> miserable <u>to</u> speak.
(그 경치는 말로써 표현할 수 없을 만큼 형편없었다.)

17

    S(주어) + V(동사) + too ~ not to 부정사 …
    S(주어) + V(동사) + so ~ that + S(주어) + can't but + 동사원형 …
    (너무 ~ 해서 …할 수 밖에 없다)

He is <u>too</u> wise <u>not</u> to solve the problem.
He is <u>so</u> wise <u>that</u> he <u>cannot but solve</u> the problem.
(그는 현명해서 문제를 풀 수 밖에 없다.)

18

    S(주어) + V(동사) + not too ~ to 부정사 …
    S(주어) + V(동사) + not so ~ that + 주어 + cannot + 동사 …
    (…하지 못할 정도로 ~ 한 것은 아니다)
    (…할수 없으리 만큼 너무 ~ 하지는 않다)

He is <u>not too</u> old to do the task.
He is <u>not so</u> old <u>that</u> he <u>cannot do</u> the task.
He is <u>not so</u> old <u>but</u> he <u>can do</u> the task.
<u>However old he may be,</u> he <u>can do</u> the task.
(그 일을 할 수 없을 만큼 늙은 것은 아니다.)

19 부정주어(No,Not) + so ~ but that …
       (…하지 못할(않을) 정도로(만큼) ~ 는 아니다)

☞ 이 경우 but that에서 but을 생략하면 that 이하의 절에 부정어(no, not)를 넣어야
한다.

<u>No</u> man is <u>so</u> old <u>but that</u> he may learn.
<u>No</u> man is <u>so</u> old <u>that</u> he may <u>not</u> learn.
<u>However old a man may be,</u> he may learn.
(배울 수 없을 만큼 그렇게 늙은 사람은 없다.)

20 S(주어) + V(동사) + only too ~ to 부정사 (…하면 매우 ~ 하다) (= extremely)

Ex) I shall be <u>only too</u> glad to help you.
          (=extremely)
   (당신을 도울 수만 있다면 대단히 기쁘겠습니다.)

cf) The rumor is <u>only too</u> true.(그 소문은 유감스럽게도 사실이다.)
          (=regrettably)

21 Hope와 To부정사와의 관계

⌈ I hope <u>that I'll succeed.</u>(O)
⌊ I hope <u>to succeed.</u>(O)

⌈ I hope <u>that he will succeed.</u>(O)
⌊ I hope <u>him to succeed.</u>(X)

☞ 이 경우에는 expect를 쓴가 또는 I hope for his success로 해야 한다.

cf) expect와 wish는 양쪽이 다 올 수 있다.
⌈ I expect <u>that he will come tomorrow.</u>
⌊ I expect <u>him to come tomorrow.</u>
⌈ I wish <u>you would succeed.</u>
⌊ I wish <u>you to succeed.</u>

cf) want와 like는 that절을 목적어로 받는 것은 가능한 피하며, 「목적어 + to부정사」로 쓴다.
⌈ I want you to study hard.(O)
⌊ I want <u>that you should study hard.</u>(X)

⌈ I like <u>her to wear long dress.</u>(O)
⌊ I like <u>that she wears her long dress.</u>(X)

cf) think동사와 to부정사와의 관계
⌈ I think <u>that he'll succeed.</u>(O)
⌊ I think <u>him to succeed.</u>(X)

$\begin{bmatrix} \text{I think } \underline{\text{that he is honest.}}\,(\text{O}) \\ \text{I think } \underline{\text{him (to be) honest.}}\,(\text{O}) \end{bmatrix}$

$\begin{bmatrix} \text{I think } \underline{\text{that I' ll succeed.}}\,(\text{O}) \\ \text{I think } \underline{\text{to succeed.}}\,(\text{X}) \end{bmatrix}$

☞ 이 경우에는 I think of my success로 써야 한다.

 ## 문장의 일부를 대신 받는 〈so〉와 〈to〉

☞ 〈so〉와 〈to〉는 아래 예시한 동사 따위의 목적어 대신 쓰인다.
  〈so〉는 문장의 절(節)을 대신 받으며, 〈to부정사〉는 구(句)를 대신 받는다. 이때의
  〈so〉와 〈to부정사〉는 앞의 내용을 긍정적으로 받을 때 쓰이는 경우이며, 부정적인
  내용을 받을 때는 〈not〉을 쓴다.

[1] 〈so〉를 받는 경우

☞ say, call, speak, tell, think, hope, expect, suppose, imagine, hear,
  guess, do, be afraid, etc.

Ex) $\begin{bmatrix} \text{She must look like a very pretty girl.} \\ \text{Yes, I imagine } \underline{\text{so.}}(= \text{that she must look like a very pretty girl}) \end{bmatrix}$
$\begin{bmatrix} \text{Do you speak English?} \\ \text{Yes, I hope } \underline{\text{so.}} \ (= \text{that I can speak English}) \end{bmatrix}$
$\begin{bmatrix} \text{Has he lost all his goods?} \\ \text{I' m afraid } \underline{\text{so.}} \ (= \text{that he has lost all his goods}) \end{bmatrix}$

[2] 〈to부정사〉를 받는 경우

☞ intend, plan, seem, mean, etc.
Ex) $\begin{bmatrix} \text{Will you take a trip to U.S.A.?} \\ \text{Yes, I plan } \underline{\text{to.}} \ (= \text{to take a trip to U.S.A.}) \end{bmatrix}$
$\begin{bmatrix} \text{Do you help him?} \\ \text{Yes, I intend } \underline{\text{to.}} \ (= \text{to help him}) \end{bmatrix}$

[3] 〈so〉와 〈to〉를 모두 받는 경우

☞ hope, wish, fear, etc.

제5장 **부정사**(Infinitive)

Ex) ┌ Can you speak English?
    ├ I hope <u>so.</u> (= that I can speak English)
    └ I hope <u>to.</u> (= to speak English)
    ┌ Can she speak English?
    ├ I hope <u>so.</u> (= that she can speak English) (0)
    ├ I hope <u>to.</u> (≠ to speak English) (X)
    ├ She hopes <u>so.</u> (= that she can speak English) (0)
    └ She hopes <u>to.</u> (= to speak English) (0)

☞ 주절과 종속절의 주어가 다른 복문을 단문으로 전환할 때 「hope」는 「to부정사」를
받지 못한다. 즉, 「hope」는 주절과 종속절의 주어가 같을 때만 가능하다.

[4] 부정의 〈not〉을 받을 때

Ex) ┌ Will he come?
    └ I'm afraid <u>not.</u> (= that he won't come)
    ┌ Will he die?
    └ I hope <u>not.</u> (= that he will not die)
    ┌ Will it be fine tomorrow?
    └ I'm afraid <u>not.</u> (= that it will not be fine tomorrow)
    ┌ Will he pass the test?
    └ I don't suppose he will. (= I suppose <u>not</u>)
    ┌ Do you think it is true?
    └ I'm afraid <u>not.</u> (= I'm afraid it is not true)
    ┌ Will he keep his promise?
    └ I guess he won't. (= I guess <u>not</u>)

23
┌ All you have(need) to do is (to) + V(동사) ~
├ S(주어) have only to + V(동사) ~
└ S(주어) need only to + V(동사) ~   (~ 하기만 하면 된다.)

┌ <u>All you have to do</u> is (to) meet her.
└ You <u>have only to</u> meet her
  (너는 그녀를 만나기만 하면 된다.)

┌ <u>All you have to do</u> is just to sign here.
├ You <u>have only to</u> sign here.

└ Just sign here. That's all you have to do.
　(당신이 해야 할 일이란 여기에 사인을 하는 것이다.)

┌ All you have to do is just to study hard.
├ You have only to study hard.
└ Just study hard. That's all you have to do.

┌ All you have to do is just to stay here and wait for him.
├ You have only to stay here and wait for him.
└ Just stay here and wait for him. That's all you have to do.

┌ All you have to do is just to go to see a dentist.
├ You have only to go to see a dentist.
└ Just go to see a dentist. That's all you have to do.

┌ All you have to do is just to drive carefully.
├ You have only to drive carefully.
└ Just drive carefully. That's all you have to do.

┌ All you have to do is just to let us know where you are.
├ You have only to let us know where you are.
└ Just let know where you are. That's all you have to do.

TEST

　* 다음의 두 문장의 의미가 같아지도록 _____을 채우시오.

┌ All you have to do is study harder.
└ You have _____ to study harder.

　(정답) only

24

All you do is (to) + V(동사) ~
You do nothing but + V(동사원형) ~ (~하기만 하다)

All he does is to complain.
He does nothing but complain.
(그는 불평하기만 한다.)

25

It takes + 시간(기간) + to 부정사 ~
It takes + 목적격(사람) + 시간(기간) + to 부정사 ~
It takes + 시간(기간) + for + 목적격(사람) + to 부정사 ~
You can + 행위 + in + 시간(기간) ~
(~ 하는데 ~ 만큼 걸린다)

Ex) How long does it take you to go to Seoul by bus?
It takes two hours to go to Seoul by bus.
It takes two hours for me to go to Seoul by bus.
It takes me two hours to go to Seoul by bus.
You can go to Seoul by bus in two hours.

cf) How far is it from here to Seoul?
It is about forty miles.
It takes about an hour by bus.

26

It costs + 돈(금액) + to 부정사 ~
It costs + 목적격(사람) + 돈(금액) + to 부정사 ~
It costs + 돈(금액) + for + 목적격(사람) + to 부정사 ~
(~ 하는데 ~ 만큼의 비용(돈)이 든다)

Ex) How much does it cost you to buy that book?
It costs five dollars to buy that book.
It costs me five dollars to buy that book.
It costs five dollars for me to buy that book.

27
```
┌ S(주어) + have + the + 추상명사 + to 부정사
├ S(주어) + be + so + 형용사 + that + 주어 + 동사
├ S(주어) + be + so + 형용사 + as + to 부정사
├ S(주어) + be + 형용사 + enough to 부정사
└ S(주어) + 부사 + 동사 (~ 하게도 ~ 하다)
```

```
┌ S + have the kindness to + V        (친절하게도 ~ 하다)
├ S + have the fortune to + V         (다행히도 ~ 하다)
├ S + have the luck to + V            (운좋게도 ~ 하다)
├ S + have the audacity to + V        (감히 ~ 하다)
├ S + have the boldness to + V        (뻔뻔히도 ~ 하다)
├ S + have the misfortune to + V      (불행히도 ~ 하다)
├ S + have the politeness to + V      (공손히도 ~ 하다)
├ S + have the impoliteness to + V    (무례하게도 ~ 하다)
├ S + have the wisdom to + V          (현명하게도 ~ 하다)
└ S + have the foolishness to + V     (어리석게도 ~ 하다)
```

```
┌ He had the kindness to help me.
├ He was so kind that he helped me.
├ He was so kind as to help me.
├ He was  kind enough to help me.
├ It was very kind of him to help me.
└ He kindly helped me.
  (그는 친절하게도 나를 도와주었다.)
```

```
┌ She had the luck to win the race.
├ She was so lucky that she won the race.
├ She was so lucky as to win the race.
├ She was lucky enough to win the race.
└ She luckily won the race.
  (그녀는 운좋게도 그 경주에서 이겼다.)
```

I had the wisdom not to borrow it from him.
I was so wise that I didn't borrow it from him.
I was so wise as not to borrow it from him.
I was wise enough not to borrow it from him.
I was wise enough that I did't borrow it from him.
I was too wise to borrow it from him.
I wisely didn't borrow it from him.
(나는 현명하게도 그에게서 그것을 빌리지 않았다.)

28 hope [want, wish, expect, intend, promise…] + 단순부정사 = 미래의 일

I hope to succeed.
I hope that I shall succeed.
(나는 성공하기를 희망한다.)

I hoped to succeed.
I hoped that I should succeed.
(나는 성공하기를 희망했다.) -성공여부는 불확실하다-

He hoped to succeed.
He hoped that he would succeed.
(그는 성공하기를 희망했다.)-성공여부는 불확실
(=He may or may not have succeed.)

29

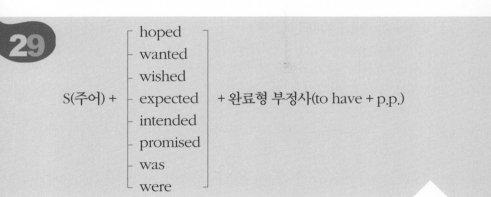

$$S(주어) + \begin{cases} \text{hoped} \\ \text{wanted} \\ \text{wished} \\ \text{expected} \\ \text{intended} \\ \text{promised} \\ \text{was} \\ \text{were} \end{cases} + 완료형 부정사(to have + p.p.)$$

```
      ┌─ ① S(주어) + had + p.p + to 부정사
=>┤─ ② S(주어) + P(과거동사) + to 부정사 ~ but + 주어 + 과거 조동사 + not
      └─ ③ S(주어) + had + p.p + that + 주어 + would ~ but + 주어 + 과거 조동사 + not
```

☞ hoped, wanted, wished, expected, intended, promised, was, were 등 「소망,
   기대, 의지, 요구」등을 나타내는 <u>과거 동사 뒤</u>에 나오는 「완료형 부정사(to have +
   P.P.)」는 「이루지 못한 사실이나 동작」을 나타낸다.

┌─ I <u>hoped to have seen</u> the show.(O)
├─ I <u>had hoped to see</u> the show.(O)
├─ I had hoped to have seen the show.(X)
├─ I hoped see the show, but I could'nt (see it).(O)
└─ I had hoped that I would see the show, but I couldn't.(O)
   (나는 쇼 구경을 하려고 했으나 할 수 없었다.)

┌─ I <u>expected to have gone.</u>
├─ I <u>had expected to go.</u>
└─ I expected to go, but I didn't go.
   (나는 가려고 했으나 가지 못했다.)

┌─ He <u>intended to have done</u> so.
├─ He <u>had intended to do</u> so.
└─ He intended to do so, but he did not.
   (그는 그렇게 하려고 했으나 하지 못했다.)

┌─ I was <u>to have called</u> on him.
└─ I was to call on him, but I didn't.
   (나는 그를 방문하려고 했으나 하지 못했다.)

30~34 부정사의 의미상의 주어를 포함한 문장의 변형 방법

30

```
It + V(동사) + 형용사 + that + S(사람주어) + (should) + 동사 ~
It + V(동사) + 형용사 + for + 목적격(사람) + to 부정사 ~
```

☞ necessary, possible, impossible, convenient, natural, etc.

```
        ┌ necessary ┐
        │ possible  │
It is   ┤ impossible ├ + that + S(주어) + V(동사) ~   ( O )
        │ convenien·│
        └ natural   ┘

        ┌ necessary ┐
        │ possible  │
It is + ┤ impossible ├ + for + 목적격(사람) + to부정사 ~ ( O )
        │ convenien·│
        └ natural   ┘
```

☞ 여기서 제시된 형용사는 「It ~ that」 또는 「It ~ for ~ to」로 양쪽 전환이 가능한
형용사이다. 그러나, 여기 제시된 형용사는 사람을 주어로 할 수 없다.

```
Ex) ┌ It is necessary that you should do it. (O)
    ├ It is necessary for you to do it. (O)
    └ You are necessary to do it.(X)
      (네가 그것을 하는 것이 필요하다.)


    ┌ It is natural that a Korean should love Korean. (O)
    └ It is natural for a Korean to love Korean. (O)
      (한국인이 한국어를 사랑하는 것은 당연하다.)
```

☞ 필요나 의무를 나타내는 형용사 necessary, essential, important, desirable 등
이 [It is + 형용사 + that + 주어 + 동사] 구문에 쓰이면, that 절에는 동사원형(미
국 영어)이나 〈should + 동사 원형〉(영국 영어)를 쓴다.

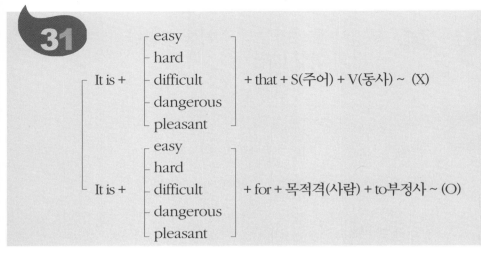

☞ 여기서 제시된 형용사는 「It ~ that」으로는 쓸 수 없으며, 오직 「It ~ for ~ to」로만 가능한 형용사이다. 또한 여기에 제시된 형용사는 사람을 주어로 할 수 없다.

- It is <u>difficult</u> that we should master English. (X)
- It is <u>difficult</u> for me to master English. (O)
- We are <u>difficult</u> to master English. (X)
- English is <u>difficult</u> to master. (O)

(영어를 마스터 하는 것은 어렵다.)

☞ 위에 제시된 형용사는 사람을 주어로 할 수 없다. 그러나, 「①타동사나 ②전치사의 의미상의 목적어」가 될 때에는 「그 의미상의 목적어」는 「주어」로 올 수 있다.

- It is <u>difficult</u> that we should master English. (X)
- It is <u>difficult</u> for me to master English. (O)
- We are <u>difficult</u> to master English. (X)
  (We는 to master의 의미상 목적이 되지 못하므로 틀린 문장임 : to master의 목적은 English임)
- English is <u>difficult</u> to master. (O) (to master의 의미상 목적은 주어인 English임)

- It's <u>hard</u> for me to read this book. (O)
- This book is <u>hard</u> for me to read. (O)
- I am <u>hard</u> to read this book. (X)

제5장 부정사(Infinitive)

It is <u>difficult</u> to please him. (O)

He is <u>difficult</u> to please. (O) (He는 to please의 의미상 목적어이

므로 맞는 문장임.)

(그는 비위를 맞추기 어려운 사람이다.)

It's pleasant to talk with her. (O)

She is pleasant to talk with. (O)

It's pleasant for me to hear from you. (O)

It's pleasant that I should hear from you. (X)

I am pleased to hear from you. (O)

It's impossible for us to work with him. (O)

He's impossible for us to work with. (O)

He's impossible to go alone. (X)

(go는 자동사이며, alone은 부사이므로 이 문장은 틀렸다)

32

It is + ┌ true
        ├ false
        ├ likely   + that + S(주어) + V(동사) ~ (O)
        ├ certain
        └ sure

It is + ┌ true
        ├ false
        ├ likely   + for + 목적어(사람) + to부정사 ~ (X)
        ├ certain
        └ sure

☞ 여기서 제시된 형용사는 「It ~ that」으로는 쓸 수 있으나, 「It ~ for ~ to」로는 쓸

수 없는 형용사이다.

It is true that he is a liar.(O)

It is true for him to be a liar.(x)

(그가 거짓말이란 말은 사실이다.)

33

It is +
good, fine, bad, kind, unkind, wise, clever,
foolish, silly, cruel, polite, thoughtful,   + of + 목적격(사람) + to부정사 ~
rude, careful, generous, stupid, considerate
(사람의 성질 · 성격 · 특성을 나타내는 형용사)

S(사람주어) + be +
good, fine, bad, kind, unkind, wise, clever,
foolish, silly, cruel, polite, thoughtful,   + to부정사 ~
rude, careful, generous, stupid, considerate
(사람의 성질 · 성격 · 특성을 나타내는 형용사)

It is very kind of you to say so. (0)
You are very kind to say so. (0)

How kind (it is) of you to say so. (0)
(당신이 그렇게 말씀하시니 친절합니다.)

It was wise of you to reject his proposal. (0)
You were wise to reject his proposal. (0)
His proposal was wise of you to reject. (X)
(당신이 그의 제안을 거절한 것은 현명했습니다.)

☞ 이때의 형용사 「wise」는 사람의 성질·성격을 나타내므로 「His proposal」이 주어로 올 수 없
된다.

34

You may come tomorrow
if you are convenient.(X)
if it is convenient to(for) you.(O)

He cannot afford to buy that house.(O)
He is unable to buy that house.(O)
It is unable for him to buy that house.(X)
It is incapable for him to buy that house.(X)
He is incapable of buying that house.(O)
He is incapable to buy that house.(X)
It is impossible for him to buy that house.(O)
(그는 그 집을 살 여유가 없다.)

☞ 「be (un)able to」와 「be capable to」의 주어는 항상 「사람」이어야 한다.

- I am sorry to hear of your father's death.(O)
- It is sorry for me to hear of your father's death.(X)
- I am a pity to hear of your father's death.(X)
- It is a pity to hear of your father's death.(O)

☞「be sorry」의 주어는 항상 「사람」이며, 「be a pity」의 주어는 항상 「It」이 된다.

35 사역동사(使役動詞 : Causative Verb)

☞ 「사역동사」란 어떤 사물이 사람에게 어떤 행위를 하게 하는 동사를 말한다.
   Ex) make, let, get, cause, have, help 등

[1] 원형부정사를 보어로 하는 사역동사 ; have, let, make

사역동사 + O(목적어) +O.C(원형부정사)

〈 make와 let의 차이 〉
- My father <u>made</u> me <u>go</u> to Brazil.
- My father <u>compelied(forced)</u> me <u>to go</u> to Brazil.
  (아버지는 내 뜻에 관계없이) 나를 브라질로 보냈다.(강요)

- My father <u>let</u> me <u>go</u> to Brazil.
- My father <u>permitted</u> me <u>to go</u> to Brazil.
- My father <u>allowed</u> me <u>to go</u> to Brazil.
  (아버지는 내 뜻을 받아들여) 나를 브라질로 보냈다.(허락)

He <u>made</u> me <u>drink</u> on that night.
(그날밤 그는 억지로 내게 술을 권해서 마시게 했다.)

Let me introduce myself.
Allow me to introduce myself.

They didn't let anyone enter the room.
They didn't force(compel) anyone to enter the room.

[2] have와 get
　(1) 능동일 때
have + 사람 + 원형부정사
　　　　O　　　O.C.
get + 사람 + to부정사
　　　　O　　　O.C.

☞ 목적어와 목적보어가 능동일 때 have와 make의 목적보어는 「동사원형」이, get의
　목적보어는 「to 부정사」가 온다.

　(2) 수동일 때(목적어와 목적보어 관계가 수동일 때
☞ 주어가 받는 경험·고통·손해를 나타내며, 목적보어는 반드시 p.p(과거분사)가 온다.
have + 사물 + p.p.
get + 사물 + p.p.

① 목적어와 목적보어 관계가 「수동」일 때 : ~을 … 당하다
☞ 주어에게 손실을 가져다 주며, 동작이 주어의 의사(意思)에 관계없이 행해진다.
　Ex) I had my watch stolen.
　　　He had his knees skinned. (신체의 일부가 피해를 받는 경우)

② 목적어와 목적보어 관계가「사역」일 때 : ~을 …해 받다〈시키다〉
　☞ 주어에게 이익을 가져오며, 동작이 주어의 의사(意思)에 따라 행해진다.
I had my watch repaired.
Where can I get it repaired?
(어디에서 수리할 수 있을까요?)
I must get my hair cut.
My mother had me clean my hands.
I had him carry the baggage.
I got him to carry the baggage.
I had the baggage carried by him.

cf) I <u>got</u> him <u>to prepare</u> for our journey.

I'll <u>get</u> him <u>to go</u> with us.

⎡ I <u>had</u> Bob <u>teach</u> Mary.(능동)

⎣ I <u>had</u> Mary <u>taught</u> by Bob.(수동)

⎡ I <u>had</u> my servant <u>clean</u> the room.(능동)

⎣ I <u>had</u> the room cleaned by my servant.(수동)

cf) 사역동사 help는 「원형부정사」또는「to부정사」모두 받을 수 있다.

I'll help her (to) translate the story.

I helped her (to)wash up at the sink.

[3] to 부정사를 보어로 하는 사역동사

☞ ask, get, like, want, wish, cause, advise, bear, believe, compel, direct, force, allow, enable, order, forbid, permit, tell, etc.

Ex) She <u>asked</u> me <u>to hand</u> this package to you.

(이 꾸러미를 당신께 전하라는 그 부인의 소청입니다.)

We must <u>get</u> some one <u>to show</u> us the way.

(길을 안내할 사람을 구해야지.)

I <u>like</u>(want, wish) you to come.

What <u>causes</u> apples <u>to fall?</u>

(무엇이 원인으로 사과는 땅으로 떨어질까?)

Elders <u>advise</u> children <u>to keep</u> their money in the bank.

(어른들은 아이들이 자기 돈을 은행에 저축하라고 조언한다.)

They firmly <u>believe</u> her <u>to be pure.</u>

(그녀가 결백함을 그들은 굳게 믿고 있다.)

The commander <u>directed</u> his men <u>to retreat.</u>

(부하들이 퇴각하도록 명령했다.)

He <u>ordered</u> his men <u>to fire.</u>

(그는 부하들에게 발포하라고 명령했다.)

36

⎡ have ⎤ + 목적어(사물) + p.p. [이익:시켜받다 (사역)]
⎣ get ⎦   [손해:당하다(수동)]

⎡ have+ 목적어(사람) + V(동사원형)[목적어와 목적보어 관계가 능동일 때] ⎤
⎣ get + 목적어(사람) + to 부정사 [목적어와 목적보어 관계가 능동일 때] ⎦

$$\begin{bmatrix} I \begin{bmatrix} had \\ got \end{bmatrix} my\ watch\ \underline{repaired}\ by\ him \\ \begin{bmatrix} I\ \underline{had}\ him\ \underline{repair}\ my\ watch. \\ I\ \underline{got}\ him\ \underline{to\ repair}\ my\ watch. \end{bmatrix} \end{bmatrix}$$

(나는 그에게 내 시계를 고치도록 시켰다.)

$$\begin{bmatrix} I \begin{bmatrix} had \\ got \end{bmatrix} my\ purse\ \underline{stolen}. \\ My\ purse\ was\ stolen. \end{bmatrix}$$

(나는 내 지갑을 도난당했다.)

37 지각동사(知覺動詞 : Verbs of Perception)

☞ 지각동사란 우리가 오감(五感)이나 심적(心的)작용에 의해 인식이나 이해를 얻는 것을 말할 때 쓰이는 동사다. 여기에는 feel, hear, see, notice, observe, perceive, smell, watch 등이 있으며, 이들 지각동사는 원형부정사(Bare-infinite root verb)를 보어로 가진다. 또는 이들은, 제5형식(불완전 타동사 ; S + V + O + O.C.)에 속하고, 이 종류의 동사는 대체로 진행형이 드물다.

[1] 지각동사 + O(목적어) + O.C.(원형부정사)
① 목적어와 목적보어 관계는 의미상 주어와 술어의 관계에 있다.
② 목적어와 목적보어 관계가 능동일 때는 => 동사원형, 현재분사(~ing)
③ 목적어와 목적보어 관계가 수동이면 => 과거분사(p.p)를 쓴다.

I <u>saw</u> the man <u>cross</u> the road.(완결된 동작)
The man <u>crossed</u> the road, and I saw him do this.

I <u>saw</u> the man <u>crossing</u> the road.(진행중인 동작)
I <u>saw</u> the man <u>while he was crossing</u> the road.

She <u>felt</u> her eyes <u>dazzled</u> by a blaze of light.
She <u>felt</u> a blaze of light <u>dazzle</u> her eyes.
(번쩍이는 광선에 그녀의 눈이 부셨다.)

<u>Watch</u> the girl <u>play</u> the violin.

We <u>noticed</u> someone <u>jump</u> over the fence.

Don't you <u>smell</u> something <u>boiling</u>?

(무엇인가 끓고 있는 냄새가 나지 않는가?)

[2] 지각동사와 함께 쓰이는 「원형부정사」는 「보어」가 된다.(5형식)

<u>We</u> <u>saw</u> <u>her</u> <u>enter</u> the music hall.

   S   V   O   O.C.

<u>I</u> <u>observed</u> <u>tears</u> <u>come</u> into her eyes.

S   V   O   O.C

<u>He</u> <u>felt</u> <u>his hands</u> <u>tremble</u>.

S   V   O   O.C.

[3] 목적보어가 be …인 때에는 to가 붙는다.

He <u>felt</u> his hands <u>to be</u> cold.

(그는 자기 손이 차다고 느꼈다.)

I <u>saw</u> the gossip <u>to be</u> false.

(그 쑥덕공론이 허위임을 나는 알았다.)

We <u>know</u> it <u>to be</u> a mistake.

(우리는 그것이 실수라는 것을 안다.)

[4] 지각동사·사역동사가 「수동태」로 쓰일 때는 「수동태」에서 「to 부정사」가 되살아난다.

⌈ I <u>heard</u> her <u>sing.</u>

⌊ She was <u>heard</u> <u>to sing.</u>

⌈ We <u>saw</u> him <u>enter</u> the room.

⌊ He was <u>seen</u> <u>to enter</u> the room.

⌈ My father <u>made</u> me <u>go</u> abroad for study.

⌊ I was <u>made</u> <u>to go</u> abroad for study by my father.

TEST

1 다음의 두 문장의 의미가 같아지도록 ____을 채우시오.

　　⌈ Our teacher made us read these books.
　　⌊ We were made _____ these books by our teacher.

　　　⌈ One might have heard a pin drop.
　　　⌊ _____ might have been _____.

(정답) to read, A pin, heard to drop

2 다음의 빈 칸에 알맞은 것은?

　Professor Kim _____ about him.
　① heard the students to talk　② heard the talk by the students
　③ heard the students' talking　④ heard the students talk.

(정답) ④

3 다음의 빈 칸에 알맞은 것은?

　Anything new?　I heard them _____ about you.
　① talked　② talking　③ to talk　④ talks

(정답) ②

4 다음의 빈 칸에 알맞은 것은?

　Tom was late yesterday.
　No wonder why I saw him _____.
　① run mad　② running madly　③ running mad　④ to run madly

(정답) ②

5 다음의 빈 칸에 알맞은 것은?

　What's the matter, Jane?
　I smell something _____.
　① burning　② burns　③ to be burned　④ to burn

(정답) ①

☞ I smell something (which is) burning.

여기서는 burn이 아니고 burning을 쓴 이유는
"타고 있는 과정"(진행중인 동작)이 비교적 짧기 때문이다.

6 다음의 빈 칸에 알맞은 것은?

What did you do in the garden?

I watched Alfred _____ his bicycle.

① to paint ② painted ③ painting ④ paints

(정답) ③

☞ ┌ I watched <u>Alfred paint his bicycle.</u>
   ├ I watched <u>Alfred painting his bicycle.</u>
   └ I watched <u>his bicycle being painted by Alfred.</u>

38 to부정사만을 목적어로 받는 타동사

원하는   약속을   계획할 때엔
want   promise   plan

바라는 날을   고르고   결정해서
wish, want choose decide

거절하거든   협박하는   체 하라.
refuse   threaten pretend

☞ hope, want, wish, expect, seek, decide, promise, care, refuse, agree,
pretend, fail, learn, choose, contrive, afford, ask, demand, deserve,
desire, endeavor, manage, refuse, threaten, seem, etc.

Ex) I <u>promised</u> not <u>to be late</u> again.
    (다시는 지각을 하지 않겠다고 약속했다.)

    The general <u>refused</u> <u>to withdraw his troops.</u>
    (그 장군은 자신의 군대를 철수하기를 거부했다.)

He pretends to be honest but he is a quite pseudologist.
(그는 정직한 체하지만 완전히 거짓말쟁이다.)

I finally managed to find what I was looking for.
(난 마침내 내가 찾던 것을 가까스로 발견했다.)

39 동명사만을 목적어로 받는 타동사

동명사의   연습은   연기하거나
          practice   postpone
회피하지 말고   중단없이   계속   즐기며
avoid, evade, escape, mind   stop, quit,   keep enjoy
끝내라는   제의를   놓치거나   부인하지 말고
finish   suggest miss   deny
잘 고려해서 인정해야 한다.
consider   admit

☞ enjoy, stop, finish, mind, miss, avoid, escape, risk, postpone, practice,
appreciate, admit, excuse, anticipate, mention, propose, suggest, doubt,
deny, pardon, mean, prevent, suffer, tolerate, resist, repent, resent,
recall, give up, keep on, go on, put off, understand, include, involve,
dislike, deny, dispute, fancy, consider, imagine, can't help ~ing, be
used to ~ing, object to ~ing, be busy ~ing, etc.

Ex) That's why I practice swimming every day.
    (그래서 나는 매일 수영을 연습했다.)

    He postponed sending an answer to her request.
    (그는 그녀의 요청에 대한 회답 발송을 늦추었다.)

    The best way to lose weight is to avoid eating fatty food.
    (체중을 줄이는 가장 좋은 방법은 지방질의 음식을 피하는 것이다.)

    Would you mind filling out this questionnaire?
    (이 설문조사에 응해 주시겠습니까?)

He <u>denies</u> <u>having stolen the watch.</u>
(그는 시계를 훔쳤음을 부인하고 있다.)

40 동명사 to부정사 양쪽을 다 목적어로 받는 동사

☞ like, love, hate, begin, start, continue, mean, try, neglect, cease, prefer, forget, remember, regret, plan, commence, can't bear, etc.

Ex) I <u>continued</u> <u>reading</u> at home all day this holiday.
(이번 휴일에는 하루 종일 집에서 책을 읽었다.)

His many talents <u>continue</u> <u>to surprise and delight audiences.</u>
(그의 많은 재능은 계속 청중을 놀라게하고 즐겁게 한다.)

I <u>prefer to eat meat</u> rather than <u>to eat vegetables.</u>
(나는 야채를 먹는 것보다 고기 먹는 것을 더 좋아한다.)

I <u>prefer</u> <u>singing</u> to <u>dancing.</u>
(나는 춤추는 것보다 노래하는 게 더 좋다.)

제6장

Essential English Grammar

분사구문
(Participial Construction)

01 분사구문(分詞構文 : Participial Construction)

☞ 「분사구문」이란 접속사 구실도 겸해 가면서, 절(節)을 (부사) 구(句)로 만드는 문장체 (Written English)표현이다. 대개 부사절이나 구로 바꿀 수 있고, 등위절에 해당하는 것도 많다. 「분사구문」은 회화체(Spoken English)로는 별로 쓰지 않는다. 「분사구문」은 순수한 부사절과는 달라서, 표현이 생략·압축되어 있어 정서적 색채가 짙다. 그 의미가 확연치 않은 것이 더러 있으나, 문맥에 따라서 해석한다.

02 (부사절을) 분사구문으로 고치는 방식 (복문=〉단문)

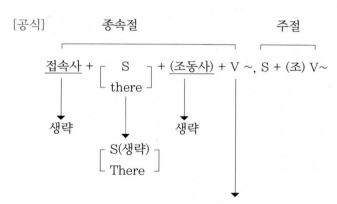

[공식]

종속절   주절

접속사 + ┌─ S ─┐ + (조동사) + V ~, S + (조) V~
          └ there ┘

↓   ↓   ↓
생략   ┌ S(생략) ┐   생략
         └ There ┘

not, never
(부정일 때)

(요점)
① 주어의 일치
② 시제의 일치
③ 능·수동형 파악
④ 접속사 파악

┌ [1] 단순형 : 주절의 시제 ≧ 종속절 시제
│   * 종속절 동사 시제와 주절의 시제가 일치할 때
│   ① 능동일 때 : V(동사원형) + ing
│   ② 수동일 때 : (being) + p.p.
└ [2] 완료형 : 주절의 시제 〈 종속절 시제
    * 종속절 동사시제가 주절의 시제보다 빠를 때
      ① 능동일 때 : having + p.p
      ② 수동일 때 : (having been) + p.p.

[1] S(주절의 주어) = S′(종속절의 주어)일 때 S를 생략

Ex)

While(as) I was walking along the street, I met John.
          S   S′

Walking along the street, I met John.

If you turn to the left, you will find the building.
   S   S′

Turning to the left, you will find the building.

Though I admit what you say, I still think you are wrong.
      S   S′

Admitting what you say, I still think you are wrong.

She smiled brightly, and extended her hands.
S.S′ 과거   과거

Smiling brightly she extended her hands.

Our train starts at six, and arrives in London at ten.
S·S′   현재   현재

Our train starts at six, arriving in London at ten.

[2] S ≠ S′일 때 S를 남긴다.

Ex)

As it was very cold, we built a fire.
  S (과거)   S′ (과거)

It being very cold. we built a fire.

As there was no bus service, we had to walk.
   S 과거   S′ (과거)

There being no bus service, we had to walk.

[3] 종속절 동사 V의 시제가 주절 동사 V와 일치하는 경우 (단순형)
① 종속절 동사 V가 능동인 경우 => V(동사원형) + ing

Ex) When she saw me, she smiled.
        S 과거   S′ 과거

└ Seeing me, she smiled.

② 종속절 동사 V가 수동인 경우 => (being) + p.p

  Ex)

┌ As he was wounded in the leg, he could hardly walk.
│   S   과거(수동)   S´ 과거
└ (Being) wounded in the leg, he could hardly walk.

┌ These dogs, if they are properly trained, will be able to do a lot of tricks.
└ These dogs, (being) properly trained, will be able to do a lot of tricks.

[4] 종속절 동사 V의 시제가 주절 동사 V보다 과거인 경우 (완료형)

① 종속절 동사 V가 능동일 때 => having + p.p

  Ex) ┌ As I ┌ have finished
│   └ finished   ┘ my work, I have nothing to do.
│   (과거 또는 현재 완료)   (현재)
│   └ Having finished my work, I have nothing to do.

② 종속절 동사 V가 수동일 때 => (having been) + p.p

  Ex) ┌ As I have been deceived so often, I am now on my guard.
│   S   현재완료(수동)   S´ 현재
│   └ (Having been) Deceived so often, I am now on my guard.

[5] 종속절 동사 V가 부정(否定)인 경우

  ☞ not, never 등은 분사구문 앞에 온다.

  Ex) ┌ As he had not received an answer, he sent a message.
│   S   과거완료(능동)   S´ (과거)
│   └ Not having received an answer, he sent a message.

03   분사구문 작성상의 주의 사항

1. 대명사 주어 뒤에 분사구문이 오지 못한다.

  Ex) ┌ The boy, being praised, worked the harder. (O)
│   S   분사구문   V

└ He, being praised, worked the harder. (X)
　　대명사주어　분사구문　　　　V

2. 분사구문에서 ┌ (being) + p.p ┐ 등은 (being),
　　　　　　　　└ (having been) + p.p ┘

(having been)이 생략되어 p.p형 분사구문이 되는 것이 보통이다.
3. 분사구문은 문장 앞, 중간, 끝에도 올 수 있다.
4. 분사구문에 주어가 남아 있는 경우 독립 분사구문이라 한다.
5. 분사구문은 문어체 어법이므로, 생활영어에서는 잘 사용되지 않는다.

 분사 구문의 종류

[1] 시간(때) : when, while, after, since, as soon as …

Ex) ┌ Arriving at the terminal, we found the bus gone.
　　└ When we arrived at the terminal, we found the bus gone.
　　　(종점에 도착했을 때 버스는 이미 떠나고 없었다.)

　　┌ Walking along the street, he met an old friend of mine.
　　└ While he walked along the street, he met an old friend of
　　　mine.
　　　(거리를 걷다가 그는 옛 친구를 만났다.)

[2] 이유, 원인(~이므로) : as, since, because …

Ex) ┌ As I desired rest, I lay down in the shade.
　　└ Desiring rest, I lay down in the shade.
　　　(나는 쉬고 싶었으므로 그늘에 누웠다.)

　　┌ Since I feel tired, I will stay at home.
　　└ Feeling tired, I will stay at home.
　　　(피곤하므로 집에 있겠다.)

　　┌ As I did not want to anger him, I pretended to agree.
　　└ Not wanting to anger him, I pretended to agree.
　　　(나는 그에게 화를 내고 싶지 않았기 때문에 동의하는 척 했다.)

☞ 부정어 not, never는 분사의 바로 앞에 온다.

[3] 조건 (~한다면) : if

Ex)
- If you turn to the right, you will find the house.
- Turning to the right, you will find the house.

- If you come tomorrow, you will be able to see him.
- Coming tomorrow, you will be able to see him.

- Born in better times, he would have become a free citizen.
- If he had been born in better times, he would have become a free citizen.

(더 좋은 시대에 태어났더라면, 그는 자유 시민이 되었을 것이다.)

[4] 양보(비록~한다 할지라도) : though, although.

Ex)
- Though I admit what you say, I still don't believe it.
- Admitting what you say, I still believe it.

- Although they were born of the same parents, they don't resemble each other.
- (Having been) Born of the same parents, they don't resemble each other.

[5] 부대상황(附帶狀況 : Attendant Circumstances) : ~하면서, ~하고서, ~한 채

① 동시동작(~하면서) ; while, as (=) 2개의 동작이 동시에 발생)

Ex)
- While she smiled brightly, she extended her hand.
- Smiling brightly, she extended her hand.

(그녀는 밝게 웃으면서 손을 내밀었다.)

- As he raised his hand, he stood up and answered.
- Raising his hand, he stood up and answered.

(그는 손을 들면서 일어나서 대답했다.)

② 연속 동작(그리고 ~ 하다) ; ~, and + V(동사)

☞ 2개의 동작이나 사건이 연속적으로 일어나는 경우이며, 일반적으로 ① 먼저 일어난 사건을 =〉「주절」로 쓰고, ② 나중에 일어난 사건을 =〉「and + V(동사)」또는 「분사구문」의 형태로 표현한다.

Ex)
- We started in the morning, and arrived in Seoul at noon.
- We started in the morning, arriving in Seoul at noon.

- A fire broke out near my house, and destroyed some five houses.
- A fire broke out near my house, destroying some five houses.

[6] 독립분사구문

☞ 분사구문의 「종속절의 주어」가 「주절의 주어」와 다를 때(S ≠ S´)
「의미상 주어(즉 종속절 주어)」를 분사구문 앞에 쓴다.

Ex) ┌ When night came on, we started for home.
     └ Night coming on, we started for home.
       (밤이 다가오자 우리는 집을 향해 떠났다.)
     ┌ When our dinner was over, we went out for a walk.
     └ Our dinner being over, we went out for a walk.
     ┌ After the sun had set, we came down the hill.
     └ The sun having set, we came down the hill.

[7] 현수 분사(Dangling Participle)

☞ 「현수 분사(懸垂 分詞:Dangling Participle)」란 분사구문에서 의미상의 주어(즉 종
속절 주어)와 주절의 주어가 일치하지 않음에도 불구하고, 분사구문의 의미상의 주
어를 생략한 구문을 말하며, 이러한 현수 분사구문은 바르게 고쳐야 한다.

Ex) ┌ Opening the door, there was a cat in the room. (X) 현수 분사
     ├ Opening the door, I found a cat in the room. (O)
     └ When I open the door, I found a cat in the room. (O)

     ┌ After finishing our work, a party was given. (X) 현수 분사
     ├ After finishing our work, we gave a party. (O)
     └ After we finished our work, we gave a party.(O)

TEST

* 다음의 대화에서 빈 칸에 알맞은 것을 고르시오.

"Why are they taking all the equipment away?"

"The job _____, they are packing up to leave."

① it to done ② did ③ being done ④ done ⑤ having done

(정답) ④

☞ The job (having been) done, … => Since the job has been done,…

*take ~ away 나르다, 옮기다, 치우다. *pack up 짐을 꾸리다, 포장하다.

[분사구문의 강조]
현재분사 (ⓥ ~ing) + (as + S + do동사) ~
과거분사(p.p.) + (as + S + be동사) ~

☞ as + S + V를 넣어 분사구문의 의미를 강조하며, 「저렇게, 이렇게」(= really)로
해석한다.

Ex) Living <u>as I do</u> in a remote village, I rarely have visitors.(= As I live)
(이렇게 외딴 마을에 살고 있으므로 나는 방문객이 별로 없다.)
Written <u>as it is</u> in plain English, the novel is fit for the beginners.
(= As it is written)
(<u>이렇게</u> 쉬운 영어로 쓰여졌기 때문에, 그 소설은 초보자에게 적합하다.)

$$\left[\begin{array}{l} \text{(Being) hidden } \underline{\text{as it was}} \\ \qquad\qquad\quad \text{(강조)} \\ \text{As it was hidden} \end{array} \right]$$ among the trees, the town was not
easily found.

(그 마을은 숲속에 가려져 <u>있으므로</u>, 쉽게 찾을 수 없었다.)

무인칭 독립분사 =〉「judging from what people say」
(사람들이 말하는 것으로 판단하면)

Ex) <u>Judging from what people say</u>, he must be a great scholar.
(사람들이 말하는 것으로 판단하면, 그는 위대한 학자임에 틀림없다.)

If we speak $\left[\begin{array}{l} \text{generally,} \\ \text{strictly,} \\ \text{frankly,} \\ \text{biologically,} \end{array} \right.$ =〉 $\left[\begin{array}{ll} \text{Generally} & \text{(일반적으로 말하면)} \\ \text{Strictly} & \text{(엄격하게 말하면)} \\ \text{Frankly} & \text{(솔직히 말하면)} \\ \text{Biologically} & \text{(생물학적으로 말하면)} \end{array} \right]$ speaking,

$\left[\begin{array}{l} \text{Talking} \\ \text{Speaking} \\ \text{If we talk(speak)} \end{array} \right]$ of movies, I don't like sad movies.

(영화에 대해 말하자면, 나는 슬픈 영화를 싫어한다.)

Judging from $\left[\begin{array}{l} \text{his appearance(그의 용모로 판단하면)} \\ \text{his accent(그의 억양으로 판단하면)} \end{array} \right.$

Granting that you were drunk, you are responsible for the accident.
(네가 술에 취했다는 것은 인정하지만, 너는 그 사고에 책임이 있다.)
Talking all things into consideration(모든 것을 고려해 볼 때)
Seeing that he is still young, he will recover soon.
(그가 아직 젊기 때문에 곧 회복될 것이다.)

┌ Considering ┐ his age, he is very tall.
└ For ┘
(그의 나이에 비하면, 그는 매우 키가 크다.)

 07 부대 상황을 나타내는 with

┌ with + O(목적어) + O.C(목적보어) ┬ ~ing(현재분사)
│   ├ p.p.(과거분사)
│   ├ 형용사
│   └ 부사(구)
│
│   ☞ 이때는 O와 O.C사이에 being을 보충한 뜻이다.
└ 「접속사(and, as 등) + S(주어) + V(동사)」로 바꾸어 쓸 수 있다.
(해석) 「~하고서, ~한 채, ~하면서, ~을 …하고, 그리고 ~ 하다」

[1] with + 목적어 + 목적보어 (-ing : 현재분사) = 접속사 + S + V
☞ 목적어와 목적보어(현재분사)는 주어와 술어 관계를 갖는다.

Ex) 1) ┌ He sat silently, with the cat dozing at his feet.
        └ He sat silently, and the cat was dozing at his feet.
    2) ┌ It was a misty morning, with little wind blowing.
        └ It was a misty morning, and little wind was blowing.
    3) ┌ He went out for a walk, with his dog following behind.
        └ He went out for a walk, and his dog followed behind.
    4) ┌ He stood with his back leaning against the wall.
        └ When he stood, his back was leaning against the wall.
    5) ┌ She was playing the piano, with her children singing around her.
        └ She was playing the piano, and her children were singing around her.
    6) ┌ The fair lady was walking along the beach, with her hair waving
        │ in the wind.

제6장 분사구문(Participial Construction)

└ The fair lady was walking along the beach, <u>and her hair was waving in the wind.</u>

[2] with + 목적어 + 목적보어(p.p. : 과거분사) = 접속사 + S + V
☞ 목적어와 목적보어(p.p)는 주어와 술어 관계를 갖는다.

Ex) ┌ He lay still, <u>with his eyes closed.</u>
└ He lay still, <u>and his eyes were closed.</u>

┌ The old man was sitting there, <u>with his legs crossed.</u>
└ The old man was sitting there, <u>and his legs were crossed.</u>

┌ He sat in the chair <u>with his eyes closed.</u>
└ When(While) he sat in the chair, <u>his eyes were closed.</u>

┌ All three astronauts were safely back on earth, <u>with their mission completed.</u>
└ All three astronauts were safely back on earth, <u>and their mission was completed.</u>

┌ <u>With an eye bandaged,</u> he could not write properly.
└ <u>As an eye was bandaged,</u> he could not write properly.

┌ He stood there, <u>with his eyes closed.</u>
│ He stood there, ┌ his eyes (being) closed (by him).
│   └ and his eyes were closed.
└ He stood there, ┌ and closed his eyes.
                 └ closing his eyes.
(그는 눈을 감은 채 거기에 서 있었다.)

[3] with + 목적어 + 목적보어(형용사 / 부사)
☞ 이때는 목적어와 목적보어 사이에 being을 보충한 뜻이 된다.

Ex) Don't speak <u>with your mouth full.</u> (입에 음식을 가득 넣은 채)
(= when your mouth is full)

He sat in his chair <u>with his mouth open.</u> (입을 벌린 채)

She went out <u>with her room empty.</u> (방을 비운 채)

He entered the room <u>with his hat on(off).</u> (모자를 쓴 채 / 벗은 채)

┌ I shall be lonely <u>with you away.</u>
└ I shall be lonely <u>when(if) you are away.</u> (네가 없다면)

[4] with + 목적어 + 목적보어(부사구;명사절, to부정사)

Ex) ┌ He was sleeping <u>with his feet on the pillow.</u> (베개 위에 두 다리를 올려놓고)
    └ When he was sleeping, <u>his feet were on the pillow.</u>

She was standing <u>with her baby on her back.</u>
            (아기를 업고)
He was standing still <u>with his hands in his pockets.</u>
            (호주머니에 손을 넣은 채)
He lay on his back <u>with his head against a cushion.</u>
            (머리를 방석에 기댄 채)
I cannot live on my wages <u>with prices what they are.</u>
(나는 물가가 지금 같아서는 나의 임금으로 살아갈 수가 없다.)
He set to work <u>with Miss Brown to help him.</u>
(그는 Brown양이 돕기로 하고 일에 착수했다.)

[5]

with ┌ a pipe in his mouth = pipe in mouth (파이프를 입에 문 채)
     │ a book in his hand = book in hand (손에 책을 든 채)
     │ a stick in his hand = stick in hand (손에 지팡이를 든 채)
     │ his hat on(off) (모자를 쓴 채(벗은 채))
     │ his hand in his pockets (손을 호주머니에 넣은 채)
     │ his feet on the pillow (두 다리를 베개에 올려놓은 채)
     └ his head against a cushion (방석에 머리를 기댄 채)

08 분사의 형용사화

☞ 분사가 형용사화 되어 분사로서 보다는 <u>형용사</u>로 취급된다.
[1] 원인격 형용사 (~한 기분을 불러 일으키는)
S(사물주어) + be + ┌ amazing, confusing, interesting, exciting,
                  └ shocking, surprising, boring, satisfactory, ect.
☞ 「원인격 형용사」는 「현재 분사」가 형용사화된 것이며, 「사물」을 수식하거나 「사물」
  이 주어인 문장의 보어로 쓰인다. 즉 원인격 형용사는 「타동사의 현재분사」로써 「능
  동·사역(~하게 하는, ~시키는, ~한 기분을 불러일으키는)」의 의미를 갖는다.

Ex) Exciting game. Surprising news. Tiring work.

　　The game was <u>exciting</u> to the boys.

[2] 경험적 형용사(~한 기분을 맛보는)

　S(사람주어) + be + amazed, bored, confused, excited, satisfied

frightened, interested, shocked, surprised, ect.

☞ 「경험적 형용사」는 「과거 분사」가 형용사화된 것이며, 항상 「사람」을 수식하는 경우
　에 쓰이거나, 「사람」이 주어인 문장의 보어로 쓰인다. 즉 경험적 형용사는 「타동사의
　과거분사」로서 「수동(~당한, ~된, ~받는, ~한 기분을 맛보는)」의 의미를 갖는다.
　Ex) Excited man. Surprised man. Tired workers.

　　The boys were <u>excited</u> over the game.

[3] 원인격 형용사와 경험격 형용사와의 관계

　Ex) ┌ An <u>exciting</u> game (관중을 열광시키는 경기 즉 열광적인 경기) (능동)
　　　└ The game <u>was exciting.</u>(능동 관계)
　　　┌ An <u>excited</u> spectator (경기를 보고 열광된 관중)
　　　└ The spectator <u>was excited.</u>(수동 관계)
　　　┌ It's <u>interesting</u> to me. (능동 관계)
　　　└ I'm <u>interested</u> in it. (수동 관계)
　　　┌ It's <u>surprising</u> to me. (능동 관계)
　　　└ I'm <u>surprised</u> at it. (수동 관계)
　　　┌ It is <u>satisfactory</u> to me. (능동 관계)
　　　└ I am <u>satisfied</u> with it. (수동 관계)
　　　┌ It was very <u>pleasant</u> for him to hear that news. (능동 관계)
　　　└ He was very <u>pleased</u> at the news. (수동 관계)
　　　┌ pleasant = pleasing ; delightful (기분좋은, 즐겁게 해주는 ; 능동)
　　　└ pleased = delighted (즐거워진 ; 수동)
　　　┌ intelligent = understanding (이해하는, 총명한 ; 능동)
　　　└ intelligible = that can be understood (이해될 수 있는 ; 수동)
　　　┌ intelligent answers to questions (질문에 대한 재치있는 대답)
　　　└ an intelligible explanation (이해하기 쉬운 설명)
☞ 과거분사로 된 형용사와 「-able(-ible)」어미를 가진 형용사는 모두 수동 형용사이다.

┌ They are <u>intolerant</u> of such a behavior (형용사의 능동)
└ They <u>can't tolerate</u> such a behavior.(그들은 그런 행동을 용서하지 못한다.)

Such a behavior is <u>intolerable</u> (형용사의 수동)
Such a behavior <u>cannot be tolerated</u> (그런 행동은 용서될 수 없다.)
intolerant「용납치 않는, 못 참는 (= can't tolerate)」
intolerable「참을 수 없는, 견딜 수 없는 (= can't be to tolerated)」

TEST

* 문맥에 알맞은 것을 고르시오.

1. He was (<u>excited</u>, exciting) by the news of the victory.
   The game was (excited, <u>exciting</u>).
2. The story is (<u>interesting</u>, interested)
   He was (<u>interested</u>, interesting) in the subject.
3. It is a (surprised, <u>surprising</u>) event.
   I was (<u>surprised</u>, surprising) to hear the news.
4. His speech was (<u>boring</u>. bored)
   I was (<u>bored</u>, boring) to hear his speech.
5. The game was (<u>exciting</u>, excited), so the audience was (exciting, <u>excited</u>).

09 의사분사(擬似 分詞) : 복합 형용사

☞ 현재분사(~ing)나 과거분사(p.p.)가 명사·형용사·부사와 결합하여 뒤에 나오는 명사를 수식하는 역할을 한다.

[1] 명사 + (타동사의) 현재분사형 + 명사
☞ 앞의 「명사」는 타동사의 「의미상의 목적어」가 된다.
have이외의 동사가 이루는 3형식을 취한다.

Ex) ┌ The drug kills pain   ┌ The visitor speaks English
    └ the pain-killing drug   └ The English-speaking visitor
      (진통제)   (영어로 말하는 방문객)

```
 ┌ a chemical which kills insects    ┌ a work which consumes time
 └ an insect-killing chemical        └ a time- consuming work.
   (살충제)                              (시간이 걸리는 일)
```

[2] 명사 + (타동사의) 과거분사형 + 명사

☞ 앞의 「명사」는 타동사의 「의미상 주어」가 된다.

　　by를 포함한 수동태 1형식을 취한다.

```
Ex) ┌ The land is owned by the government    ┌ The fruit is dried by the sun
    └ the government-owned land              └ the sun-dried fruit
      (정부 소유지:所有地)                        (햇볕으로 건조시킨 과일)
      ┌ a cart which is drawn by a horse
      └ a horse-drawn cart
        (말이 끄는 마차)
      ┌ a society which is dominated by science
      └ a science-dominated society
        (과학이 지배하는 사회)
```

[3] 형용사 + (자동사의) 현재분사 + 명사

☞ 앞의 「형용사는」는 「자동사의 보어」가 된다.

　　형용사 보어를 가진 2형식을 취한다.

```
Ex) ┌ The village appears odd       ┌ The rose smells sweet
    └ the odd-appearing village     └ the sweet-smelling rose
      (이상하게 보이는 마을)              (향기가 나는 장미)
      ┌ the wine which tastes nice    ┌ a gentleman who looks handsome
      └ the nice-tasting wine.        └ a handsome-looking gentleman.
        (맛좋은 포도주)                    (잘생긴 신사)
```

[4] 형용사 + 명사-ed + 명사

☞ 앞의 「분사형」은 뒤에 오는 명사의 성질·특징을 나타낸다.

　　have동사가 이루는 3형식을 취한다.

```
Ex) ┌ A girl has blue eyes.          ┌ a doll which has blue eyes
    └ a blue eyed-girl               └ a blue-eyed doll
      (파란 눈을 가진 소녀)                (파란 눈을 가진 인형)
      ┌ A stool has three legs
      ├ a stool that has three legs => a three-legged stool
      └ a stool with three legs
        (다리가 3개인 의자)
```

[5] 「부사 + 과거분사」 + 명사

☞ 부사는 「과거분사」를 수식한다.

「be + 부사 + p.p.」꼴의 수동태 1형식을 취한다.

Ex) ┌ The house was newly painted.　┌ The worker is well trained.
　　└ the newly-painted house　　　└ the well-trained worker
　　　(갓 페인트 칠한 집)　　　　　　(잘 훈련된 일꾼)

　　┌ a man who is well educated　┌ a couple who are newly married
　　└ a well-educated man.　　　　└ a newly-marred couple.
　　　(교양있는 사람)　　　　　　　(신혼 부부)

TEST

1 밑줄 친 곳이 잘못된 것은? (　　)

① I met a one-eyed man.　　② I met a brown-haired lady

③ I met a one-arming robber.　④ I met a happy-looking girl.

⑤ I met a well-educated man.

(정답) ③

☞ ①, ②, ⑤는 「명사 + ed」의 유사분사이며, ③은 「a one-armed robber」 (외팔 강도)로 고쳐써야 한다.

2 밑줄 친 부분의 잘못된 것은? (　　)

① I met a happy-looked girl.　② I saw a one-armed robber.

③ He is a good-natured man.　④ She is a brown-haired lady.

⑤ It is a tree-legged stool.

(정답) ①

☞ ①은 「a happy-looking girl」(=> a girl who looks happy)로 고쳐써야 한다.

3 다음중 문장을 구로 고친것 중 잘못된 것은? (　　)

① ┌ The animal has four legs.　② ┌ The animals have long ears.
　 └ the four-legged animal.　　　└ the long-eared animals.

③ ┌ The wine tastes nice.　　　④ ┌ The birds eat insects.
　 └ the nice-tasting wine.　　　　└ the insect-eaten birds.

⑤ ┌ A girl has blue eyes.
　 └ a blue eyed-girl.

(정답) ④

☞ ┌ he birds eat insects.
  ├ the birds <u>which</u> eat insects(형용사절)
  ├ the birds <u>eating</u> insects(분사구)
  ├ the birds <u>insect-eating</u> (복합 형용사 : 의사분사)
  └ the <u>insect-eating</u> birds(어순조정)

[6] 학습 요점

☞ 아래 설명 중 (1)은 주어, (2)는 동사 =〉 ┌ 능동 = 현재분사 ┐ (3)은 보어,
                                        └ 수동 = 과거분사 ┘

목적어, 수식어 등을 나타낸다.

=〉 즉 절(節)을 구(句)로 전환하는 것으로서, (2)가 부사이고 (3)이 과거분사이면
(2)(3)(1)의 순서가 된다.

(1)<u>주어</u>	(2)<u>동사</u>	3) 보어/목적어 /수식어	〈=〉	(3)	(2)	(1)	
1. the man	looks	good	=	the good - looking man			(인상이 좋은 사람)
the wine	tastes	nice	=	the nice - tasting wine			(맛좋은 포도주)
2. the drug	kills	pain	=	the pain - killing drug			(진통제)
people	love	peace	=	peace - loving people			(평화를 사랑하는 사들)
3. the fruit	is dried	by the sun	=	the sun - dried fruit			(햇볕에 말린 과일)
rule	are made	by man	=	man - made rules			(인간이 만든 법률)
4. a man	works	hard	=	a hard - working man			(근면한 사람)
a man	did	well	=	a well - doing man			(잘 살아가는 사람)
5. people	are	well dressed	=	well - dressed people			(잘 차려입은 사람들)
the house	is	newly painted	=	the newly - painted house			(새로이 단장을 한 집)

제7장
Essential English Grammar

조동사
(Auxiliary Verb)

01 현재의 추측 =〉「will + 동사원형」(~일 것이다)
과거의 추측 =〉「will + have + p.p」(~였을 것이다)

This will be mine.
Perhaps this is mine.
(이것은 내 것일 거야.[내 것이겠지])

You will have heard the news.
I suppose you have heard the news.
(너는 그 뉴스를 들었을 것이다.)

02 현재의 추측 =〉 S(주어) + may + V(동사)
〈 ~ 일런지도 모른다 : 막연한 추측 〉
과거의 추측 =〉 S(주어) + may + have + p.p.
〈 ~ 였을지도 모른다.〉

It is possible(probable) that he is rich.
He may be rich.
Maybe he is a rich man.

Maybe
Perhaps   he is a rich man.
Possibly
(그는 부자일런지도 모른다.)

It is possible(probable) that he was a rich man.
He may have been a rich man.
Maybe he was a rich man.

Maybe
Perhaps   he was a rich man.
Possibly
(그는 부자였을지도 모른다.)

03 현재의 추측 =〉 S(주어) + must + V(동사)
〈 ~ 임에 틀림없다 : 강한 추측 〉
과거의 추측 =〉 S(주어) + must + have + p.p.
〈 ~ 였음에 틀림없다 〉

I am sure that he is ill.
It is certain that he is ill.
He must be ill.
(그는 아픈게 틀림없다.)

I am sure that he was ill.
It is certain that he was ill.
He must have been ill.
(그는 아팠음에 틀림없다.)

04 S(주어) + cannot + V(동사) (~ 일리가 없다 : 강한 부정)
S(주어) + cannot + have + p.p (~ 였을리가 없다)

I am sure that he is not rich.
He cannot be rich.
It is impossible that he is rich.
(그가 부자일리가 없다.)

Can it be true?
Is it possible that it is true?
(그것이 사실일까?)

It can not be true.
It is impossible that it is true.
(그것은 사실일리가 없다.)

제7장 조동사(Auxiliary Verb)

I am sure that he <u>was not</u> rich.

He <u>cannot have been</u> rich.

It is impossible that he <u>was</u> rich.

(그가 부자였을 리가 없다.)

<u>Can</u> he <u>have done</u> such a thing?

<u>Is it possible</u> that he <u>did</u> such a thing?

(그가 그런 짓을 하였을까?)

05   S(주어) + need not have + p.p.
(~ 할 필요가 없었는데 (그런데) ~ 했다)

You paid the money, but it was not necessary.

You <u>need not have paid</u> the money.

(너는 그 돈을 지불할 필요가 없었다 - 그런데도 그 돈을 지불했다.)

He <u>needn't have done</u> it.

He did it, but it was not necessary.

(그는 그것을 할 필요가 없었는데 - 그런데 했다.)

    cf) S(주어) + do not need + to + ⓥ   (~ 할 필요가 없어서 안했다.)

    Ex) He <u>did not need to help</u> her.

        (그는 그녀를 도와줄 필요가 없었다 - 그래서 도와주지 않았다.)

        You <u>didn't need to pay</u> the money.

        (너는 그 돈을 지불할 필요가 없었다 - 그래서 지불하지 않았다.)

두 문장의 의미가 같아지도록 _____ 에 알맞은 말을 고르시오.

You met her again, but it was not necessary.

You _____ her again.

① need not have meet　　② did not need to meet

③ need not meet　　④ did not have to meet

⑤ cannot have meet

(정답) ①

06　S(주어) + ⌈ should ⌉ + have + p.p
　　　　　 ⌊ ought to ⌋
(~ 했어야 했는데 안해서 유감이다)

☞ 과거에 대한 유감이나 비난을 나타낸다.

⌈ I am sorry that you did not study hard.
⌊ I wish you had studied hard.
　 You should have studied hard.
　 (너는 공부를 열심히 했어야만 했다 −그런데도 안해서 유감이다.)

⌈ You ⌈ ought to ⌉ have helped her.
│　　　 ⌊ should ⌋
│ Why didn't you help her?
│ I wish you had helped her.
│ I am sorry you didn't help her.
│ You had to help her but you didn't.
│ Would to God ⌉
│ I wish　　　 │ you had helped her.
│ Would that　 │
⌊ If only　　　⌋

└ It is regrettable that you didn't help her.
(너는 그녀를 도와주었어야 했다.)

07 S(주어) + could have + p.p
(~ 할 수 있었으나 하지 않았다)

┌ We could buy the car, but we did not.
└ We could have bought the car.
(우리는 그 차를 살 수 있었으나 사지 않았다.)

08
┌ S(주어) + may well + V(동사원형) ~   (~하는 것은 당연하다,
├ S(주어) + have good reason to + V(동사) ~   ~할만도 하다)
└ It's natural that S(주어) + (should) + V(동사원형)~

┌ He may well get angry.
├ He has good reason to get angry.
└ It's natural that he (should) get angry.
(그가 화를 내는 것은 당연하다.)

┌ You may well say so.
├ I take it for granted that you say so.
├ You have good reason to say so.
│   ┌ no wonder ┐
└ It is │ natural │ that you should say so.
        │ a matter of course │
        └ not surprising ┘
(그렇게 말하는 것도 당연하다.)

*take it for granted that + S + V [that 이하를 당연하다고 여기다]

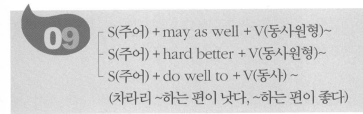

09
S(주어) + may as well + V(동사원형)~
S(주어) + hard better + V(동사원형)~
S(주어) + do well to + V(동사) ~
(차라리 ~하는 편이 낫다, ~하는 편이 좋다)

You <u>may as well go</u> at once.
You <u>had better go</u> at once.
You <u>do well to go</u> at once.
It <u>would be better</u> for you to go at once.
(즉시 가는 것이 더 좋다.)

10
S(주어) + may as well A as B (실현 가능)
S(주어) + might as well A as B (실현 불가능)
(B 하느니 차라리 A 하는게 낫다)
(B 해도 좋은 것 처럼 A 라고 할 수 있다)

Ex) You <u>may as well</u> not know a thing at all <u>as</u> know it but imperfectly.
(그것을 불완전하게 아느니, 차라리 전혀 모르는 게 났다.)

You <u>might as well</u> expect the river to flow backward <u>as</u> expect me to agree.
(내가 동의하기를 기대하는 것보다, 강물의 흐름을 되돌려 놓으려고 하는 것이 났다.)

You <u>may as well</u> call a cat a little tiger <u>as</u> call a tiger a big cat.
(호랑이를 큰 고양이라 불러도 좋은 것처럼, 고양이를 작은 호랑이라고 할 수 있다.)

 would rather A than B
(B 하느니 차라리 A 하다)

I ┌ would rather ┐
┤ would sooner ├ die <u>than</u> live in dishonor.
└ had rather ┘
I <u>would as soon</u> die as live in dishonor.
I <u>would choose</u> death <u>before</u> life in dishonor.
I <u>prefer</u> dying <u>to</u> living in dishonor.
I <u>prefer</u> to die <u>rather than</u> (to) live in dishonor.
(불명예스럽게 사느니 차라리 죽는게 났겠다.)

I <u>would choose</u> death <u>before</u> disgrace.
I <u>would rather</u> die <u>than</u> disgrace myself.
I <u>would sooner</u> die <u>than</u> disgrace myself.
I <u>would soon</u> as die <u>as</u> disgrace myself.
(수모를 당하느니 오히려 죽겠다.)

12 lest ~ should ··· =〉 for fear that ~ should (~가 ···하지 않도록)

Ex) Write it down in your note book ┌ <u>lest</u> you <u>should</u> forget it.
                                    └ <u>so that</u> you <u>may not</u> forget it.
(네가 그것을 잊지 않도록 노트에 적어 두어라.)

He lowed his voice ┌ for fear that he should ┐ be heard.
                   └ so that he might not ┘
(그는 자기말을 남이 듣지 않도록 목소리를 낮추었다.)

13 ┌ can ~ (~ 할 수 있다)
├ be able to + V(동사)
├ be capable of ~ing
├ be equal to ~ing
└ be in a position to + V(동사)

I can(not) swim.
I am (un)able to swim.
I am (in)capable of swimming.
I am (un)equal to swimming.
It is (im)possible for me to swim.
Swimming is within(beyond) my ability.
(나는 수영을 할 수 있다.[없다])

I'm sorry, but I can't help you.
I'm sorry, but I'm not able to help you.
I'm sorry, but I'm not in a position to help you.
(미안하지만, 도와줄 수가 없구나.)

We can prevent or control it much better.
We are able to prevent or control it much better.
We are in a position to prevent or control it much better.
We are in a much position to prevent or control it much better.
(우리는 그것을 더욱 효율적으로 방지하거나 통제할 수 있다.)

14 Used to 와 Would

[1] Would : 과거의 불규칙적인 습관을 나타낸다(~하곤 했다)

☞ would는 보다 개인적인 회상이고, 비교적 짧은 기간 동안의 습관을 나타낸다.

Ex) He <u>would</u> often sit for hours without saying a word.
(그는 말 한마디하지 않고 몇 시간씩 앉자 있곤 했다.)

[2] Used to [juːstə] + V(동사)

(1) 동작을 나타낼 때 : 과거의 규칙적인 습관을 나타낸다.

(~ 하는 습관이 있었다, ~하는 것이 예사였다, ~하곤 했다.)

Used to는 보다 객관적이고 긴 기간 동안의 규칙적인 습관을 나타낸다.

제7장 조동사(Auxiliary Verb)

Ex) He <u>used to</u> take a walk in the morning.
  (그는 아침이면 산보를 하곤 했다.)
  When I was a child, I <u>used to</u> drink milk.
  (내가 어렸을 때는 우유를 마시곤 했다.)

(2) 상태를 나타낼 때 : 과거의 사실, 상태를 나타낸다.[과거(이전, 옛날)
  에는 ~있었다, ~하였다]

☞ 과거에 계속 되어온 상태를 나타낸다. 보통 무의지 동사(無意志 動詞)와 함께 사용
  된다. 단순 과거형 시제로 표시할 수 있으며, used to를 사용하면 그만큼 「현재와
  의 대비(對比)」를 강조하는 것이 된다.

  Ex) There <u>used to be</u> a castle on this hill.
              (= was)
    (과거에는 이 언덕에 성(城)이 하나 있었다.- 즉 지금은 성이 없다.)
    There <u>used to be</u> a pond in the garden.
                (= was)
    (이 정원에는 과거에 연못이 있었다.- 즉 지금은 연못이 없다는 뜻이다.)
    That's where I <u>used to live</u> when I was a child
                  (= lived)
    (그곳은 내가 어렸을 때 살았던 곳이다.- 즉 지금은 그곳에 살고 있지 않
    다는 뜻이다.)
    What I am is different from <u>what I used to be.</u>
                      (= what I was)
    (현재의 나는 과거의 나와는 다르다.)
    That house over there <u>used to belong</u> to my uncle.(= belonged)
    (저기에 있는 저 집은 과거에는 우리 아저씨 집이었다.- 즉 지금은 아저
    씨 집이 아니다.)

[3] ┌ I <u>used to get</u> up early.
    ├ I <u>was accustomed to getting</u> up early.
    ├ I <u>was in the habit of getting</u> up early.
    ├ I <u>made a point of getting</u> up early.
    └ I <u>made it (a rule, a point) to get</u> up early.
    (나는 과거에 일찍 일어났었다.)

15

S(주어) + cannot + ⓥ(동사) ~ too + 형용사/부사 …
S(주어)가 아무리 (형용사/부사)… ⓥ해도 지나친 것은 아니다(=좋다)]

[1] ┌ cannot + ⓥ
│ ├ can hardly
│ S + ├ can scarcely ┤ ~ too + 형용사/부사
│ ├ can never
│ └ 부정어
├ It's impossible to + ⓥ ~ too + 형용사/부사
├ It's impossible to + over + ⓥ ~
└ The + 비교급 ~ the + 비교급(즉 비례 비교급으로 표현)

┌ 아무리 ~ 해도(결코) 지나치지 않다.
├ 아무리 ~ 해도(결코)지나치다고 할 수 없다.
├ 아무리 ~ 해도 오히려 부족하다.
├ 아무리 ~ 해도 부족할 정도다.
└ ~ 하면 할수록 더 좋다.(즉 비례 비교급으로 표현)

    Ex) We <u>cannot</u> praise him too much.
       (아무리 그를 칭찬해도 지나치지 않다 – 즉 「그는 칭찬을 들을 가치가 있
       다」는 의미임)
       We <u>cannot</u> speak too severely of his conduct.
       (우리가 아무리 그를 혹평해도 지나치지 않다.)

**[2] 조동사 <u>cannot</u>의 표현은 It's impossible to + V구문으로
나타낼 수 있다.**

┌ We <u>cannot</u> be <u>too</u> careful in this world.
└ It's impossible (for us) to be <u>too</u> careful in this world.
  (아무리 조심해도 오히려 부족하다.)

┌ I <u>can't</u> speak <u>too</u> highly of its value.
└ It's impossible for me to speak <u>too</u> highly of its value.
  (그것의 가치를 아무리 높이 평가해도 지나치지 않다.)

[3] 부사 <u>too</u> 대신 <u>to excess</u>, <u>excessively</u>, <u>enough</u> 등을 써도 같은 뜻이 된다.

We <u>cannot</u> state the importance of health ⌐ <u>to excess</u>.
                                     ├ too
                                     ├ enough
                                     └ excessively

(건강의 중요성을 아무리 말해도 오히려 부족하다.)

I <u>cannot</u> thank you ⌐ <u>too much</u>.
                   ├ enough
                   ├ to excess
                   └ excessively

(당신에게 아무리 감사해도 지나치지 않다.)

[4] 부사 too(much, highly, strongly)와 cannot 다음의 본동사가 하나의 동사로 표현될 수 있다.

즉 ⌐ cannot + ⓥ ~ too much
    └ cannot over + ⓥ (over를 접두어로 하는 동사) ┘ 로 표현할 수 있다.

⌐ We <u>cannot</u> praise his merits <u>too much.</u>
├ We <u>cannot</u> <u>overpraise</u> his merits.
├ <u>It's impossible</u> to praise his merits <u>too much</u>.
└ <u>It's impossible</u> to <u>overpraise</u> his merits.
    (그의 공적을 아무리 찬양해도 오히려 부족할 정도다.)

We <u>cannot</u> <u>overestimate</u> his ability.
cf) overpraise = praise ~ too highly(much, strongly)
             = speak too highly of (지나치게 칭찬하다)
    overestimate = estimate ~ too highly (much, strongly)
               = overvalue, overrate. (과대평가하다)
    overstate = state(express) ~ too highly (much, strongly)(과장하다)

[5] 종합

- S + <u>cannot</u> + V ~ <u>too much</u>
- S + <u>cannot</u> + V ~ <u>enough</u>(to excess, excessively)
- S + <u>cannot</u> + <u>over</u> + ⓥ ~
- S + <u>cannot</u> + <u>exaggerate</u> ~
- It's impossible to + ⓥ ~ <u>too</u> + 형용사/부사
- It's <u>impossible</u> (for + 목적격) to <u>over</u> + ⓥ ~
- It's <u>no exaggeration</u> to ⓥ ~
- The + 비교급 ~ the + 비교급 (비례 비교급으로 표현가능)

Ex)
- We <u>can't</u> praise him <u>too much</u>(too strongly, too highly)
- We <u>can't</u> praise him <u>enough</u>(to excess, excessively)
- We <u>can't</u> <u>overpraise</u> him.(= He <u>cannot</u> be <u>overpraised</u>)
- We <u>can't</u> <u>exaggerate</u> him.
- It's <u>impossible</u> (for us) to <u>overpraise</u> him.
- It's <u>no exaggeration</u> to praise him.
- <u>The more</u> we praise him, <u>the better</u> it is.
- It's <u>not too much</u> to praise him.
  (그를 아무리 칭찬한다 해도 과언은 아니다.)

- I <u>can't</u> emphasize the importance of this <u>too strongly</u>.
- I <u>can't</u> <u>overemphasize</u> the importance of this.
- It's <u>impossible</u> for me to emphasize the importance of this <u>too strongly</u>.
- It's <u>impossible</u> for me to <u>overemphasize</u> the impotance of this.
- <u>The more</u> strongly I emphasize the importance of this, <u>the better</u> it is.
  (나는 이것의 중요성을 아무리 강조해도 오히려 부족하다.)

- What should be done <u>cannot</u> be done too soon.
- <u>The sooner</u> we do <u>what should be done</u>, the better it is.
  (=what we should do)
  (마땅히 할 일은 아무리 빨리해도 너무 빠르다고 할 수 없다.)

- The influence of imitation in human society can hardly be overestimated.
  (인간 사회에 있어서 모방의 영향은 아무리 과대 평가해도 지나치지 않다.)

It is no exaggeration to say that he is the greatest novelist in America.
It is not too much to say that he is the greatest novelist in America.
(그가 미국에서 가장 훌륭한 소설가라고 해도 과언은 아니다.)

It is no exaggeration to say that he saved my life.
It is not too much to say that he saved my life
 (그가 나의 생명을 구했다고 해도 과언은 아니다.)

It is no exaggeration to say that he values honor above life.
It is not too much to say that he values honor above life.
(그는 명예를 목숨보다 중히 여긴다 해도 과언은 아니다.)
 * value A above B (A를 B보다 중히 여기다)

TEST ㅣㅓㅣㅓㅣㅓㅣㅓㅣㅓㅣㅓㅣㅓㅣㅓㅣㅓㅣㅓㅣㅓㅣㅓㅣㅓㅣㅓ

1 다음의 문장과 뜻이 같은 문장을 하나 고르시오.

What is good to be done can hardly be done too soon.

① We must take time in doing what is good.
② The sooner we do what is good, the better it is.
③ It takes lots of time to do what is good.
④ We must be very careful to do what is good to be done.

(정답) ②

*do good ~ 에 이롭다
*do harm ~ 에 해롭다

2 다음의 두문장이 같은 뜻이 되도록 _____을 채우시오.

We cannot emphasize the importance of the matter too strongly.
It is _____ to overemphasize the importance of the matter.

(정답) impossible

16 미래시제 will, shall 의 용법

[1] 단순미래(單純未來)의 경우 (ⓥ 할 것이다, ⓥ 할 것인가?)

분류 인칭	미 국		영 국	
	평서문	의문문	평서문	의문문
1인칭	I will	Will I?	I shall	Shall I
2인칭	You will	Will you?		
3인칭	He will	Will he?		

Ex) I will(shall) be 17 on my next birthday.
   Will(shall) we be back in time?
   We will(shall) be delighted if you come.
   Where will(shall) we find him?
   That will cost a lot of money.

[2] 의지미래(意志未來)의 경우

Shall I + ⓥ? (ⓥ 할까요?)

Will you + ⓥ? (ⓥ 하시겠습니까?) (ⓥ 해 주시겠습니까?)

Shall he + ⓥ? (ⓥ 시킬까요?)   (ⓥ 하게 할까요?)

분류 ＼ 문장	평서문	의문문	해석
① 주어의 의지 표시	S(주어) + will	Will + S(주어)?	~하겠다
② 상대방의 의지를 묻는 경우 Do you want him to + ⓥ Will you let him ⓥ ~		Shall I ~? Will you ~? Shall he ~?	~시킬까요(원합니까)? ~해 주시겠습니까? ~시킬까요(원합니까)?
③ 말하는 사람(話者)의 의지표지 I will let + 목적어 + ⓥ	You shall ~ He shall ~		나는 당신에게 ~시키겠다 나는 그에게 ~시키겠다

(1) 주어 자체의 의지 표시

☞ 주어 자체의 의지·고집·희망(소망)·거절(부정문에서) 등을 나타낸다.
   이때의 조동사는 모두 Will이고 Will에 강세가 온다.

① 의지 : I will do what I can.(내가 할 수 있는 것을 하겠다.)
　　　　I will go, no matter what you say.
　　　　(네가 뭐라고 하던 나는 가겠다.)
　　　　He will have his own way.(그는 제멋대로 하려고 한다.)
② 고집 : The door will not open.(문이 도무지 열리지 않는다.)
③ 희망 : You will help me, I'm sure.(도와주시겠지요, 틀림없이.)
④ 요구·명령 : You will leave this room at once.
　　　　　　(즉시 방을 나가시오.)
⑤ 부탁 : The audience will kindly be seated.(여러분 앉아 주십시오.)
⑥ 거절 : They won't accept your offer.(당신의 제의를 받아들이려
하지 않는다.)

[2] 상대방(You)의 의지를 묻는 경우와 제3자(The Third)의 의지
　　를 묻는 경우
　☞ 「~ 가 ~ 하도록 할까요 」 「~시킬까요(원합니까)」의 뜻으로 상대방의 의지를 묻는
　　의문문으로 나타낸다.

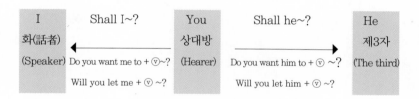

① 상대방(You)의 의지를 묻는 경우
　Ex)┌ Shall I open the window?
　　　├ Do you want me to open the window?
　　　└ Will you let me open the window?
　　　(제가 창문을 열어도 될까요? ; 제가 창문을 열기를 원하십니까?)

② 제3자(The Third)의 의지를 묻는 경우
┌ Shall he contact you by telephone?
├ Do you want him to contact you by telephone?
└ Will you let him contact you by telephone?
(그에게 전화하라고 시킬까요? ; 당신은 그가 전화 연락을 하기를 원하

십니까?)

What <u>shall he</u> do?
What <u>do you want him to</u> do?
What <u>will you let him</u> do?
(그에게 무엇을 시킬까요? ; 당신은 그가 무엇을 하기를 원합니까?)

③ 권유·부탁을 나타내는 경우
Let's do it again, <u>shall we?</u> (간접 명령)
<u>Will you</u> have some coffee? (권유)
<u>Will you</u> do me a favor? (부탁)
Help me with this baggage, <u>will you?</u> (부탁)
<u>Won't you</u> stay a little longer? (초대)

(3) 말하는 사람(話者:Speaker)의 의지 표시

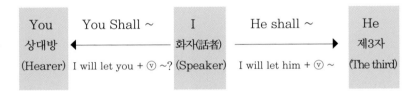

① 상대방(You)에 대한 말하는 사람(話者:Speaker)의 의지 표시
☞ Shall은 2인칭(You)을 쓰면 말하는 사람(Speaker)의 의지를 나타낸다. 약한 뜻일
때 「허가」, 강한 뜻일 때 「주장·명령」을 나타낸다.
You shall ~ 형은 문어체(Written English)에는 남아 있으나, 실생활 영어(구어
체:Spoken English)에서는 거의 사용되지 않고 있다.

Ex) <u>You shall have</u> this watch.
<u>I will give you</u> this watch.
<u>I will let you have</u> this watch.
(내가 이 시계를 너에게 주겠다.)

<u>You shall have</u> a nice present.
<u>I will let you have</u> a nice present. (문어체)

$\begin{bmatrix} \text{I will give you a nice present.(구어체)} \\ \text{I promise you a nice present.(구어체)} \end{bmatrix}$
(내가 너에게 멋진 선물을 주마.)

② 제3자(The Third)에 대한 말하는 사람(Speaker)의 의지 표시

☞ 3인칭(He, She, It 등)의 Shall은 제3자에 대해 「~ 하겠다」는 말하는 사람 (Speaker)의 의지를 나타낸다.

He shall~ 형은 문어체(Written English)에서는 남아 있으나 구어체(Spoken English) 에서는 거의 사용되지 않는다.

Ex) ┌ He shall be scolded.
├ I will let him be scolded at once.
└ I will scold him.
(나는 그를 혼내 주겠다.)
┌ It shall be done at once.
├ I will let it be done at once.
└ I will do it at once.
(내가 당장에 그것을 하겠다.)
┌ They shall go at once.
├ They must go at once.
├ They have to go at once.
├ They have got to go at once.
├ They are to go at once.
└ I will let them go at once.
(지금 즉시 그들을 가게 하겠다.)

TEST ╰╮╭╰╮╭╰╮╭╰╮╭╰╮╭╰╮╭╰╮╭╰╮╭╰╮╭╰╮╭╰╮╭╰╮

* 다음의 두 문장의 의미가 같아지도록 ____에 적당한 말을 쓰시오.

1. ┌ I will give you my last stamp.
   └ You ____ ____ my last stamp.
(정답) shall have

2. ┌ I will let someone open the door.
   ├ The door ____ be opened.
   └ Someone shall open the door.
(정답) shall

제8장
Essential English Grammar

태(態:Voice =〉
수동태/능동태)

┌ 능동태 : 동작을 하는 쪽에 중점을 둠
└ 수동태 : 동작을 받는 쪽에 중점을 둠

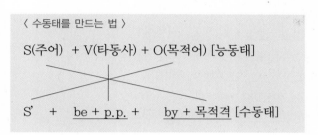

〈 수동태를 만드는 법 〉

S(주어) + V(타동사) + O(목적어) [능동태]

S' + be + p.p. + by + 목적격 [수동태]

[능동] We respect him. (능동태 : 3형식)

[수동] He is respected by us. (수동태 : 1형식)

① 능동태의 목적어가 수동태의 주어로 간다.
② 타동사는 be + p.p 형식으로 바꾼다.(자동사는 수동태가 될 수 없다.)
③ 능동태의 주어를 by + 목적격으로 표현한다.

Ex) ┌ He wrote this letter.
    └ This letter was written by him
    ┌ I love her.
    └ She is loved by me.

[1] 조동사가 있는 문장의 수동태

☞ 조동사를 그대로 쓰고, 조동사 뒤에는 원형 be동사가 온다.

Ex) ┌ We can see stars at night.
    └ Stars can be seen at night.

[2] 수동형의 8가지 시제

① S + V + O

=〉 S′ + <u>be + p.p</u> + by + O′

His family <u>love</u> him.

He <u>is loved by</u> his family.

② S + be ~ing + O

=〉 S′ + <u>be + being + p.p</u> + by + O′ (진행형일 때)

The novelist <u>is writing</u> a novel.

A novel <u>is being written by</u> the novelists.

The novelist <u>was writing</u> a novel.

A novel <u>was being written by</u> the novelists.

③ S + have been + O

=〉 S′ + <u>have been + p.p</u> + by + O′ (완료형일 때)

Many fans <u>have loved</u> him.

He <u>has been loved by</u> many fans.

A beautiful woman <u>had loved</u> him.

He <u>had been loved by</u> a beautiful woman.

④ S + 조동사 + 동사 + O

=〉 S′ + 조동사 + be + p.p + by + O′ (조동사가 있을 때)

His new neighbors <u>will love</u> him.

He <u>will be loved by</u> his new neighbors.

[3] 수동형에는 ┌ ①미래 진행형
②현재완료 진행형   등의 4개 시제는
③과거완료 진행형   수동형이 없다.
└ ④미래완료 진행형

[4] 수동형이 될 수 없는 동사

☞ have(가지다), resemble, lack, enjoy, belong, cost, last,

escape, fit, suit, become, meet 등

Ex)┌She <u>resembles</u> her mother.(O)
　　└Her mother <u>is resembled by</u> her.(X)
　　┌This umbrella <u>belongs</u> to me.(O)
　　└This umbrella <u>is belonged</u> to me.(X)

[정리]　S　＋　V　＋　O

=> S′ + ┌ be + p.p　　　　　┐ + by + O′
　　　　├ be + being + p.p　│
　　　　└ have + been + p.p ┘

02 태(態)의 전환

[1] 제3형식일 때 (S + V + O)

┌ He <u>painted</u> the famous picture.
└ The famous picture <u>was painted by</u> him.

[2] 제4형식일 때 (S + V + I.O. + D.O.)

☞ 목적어가 둘이므로 직접 목적어나 간접 목적어를 주어로 하는 두 가지 수동태가 가능하다.

┌ He <u>gave</u> me the money.
├ <u>I was given</u> the money by him.
└ <u>The money was given</u> (to) me by him.

☞ 직접 목적어를 주어로 하고 간접 목적어가 목적어로 그대로 남아있는 경우는 (간접 목적어가 보류 목적어로 될 때는) 흔히 그 앞에 to, for, of 등을 놓는다.

Ex) A letter was sent <u>(to)</u> me by her.
　　A watch was bought <u>for</u> me by him.
　　Some question were asked <u>of</u> me by him.

① 직접 목적어만 수동태의 주어로 올 수 있고,
　 간접 목적어는 수동태의 주어로 올 수 없는 경우

☞ bring, afford, buy, carry, do, get, make, read, sell, sing, write 등

I wrote him a letter.(O)
A letter was written to him by me.(O)
He was written a letter by me.(X)

He made me a box.(O)
A box was made (for) me by him.(O)
I was made a box by him.(X)

② 간접 목적어만 수동태의 주어가 될 수 있고, 직접 목적어는 수동태의 주어가 될 수 없는 경우

☞ spare, save, envy, call, kiss, strike 등

This device <u>spared</u> me a lot of trouble.(O)
<u>I was spared</u> a lot of trouble by this device.(O)
<u>A lot of trouble was spared</u> me by this device.(X)

[3] 제5형식 문장의 전환(S + V + O + O.C.)

☞ 목적어가 주어로 되고, 목적격 보어는 그대로 남아서 주격보어가 된다.(목적격 보어를 수동태의 주어로 할 수 없다.)

① 보어가 명사인 경우

We elected him president.(O)
He was elected president (by us).(O)
Presdent was elected him (by us).(X)

  cf) <u>He made</u> her happy.
      <u>She was made</u> happy by him.

② 보어가 부정사인 경우

(i) 지각동사·사역동사가 쓰일 때는 능동태에서 생략되었던 to부정사가 되살아난다.

I heard her <u>sing.</u>
She was heard <u>to sing</u> by me.

We <u>saw</u> him <u>enter</u> the room.
He was seen <u>to enter</u> the room.

Our teacher <u>made</u> us <u>read</u> these books.
We were made <u>to read</u> these books by our teacher.

One <u>might</u> have heard a pin <u>drop.</u>
<u>A pin</u> might have been <u>heard to drop.</u>
(ii) let은 수동태에서 be allowed to로 바꾼다.
I will <u>let</u> you know the secret.
You shall <u>be allowed to know</u> the secret.
I will let the secret <u>be known to</u> you.

cf) ┌ be known to (~에 의해 알려지다)
└ be known by (~에 판단되어지다)
┌ People know us by the company we keep.
└ We are known by the company we keep.
(친구를 보면 그 사람의 인품을 알 수 있다.)
┌ We know a tree by its fruit.
└ A tree is known by its fruit.
(나무는 그 열매를 보면 안다. – 나무의 가치는 그 열매로 판정된다.)

03 부정문의 수동태

☞ 수동태의 be의 시제는 능동태의 do 시제에 일치한다.
His pupils <u>do not like</u> him.
He <u>is not liked</u> by his pupils.

04 조동사가 있는 수동태

☞ can, may, must 따위의 조동사 등이 있는 능동태는 수동태에서도 같은 조동사를
사용한다.
┌ 조동사 + V
└ 조동사 + be + p.p

We <u>can see</u> a full moon tonight.
A full moon <u>can be seen</u> (by us) tonight.

Tom <u>will repair</u> this car.
This car <u>will be repaired</u> by Tom.

~ do it 　　~ have done it 　　~ be doing it
It is done by~ 　It had been done it by~ 　It is being done~

명령문의 수동태

☞ Let을 이용한 명령문의 수동태는 현대 일상 영어에서는 거의 사용되지 않고 있다.
① 긍정 명령문일 때 => Let + O + be + p.p

Do it at once.
<u>Let</u> it <u>be done</u> at once.

Sign the paper.
<u>Let</u> the paper <u>be signed.</u>

② 부정 명령문 일 때 => 　Let + O(목적어) + not + be + p.p.
　　　　　　　　　　　　Don't + let + O(목적어) + be + p.p.

Don't touch this stone.
<u>Let</u> this stone <u>not be touched.</u>
<u>Don't let</u> this stone <u>be touched.</u>

Don't set the dog free.
<u>Let</u> the dog <u>not</u> be set free.
<u>Don't</u> let the dog <u>be set free.</u>

Don't cut down the tree.
<u>Don't let</u> the tree <u>be cut</u> down.
<u>Let</u> the tree <u>not be cut</u> down.

cf) 　Let him <u>play</u> the piano.
　　　Let the piano <u>be played by</u> him.

☞ Let으로 시작하는 간접 명령문의 수동태 : Let + O + be + p.p.

① 의문사가 없는 의문문 => be + O + p.p
☞ 능동태에서 아무런 의미가 없이 의문문·부정문을 만들기 위해서 쓰인 do, does, did를 수동태에서는 사용할 필요가 없어지고, 「be + p.p」 형태만 남는다.

┌ Did he make a box?
└ Was a box made by him?

┌ Did his pupils like him?
└ Was he liked by his pupils?

② 의문사가 있는 의문문 => ┌ 의문사 + be + S + p.p
                               └ By + 의문사 + be + S + p.p

☞ 주격 who일 때만 By whom으로 쓰고, 그 외는 의문사가 그대로 문두에 온다.

┌ What did Tom plant there?
└ What was planted there by Tom?

┌ When did you finish it?
└ When was it finished by you?

┌ Who invented this machine?
└ By whom was this machine invented?

┌ Who broke the window?
└ By whom was the window broken?

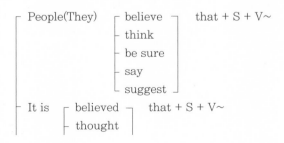

┌ People(They) ┌ believe ┐ that + S + V~
│   ├ think
│   ├ be sure
│   ├ say
│   └ suggest ┘
┌ It is ┌ believed ┐ that + S + V~
       └ thought ┘

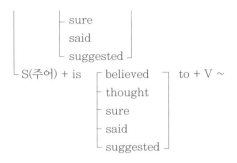

```
            ┌ sure
            ├ said
            └ suggested
  └ S(주어) + is  ┌ believed ┐  to + V ~
                ├ thought
                ├ sure
                ├ said
                └ suggested ┘
```

They say that he is a liar.
People say that he is a liar.
It is said that he is a liar.
He is said to be a liar.

They say that she was beautiful.
It is said that she was beautiful.
She is said to have been beautiful.

It is believed that he was diligent when young.
He is believed to have been diligent when young.

People think that Americans chew gum and talk through their noses.
It is thought that Americans chew gum and talk trough their noses.
Americans are thought to chew gum and talk through their noses.

They say that honesty is the best policy.
It is said that honesty is the best policy.
Honesty is said to be the best policy.

It is certain that he will turn up.
I am sure that he will turn up.
He is sure to turn up.

I am sure that he will live to eighty.
I am sure of his living to eighty.
He is sure to live to eighty.

I am sure that you will need more money.
You are sure to need more money.
You will surely need more money.

TEST

1 다음 빈칸에 알맞은 것을 고르시오.

⌈ They say that he drew this picture.
⌊ This picture is said _____ by him.

① to have drawn ② to draw ③ to have been drawn ④ to be drawn
(정답) ③

⌈ They say that <u>he drew this picture.</u>
⌈ They say that <u>this picture was drawn by him.</u>
⌊ This picture is said <u>to have been drawn by him.</u>
⌈ <u>They say</u> that he drew this picture.
⌈ <u>It is said</u> that he drew this picture.
⌊ He <u>is said to have drawn</u> this picture.

2 두 문장의 뜻이 같도록 아래 문장들을 완성하시오.

1. ⌈ They believe that he is sick.
   ⌊ He is believed to _____.

2. ⌈ They say that Mary was very lucky to win the beauty contest.
   ⌊ Mary is said to _____.

3. ⌈ I am very sorry that I did not answer your letter sooner.
   ⌊ I am very sorry not to _____.

4. ⌈ I am very pleased that I met a good friend to travel with.
   ⌊ I am very pleased to _____.

(정답) 1. be sick.

2. have been very lucky to win the beauty contest.

3. have answered your letter sooner.

4. have met a good friend to travel with.

08 [부정주어 능동태의 수동태로의 전환]

$$by \begin{bmatrix} anything(O) \\ anybody(O) \\ anyone(O) \end{bmatrix} \quad by \begin{bmatrix} nothing(X) \\ nobody(X) \\ no\ one(X) \end{bmatrix}$$

☞ nobody, no one 등 「부정 주어」가 있는 능동형의 문장을 수동문으로 전환시킬 때
는 「not ~ by anyone(anybody)」의 형식이 된다. 즉 수동태에서는 「by
nobody」형태로는 쓸 수 없다.
또한 능동태에서는 「Anybody ~ not …」의 형태로 쓸 수 없다.

Nobody could solve the problem.(O)
The problem could <u>not</u> be solved <u>(by anybody)</u>.(O)
The problem could be solved by <u>nobody</u>.(X)
<u>Anybody</u> could <u>not</u> solve the problem.(X)
(아무도 이 문제를 풀지 못했다.)

<u>Nothing</u> satisfied her.(O)
She was <u>not</u> satisfied with <u>anything</u>.(O)
She was satisfied with <u>nothing</u>.(X)
(아무것도 그 여자를 만족시켜 주지 않았다.)

<u>Nobody</u> took any notice of the fact.(O)
The fact was <u>not</u> taken any notice of <u>(by anybody)</u>.(O)
The fact was taken <u>no</u> notice of <u>(by anybody)</u>.(O)
<u>Any</u> notice was taken of the fact <u>by nobody</u>.(X)
<u>No</u> notice was taken of the fact <u>by anybody</u>.(O)
(아무도 그 사실을 주목하지 않았다.)

* 다음 주어진 문장과 뜻이 같은 것은?

<u>Nobody paid attention to the sign.</u>

① Attention was paid to the sign by nobody.
② The sign was paid attention to by nobody.
③ No attention was paid to the sign by anybody.
④ The sign was not paid attention by anybody.

He did not pay any attention to my advice. (O)

Any attention was not paid to my advice by him. (O)

No attention was paid to my advice by him. (O)

☞ 위 문제 ④는 The sign was not paid attention to by anybody로 써야 한다.

cf) We took good care of the garden.(O)

The garden was taken good care of by us.(O)

Good care was taken of the garden by us.(O)

09 동작 수동태와 상태 수동태

Our house is painted every year.(동작 수동태)

We paint our house every year.

(우리 집은 매년 페인트칠하여 진다.)

Our house is painted white.(상태 수동태)

We have painted our house white.

(우리 집은 하얀 색으로 칠하여져 있다.)

10 동사구의 수동태

① 동사 + 전치사(부사)를 하나의 타동사로 생각하고 고친다.

A car ran over the child.

The child was run over by a car.

The villagers laughed at him.

He was laughed at by the villagers.

The villagers <u>looked down upon</u> him.

He <u>was looked down upon by</u> the villagers.

② 동사 + 명사 + 전치사 + 명사

i) 동사의 주어가 수동태의 주어로 나온다.

ii) 동사구속의 명사가 주어로 나온다.

☞ 즉 「동사 + 명사 + 전치사」형의 동사구의 명사에 any, some, every, much, little, no 따위의 형용사가 있으면 그 「형용사 + 명사」를 수동태의 주어로 할 수 있다.

The hunters <u>paid no attention to</u> his warning.

<u>His warning</u> was paid no attention to by the hunters.

<u>No attention</u> was paid to his warning by the hunters.

They <u>took good care</u> of him.

<u>He</u> was taken <u>good care</u> of by them.

<u>Good care</u> was taken of him by them.

We <u>took great care of</u> the boy.

<u>The boy</u> was taken <u>great care</u> of by us.

<u>Great care</u> was taken of the boy by us.

11 by ~의 생략

① 주어가 one, we, they 등 일반적인 사람의 경우

② 행위자가 불분명한 경우

③ 행위자가 문맥상 분명한 경우에 by ~가 생략된다.

One should keep promises.

Promises <u>should be kept</u> (by one).

He is said to have died young.

They say that he died young.

It <u>is said</u> that he died young (by them).

All the goods were sold in a day. (행위자 불분명)

(상품이 하루만에 다 팔렸다.)

His son was killed in the railway accident. (행위자 불분명)
(그의 아들은 철도 사고로 죽었다.)

I trod upon a snake and was bitten on the leg.(행위자 분명)
(뱀을 밟아서 다리를 물렸다.)

12 by 이외의 전치사를 사용하는 경우

① 감정을 나타내는 동사는 대개 전치가 「at, with」를 사용한다.

The news <u>surprised</u> me.　　The result <u>satisfied</u> him.
I <u>was surprised at</u> the news.　He <u>was satisfied with</u> the result.
I <u>was acquainted with</u> him.
I <u>was much interested in</u> the detective story.
My father <u>is displeased with</u> me.
I <u>am rejoiced at</u> your success.
He <u>is always worried about</u> the result.

② be known to (~에게 알려지다)
　be known by (~을 보면 알다, ~에 의하여 판단되어 지다)
　be known as (~으로 알려지다)
　be known for (=be famous for)

Everybody knows the poet.
The poet <u>is known to</u> everybody.

We know a man <u>by</u> the company keeps.(by는 판단의 기준을 나타냄)
A man <u>is known by</u> the company he keeps.
(사람은 그가 사귀는 친구를 보면 알 수 있다.)

We know the tree <u>by</u> its fruit.(by는 판단의 기준을 나타냄)
The tree <u>is known by</u> its fruit.
(나무는 그 열매를 보면 알 수 있다.)

He is known as a successful architect.
He is known for his novel.(= be famous for, be renowned for, be celebrated for)

 기타 문장 중의 수동태

┌ I've heard her spoken ill of by Mary.
└ I've heard (that) Mary speak ill of her.

┌ I've heard it admired by many foreigners.
└ I've heard (that) many foreigners admire it.

cf) ┌ She looks forward that they will visit her.
    ├ She looks forward to their visiting her.
    ├ She looks forward that she will be visited by them.
    └ She looks forward to being visited by them.

TEST

* 보기와 같이 "being + 과거분사"의 형으로 된 동명사를 사용해서 빈 곳을 완성하시오.

[보기] She looks forward to their visiting her.
        She looks forward to being visited by them.

1. ┌ She likes their asking her opinion.
   └ She likes _____.

2. ┌ She hates their serving her at the table.
   └ She hates _____.

3. ┌ She looks forward to their inviting her to the party.
   └ She looks forward to _____.

4. ┌ She enjoys the family taking care of her.
   └ She enjoys _____.

제8장 태(態:Voice =) 수동태/능동태)

Take A Break!

[한국 풍속화 감상 1 – 맥추(Barley in the Autumn)]

누런 보리밭에 꿩이 알을 품는다. 인적 소리에 푸드득 날개 치는 소리. 사람과 새가 서로 놀란다.

A pheasant is brooding eggs in a golden barley field. At a man's noise it flaps its wings. The man and the bird surprised each other.

제9장
Essential English Grammar

가정법
(Subjunctive Mood)

01 현재시제의 미래시제 대용
(代用:대신 쓰이는 경우)

☞ If, When, While, Until 등 「때나 조건」을 나타내는 「부사절」에 있어서는 「미래시제」 대신에 「현재시제」를 쓴다.

[1] 시간(때)나 조건을 나타내는 부사절에서는 현재시제가 가까운 미래시제를 대신한다.

Ex) If it <u>rains</u>, I won't go.

[You may not go out until you <u>finish</u> your homework. (O)
[You may not go out until you <u>will finish</u> your homework. (X)

[It will not be long before we <u>graduate</u> from high school. (O)
[It will not be long before we will <u>graduate</u> from high school. (X)

[We are waiting till he <u>comes</u>. (O)
[We are waiting till he <u>will come</u>. (X)

[We will eat when he <u>comes</u> back. (O)
[We will eat when he <u>will come</u>. (X)

TEST

다음 글을 읽고 _____에 들어갈 적당한 말을 고르시오.

"Johnny is supposed to visit me this afternoon."

"If he _____, tell him I said 'hello'."

① coming ② come ③ comes ④ will come ⑤ shall come

(정답) ③

[2] (시간·때의) 부사절에서는 미래시제를 못쓰므로 미래완료에 는 현재완료로 대신 쓴다.

[I will come as soon as I <u>have finished</u> writing this letter. (O)
[I will come as soon as I <u>will have finished</u> writing this letter. (x)

| Essential English Grammar | **187**

[3] 근접미래(近接未來:가까운 미래)

☞ 왕래발착동사(往來發着動詞:go, come, leave, start, arrive 등)가 미래부사와 함께
   쓰일때는 현재시제가 가까운 미래를 나타낸다.

Ex) He starts(=will start) tomorrow morning.
    We leave(=will leave) tomorrow.

[4] 현재 진행형이 가까운 미래, 예정을 나타내는 경우.

Ex) We are having a party tonight.
    (=will have)
    We are leaving for Busan tonight.
    (=will leave)
    Are you staying here till next week?
    (=Will you stay)
    Father is taking us to the zoo next Sunday.
    (=will take)
    We're getting married in June.
    (=will get)
    I'm dining out today. *dine out 외식하다.
    (=will dine)

02 명령문 + and (이익 : 그러면) => if + S(주어) + V(동사)
명령문 + or (손해 : 그렇지않으면) => ⌈ if + S(주어) + not + V(동사)
                                  ⌊ unless + S(주어) + V(동사)

Hurry up, and you will be in time for the train.
If you hurry up, you will be in time for the train.
(서둘러라, 그러면 기차시간 안에 도착할 것이다.)

Work hard, or you will fail.
If you do not work hard, you will fail.
Unless you work hard, you will fail.
(열심히 공부하라, 그렇지 않으면 실패할 것이다.)

03 otherwise + S + 가정법 과거 (만일에 그렇지 않다면)

He works hard ; otherwise he would fail.
He works hard ; if he did not work hard, he would fail.

04 otherwise + S + 가정법 과거완료 (만일에 그렇지 않았다면)

He left at once ; otherwise he could not have caught the train.
He left at once ; if he had left a little later he could not have caught the train.

TEST

1 빈 칸에 가장 알맞은 표현을 고르시오.

Using this method, men discovered laws of nature that otherwise

_____.

① remained unknowing

② remained unknown

③ would have remained unknowing

④ would have remained unknown

⑤ would remained unknown

(정답) ④

☞ 여기서 key word는 otherwise (만약 그렇지 않으면 = if ~ not)이며, 이때
「otherwise」는 「if they had not discovered laws of nature」로 바꾸어 쓸
수 있다.

◀ NOTES ▶

＊method 방법　＊laws of nature 자연 법칙

[전문 해석] 이 방법을 사용함으로써, 만약 그렇지 않았더라면, 아직 알려지지
않은 채로 있을 자연법칙을 인간은 발견했다.

2 다음 문장의 밑줄 친 부분을 절로 옮기시오.

He did as advised ; <u>otherwise</u> he would not have made it.

(　　　　　　　　)

(정답) if he had not done as advised.

05
$$\left[\begin{array}{c} \text{But for} \\ \text{Without} \end{array}\right] + \text{N(명사), S(주어)} + \text{(would, should, could, might)} + \text{동사원형} \cdots$$

「가정법 과거」 (~이 없다면, …일텐데)

$$\left.\begin{array}{l} \left[\begin{array}{c} \text{But for} \\ \text{Without} \end{array}\right] \text{my illness} \\ \text{If I were not ill,} \\ \text{Were I not ill,} \\ \text{If it were not for my illness,} \\ \text{Were it not for my illness,} \end{array}\right\} \quad \text{I could go there.(가정법 과거)}$$

As I am ill, I can not go there. (직설법 현재)
(아프지만 않다면 나는 거기에 갈 수 있을 텐데)

06
$$\begin{bmatrix} \text{But for} \\ \text{Without} \end{bmatrix} + \text{N(명사), S(주어)} + \begin{bmatrix} \text{would, should} \\ \text{could, might} \end{bmatrix} + \text{have} + \text{p.p.}$$

[가정법 과거완료]   (~이 없었다면, …였을 텐데)

$$\begin{bmatrix} \text{But for} \\ \text{Without} \end{bmatrix} \text{your help,}$$
It it had not been for your help,
Had it not been for your help,
If you had not helped me,   I would have failed.
Had you not helped me,   (가정법 과거완료)
If there had been no your help,
If there had not been your help,
As you helped me, I did not fail.(직설법 과거)
(너의 도움이 없었다면 나는 실패했을 것이다.)

07 It is (high/about) time + that + S(주어) + 과거동사
[또는 should + V(동사원형)] (~할 시간(때)이다)

☞ 긴급, 당연, 필요,재촉을 나타내며, 이때의 that이하는 형용사절이며, should는 생
   략할 수 없다.

It's (high) time that we <u>left</u>.
It's (high) time that we <u>should leave</u>.
It's (high) time for us <u>to leave</u>.
(우리가 떠나야 할 시간이다.)

It is time that you <u>went</u> to bed.
It is time that you <u>should go</u> to bed.
It is time for you <u>to go</u> to bed.
(너는 이제 자야 할 시간이다.)

It is (about) time we <u>were</u> off.
(이제 우리가 떠날 시간이다.)

08 I wish가 이끄는 가정법 문장

```
┌ I wish
├ If only
├ Would that        he were here with us
└ Oh that
```

[1] I wish + 가정법 과거(명사절)

☞ 현재사실의 반대되는 소원을 나타낸다. 이때의 be동사는 항상 「were」다.

```
Ex) ┌ I wish it were true. (가정법)
    ├ I am sorry (that) it is not true. (직설법)
    └ It's a piety that it is not true. (직설법)

    ┌ I wish I were a bird.
    └ I am sorry (that) I am not a bird.

    ┌ I wish you get up early. (가정법)
    ├ I am sorry that you don't get up early. (직설법)
    └ You should get up early. (가정법)
```

[2] I wished + 가정법 과거

```
Ex) ┌ I wished it were true. (가정법)
    ├ I was sorry (that) it was not true. (직설법)
    └ It was a piety that it was not true. (직설법)
```

☞ that 이하의 과거형은 시제의 일치에 따른 것임.

```
    ┌ I wished you got up early.
    └ I was sorry that you didn't get up early.
```

[3] I wish + 가정법과거완료 (과거사실의 반대되는 가정 또는 상상)

```
Ex) ┌ I wish I had been rich. (가정법)
    ├ I am sorry (that) I was not rich. (직설법)
    └ It's a piety that I was not rich. (직설법)

    ┌ I wish you had got up early. (가정법)
    ├ I'm sorry that you didn't get up early. (직설법)
    └ You should have got up early. (가정법)
```

1 다음 대화에서 _____에 알맞은 것은?

A : Did you enjoy the dance last night?

B : Yes, but I wish I _____ a cold.

① hadn't   ② didn't have

③ hadn't had   ④ haven't had

⑤ had

(정답) ③

2 다음 두 글의 뜻이 같도록 ____에 알맞은 것을 써 넣으시오.

A : I wish I hadn't invited her to the party.

B : I am sorry that _____ to the part.

① I do not invite her   ② I invited her

③ I did not invite her   ④ I had invited her

⑤ I invited her

(정답) ②

[4] I wished + 가정법 과거완료

Ex) ┌ I wished I had been rich.
    ├ I was sorry (that) I had not been rich.
    └ It was a pity that I had not been rich.

☞ that 이하의 과거완료는 시제의 일치에 따른 대과거.

    ┌ I wished you had got up early.
    └ I was sorry that you hadn't got up early.

[5]

I wish + S + ┌ would ┐
             ├ should ┤ (가정법 미래)
             └ might ┘

☞ 미래의 일에 대해서 어떻게 되기를 소원할 경우에는 wish 다음에 「would, should, might」를 쓴다.

    Ex) I wish I would be strong.
        (힘이 세었으면 좋을 텐데.)

09
```
┌ as if      ┐ + S(주어) + 과거동사 ~ (가정법 과거)
│            │         = In fact(Actually) S + V(현재동사)
└ as though ┘ (마치 ~인것처럼)
```

```
┌ He talks as if he knew everything.
└ In fact(=Actually) he doesn't know everything.
```
(그는 마치 모든 것을 아는 것처럼 말한다.)

```
┌ He talks as if he were rich.
└ In fact(=Actually) he is not rich.
```
(그는 마치 부자인 것처럼 말한다.)

```
┌ He talked as if he knew everything.
└ In fact(=Actually) he did not know everything.
```
(그는 마치 모든 것을 알고 있었던 것처럼 말했다.)

```
┌ He talked as if he were rich.
└ In fact(=Actually) he was not rich.
```
(그는 마치 부자인 것처럼 말했다.)

10
```
┌ as if      ┐ + S(주어) + had + p.p.~ (가정법 과거완료)
│            │         = In fact + S + 과거동사 또는 현재완료
└ as though ┘ (마치 ~ 이었던 것처럼)
```

```
┌ He talks as if he had seen her.
└ In fact he has not seen her.
```
(그는 마치 그 이전에 그 여자를 만나보았던 것처럼 말한다.)

```
┌ He talks as if he had known everything.
└ In fact(=Actually) he has not known everything.
```
(그는 마치 모든 것을 알고 있었던 것처럼 말한다.)

He <u>talked</u> as if he <u>had seen</u> her.
In fact he <u>had not seen her.</u>
(그는 마치 그 이전에 그 여자를 보았던 것처럼 말했다.)

He <u>talked</u> as if he <u>had known</u> everything.
In fact(=Actually) he <u>had not known</u> everything.
(그는 마치 모든 것을 알고 있었던 것처럼 말했다.)

11
┌ In cause(that) + S(주어) + ┌ V(직설법 현재동사) ┐
│   └ should + V(동사원형) ┘
├ In case of + N(명사)
└ In the event of + N(명사)   (~할 경우에만, 만일 한다면)

EX) ┌ <u>In case of his failure</u>, should he try again?
    ├ <u>Should he fail</u>, should he try again?
    └ <u>If he should fail</u>, should he try again?
    (만일 그가 실패하면 또 다시 시작할까?)

<u>In case</u> he does not come will you go alone?
(만일 그가 오지 않는다면 당신 혼자 가겠는가?)

<u>In case of</u> trouble, call for my help.
(문제가 생겼을 경우에는 내 도움을 청하시오.)

Take your umbrella <u>in case</u> it should rain.
(비가 올 경우를 대비해서「비가 오면 안되니까」우산을 가지고 가거라.)

<u>In the event of</u> fire, ring the alarm bell.
(화재가 날 경우에는 경종을 울리시오.)

12 Provide(that) + S(주어) + V(직설법 현재동사)

Provide(that)
Providing (that)
So that
On condition that(=If)
So long as(=If only)
If only
In case(that)(=If)
+ S(주어) + V(직설법 현재동사)
(~하기만 한다면)

Suppose(that)
Supposing(that)
+ S(주어) + V(직설법 현재동사)/또는 가정법 과거동사
(~ 한다면)

Granted(that)
Granting(that)
+ S(주어) + V(직설법 현재동사)

☞ 양보(even if)를 나타냄. (설령 ~한다 할지라도)

Ex) In case of his failure, should he try again?
Should he fail, should he try again?
If he should fail, should he try again?

I will go there, providing (that) my expenses are paid.
(내 경비만 지불해 준다면, 나는 거기에 가겠다.)

I will consent, provide that all the others agree.
(모든 다른 사람들이 찬성한다면 나도 동의하겠다.)

So that it is done, it matters not how.
(그것이 이루어지기만 하면, 어떻게 이루어지던 상관없다.)

I will accept the post, on the condition that you assist me.
(네가 나를 도와준다면 나는 그 자리를 수락하겠다.)

You may stay here, so long as you keep quiet.
(네가 조용히만 있는다면, 여기 남아 있어도 좋다.)

In case I forget, please remind me of it.
(내가 잊어버리면, 그것을 나에게 일러주시오.)

Suppose that he refuse, what shall we do?
(만일 그가 거절한다면 우리는 어떻게 할까?)

Granted that it is true, it does not matter to me.
(비록 그것이 사실일지라도, 나에게는 별로 중요하지 않다.)

Suppose (that) I were your teacher, what would you want me to teach?
(만일 내가 너의 선생이라면, 너는 무엇을 가르치기를 원하겠는가?)

Suppose (that) it were true, what would you happen?
(만일 그것이 사실이면, 어떤 일이 발생할까?)

13

S(주어) +
- 제안·충고(suggest, advise, recommend)
- 주장(insist, urge)
- 요구(demand, require, desire,
- 명령(order, command, instruct)
- 결정(decide)
- 이성적인 판단(necessary, important, proper, natural, ight, well, good, wrong, rational)
- 감정적 판단(strange, curious, odd, wonderful, a pity, surprising, regrettable)

that + 주어 + (should) + 동사 ~

☞ 위와 같은 뜻을 갖는 동사, 형용사, 명사가 올 때는 목적절인 that절을 받는 경우 그 내용이 사실적이 아니기 때문에 「가정법 현재」로 취급하여, 주어의 인칭에 관계없이 종속절인 that절에서는 ①동사원형이나 ②(should) + 동사원형을 쓰며, 이때의 「should」는 생략해도 된다.

[1] 주절이 제안, 충고, 주장, 요구, 명령, 결정을 나타내는 경우

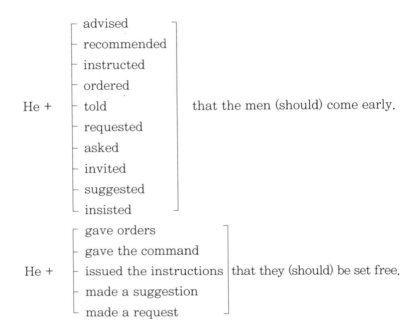

He +
- advised
- recommended
- instructed
- ordered
- told
- requested
- asked
- invited
- suggested
- insisted

that the men (should) come early.

He +
- gave orders
- gave the command
- issued the instructions
- made a suggestion
- made a request

that they (should) be set free.

☞ suggest(제안하다), propose, demand, insist, recommend와 같은 동사의 목적어로 쓰인 that절에서는 「should + 동사 원형」을 쓴다. 단, that절의 내용이 그렇게 되었으면 하는 「의향」을 나타내지 않고 「단순 사실」는 주제의 시제에 일치시킨다.
즉, 명령, 요구, 주장, 충고, 제안, 등의 동사들이 that절을 동반할 때에 뒤의 문장에는 동사 원형이 온다. 그러나, that절의 내용이 「미래의 내용」일 때에만 적용된다. suggest의 경우 「제안하다」로 사용될 때만 적용되며, 동사 suggest가 that절 이하의 사실을 '제시하는' 것이 아니라, 「보여주다, 암시하다」의 뜻으로 쓰이는 경우 정상적으로 내용에 시제일치를 시켜서 완성해야 한다. 또한 insist(주장하다)가 뒤에 that절을 취할 때, 그 내용이 「미래의 사실」이면 that절의 동사는 원형 동사가 와야한다. 하지만, that절이 「미래의 사실」이 아니라, 「과거의 사실」을 말하고 있다면 시제를 내용에 일치시켜야 한다. 즉, 내용이 과거일 경우 「과거」에 일치시켜야 한다.

Ex)
- Many witnesses <u>insisted</u> that the car accident <u>had taken place</u> on the crosswalk.(O)
- Many witnesses <u>insisted</u> that the car accident <u>should take place</u> on the crosswalk.(X)

(많은 목격자들이 그 자동차 사고는 횡단보도에서 일어났다고 주장했다.)

[2] 이성적 판단(理性的 判斷)을 나타내는 경우(이때의 should는 해석하지 않는다.)

It is +
- necessary
- important
- proper
- natural
- right
- wrong
- well/good
- rational

that he (should) go there.

[3] 감정적 판단(感情的 判斷)을 나타내는 경우(이때의 should는 「~하다니」로 해석한다.)

It is +
- strange
- curious
- odd
- wonderful
- surprising
- regrettable
- a pity

that we should meet here.

cf) It is strange <u>that he has not come.</u>(그가 오지 않다니)

  It is strange <u>that we should meet here.</u>(우리가 여기서 만나다니)

☞ should가 없는 경우는 「차분한 기분」인 데 대해 should가 있는 경우는 「뜻밖의 감정」을 강조함.

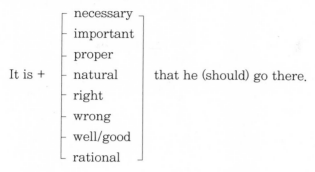

1. 다음 글의 밑줄 친 부분 중. 어법상 <u>틀린</u> 것을 고르시오.

Analysis of sales figures for this year (A)<u>suggests</u> that the (B)<u>majority</u> of customers (C)<u>be remaining</u> loyal to their favorite brands (D)<u>despite</u> a substantial increase in the price.

(정답) (C)be remaining => are remaining

☞ 동사 suggest가 that절 이하의 사실을 '제시하는' 것이 아니라, 「보여주다, 암시하

다」의 뜻으로 쓰였기기 때문에 정상적으로 내용에 시제 일치를 시켜서 완성해야 한다. 즉, 소비자들의 현재 상태를 보여주는 것이기 때문에 현재 시제가 작합하다.

◀ NOTES ▶

＊analysis 분석 ＊figure 수치, 숫자 ＊the majority of customers 대다수의 소지자들 ＊substantial 상당한

[전문 해석] 올해 영업 수치를 분석해 본 결과, 고객들 대부분은 상당한 가격 인상에도 불구하고 자신들이 좋아하는 브랜드를 고집하는 것으로 나타났다.

2. 다음 글의 밑줄 친 부분 중, 어법상 **틀린** 것을 고르시오.

Mr. Johnson insisted that the housekeeping staff never (A)<u>comes</u> to clean his suite (B)<u>during</u> the (C)<u>entire</u> time he was (D)<u>at the hotel</u>.

(정답) (A) comes =〉 came
☞ 동사 insist(주장하다)가 뒤에 that절을 취할 때, 그 내용이 「미래의 사실」이면 that절의 동사는 원형 동사가 와야 한다. 하지만, 위의 문장에서 that절은 「미래의 사실」이 아니라, 「과거의 사실」을 말하는 것이기 때문에 시제를 내용에 일치시켜야 한다. 즉, 내용이 과거이므로 「과거」에 일치시켜야 한다.

◀ NOTES ▶

＊housekeeping staff (호텔의) 청소, 관리 등을 담당하는 직원 ＊suite (여러 개) 붙은 방, (호텔의) 특별실(스위트 룸)

14 조건절 대용어구(전치사일 때) =〉 [with, in, in case of]

With guns,
If we had guns,
⎱ we could defeat the enemy.
(만일 우리가 총을 가지고 있다면 우리는 적을 물리칠 수 있을 것이다.)

With little more industry,
If he had had a little more industry,
If he had been a little more industrious,
⎱ he would not have been poor.

제9장 **가정법**(Subjunctive Mood)

(만일 조금만 근면했더라면, 그는 그렇게 가난하지는 않았을 것이다.)

I would not do such a thing ┐   in your place.
if I were in your place. ┘
(만일 내가 네 입장이라면, 그런 일을 하지 않을 것이다.)

In case of my husband's death, ┐
If my husband were to die,   ├ how could I bring up my little kids?
If my husband should die, ┘
(만일 내 남편이 사망한다면, 어떻게 내가 어린 자식들을 양육할 수 있
겠는가?)

15 조건절 대용어구(단어:명사구일 때)

A Korean would not do such a thing.
If he were a Korean, he would not do such a thing.
(한국 사람이라면 그러한 일을 하지 않을 것이다.)

An able doctor would have relieved her of pain.
If he had been an able doctor, he would have relieved her of pain.
(만일 그가 유능한 의사였더라면, 그녀의 고통을 제거했을 것이다.)

16 조건절 대용어구(접속사 I)
=> [or, or else, otherwise]

                          ┌ or
                          ├ or else   ┐ I would accept
I am engaged now,   ├ otherwise   ┤ your invitation.
                          └ if I were not engaged now, ┘
(나는 지금 약속이 되어 있다. 만일 지금 약속이 없다면 〈그렇지 않다면〉,

너의 초대를 수락할텐데.)

I went at once,
- or else
- otherwise
- if I had not gone at once

I would have missed the train.

(나는 즉시 갔다. 그렇지 않았다면, 나는 그 기차를 놓쳐 버렸을 텐데.)

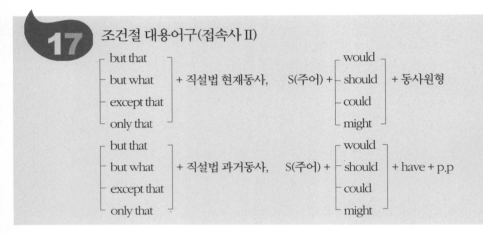

17 조건절 대용어구(접속사 II)

- but that
- but what
- except that
- only that

+ 직설법 현재동사,　S(주어) +
- would
- should
- could
- might

+ 동사원형

- but that
- but what
- except that
- only that

+ 직설법 과거동사,　S(주어) +
- would
- should
- could
- might

+ have + p.p

- But that I am poor
- If I were not poor
- Were I not poor

I could go abroad.

- As I am poor, I can not go abroad.

(내가 가난하지 않다면, 나는 외국에 갈 수 있을 텐데.)

- I would come <u>only that</u> I am engaged to dine out.
- I would come <u>if I were not</u> engaged to dine out.

(밖에서 만찬 약속이 없으면 오겠습니다.)

- But that I was busy,
- If I had not been busy,
- Had I not been busy,

I would have attended the meeting.

- As I was busy, I did not attend the meeting.

(만일 내가 바쁘지 않았더라면, 그 모임에 참석했을 텐데.)

　　　　　　　　　　　　　　　　제9장 **가정법**(Subjunctive Mood)

18 조건절 대용어구(부정사일 때) =〉「to + 동사원형」 과 「to + have + p.p」

To hear her sweet voice,
If you heard her sweet voice, you would fall in love with her.
If you were to hear her sweet voice,
(만일 네가 그녀의 달콤한 목소리를 들으면, 너는 그녀와 사랑에 빠질 것이다.)

He would have been foolish <u>to have done it</u>.
He would have been foolish <u>if he had done it</u>.
(만일 그가 그 일을 했더라면, 그는 바보였을 것이다.)

I should be glad <u>to go with you</u>.
I should be glad <u>if I could go with you</u>.
(너와 함께 갈 수 있다면 좋겠는데.)

<u>To hear him speak English</u>, you would take him for American.
<u>If you heard him speak English</u>, you would take him for American.
(만약 그가 영어를 말하는 것을 듣는다면, 그를 미국인으로 착각할거다.)

19 조건절 대용어구(형용사절/분사구문)

A men <u>who had common sense</u> would not do such a thing.
A men, <u>if he had common sense</u>, would not do such a thing.
(상식이 있는 사람이라면, 그런 일을 하지 않을 텐데.)

The same thing, ┌ happening in wartime,
                └ if it should happen in wartime, ┘

would amount to great disaster.

(그와 같은 일이 만일 전시 때 발생한다면, 큰 재난이 될 것이다.)

 20 가정법의 관용어구 =〉
┌ if any, what if, as it were, if ever, if not all, ┐
└ if at all, if anything ┘

Ex) There are few, <u>if any</u>, mistakes. (=if there are any mistakes)
(비록 있다해도 잘못은 얼마 안된다.)

<u>What if</u>, I should fail in the examination? (=What should I do if)
(시험에 실패하면 <u>어떻게 할까?</u>)

He is, <u>as it were</u>, an endless dreamer. (=so to speak, that is to say, namely)
(그는 <u>말하자면</u> 끝 없는 공상가이다.)

cf) 「as it is」는 직설법으로 「그런데 사실은 ~ 이다」의 뜻이다. 이것의 과거는 「as it was」이다.

He seldom, <u>if ever</u>, goes to church. (=if he ever goes to church)
(<u>비록 간다 할지라도</u> 그는 교회에 아주 드물게 간다.)

He spent more than half the money, <u>if not all</u>.
(<u>비록 전부는 아니지만</u> 그는 반.이상의 돈을 썼다.)

He is little, <u>if at all</u>, better than a beggar.
(<u>조금 낫더라도</u> 그는 거지나 다름없다.)

True greatness has little, <u>if anything</u>, to do with power.
(<u>비록 있다해도</u> 참된 위대성은 권력과 관계가 그렇게 많은 것은 아니다.)

제9장 *가정법*(Subjunctive Mood)

21

If(When) + S(주어) + V(동사) + once(부사) ~ , S′ + V′ ···
Once(접속사) + S(주어) + V(동사) ~ , S′ + V′ ···
(일단 ~ 하면···)

☞ 「Once」가 「부사」로 쓰인 문장을 「접속사」로 쓰인 문장으로 전환.

If you have <u>once</u> started, you must finish it.
<u>Once</u> (you have) started, you must finish it.

If I had <u>once</u> begun, I had to continue with my study.
<u>Once</u> I had begun, I had to continue with my study.

If you have <u>once</u> made up your mind, you must not change it.
<u>Once</u> you have made up your mind, you must not change it.

If you <u>once</u> understand this rule, you will have no problem.
<u>Once</u> you understand this rule, you will have no problem.

<u>When</u> I had <u>once</u> mastered the skill, I was able to enjoy it.
<u>Once</u> I had mastered the skill, I was able to enjoy it.
<u>Once</u> having mastered the skill, I was able to enjoy it.

<u>When</u> he has <u>once</u> remembered a name, he never forgets it.
<u>Once</u> he has remembered a name, he never forgets it.
<u>Once</u> having remembered a name, he never forgets it

제10장
Essential English Grammar

화법
(話法:Narration)

전달동사 Say 와 Tell

[1] say
① 사람의 실제적인 말을 인용할 때 쓴다. (즉 직접화법에서)
  Ex) He said, "I shall go home." (O)
    I told, "I shall go home." (X)

② 간접목적어가 포함되지 않은 문장의 간접화법에서 쓰인다.
  Ex) He said that he would go home. (O)
    He said to me that he would go home. (X)

[2] tell
① 간접 목적어가 들어있는 문장의 간접화법에서 쓰인다.
  Ex) He told me that he would go home. (O)
    He said to me that he would go home. (X)
    He told that he would go home. (X)

② 직접 화법에서는 쓰이지 않는다.
  Ex) I told, "I shall go home."(X)

화법의 기본 형태와 종류

I. 화법의 기본형태

[형식] S   +   say   +   (to 사람)   +   "문장"
     (전달자) (전달동사)   (피전달자)   (피전달문)

① 직접화법(Direct narration) => 어떤 사람의 말을 그대로 전하는 것.
    Ex) He said to me, "I am happy."

② 간접화법(Indirect narration) =〉자기의 말로 바꿔서 전하는 형식.
  Ex) He told me that he was happy.

(화법 전환시 주의할 사항)
①인칭 → ②시제 → ③부사어구 → ④문장의 형태

II. 화법(話法)의 종류(문장의 형태)

	직 접 화 법	간 접 화 법
서 술 법	Tom says, "I am safe."	Tom says (that) he is safe.
의 문 문	Jack said to me, "why did you not go?"	Jack asked me why I had not gone.
명 령 문	Miss Kim said to them, "Please be quiet."	Miss Kim requested them to be quite.
기 원 문	He said, "May you be prosperous."	He expressed his wish that I might be prosperous.
감 탄 문	She said, "How happy I am!"	She said that she was very happy.

III. 전달동사의 위치

[1] 문두(文頭)에 올 때 : say, ask 같은 전달동사가 인용문 앞에
  올 때. =〉S(주어) + V(동사)
  Ex) She said, "He is the boss."

[2] 문중(文中)에 올 때 : say, ask 같은 전달동사가 인용문 사이
  에 올 때. =〉V(동사) + S(주어)
  Ex) "As a result." said John, "I am very angry."

[3] 문미(文尾)에 올 때 : say, ask 같은 전달동사가 인용문 다음에
  올 때. 「S + V」,「V + S」의 2가지 모두 사용할 수 있다.
  Ex) "I am your friend." ┌ said John.
      (피 전달문)   ├ John said.
                            └ he said.

03 직접화법을 간접화법으로 전환할 때 변화하는 것

[1] 인칭

① 1인칭은 「전달문의 주어」와 일치한다.

Ex) ┌ "I'll behave myself." he promised.   (1인칭일 때)
   │   (1인칭)   (전달문의 주어)
   └ He promised that he would behave himself.

② 2인칭은 전달문의 간접목적어의 인칭과 일치한다. (2인칭일 때)

Ex) ┌ "You are beautiful." he whispered to her.
   │   (2인칭)   (전달문 주어)   (전달문의 간접목적어)
   └ He whispered to her that she was beautiful.

③ 3인칭은 인칭의 변화가 없다.
   또 문미(文尾)에 있는 화자(話者)는 문두(文頭)에 온다.

Ex) ┌ She said, "He is the boss."
   │   (3인칭)
   └ She said that he was the boss.
                (3인칭)

[2] 시제 및 부사

① 전달동사가 「현재, 현재완료, 미래시제」인 경우는 피전달문의 동사 시제는 변하지 않는다.

② 전달동사의 시제가 「과거」인 경우 => 피전달문의 동사시제는 「시제의 일치법칙」을 따른다.

(i) 직접화법동사가 「현재」이면 => 간접화법에서는 「과거」로 바꾼다.

(ii) 직접화법동사 ┌ 과거 ┐
              │ 현재완료 │ 이면 => 간접화법에서는 모두 「과거완료」
              └ 과거완료 ┘   로 바꾼다.

③ 전달동사의 시제가 「과거」인 경우 => 피전달문중의 「부사」는 다음과 같이 변한다.

(즉 대명사와 때, 곳(장소)에 관한 부사는 전달자의 입장에서 본 것으로 바뀐다.)

직접화법	간접화법	직접화법	간접화법
yesterday	the previous day the day before	ago	before
last night	the previous night the night before	now	then
next week	the following week the next week	today	that day
tomorrow	the next day the following day	here	there
thus	so	this(these)	that(those)
last + 시간	the previous + 시간	next + 시간 the	following + 시간

Ex) ┌ She <u>said</u> to us, "<u>I met</u> him in this room a week <u>ago</u>."
　　└ She <u>told</u> us that <u>she had met</u> him in <u>that</u> room a week <u>before</u>.

☞ 이러한 부사어의 전환은 기계적으로 변하는 것이 아니고, 말한 때와 장소가 표시되는 경우 그때와 장소에 연관하여 생각해야 하므로 변하지 않는 경우도 있다.

Ex) ┌ She was <u>here</u> last week and said, "I like <u>this</u> room very much."
　　└ She was <u>here</u> last week and said that she liked <u>this</u> room very much.

　　┌ When he came <u>last night</u>, he said, "I saw a strange sight <u>today</u>."
　　└ When he came <u>last night</u>, he said that he had seen a strange sight <u>yesterday</u>.

　　┌ She said <u>just now</u>, "I will come again <u>tomorrow</u>."
　　└ She said <u>just now</u> that she would come again <u>tomorrow</u>.

04 피전달문이 평서문(서술문)인 경우

[공식] S(주어) + say (to 사람), "S´ + (조) V´ ··· "
       S + ┌ tell   ┐ + 사람 + (that) + S + ···
            │ say   │
            │ remark │
            └ state ┘

☞ 간접화법의 전달동사는 say, tell, remark, state 등이다.
  다만 직접화법의 「say to」는 => 대개 「tell」로 고친다.
  간접화법에서도 「say to + 사람」으로 할 수 있으나, 「tell + 사람」이 일반적이다.

① 전달동사가 현재, 현재완료, 미래시제인 경우와 가정법 시제의 경우
   피전달문의 동사시제는 변하지 않는다.

┌ She <u>keeps</u> saying, "I <u>am</u> a failure."
│   (현재시제)   (현재)
└ She <u>keeps</u> saying that she <u>is</u> a failure.

┌ He <u>has said</u>, "It <u>is</u> too difficult."
│   (현재완료)
└ He <u>has said</u> that it <u>is</u> too difficult.

┌ He said, "<u>If</u> I <u>were</u> rich, I <u>would</u> buy it."
│   (가정법)
└ He said that if he <u>were</u> rich, he <u>would</u> buy it.

┌ She said, "He <u>must</u> study harder."
│   (조동사)
└ She said that he <u>must</u> study harder.

② 피전달문의 must, ought to는 전달동사가 <u>과거인</u> 경우에도 그대로
  사용할 수 있다.

┌ Mother said (to me), "Your sweater <u>must</u> be dry-cleaned."
└ Mother said that my sweater <u>must</u> be dry-cleaned.

He said to me, "You <u>ought to</u> be ashamed of yourself."
He told me that I <u>ought to</u> be ashamed of myself.

③ 전달동사의 시제가 「과거」인 경우 => 피전달문의 동사시제는 「시제
   의 일치법칙」을 따른다.
  (i) 직접화법동사가 「현재」이면 => 간접화법에서는 「과거」로 바꾼다.

  (ii) 직접화법동사 $\left[\begin{array}{l}\text{과거} \\ \text{현재완료} \\ \text{과거완료}\end{array}\right]$ 이면 => 간접화법에서는 모두
                                           <u>과거완료</u>로 바꾼다.

He <u>said</u>, "I <u>am</u> sick."
He <u>said</u> that he <u>was</u> sick.
He said, "I <u>bought</u> this book yesterday."
He said that <u>he had bought that</u> book <u>the day before</u>.
He said, "I <u>have written</u> it."
He said that he <u>had written</u> it.

④ 주의사항
☞ 불변의 진리, 현재의 사실, 습관, 역사적인 사실을 말할 때는 시제는 그대로 둔다.
He said, "Honesty <u>is</u> the best policy."
He said that honesty <u>is</u> the best policy.
He said, "She <u>is</u> always complaining."
He said that she <u>is</u> always complaining.
My teacher said, "Columbus <u>discovered</u> America."
My teacher said that Columbus <u>discovered</u> America.

⑤ 전달동사의 시제가 「과거」인 경우 => 피전달문중의 「부사」는 즉 대명
   사와 때, 곳(장소)에 관한 부사는 전달자의 입장에서 본것으로 바꾼다.
He said, "I reached <u>here</u> <u>yesterday</u>."
He said that he had reached <u>there</u> <u>the day before</u>.
She said, "I am busy <u>today</u>."
She said that she was busy <u>that day</u>.

He said, "I saw her three years <u>ago</u>."
He said that he had seen her three years <u>before</u>.

⑥ 「시간, 공간」의 변화가 없는 경우는 그대로 둔다.
(즉 같은 날, 같은 장소에서 전했다면 변동이 없다.)

He said, "It rained <u>here yesterday</u>."
He said that it rained <u>here yesterday</u>.

05 단순 미래와 의지 미래의 화법

☞ 피전달문 중의 「will, shall」은 전달동사가 과거인 경우 시제의 일치법칙을 따르고, 「단순 미래」는 주어의 인칭변화에 따른 변화를 한다. (사실상 You will (would) => I shall (should)의 경우뿐이다.)

[1] 단순 미래

He said (to me), "You <u>will</u> be able to pass the examination."
He said that I <u>should</u>(미국:I would) be able to examination.

He said he <u>should</u> be free tomorrow.
He said, "I <u>shall</u> be free tomorrow."

[2] 의지 미래

He said, "I <u>will</u> never do it again."
He said that he <u>would</u> never do it again.

I told him that if he was a good boy he <u>should</u> have a book.
I said to him, "If you are a good boy, you <u>shall</u> have a book."

cf) 의지미래 => 말하는 사람의 의지가 들어 있다.

Ex) I <u>will do</u> my best.

You <u>shall have</u> this watch.
I <u>will let you have</u> this watch.
I <u>will give you</u> this watch.

06 피전달문이 의문문인 경우의 간접화법

☞ 간접화법의 전달동사를 「ask, inquire of, demand of」로 고친다. inquire의 경우 전달을 받는 사람앞에 of를 붙인다. 또한 ①피전달문이 「의문사」로 시작되면, 의문사가 바로 「종속의문사」로서 접속사 역할을 한다. ② 의문사가 없는 의문문은 「If, Whether (or not)」 등을 쓴다.

[공식] ┌ S(주어) + say (to 사람; to oneself), "의문사 + (조) V´ + S´ …"
　　　　└ S(주어) + ┌ ask (사람)
　　　　　　　　　　├ wonder 　　　　　　┤ + 의문사 + 평서문 순서 …
　　　　　　　　　　└ inquire of 사람 ┘

☞ 「wonder」는 전달동사가 「say to oneself」의 경우에 쓴다.

Ex) ┌ I said to myself, "where can I find her?"
　　 └ I wondered where I could find her.

[1] 의문사가 있는 경우

┌ He said to me, "Who are you?"
└ He asked me who I was.

┌ He said to her, "How long have you been ill?"
└ He inquired of her how long she had been ill.

┌ She said to me, "Why did you strike my boy?"
└ She demanded of me why I had struck her boy.

┌ She said to me, "When will my dress be finished?"
└ She asked me when her dress would be finished.

┌ He said to me, "What do you think of my new book?"
└ He asked me what I thought of his new book.

　☞ 직접화법의 do는 의문문 작성을 위한 조동사이므로 없어진다.

┌ He said to me, "Which is the shortest course?"
└ He inquired of me which the shortest course was.

[2] 의문사가 없는 경우

We asked her, "Is this your first visit here?"
We asked her if(또는 whether) that was her first visit there.

"Do you know my name?" said he.
He asked if(또는 whether) I knew his name.

He said to me, "Did you hear him go out?"
He asked me if(또는 whether) I had heard him go out.

cf)「형태」는「의문문」이나,「내용」이「부탁, 의뢰」등의 경우는「명령문의 간접화법」에 준하여 바꾸기도 한다.

She said to him "Will you please turn off the radio?"
She asked him to turn off the radio.
She asked him if he would turn off the radio.

He said to me, "Could you give me a cigarette?"
He asked me to give him a cigarette.
He asked me if I could give him a cigarette.

07 피전달문이 기원문인 경우의 간접화법

☞ 피전달문 내에서 God의 유무(有無)에 따라

① God이 있으면 ; 전달동사 =〉 pray
② God이 없으면 ; 전달동사 =〉 express one's wish

[공식] S(주어) + say (to 사람) (May) S´ + V´ …!

S(주어) + ⌈ pray   ⌉ that S´ + may V´ …
         ⌊ express one's wish ⌋

He said, "(May) God bless this child."
He prayed that God might bless that child.

He said to me, "May you be happy!"
He expressed his wish that I might be happy.

She said to me, "May you live long!"
She expressed her wish that I might live long.

08 피전달문이 명령문인 경우의 간접화법

☞ 전달동사 「say to」는 「tell, ask, request, beg, advise, order, command」 등으로 변한다. 일반적으로 「tell(명령의 경우), ask(부탁, 의뢰의 경우), advise(충고의 경우)」를 주로 사용한다.

[공식]   S(주어) + say (to 사람), "(Don't) V ……"

   S(주어) + ⌈ tell(order, command) ⌉
              │ ask(request, beg) │ + 사람 + (not) to + V ~
              ⌊ advise ⌋

☞ 즉 " "를 떼고 (접속사 필요 없이) 피전달문을 「to + V」 형식으로 하며, 부정문에서는 「not + to + V」로 한다.

┌ He said to me, "Study hard."
└ He told me <u>to study</u> hard.
┌ She said to him, "Please open the window."
└ She asked him <u>to open</u> the window.
┌ She said to him, "Please get me a glass of water."
└ She asked(requested, begged) him <u>to get</u> her a glass of water.
┌ The teacher said to the pupils, "Read aloud."
└ The teacher commanded(ordered) the pupils <u>to read</u> aloud.
┌ He said to us, "Wait; don't be in such a hurry."
└ He told us <u>to wait and not to be</u> in such a hurry.
┌ He said to us, "Don't smoke on the classroom."
├ He told us <u>not to smoke</u> on the classroom.
├ He forbade us <u>to smoke</u> in the classroom.
└ He prohibited <u>our smoking</u> in the classroom.

   cf) 문장형태는 평서문이나 내용이 실질적인 명령문인 경우는, 명령문에 준하여 바꿀 수도 있다.

┌ The doctor said to him, "<u>You had better go somewhere for a change
│ of air.</u>"

216   제10장 화법(話法:Narration)

$\lceil$ The doctor advised him to <u>go somewhere for a change of air.</u>
$\lfloor$ The doctor told him <u>that he had better go somewhere for a change</u>
<u>of air.</u>

09 피전달문이 감탄문인 경우의 간접화법

☞ 전달동사는 「cry(out), exclaim, shout + 감탄사」와 같은 의미를 표시하는 어구로
나타난다.

[공식 1] $\lceil$ S(주어) + say, "<u>감탄사</u>! S' + V' ……"

$\lfloor$ S(주어) + $\lceil$ cry out (shout) $\rceil$
         exclaim   + <u>전치사 + N(명사) + that</u> ~
         $\lfloor$ say $\rfloor$

☞ 감탄사가 「전치사 + N(명사) = 부사구」로 변하는 경우는 다음과 같다.
① Alas ! => with a sigh
② Hurrah ! or Bravo! => with joy, with delight
③ Oh! Ah! => $\lceil$ with regret (후회의 경우)
           in surprise (놀람의 경우)
           $\lfloor$ in anger (화난 경우)

$\lceil$ He said, "<u>Alas</u>! I have ruined again."
$\lfloor$ He cried out(exclaimed) <u>with a sigh</u> that he had ruined again.

$\lceil$ The boys said, "<u>Hurrah</u>! we have won."
$\lfloor$ The boys exclaimed(shouted) <u>with joy</u> that they had won.

$\lceil$ She said, "<u>Alas</u>! How foolish I have been!"
$\lfloor$ She confessed <u>with regret</u> that she had been very foolish.

$\lceil$ They said, "<u>Hurrah</u>! We have arrived at the top."
$\lfloor$ They cried out <u>with delight</u> that they had arrived at the top.

[공식 2] S(주어) + say "What + (관사) + 형 + 명사 + S´ + V´ … "

"How + 형/부 + S´ + V´ …!"

$$
\text{S(주어) + } \begin{cases} \text{cry out (shout)} \\ \text{exclaim} \\ \text{say} \end{cases} \begin{array}{l} + \text{what} \sim \text{명사 + S´ + V´ …} \\ (\text{how} \sim + S´ + V´ ….) \end{array}
$$

$$
\text{S(주어) + } \begin{cases} \text{cry out (shout)} \\ \text{exclaim} \\ \text{say +} \end{cases} \begin{array}{l} \text{that + S´ + V´ (관)} \\ + \text{very (형) + 명사} \\ (S´ + V´ + \text{very 형/부}) \end{array}
$$

He said, "What a beautiful girl she is!"
He exclaimed (said) ┌ what a beautiful girl she was.
                    └ that she was a very beautiful girl.

She said "Ah! How foolish I have been."
She exclaimed(confessed) with regret how foolish she had been.
She exclaimed (confessed) with regret that she had been very foolish.

I said to them, "What a fine fellow Parker is!"
I told them ┌ what a fine fellow Parker was.
            └ that Parker was a very fine fellow.

10 관용적 용법의 화법

He said, "Yes."
He agreed.
He answered in the affirmative.
He assented.
(그는 동의했다.)

She said "No."
She denied.
She disagreed.
She refused.
She answered in the negative.
(그 여자는 부인했다.)

He said, "Yes, I do."
He said that he did.

He said, "Good morning."
He wished me a good morning.

He said, "No I don't."
He said that he didn't.

He said to me, "Congratulations on your success!"
He congratulate me on my success.

11 특수한 경우의 화법

[1] S(주어) + say (to + 사람), "Let's + V(동사) + … (shall we?)"
S(주어) +┌ suggest ┐(to + 사람) that we(they) should + V(동사) …
　　　　 └ propose ┘

Ex) ┌ He said to us, "Let's have a drive to the lake." (O)
　　└ He suggested(proposed) (to us) that we should have a drive to the lake." (O)
　　┌ He proposed to have a drive to the lake." (O)
　　└ He suggested to have a drive to the lake." (X)
　☞ 간접화법에서 suggest는 반드시 that절을 받는다.

[2] ┌ S(주어) + say (to 사람), "Which + (조동사) + S´(주어) +
   │   V´(동사)…, ┌ this or that?
   │   └ A or B?
   └ S(주어) + ask + (사람) + which of ┌ the two ┐ +
                                        └ A and B ┘

       S´(주어) + V´(동사)

Ex) ┌ He said to me, "<u>Which</u> do you like better, <u>this or that?</u>"
    └ He asked me <u>which of the two</u> I liked better.

12 피전달문이 and, but, or 등으로 연결된 중문(重文)인 경우의 화법

☞ 피전달문이 and, but, or 등으로 연결된 중문(重文 : Compound Sentence)인 경우,
뜻을 잘못 오해하지 않기 위하여 and, but, or 뒤에「that」을 반복하는 것이 보통
이다. 그러나 and, but, or 뒤가 주어 없이 바로 동사인 경우는 that을 반복하지 않
아도 뜻에 오해가 생기지 않는다. 즉, 접속사인 and, but, or 다음에는「that」이 오
며, 첫 번째 나오는「that」은 생략하여도 좋다.

Ex) ┌ She said, "I have been sick for a week, <u>but</u> I'm getting better."
    └ She said (that) she had been sick for a week, <u>but that</u> she was
      getting better.
    ┌ He said, "I'm busy <u>and</u> I cannot comply with your request."
    └ He said (that) he was busy <u>and that</u> he could not comply with
      my request."

☞ 여기서 두 번째의「that」을 빼면,「he could not comply with my request」가
「he」의 말인지 전달자의 말인지 분명하지 않다.

┌ He said, "The watch is very expensive, <u>and</u> I can't buy it."
└ He said (that) the watch was very expensive, <u>and that</u> he
  could not buy it."

☞ 위 예문의 경우, and 뒤의「that」이 없으면「He said」는「expensive」까지이고,
and 이하는 별개의 문장으로 분리되어「그는 그 시계가 너무 비싸다고 말했다. 그
리고, 그는 그것을 살 수 없었다」로 잘못 이해할 수도 있다.

He said, "We have changed our minds, <u>and</u> are going to the mountains."

He said (that) they had changed their minds, <u>and</u> were going to the mountains."

☞ 위의 예문의 경우처럼 and (but, or) 뒤에 <u>주어 없이</u> 연결된 문장의 경우에는 「that」을 반복하지 않으며, 「that」을 반복하려면 주어를 보충해야 한다.

13 접속사가 for, as인 경우의 화법

☞ 접속사가 for, as인 경우는 「that」을 반복하지 않는다.

Ex) ┌ He said, "I would say no more, <u>for</u> I hate explanation."
　　 └ He said (that) he would say no more, <u>for</u> he hated explanation.

14 「명령문, and(or) + S(주어)+ V(동사)」인 경우의 화법

☞ 「명령문, and(or) + S(주어)+ V(동사) …」의 경우에는「that」을 반복하지 않는다.

Ex) ┌ He said to me, "Hurry up, <u>and</u> you will be in time."
　　├ He told me to hurry up, and I <u>should</u> be in time.
　　├ He told me (that) <u>if</u> I hurried up I <u>should</u> be in time.
　　└ He told me to hurry up, <u>saying(또는 adding) that</u> I <u>should</u> (then) be in time.

　　┌ He said to me, "Hurry up, <u>or</u> you will be late."
　　├ He told me to hurry up <u>or</u> I <u>should</u> be late.
　　├ He told me (that) if I didn't hurry up I <u>should</u> be late.
　　└ He told me to hurry up, <u>saying(또는 adding) that</u> I <u>should</u> (otherwise) be late.

15 피전달문이 접속사 없이 여러 개의 문장으로 연결되어 있는 화법

☞ 피전달문이 접속사 없이 여러 개의 평서문이거나, 종류가 다른 문장인 경우는 그 문장마다 전달동사가 달라지며, 문장과 문장은 「and, but, or, because」 등의 접속사로 연결하거나 또는 분사 구문 등을 이용하여 연결한다.

Ex) ┌ She said, "It isn't my fault. I've done nothing wrong."
└ She said (that) it wasn't her fault <u>and that</u> she had done nothing wrong.

┌ "This isn't the first time he lied," she said, "I don't believe him."
└ She said (that) that wasn't the first time he had lied <u>and that</u> she didn't believe him.

┌ Mother said, "Please be quiet, boys ! The baby has just gone to sleep."
└ Mother asked the boys to be quiet <u>because(또는 saying that)</u> the baby had just gone to sleep.

┌ He said, "How long have you been learning English? Your accent is very good."
└ He asked how long I had you been learning English <u>and said that</u> my accent was very good.

┌ They said, "We are going for a country walk. Would you like to join us?"
└ They said (that) they were going for a country walk <u>and asked me if</u> I would like to join them

16 묘출화법과 혼합화법 => 소설 등에서 등장인물의 생각이나 심리를 생생하게 표현하는 형식

┌ 문장의 어순과 구두점(?!) : 직접화법에 준함
└ 인칭과 시제 : 간접화법에 준함

[1] 혼합화법

☞ 혼합화법은 전달동사는 있으나 직접화법의 공식적인 형태를 갖추지 않고, 간접화법 전환시의 인칭 대명사의 변화, 시제의 일치 등의 법칙을 따르면서 피전달문 형식을 유지하고 있어, 직접화법과 간접화법의 중간적인 형태를 취하고 있다.

He said to me, "Will you go to the movies?"(직접화법)
He asked me if I would go to the movies.(간접화법)
He asked me would I go to the movies.(혼합화법)
〈전달동사(asked)가 있음〉
("그는 나에게 내가 극장에 갈 것인가?"라고 물었다.)

He said, "Is that enough?"(직접화법)
He asked if that was enough.(간접화법)
He asked was that enough.(혼합화법) 〈전달동사(asked)가 있음〉
("그는 그것으로 충분하냐?"고 물었다.)

[2] 묘출화법

☞ 묘출화법의 형식도 혼합화법과 같으나, 다만 전달동사가 없는 것이 다르다. 이 묘출 화법은 작가가 작중인물의 생각을 제3자적인 입장에서 대변하는 형식으로서, 심리 묘사의 수법으로 소설 등의 작품에서 많이 사용되는 형식이다.

He felt sorry for her. He said to himself, "It must have been a terrible blow for her to lose her mother."(직접화법)
He felt sorry for her. He thought(wondered) it must have been a terrible blow for her to lose her mother.(간접화법)
He felt sorry for her. It must have been a terrible blow for her to lose her mother.(묘출화법)〈전달동사가 없다〉
(그는 그녀가 불쌍하게 느껴졌다. 그녀가 어머니의 죽음을 당한 것은 커다란 타격이었음에 틀림없다고 그는 생각했다.)

She stared at him in speechless amazement.
She said to herself, "How could he come back so soon? Why didn't he inform me of his return?" (직접화법)

She stared at him in speechless amazement.

She thought(wondered) how he could come back so soon and why had he not informed me of his return?" (직접화법)

She stared at him in speechless amazement.

How he could come back so soon? Why had he not informed me of his return? (묘출화법) 〈전달동사가 없다〉

(그녀는 놀라서 말도 못하고 그를 쳐다봤다. 어떻게 이렇게 일찍 돌아올 수 있었을까? 왜 나에게 돌아오는 것을 그는 알리지 않았을까? (하고 그녀는 마음속으로 중얼거렸다.)

제11장
Essential English Grammar

관계 대명사
(Relative Pronoun)

01 관계 대명사(Relative Pronoun)

[1] 관계 대명사의 역할

☞ 「관계 대명사(Relative Pronoun)」는 주절과 종속절을 연결하는 「접속사」의 역할을 하는 동시에 주절에 있는 명사·대명사를 받는 「대명사」의 역할을 한다. 즉 관계 대명사란 「접속사+대명사」의 구실을 겸하는 것으로 여기에는 「주격, 소유격, 목적격」 등이 있다. 관계 대명사는 선행사를 수식하는 형용사절을 이끈다. 단 what만은 명사절을 이끈다. 「선행사」란 관계 대명사절에 의해 수식되는 명사·대명사로서 보통 관계 대명사 바로 앞에 온다. 따라서 관계 대명사는 반드시 선행사 뒤에 온다. 아래의 예문에서는 「a son」이 선행사이다.

[A] He has a son   +   [B] The son is very wise.
  He has a son <u>and he</u> is very wise.
  He has <u>a son</u> <u>who</u> is very wise.
   〈선행사〉 〈관계 대명사〉
  (그는 매우 현명한 아들이 있다.)

[2] Special Guide 특강

(1) 왼쪽의 그림처럼 [A][B] 두 문장에서 먼저 공통되는 부분(그림에서 빗금부분)을 찾아낸다 (위의 예에서 a son과 the son)

(2) 공통되는 부분을 접속사+대명사 로 연결한다.(위의 예에서 and he)

(3) 접속사+대명사를 관계 대명사로 전환한다.
   (여기서 관계란 접속사를 의미한다.)

(4) 관계 대명사의 격(格 : 주격·소유격·목적격)을 따진다.

(5) 관계 대명사는 반드시 「선행사 뒤」에 와야 한다.

02 관계 대명사의 종류

☞ 관계 대명사는 선행사가 사람과 사물 중 어느 것을 나타내느냐에 따라서 다음과 같은 종류가 있다.

선행사의 종류	주 격	소 유 격	목 적 격
사람	who	whose	whom
사물·동물	which which	whose of which	which
사람·동물·사물	that	–	that
사물(선행사 포함)	what	–	what

[1] who의 용법
관계 대명사 who는 선행사가 사람인 경우에 쓰이며, who, whose, whom의 격변화가 있다.

(1) 주격(who)일 때(who = and + 주어)

> I know the girl. The girl wrote me a letter.
>   (같은 사람)
> I know the girl and she wrote me a letter.
> I know the girl who wrote me a letter.
> (선행사)┗━━━┛   (형용사절)
> (나에게 편지를 보낸 그 소녀를 안다.)

(2) 소유격 (whose)일 때 (whose = and + 소유격)

> I have a friend. His father is a teacher.
> I have a friend and his father is a teacher.

I have a friend　whose　father is a teacher.
〈선행사〉↑_____|(형용사절)
(내게는 아버지가 교사인 친구가 있다.)

*관계 대명사는 선행사 바로 뒤에 온다.

A child　is called　an orphan.　His　parents　are dead.
A child　is called　an orphan　and his　parents　are dead.
A child whose parents are dead is called an orphan.
〈선행사〉↑_____| 〈형용사절〉
(부모가 돌아가신 아이는 고아라 부른다.)

(3) 목적격(whom)일 때 (whom = and + 목적격)
This is　the boy　I spoke of　him　yesterday.
This is the boy and I spoke of　him　yesterday.
This is the boy　whom I spoke of　him yesterday.
　〈선행사〉↑_____| 〈형용사절〉

This is the boy　of whom　I spoke yesterday.
〈선행사〉↑_____|〈형용사절〉
(이 아이는 내가 어제 말한 소년이다.)
　☞ 이때는 전치사가 관계 대명사 앞에 올 수 있다.

03 소유격 관계대명사
=〉 [whose와 of which]

┌ He bought a book + ┌ Its cover was blue.
│　　　　　　　　　　└ The cover of it was blue.
└ He bought a book　┌ whose cover　┐ was blue.
　　　　　　　　　　└ of which the cover ┘
　　(그 사람은 표지가 파란 책을 샀다.)

This is the word + ⌈ I don't know the meaning of it.
⌊ I don't know its meaning.

This is the word ⌈ which I don't know the meaning of.
├ of which I don't know the meaning.
├ the meaning of which ⌉
├ of which the meaning │ I don't know.
⌊ whose meaning ⌋

(이것이 내가 그 의미를 모르는 단어이다.)

04 「선행사, + 관계대명사」 =〉「선행사, + 접속사 + 대명사」

Ex) I will employ him, ⌈ who ⌉ can speak English.
⌊ for he ⌋
(나는 그 사람을 고용하겠다. 왜냐하면 그가 영어를 말할 수 있으니까)

I met a man, ⌈ who ⌉ showed me a way.
⌊ and he ⌋
(어떤 남자를 만났는데, 그가 나에게 길을 안내해 주었다.)

I met the boy, ⌈ who ⌉ did not tell me the news.
⌊ but he ⌋
(그 소년을 만났으나 그 소식을 알려주지 않았다.)

I dislike the man, ⌈ who ⌉ is a gentleman.
⌊ though he ⌋
(나는 그를 싫어한다. 비록 신사이지만)

⌈ I don't know Mr. Kim, whom I had not seen before
⌊ I don't know Mr. Kim, for I had not seen him before.
(나는 김 선생님을 몰라봤다. 왜냐하면 그 이전에 본 적이 없었기 때문이다.)

05 선행사 + 관계대명사(주격) + V(동사) =〉 선행사 + to부정사

He was the first man <u>who set</u> foot on the moon.
He was the first man <u>to set</u> foot on the moon.
(그는 달 위에 발을 내딛은 최초의 인간이었다.)

Korea was the first country <u>that used</u> movable metal type.
Korea was the first country <u>to use</u> movable metal type.
(한국은 이동식 금속활자를 사용한 최초의 국가다.〈제일 먼저 사용한 나라다.〉)

Who was the first man <u>who flew</u> across the Atlantic?
Who was the first man <u>to fly</u> across the Atlantic?
(대서양을 횡단 비행한 최초의 사람은 누구인가?)

He was the first man <u>who won</u> a gold medal in the Olympics.
He was the first man <u>to win</u> a gold medal in the Olympics.
(그는 올림픽에서 금메달을 탄 최초의 인물이었다.)

She was among the first people <u>who collected</u> coins.
She was among the first people <u>to collect</u> coins.
(그녀는 동전을 수집한 최초의 사람들 중에 하나다.)

I was the first guest <u>who arrived</u> at the party.
I was the first guest <u>to arrive</u> at the party.
(나는 그 파티에 도착한 최초의 손님이었다.)

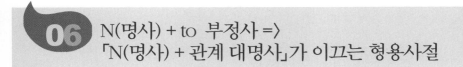

06 N(명사) + to 부정사 =〉 「N(명사) + 관계 대명사」가 이끄는 형용사절

Ex) I have no friend ┌ to help me.
                      └ who will help me.
(나에게는 나를 도와줄 친구가 없다.)

I have nothing ⌐ to do today.
                 └ that I should do today.
(나는 오늘은 해야 할 일이 없다.)

⌐ He was the first Korean <u>that flew</u> across the Pacific.
└ He was the first Korean <u>to fly</u> across the Pacific.
(그는 태평양을 횡단 비행한 최초의 한국인이다.)

⌐ I was the first guest <u>who arrived</u> at the party.
└ I was the first guest <u>to arrive</u> at the party.
(나는 그 파티에 도착한 최초의 손님이다.)

cf) ⌐ You have no reason <u>why you should resign</u>.
    └ You have no reason <u>to resign</u>.
       (당신은 사임할 이유가 없습니다.)

07 〈관계 대명사 + to 부정사(=관계 대명사 + S(주어) + can(will) + V(동사)〉

⌐ 명사/대명사 + to 부정사 + 전치사(이때 to 부정사는 형용사적 용법이다)
├ 명사/대명사 + 전치사 + 관계 대명사 + to 부정사
├ 명사/대명사 + 관계 대명사 + S(주어) + V(동사) + 전치사
└ 명사/대명사 + 전치사 + 관계 대명사 + S(주어) + V(동사)

Ex) ⌐ He has no house <u>to live in</u>.
    ├ He has no house <u>which to live in</u>.
    ├ He has no house <u>in which to live</u>.
    ├ He has no house <u>where to live</u>.
    ├ He has no house <u>which he can live in</u>.
    ├ He has no house <u>in which he can live</u>.
    ├ He has no house <u>where he can live</u>.
    └ He has no house <u>(which) he can live in</u>.(관계 대명사의 목적격은 생략 가능)
       (그는 살 집이 없다.)

⌐ He had no money <u>to buy food with</u>.
├ He had no money <u>with which to buy food</u>.
├ He had no money <u>with which he had to buy food</u>.
└ He had no money <u>which he had to buy food with</u>.

(그는 음식을 살 돈이 없다.)

I have no pen to write with.
I have no pen with which to write.
I have no pen which I can write with.
I have no pen with which I can write.
(나는 가지고 쓸 펜이 없다.)

I have no friend to depend on.
I have no friend on whom to depend.
I have no friend whom I can depend on.
I have no friend on whom I can depend.
(나는 의지할 친구가 없다.)

a chair to sit on (앉는 의자)
a chair on which to sit
a chair which we can sit on
a chair on which we can sit
a chair where we can sit

some income to live on (살아가야 하는 수입)
some income on which to live
some income which we can live on

a stick to walk with (짚고 걸어 다닐 지팡이)
a stick with which to walk
a stick which we can walk with

money to buy something with (구입할 돈)
money with which to buy something
money which we buy something

a friend to talk with(이야기할 친구)
a friend with whom to talk
a friend whom we can talk with

I cannot find words ┌ to thank you in. (O)
                    ├ in which to thank you. (O)
                    └ to thank you.   (X)
(나는 너에게 어떻게 감사의 말을 해야 할지 모르겠다.)

I looked for a shade
- which I could take a rest <u>in</u>.
- <u>in which</u> I could take a rest.
  (=where)
- <u>in which</u> to take a rest.
  (=where)
- to take a rest <u>in</u>.

(나는 휴식을 취할 수 있는 그늘을 찾았다.)

08 관계대명사와 전치사의 위치

Ex) This is the poet
- of whom we spoke.
- whom we·spoke of.
- we spoke of.
- that we spoke of.(관계 대명사 that 앞에는
  전치사가 올 수 없다.)

(이 분이 우리가 말한 그 시인이다.)

- This is <u>the house</u>. And I spoke of <u>it</u>.
- This is the house <u>which</u> I spoke <u>of</u>.
- This is the house (which) I spoke <u>of</u>. (이때의 which는 생략 가능)
- This is the house <u>of which</u> I spoke.(이때는 which의 생략이 불가능하다)

☞ 전치사는 관계 대명사 앞에 올 수 있다. 그러나, 「전치사 + 관계 대명사」에서는 관계
   대명사의 생략이 불가능하다.

- This is the house of I spoke.(X)
- This is the house of that I spoke.(X)

☞ 관계 대명사 that앞에서는 전치사를 쓸 수 없다.

09 의사(유사) 관계 대명사(as / but)

의사 관계 대명사(as) => as ~ as / the same ~ as

의사 관계 대명사(but) =>
- but = that ~ not
- but = who ~ not

종속 접속사 (but)   => but = that ~ not

He is <u>as</u> great a poet <u>as ever lived</u>.
He is one of <u>the greatest</u> poets <u>that</u> ever lived.
(그는 누구에게도 못지않은 훌륭한 시인이다.)

This is <u>the same</u> watch <u>as</u> I lost.(동종류:同種類)
This is <u>the same kind of watch as</u> I lost.
(이것은 내가 잃어버린 것과 같은 종류의 시계이다.)

   cf) This is <u>the same</u> watch <u>that</u> I lost.(동일물:同一物)
        This is <u>the very watch that</u> I lost.
        (이것은 내가 잃어버린 바로 그 시계이다.)

☞ 부정어(no, not) 뒤에 나오는 「but」은 「that ~ not」의 의미를 지닌다.
There is <u>no</u> rule <u>but</u> has some exceptions.
There is <u>no</u> rule <u>that</u> does <u>not</u> have some exceptions.
There is <u>no</u> rule <u>without</u> some exceptions.
<u>Every rule</u> has some exceptions.
(예외 없는 규칙은 없다.)

There is <u>no</u> parents <u>but</u> love their son.
There is <u>no</u> parents <u>who</u> do not love their son.
<u>All parents</u> love their son.
(자기 자식을 사랑하지 않는 부모는 없다.)

There is <u>scarcely</u> a man but speaks well of Tom.
There is <u>scarcely</u> a man <u>that(who) doesn't</u> speak well of Tom.
<u>Everybody</u> speaks well of Tom.
(Tom을 칭찬하지 않는 사람은 거의 없다.)

There is <u>no</u> one <u>but</u> knows it.
There is <u>no</u> one <u>who does not</u> know it.
<u>Everybody</u> knows it.
(그것을 모르는 사람은 아무도 없다.)

No one is old <u>but</u> he may learn.
(but은 종속 접속사로서 that ~ not의 의미이다.)
No one is so old <u>that</u> he may <u>not</u> learn.
(배우지 못할 만큼 나이가 많은 사람은 없다.)

He is not such a fool <u>but</u> he knows it.
(but 은 종속접속사로서 that ~ not의 의미이다.)
He is not such a fool <u>that</u> he does <u>not</u> know it.
(그는 그것을 모를 정도로 그런 바보는 아니다.)

10 관계 형용사 What =〉 ┌ all the + N(명사) + that ~
├ that(those) + N(명사) + that(which) ~
└ as much(many) + N(명사) + as ~

I gave him <u>what money</u> I had.
I gave him <u>all the money that</u> I had.
(내가 가지고 있던 돈 전부를 그에게 주었다.)

He saved <u>what little money</u> he earned.
He saved <u>all the little money that</u> he earned.
(그가 번 얼마 되지 않는 모든 돈을 저축했다.)

The leaves were trembling with <u>what little breeze there was</u>.
The leaves were trembling with <u>all the little breeze</u> there was.
(있을까 말까하는 미풍에 잎이 흔들리고 있었다.)

She waited with <u>what patience</u> she could command.
She waited with <u>as much patience as</u> she could command.
(자기가 할 수 있는 최대한의 인내심으로 그녀는 기다렸다.)

Lend me <u>what books</u> you can.
Lend me <u>as many books as</u> you can.
(될 수 있는 한 많은 책을 빌려 주시오.)

Wear <u>what clothes</u> you please.
Wear <u>those clothes which</u> you please.
(네가 좋아하는 옷을 입어라.)

I will give you <u>what help</u> I can.
I will give you <u>all the help that</u> I can.
I will give you <u>as much help as</u> I can.
(내가 줄 수 있는 만큼의 도움이야 줄 수 있다.)

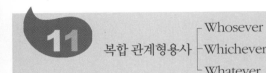

11 복합 관계형용사 ⎡ Whosever ⎤
                    ⎢ Whichever ⎥ + N(명사) = any + N(명사) + that
                    ⎣ Whatever ⎦

You may read <u>whatever book</u> you like.
You may read <u>any book that</u> you like.
(네가 좋아하는 어떤 책을 읽어도 좋다.)

<u>Whosever horse</u> comes in first wins the prize.
<u>Any horse that</u> comes in first wins the prize.
(먼저 들어오는 것이 누구의 말이든 상을 받는다.)

Read well to the end <u>whichever book</u> you choose one.
Read well to the end <u>any book that</u> you choose one.
(네가 선택한 책은 어느 것이나 끝까지 읽어라.)
☞ 선택의 뜻이 강할 때는 「whatever」보다 「whichever」를 쓴다.
  cf) <u>Whatever book</u> you may read, you should read it throughly.
    <u>No matter what book</u> you may read, you should read it throughly.
    (네가 무슨 책을 읽을지라도 끝까지 읽어야 한다.)

 12 복합 관계사 => ⎡ whosever ⎤
                              ⎢ whichever ⎥
                              ⎣ whatever ⎦

☞ 「복합 관계사」란 「who, which, what」 등과 같은 의문사에 「ever」를 붙인 것을 말하며, 선행사를 포함하고 ① 명사절 ② 부사절을 인도한다.

[1] 명사절을 인도할 때 (복합 관계 대명사)

☞ whoever, whomever, whosever, whatever, whichever 등이 있으며, 주어, 목적어, 보어 역할을 한다.

> whoever = anyone who,   whomever = anyone whom
> whosever = anyone whose,   whatever = any + N(명사) + that
> whichever = anything that = any + N(명사) + that

Whatever he said was true.
Anything that he said was true.
(그가 말한 것은 무엇이든지 사실이었다.)

Whoever does his best will be blessed.
Anyone who does his best will be blessed.
(최선을 다하는 사람은 누구나 축복 받는다.)

Whatever he says is very important.
Anything that he says is very important.
(그가 말하는 것은 무엇이나 아주 중요하다.)

Give the book to whoever wants it.
Give the book to anyone who wants it.
(그 책을 원하는 사람이면 아무에게나 주어라.)
　　☞ 이 문장에서는 to의 목적어로 착각하여 「whomever」로 하면 안된다. 여기서는 to 뒤의 문장에서 「wants」의 주어 역할을 하고 있기 때문이다.

Give the book to whomever you like.
Give the book to anyone whom you like.
(그 책을 당신이 좋아하는 사람이면 아무에게나 주어라.)
　　☞ 여기서의 「whomever」는 뒤에 나오는 「like」의 목적어 역할을 하고 있다.

[2] 부사절을 인도할 때 (복합 관계부사)

☞ 주로 may(will)를 수반하여 「no matter + 의문사」의 의미로 「의문사의 뜻 + 양보의 뜻」(아무리~일지라도)이 결합된 경우다.

> 의문사 + ever = no matter + 의문사

- Whatever you may do, do your best.
- No matter what you may do, do your best
  (네가 무엇을 할지라도 최선을 다해라.)

- Whoever may object, I will do it.
- No matter who may object, I will do it.
  (아무리 누가 반대할지라도 나는 그것을 할 것이다.)

- Whichever you may choose, you will love it.
- No matter which you may choose, you will love it.
  (네가 어떤 것을 선택한다 할지라도 좋아하게 될거다.)

- However much he eats, he never gets fat.
- No matter how much he eats, he never gets fat.
  (그는 아무리 많이 먹더라도 전혀 살이 찌지 않는다.)

- Whenever I may call on him, I find him working.
- No matter when I may call on him, I find him working.
  (내가 그를 언제 찾아가더라도 그는 일을 하고 있다.)

13 관계대명사 what ⇒ the thing which; that which; all that

☞ 관계 대명사 「what」은 그 자체에 선행사를 포함하고 있으며(즉, 따로 가르키는 선행사가 없음), 해석은 「~ 것」으로 한다.

- That which is beautiful is not always good.
- What is beautiful is not always good.

(아름다운 것이라고 해서 항상 좋은 것은 아니다.)

┌ I will do <u>all that I can</u>.
└ I will do <u>what I can</u>.
  (내가 할 수 있는 것을 모두 하겠다.)

┌ This is <u>the thing which I want</u>.
└ This is <u>what I want</u>.
  (이것은 내가 원하는 것이다.)

TEST

* ＿＿＿＿에 들어갈 적당한 말을 고르시오.

We are not completely sure ＿＿＿ causes booms and
depressions in free economies.

① how ② whom ③ what ④ why ⑤ that

(정답) ③

☞ what이 이끄는 간접 의문문이 are sure의 목적어이다. 따라서 명사절이 목적절로
오기 위해서는 빈 칸에는 선행사를 포함하는 what이 와야 한다.

(전문 해석) 우리는 무엇이 자유 경제의 활성화 침체를 가져 오는지 확신하지
못한다.

14

what he is (그의 인물 : his character) ↔ what he has (그의 재산 : his wealth)
what he is(현재의 그 사람) ↔ what he was (과거의 그 사람)
                                  what he should be (미래의 그 사람)
what he is (본연의 그 사람) ↔ what he seems (외양의 그 사람)
what he is (그의 인물) ↔ what he does (그의 행위)
what he is (그의 인물) ↔ what he has achieved (그의 업적)

Ex) <u>What you do</u> more important than <u>what you say</u>.
   (행동〈하는 것〉은 말〈하는 것〉보다 중요하다.)

Jim is not <u>what he was</u>.
(Jim은 옛날의 그가 아니다.)

A man is not always <u>what he seems</u>.
(사람은 반드시 외관만으로는 판단할 수 없다.)

It is not <u>what a man has</u> but <u>what he is</u> that is really important.
(정말로 중요한 것은 재산(사람이 갖고 있는 것)이 아니고 됨됨이(인물)이다.)

I respect <u>what tom is</u>, not <u>what Tom has</u>.
(나는 Tom의 재산이 아닌 인격을 존중한다.)

TEST

* _____에 들어갈 적당한 것을 고르시오.

He is not _____ he was 10 years ago.

① that ② what ③ which ④ who ⑤ whom

(정답) ②

☞ 위 문장은 선행사가 따로 없으므로, 보어 역할을 할 수 있는 관계 대명사 what이
필요하다. 즉, what he was 10 years ago은 보어절이 된다.

[전문 해석] 그는 더 이상 10년 전의 그가 아니다.

15

A is to B ⌈ what ⌉ C is to D
        ⌊ (just) as ⌋

- (Just) As C is to D, so is A to B
- (Just) As C is to D, A is to B
- What C is to D, that is A to B
- What C is to D, A is to B

(A가 B에 대한 관계는 C가 D에 대한 관계와 같다 =〉 A : B = C : D)

☞ 이때의 「be to」는 「be with = do(es) for = be applicable to」와 같으며 「~에
해당되다(= be true of)」의 의미이다.

Reading is to the mind <u>what</u> exercise is to the body.

Reading is to the mind <u>(just) as</u> exercise is to the body.

<u>(Just) As</u> exercise to the body, <u>so</u> is reading to the mind.

<u>(Just) As</u> exercise is to the body, reading is to the mind.

<u>What</u> exercise is to the body, reading is to the mind.

<u>What</u> exercise is to the body, <u>that</u> is reading to the mind.

(독서가 마음에 대한 관계는 운동이 신체에 대한 관계와 같다.)

16 what we call 〈소위 말하자면〉

He is $\begin{cases} \text{what we cell} \\ \text{what you call} \\ \text{what they call} \\ \text{what is called} \end{cases}$ a self-made man.

(그는 소위 자수성가한 사람이다.)

17 what with A and what with B (한편으로는 A때문에, 또 한편으로는 B때문에) - 원인, 이유
what by A and what by B (한편으로는 A에 의해, 또 한편으로는 B에 의해) - 수단, 방법

Ex) <u>What with</u> fatigue and <u>what with</u> hunger, he fell down as if he were dead.
(피곤도 하고 배도 고프고 해서 그는 죽은 것처럼 쓰러졌다.)

<u>What by</u> threats and <u>what by</u> entreaties, he achieved his arm.
(협박도 하고 또 간청도 해서 그는 그의 목적을 달성했다.)

제12장
Essential English Grammar

관계 부사
(Relative Adverbs)

01 관계 부사(Relative Adverbs)

[1] 관계 부사의 역할

☞ 관계 부사란 「접속사 + 부사」의 구실을 겸하는 것으로 여기에는 시간(때), 장소, 방법, 이유 등이 있다. 「관계 부사」는 선행사를 수식하는 「형용사절」을 이끈다. 「선행사」란 관계 부사절에 의해 수식되는 명사·대명사로서 보통 관계 부사 바로 앞에 온다. 따라서 관계 부사는 반드시 선행사 뒤에 온다. 아래의 예문에서는 「The office」가 선행사이다.

[A] This is the office.   +   [B] He works in the office.
This is the office <u>and</u> he works <u>in the office</u>.
This is the office <u>and</u> he works <u>there</u>.
This is the office <u>which</u> he works <u>in</u>.
This is the office <u>in which</u> he works.
This is <u>the office</u> <u>where</u> he works.
　　　〈선행사〉〈관계부사〉
(이곳이 그가 일하는 사무실이다.)

[2] Special Guide 특강

(1) 왼쪽의 그림처럼 [A][B] 두 문장에서 먼저 공통되는 부분(그림에서 빗금부분)을 찾아낸다.(위의 예에서 the office와 the office)

(2) 공통되는 부분을 접속사+부사로 연결한다.(위의 예에서 the office)

(3) 접속사+부사 를 「관계 부사」로 전환한다.
(여기서「관계」란 「접속사」를 의미한다.)

(4) 관계 부사의 「선행사(시간, 장소, 방법, 이유)」를 따진다.

(5) 관계 부사는 「전치사 + 관계 대명사」로 전환할 수 있다.

(6) 관계 부사는 반드시 「선행사」뒤에 온다.

02 관계 부사의 종류

☞ 관계 부사는 선행사가 시간(때), 장소, 방법, 이유 어느 것을 나타내느냐에 따라서 다음과 같은 종류가 있다.

선행사 ＼ 관계부사	관계부사	전치사 + 관계대명사
시간(때) (the time)	when	at(on, in) which
장 소 (the place)	where	in(to, at, on) which
방 법 (the way)	how	in which
이 유 (the reason)	why	for which
공 통	that	—

I. 시간(때:when)

- Monday is <u>the day</u>. + People feel blue on <u>the day</u>.
- Monday is the day <u>and</u> people feel blue on <u>the day</u>.
- Monday is the day <u>and</u> people feel blue <u>then</u>.
- Monday is the day <u>on which</u> people feel blue.
- Monday is the day <u>when</u> people feel blue.

(월요일은 사람들이 우울하게 느끼는 날이다.)

☞ 「전치사 + 관계 대명사」는 선행사에 따라 「관계 부사」로의 전환이 가능하다.

- I know <u>the time</u>. + He will arrive at <u>the time</u>.
- I know the time <u>and</u> he will arrive at <u>the time.</u>
- I know the time <u>which</u> he arrive <u>at</u>.
- I know the time <u>at which</u> he will arrive.
- I know the time <u>when</u> he will arrive.
- I know the time <u>that</u> he will arrive.

(나는 그가 도착할 시간을 알고 있다.)

II. 장소(Where)

- This is <u>the place</u>. + He was born in <u>the place</u>.
- This is the place <u>and</u> he was born in <u>the place</u>.
- This is the place <u>and</u> he was born <u>there</u>.
- This is the place <u>which</u> he was born <u>in</u>.
- This is the place <u>in which</u> he was born.
- This is the place <u>where</u> he was born.

(이곳은 그가 태어난 곳이다.)

III. 방법(How)

- This is <u>the way</u>. + They did it in <u>the way</u>.
- This is the way <u>and</u> they did it in <u>the way</u>.
- This is the way <u>in which</u> they did it.
- This is the way <u>how</u> they did it.(X)
- This is the <u>way</u> that they did it.(O)

- He told me the way. + He had succeed in that way.
- He told me the way ┌ in which (O) ┐ he had succeed.
  ├ how (X) ┤
  └ that (O) ┘
- He told me <u>how</u> he had succeed.

(그는 나에게 성공한 방법을 말해 주었다.)

☞ 현대 영어에서는 관계 부사 how는 선행사 the way와 함께 쓰이지 않는다. 즉, 선
행사(the way)를 생략하거나 관계부사(how) 그 자체를 생략해서 쓴다.

He told me ┌ how ┐ he had succeed.
          └ the way ┘

IV. 이유(Why)

- This is <u>the reason</u>. + He was late for <u>the reason</u>.
- This is the reason <u>and</u> he was late for <u>the reason</u>.
- This is the reason <u>which</u> he was late <u>for</u>.
- This is the reason <u>for which</u> he was late.
- This is the reason <u>why</u> he was late.

(이것이 그가 늦은 이유이다.)

┌ That is the reason. + He was absent for the reason.
├ That is the reason and he was absent for the reason.
├ That is the reason which he was absent for.
├ That is the reason for which he was absent.
├ That is the reason why he was absent.
└ That is the reason that he was absent.
　That is why he was absent.
(그것이 그가 결석한 이유이다.)

Take A Break!　[한국 풍속화 감상 2 – 회초리(Switch)]

어렸을 때 할아버지나 아버지가 아끼던 물건을 깨뜨린 벌로 매를 맞아 본 경험이 있는 사람이 이 그림을 본다면 먼저 즐거운 웃음이 나올 것이다. 할아버지가 아끼고 아끼던 청자 항아리를 깨뜨리고 목침 위에 올라서서 회초리 맞기를 기다리고 있는 손자의 얼굴은 측은해 보인다. 그러나 할아버지의 회초리는 허공에 원만 그릴 뿐이다.

It is still memorable that young children were frequently switched by their grandfathers when they committed a wrongdoing. The face of the child is very pitiful as he is waiting for the whipping standing on the wooden pillow, because he broke a blue celadon highly cherished by the grandfather.

제13장
Essential English Grammar

접속사(Conjunction)와
절(節:Clause)

01 And의 주의할 용법

[1] come (go, try, run) and R.V. (Root Verb : 동사원형) 꼴에서 and는 「to의 뜻」이며 근대영어에서는 생략하여 쓴다.

Ex) ┌ Try and get on in the world.
　　└ Try (to) get on in the world.
　　He went (to) have a look at the house.
　　(그는 그 집을 보기 위해서 갔다.)

[2] 「형용사 and 형용사」 꼴이 주격보어로 쓰일 때는 앞에 있는 형용사가 어떤 뜻이라도 「very(=nicely)」의 뜻이다. 즉 형용사 rare, nice, good 등이 and와 결합하여 부사적으로 사용되어 다음에 나오는 형용사를 강조해주는 용법이 있다.

Ex) rare and hungry = very hungry (아주 배가 고픈)
　　good and tired = very tired (몹시 피곤한)
　　nice and warm = very warm (아주 따뜻해서)
　　The water is cool and warm.
　　　　　　(=very warm)
　　I am nice and tired.
　　　　　　(=very tired)

02 Neither A nor B (A도 B도 아니다)

I am not rich, ┌ nor 　　┐ do I wish to be.
　　　　　　　└ neither ┘

I am not rich and I do not wish to be, either.
(나는 부자도 아니고 또한 부자가 되고 싶지도 않다.)

Neither he nor I am rich.
(그도 나도 둘 다 부자가 아니다.)

03 상관 접속사의 인칭과 수(단수/복수)의 일치

＊인칭과 수(단수/복수)의 일치＊

주 어	동 사
both A and B	복수 동사
not only A but also B either A or B neither A nor B	B에 일치
B as well as A	B에 일치

Ex) Both you and I <u>are</u> right.
(너와 나 모두 옳다.)
Not only I but also you <u>are</u> wrong.
(나뿐만 아니라 너도 또한 잘못이다.)
I as well as you <u>am</u> wrong.
(나뿐만 아니라 너도 또한 잘못이다.)
Neither I nor he <u>is</u> rich.
(나도 그도 부자가 아니다.)
Either you or I <u>am</u> in the wrong.
(너든 나든 어느 한 명이 잘못이다.)

 TEST

＊ 다음의 문장중 밑줄친 부분이 맞는지 틀리는지 판단하고 틀리면 고쳐 쓰세요.

1. Every students <u>have</u> a right to be treated fairly. => has

2. Each child <u>was</u> given a small gift. => O

3. Neither you, nor I, nor anyone else <u>knows</u> the solution. => O

4. Either you or John <u>has</u> to go with Jane. => O

5. Not only our principal but also all the other teachers <u>were</u> invited.
=> O

6. He as well as you <u>are</u> strong enough to lift the barbell. => is

| Essential English Grammar |

04 nor와 neither의 구별

☞ nor는 「and + not」이 되어 「접속사」로 쓰이며, neither는 「not + either」이 되어 「부사」로 쓰이는 것이 원칙이다. 따라서 아래의 두 번째 예문에서는 semi-colon(;)이 접속사 역할을 한다.

I am not a scholar, <u>nor</u> do I wish to be.
I am not a scholar, <u>and</u> I do not wish to be.
I am not a scholar; <u>neither</u> do I wish to be.
I am not a scholar; I do <u>not</u> wish to be, <u>either</u>.

05 Now that/Seeing that/In that/On the ground that

[1] now나 now that은 접속사로서 대개 다음 세 가지 뜻으로 쓰인다.
  ① '이제…이니까'('때'와 '이유' 두 가지 뜻을 나타냄)
  ② '…이유는(~때문에)'('이유'를 나타냄)(=since)
  ③ '…한 지금은'('때'를 나타냄)

☞ 물론 이러한 의미상의 구별은 절대적인 것은 아니다. 문맥에 따라서 적절하게 옮겨야 한다.
  Ex) <u>Now(that)</u> we've eaten all the sandwiches, we'll have to make do with potato chips.(샌드위치를 다 먹었으므로 우리는 감자 칩으로 끼니를 때워야 한다.)

[2] seeing that…은 「…이니까」로 역시 이유를 나타내는 since와 마찬가지로 that 이하의 내용이 진실임을 알고 있는 경우에만 사용한다. 이것은 원래는 「무인칭 독립 분사」로서 「…이라는 사실로 보아서(=if we see that…)」의 의미에서 「…이니까(~때문에)」라고 옮기기에 이르렀다고 볼 수 있다.
  Ex) <u>Seeing that</u> you don't know it yourself, the report cannot be

true. (네 자신도 그것을 모르므로 그 보고는 사실이 아닐 것이다.)

[3] in that…은 「…이라는 점에 있어서」란 뜻에서 「…이라는 것 때문에」라고 이유를 나타낸다.

Ex) In that he killed Abel he was a murderer.
(그는 아벨을 죽였기 때문에 살인자였다.)

☞ 주의 : that로 시작되는 절 앞에서는 전치사를 둘 수 없다는 게 원칙이다. 그러나 예외가 있다. 다음의 두 가지 전치사는 that로 시작하는 절 앞에 둘 수가 있다.

① I like you in that you are honest and candid.
Men differ from brutes in that they can think and speak(= since, because)
The higher income tax is harmful in that it may discourage people from trying to earn more.

② except, but, save 등은 『~을 제외하고, 이외는』이라는 뜻의 전치 사이다. but that(=but what = except that = only that ~ (~ 이 아니라면)) 다음에는 「가정법」이 아닌 「직설법」이 온다.

Ex) The child knows nothing but that his mother was married again.
(그 아이는 어머니가 재혼했다는 것 이외는 아무것도 모른다.)
He is a good husband except that he comes drunk every night.
(그는 매일 밤 술취해 귀가하는 것 말고는 다정한 남편이다.)
That will do except that it is too long.
(그것은 너무 길다는 것을 제외하고는 좋다.)
⌈ He would have helped you but that he was short of money.
⌊ He would have helped you if he had not been short of money.
⌈ But that I am poor I could go abroad.
⌊ If I were not poor, I could go abroad.
⌈ I would come only that I am engaged to dine out.
⌊ I would come if I were not engaged to dine out.

[4] 「on the ground that…」은 원래는 「 '…이라고 하는 근거를 바탕으로' 」의 뜻이므로 「…이니까」라고 옮긴다. 이 경우의 ground는 '근거, 이유' 란 뜻이고, 「on」은 「depend on」이나 「live on」 따위의 「on」으로서 「…을 근거로」란 뜻이다.

Ex) He wishes to resign <u>on the ground that</u> his health is failing.
(그는 건강이 쇠약해졌다는 이유로 사임을 원하고 있다.)

06 at once A and B 「A이기도하고 B이기도 하다」

He is <u>both</u> brave <u>and</u> wise.
He is <u>at once</u> brave <u>and</u> wise.
He is <u>alike</u> brave <u>and</u> wise.
He is brave <u>and</u> wise <u>alike</u>.
He is brave <u>and</u> wise <u>as well</u>.
He is <u>not only</u> brave but also wise.
He is wise <u>as well</u> as brave.
(그는 용감할 뿐만 아니라 현명하다.)

He gave me
  <u>both</u> food <u>and</u> money
  <u>not only</u> food but also money
  <u>not only</u> food <u>but</u> money <u>as well</u>
  <u>not merely</u> food but also money

He gave me money <u>as well as</u> food.

He gave me food, and money
  as well
  besides
  into the bargain
  in addition
  additionally

(그는 음식은 물론 돈도 주었다.)

<u>Not only</u> you but also he is in danger.
He <u>as well as</u> you is in danger.
(너 뿐만 아니라 그도 위험에 처해 있다.)

He <u>not only</u> teaches English, <u>but also</u> writes many novels.
<u>Besides</u> teaching English, he writes many novels.
<u>In addition to</u> teaching English, he writes many novels.
(그는 영어를 가르치는 것 이외에도 소설을 많이 쓴다.)

 ## 07   Not A until B   (B 해서야 비로소 A 하다)

I did <u>not</u> fall asleep <u>until</u> the dawn began to appear.
<u>Not until</u> the dawn began to appear <u>did</u> I fall asleep.(도치 강조 구문)
<u>It</u> was not until the dawn began to appear <u>that</u> I <u>fell</u> asleep.
(It ~ that 강조 구문)

☞ 강조 구문에서는 「not until」이 붙어 다니며, 이때에는 「not until」을 「only after (=only when)」으로 바꾸어 써도 된다.

I fell asleep <u>only after(only when)</u> the dawn began to appear.
(only after를 이용한 긍정문)
<u>Only after(Only when)</u> the dawn began to appear did I fall asleep.(도치 강조 구문)
It was only after(only when) the dawn began to appear that I fell asleep.(It ~ that 강조 구문)
The dawn began to appear <u>before</u> I fell asleep.(before를 이용한 긍정문)
(새벽이 되어서야 비로소 잠이 들었다.)

We do not know the value of health <u>until</u> we lose it.
(우리는 건강을 잃고서야 그 가치를 안다.)

He did <u>not</u> arrive <u>until</u> it grew dark.
<u>Not until</u> it grew dark <u>did he</u> arrive.
<u>It</u> was not until it grew dark <u>that</u> he arrived.
He arrived <u>only after</u> it grew dark.

(날이 어두워지고 나서야 비로소 그는 도착했다.)

I did <u>not</u> realize the value of the documents <u>until</u> yesterday.

<u>Not until</u> yesterday <u>did I realize</u> the value of the documents.

<u>It</u> was not until yesterday <u>that</u> I realized the value of the documents.
(이제서야 나는 그 문서의 가치를 깨달았다.)

08 양보 부사절의 접속사
=〉 though, although, if, even if

Though
Although   he is poor, he is happy.
If
Even if

In spite of
Despite
After all
For all   his poverty, he is happy.
With all
In the face of
Notwithstanding

<u>Poor as he is</u>, he is happy.
(비록 그는 가난하지만 행복하다.)

☞ [보어 + as + S(주어) + V(동사) = Though + S(주어) + V(동사)+ 보어]

09 양보 부사절

(보어)
┌ 형용사
├ 부사   ┐
├ 무관사 명사   │ + as + S(주어) + V(동사)
└ 과거분사(P.P) ┘

(보어)
┌ 형용사
│ 부사
=> Though + S(주어) + V(동사) + ├ 무관사 명사
└ 과거분사(P.P)

┌ Young as he is, he has much sense.
├ Young though he is, he has much sense.
└ Though he is young, he has much sense.
(그는 비록 어리지만 분별력이 있다.)

┌ Coward as he was, he could not bear such an insult.
├ Coward though he was, he could not bear such an insult.
└ Though he was coward, he could not bear such an insult.
(비록 그는 겁쟁이었지만, 그러한 모욕을 참을 수가 없었다.)

┌ Hard as he studied, he failed in the exam.
└ Though he studied hard, he failed in the exam.
(비록 그는 열심히 공부했지만, 시험에 떨어졌다.)

┌ Startled as he was, he didn't lose his balance.
├ Startled though he was, he didn't lose his balance.
└ Though he was startled, he didn't lose his balance.
(그는 비록 놀랐지만 마음의 안정을 잃지 않았다.)

10 부사절·부사구의 여러 형태

As
Since
Because
Now that
Seeing that
On the ground that
he is poor, he cannot buy the car.

Because of
Owing to
On account of
On the ground of
his poverty, he cannot buy the car.

He is <u>so</u> poor <u>that</u> he <u>cannot</u> buy the car.

He is <u>too</u> poor to buy the car.

He is <u>so</u> poor <u>as not to</u> buy the car.

His poverty is <u>such that</u> he <u>cannot</u> buy the car.

His poverty
prevents
prohibits
hinders
keeps
him from buying the car.

His poverty <u>forbids</u> him <u>to buy</u> the car.

(그는 대단히 가난해서 차를 살 수가 없다.)

11 owing partly to A and partly to B
partly (because) A and partly because B
(일부분은 A 때문에, 일부분은 B 때문에)

Ex) I employed him <u>partly</u> out of compassion, and <u>partly because</u> I
was short of hands.
(나는 일부는 동정심에서, 일부는 일손이 모자라서 그를 고용했다.)

12 as it is

[1] (보통 假定的 表現 뒤에서, 또는 文頭에서) 사실은, 실제로는
(= in reality, in fact)

Ex) I thought the inflation would go down, but as it is it's going up again.
(나는 인플레이션이 내려가리라 생각했는데, 사실은 다시 올라가고 있었다.)

[2] (대개 文尾에서) 현재의 상태로, 있는 사실 그대로

Ex) You have too many friends as it is.
(현재 상태로 볼 때 너는 친구가 너무 많다.)

Leave it as it is.
(현재의 상태 그대로 놔두라.)

State the fact as it is.
(사실을 있는 그대로 진술하라.)

We must learn to see things as they are.
(우리는 사물을 있는 그대로 볼 줄 알아야 한다.)

[3] as it was (= as it used to be) 「과거의 상태로, 그 당시 그대로, 그 모습 그대로」

Ex) The village remains as it used to be(= as it was).
(그 마을은 이전에 있던 그대로 남아 있다.)

[4] as it were 「즉, 말하자면 (= so to speak, that is to say, namely)」

Ex) He is, as it were, a bookworm.
(그는 말하자면 책벌레다.)

13 As(so) long as 와 As(so) far as

[1] As long as S(주어) + V(동사) ~

(1) 시간 : 「~ 하는 한, ~ 하는 동안(= while)」

Ex) I shall not forget your kindness <u>as long as</u> I live.
(내가 살아 있는 한 너의 친절을 잊지 않겠다.)

You can keep the book <u>as long as</u> you need it.
(네가 그 책이 필요한 동안 가지고 있어도 좋다.)

☞ as(so) long as는 「~하는 동안(=while)」으로 해석될 때, 이 경우 「기간」을 나타낸다. as(so) long as가 「~이나」와 같이 「시간의 길이」를 강조하는 경우(전치사구일 때)에도 쓰인다.

Ex) The boy stayed with us <u>as long as</u> three weeks.
(그 아이는 우리와 함께 3주일이나 머물렀다.)

(2) 조건 : 「~ 하기만 하면(= If only, Provided that)」

Ex) You may stay here <u>as long as</u> you keep quiet.
(조용하기만 하면 여기 있어도 좋다.)

You need not fear <u>so long as</u> you are innocent.
(죄가 없다면 두려워 할 필요가 없다.)

Any book will do <u>as long as</u> it is interesting.
(재미만 있으면 아무 책이라도 좋다.)

[2] So(as) far as S(주어) + V(동사) ~ (= In so far as S + V ~)

(1) 한도(범위) : 「~ 하는 한, ~한 범위 내에서」(접속사로 쓰일 때)

Ex) <u>As far as</u> we know, the birds came back again each year.
(우리가 아는 한 새는 해마다 다시 돌아온다.)

He will help you <u>as far as</u> he can.
(그가 할 수 있는 범위내에서 너를 도와 줄 것이다.)

[<u>As far as I know</u>, he is reliable.
[<u>To the best of my knowledge</u>, he is reliable.
(내가 아는 한, 그는 믿을 수 있는 사람이다.)

(2) 장소 : 「~ 까지」 (전치사구일 때)

Ex) We walked <u>as far as</u> the post office.
(우리는 우체국까지 걸어갔다.)

He accompanied her <u>as far as</u> the station.
(그는 역까지 그녀를 배웅했다.)

I kept standing <u>as far as</u> the next station.
(나는 다음 역까지 계속 서 있었다.)

(3) 정도 : 「~ 까지도 하다」(= even)
☞ so far as가 go와 함께 쓰일 때는 「~ 까지도 하다」의 의미로서 「정도」를 강조한다.
Ex) ┌ He <u>went so far as</u> to make fun of us.
    └ He <u>even</u> made fun of us.
       (그는 우리를 조롱하기까지 했다.)

[3] 주의 : 「as ~ as」동등 비교 구문과 혼동하지 말 것.
Ex) This is <u>as</u> long <u>as</u> that.
(이것은 저것만큼 길다.)

Incheon is <u>as</u> far <u>as</u> Seoul from here.
(여기서 인천은 서울만큼 멀다.)

[4] ┌ So far as + S(사람.사물주어) + be concerned (~에 관한 한)
    └ So far as + S(사물주어) + goes
☞ 사람이 주어인 구문에서는 go는 쓰지 못한다.

Ex) ┌ So far as I am concerned (O)
    ├ To the extent that I am concerned (O)
    ├ For my part (O)
    └ So far as I go (X)
       (나에 관한 한)

    ┌ So far as mathematics is concerned (O)
    └ So far as mathematics goes (O)
       (수학에 관한 한)

1 밑줄 친 as(so) long as의 의미가 나머지와 다른 하나는?

① You may take any exercise <u>so long as</u> you do regularly.

② I will never speak to you <u>as long as</u> I live.

③ Any book will do <u>as long as</u> it is interesting.

④ You may eat anything <u>so long as</u> you don't eat too much.

⑤ You need not fear <u>so long as</u> you are innocent.

(정답) ②

☞ ②는 「시간」을 나타내며, 그외 나머지는 「조건」을 나타내고 있다.

2 밑줄 친 as(so) far as 와 의미가 나머지와 다른 하나는?

① <u>As far as</u> I know, he is trustworthy.

② I went by train <u>as far as</u> Incheon, where I took ship.

③ <u>As far as</u> the eyes can reach, nothing can be seen.

④ <u>As far as</u> I am concerned, English is easier than French.

⑤ He will help you <u>as far as</u> he can.

(정답) ②

☞ ②는 「장소」를 나타내며, 그외 나머지는 「한도(범위)」를 나타낸다.

3 밑줄 친 곳을 (   )속의 말로 대치할 수 <u>없는</u> 것은?

① I shall never forget it <u>as long as</u> I live. (while)

② You can go there <u>so long as</u> you get back before dark. (if only)

③ This is not true, <u>so far as</u> I can tell. (as far as)

④ My baby can toddle <u>as far as</u> yours do. (in so far as)

⑤ <u>So far as I am concerned</u>, I'm perfect. (For my part)

(정답) ④

☞ ④는 「동등비교(~만큼)」를 나타낸다.

4 다음의 두 문장의 의미가 같아지도록 _____에 알맞은 단어를 쓰시오.

　<u>As far as I know</u>, he is honest and reliable.

　To the _____ of my _____, he is honest and reliable.

(정답) best, knowledge.

14 명령문형의 양보부사절 => ┌ 동사 원형 + wh-clause
┌ 동사 원형 + as-clause
├ Be + S(주어) + ever
└ Let + 목적어 + 동사 원형

☞ 「원형동사」로 시작되는 명령문이 「양보의 내용」을
나타내는 경우는 다음의 4가지가 있다.

[1] ┌ 원형 동사 + 의문사(wh-절) + S(주어) + may(will) ~
├ 복합 관계 부사(Wh-ever) + S(주어) + may(will) ~   ┐ (~ 가 ~하더라도)
└ No matter + wh-절 + S(주어) + may(will) ~

☞ ① may 대신 will을 사용하기도 한다. ② S(주어)가 1인칭일 때 V(동사)앞에 「Let's」를
더하거나, S(주어)가 3인칭일 때 V(동사) 앞에 「Let + O(목적격)」을 더할 때가 있다.

┌ Go where you may, you will be welcomed.
├ Wherever you may go, you will be welcomed.
└ No matter where you may go, you will be welcomed.
(너는 어디를 가더라도 환영받을 것이다.)

┌ Come what may, we must remain cheerful.
├ Whatever may happen, we must remain cheerful.
└ No matter what may happen, we must remain cheerful.
(무슨 일이 생기더라도 우리는 명랑해야 한다.)

┌ Come what may, we must not lose courage.
├ Whatever may come, we must not lose courage.
└ No matter what may come, we must not lose courage.
(어떤 일이 일어나도 용기를 잃어서는 안된다.)

┌ (Let's) Say what we will, he won't change his mind.
├ Whatever we may say, he won't change his mind.
└ No matter what we may say, he won't change his mind.

(우리가 뭐라고 말해도, 그는 그의 생각을 바꾸지 않을 것이다.)

<u>(Let him) Say what he will</u>, we don't believe him.
<u>Whatever we may say</u>, we don't believe him.
<u>No matter what we may say</u>, we don't believe him.
(그가 무슨 말을 해도 우리는 그를 믿지 않는다.)

[2] V(원형 동사) + as + S(주어) + may(will) ~
     However + 형용사/부사 + S(주어) + may(will) ~   (아무리 ~하더라도)
     No matter how + 형용사/부사 + S(주어) + may(will) ~

☞ ① may 대신 will을 사용하기도 한다.
   ② 부사가 없을 때는 뜻에 따라서 hard나 carefully 등을 사용할 수 있다.

<u>Try (as hard) as you may</u>, you can never do it in a week.
<u>However hard you may try</u>, you can never do it in a week.
<u>No matter how hard you may try</u>, you can never do it in a week.
(네가 아무리 노력 해볼지라도, 너는 그것을 일주일 안으로는 해낼 수 없다.)

<u>Work (as hard) as he will</u>, he is slow of making progress.
<u>However hard he may work</u>, he is slow of making progress.
<u>No matter how hard you may try</u>, he is slow of making progress.
(아무리 열심히 일을 해도 그는 진보가 느리다.)

[3] Be 또는 V(원형 동사) + S(주어) + ever so + 형용사/부사 ~
     Let + 목적격 + be ever so + 형용사/부사 ~
     However + 형용사/부사 + S(주어) + may(will) be   ~(아무리 ~하더라도)
     No matter how + 형용사/부사 + S(주어) + may(will) be ~

<u>Be a man ever so poor</u>, he should not be mean.
<u>Let a man be ever so poor</u>, he should not be mean.
<u>However poor a man may be</u>, he should not be mean.
<u>No matter how poor a man may be</u>, he should not be mean.
(아무리 가난하더라도 비굴해서는 안된다.)

Be it ever so humble, there is no place like home.
Let it be ever so humble, there is no place like home.
No matter how humble it may be, there is no place like home.
However humble it may be, there is no place like home.
(아무리 누추하다 할지라도 내집 같은 곳은 없다.)

Sing he ever so well, he will never equal his brother.
Let him sing ever so well, he will never equal his brother.
No matter how well he may sing, he will never equal his brother.
However well he may sing, he will never equal his brother.
(그가 아무리 노래를 잘해도 그의 형보다는 못하다.)

[4] ┌ Be + 목적격 + 의문사(wh-절) + S(주어) + may(will) ~ ┐
    ├ Let + 목적격 + be + 의문사(wh-절) + S(주어) + may(will) │ ~(~가 ~하더라도)
    ├ 복합 관계 부사(Wh-ever) + S(주어) + may(will) ~   │
    └ No matter + wh-절 + S(주어) + may(will) ~   ┘

Be the motive what it may, I cannot agree to such a plan.
Let the motive be what it may, I cannot agree to such a plan
Whatever motive it may be, I cannot agree to such a plan
No matter what motive it may be, I cannot agree to such a plan.
(동기가 무엇이든 나는 그 계획에 동의할 수 없다.)

Be the work what it may, you must do it yourself.
Let the work be what it may, you must do it yourself.
Whatever work it may be, you must do it yourself.
No matter what work it may be, you must do it yourself.
(너의 일이 어떠한 것이든 최선을 다하라.)

[5] ┌ Be + S(주어) + A or B
    └ Whether + S(주어) + be + A or B

Be a life long or short, its completeness depends on what it
was lived for.

└ Whether a life is long or short, its completeness depends on what it was lived for.
(인생이 길든 짧든, 인생의 완성은 무엇을 위하여 살았느냐에 달려 있다.)

┌ Be it true or not, it is not worth considering.
└ Whether it is true or not, it is not worth considering.
(그것이 사실이든 아니든, 고려할 가치가 없다.)

 ## 15 종속절의 부정어가 주절(主節)로 자리를 옮긴 부정(否定)의 전이(轉移) (Transferred Negation)

☞ 영어에서 「부정의 전이(Transferred Negation)」란 주절(主節)을 부정(否定)해서 종속절의 내용을 부정하는 경향을 말한다. 즉 「think, believe, suppose, imagine, expect」 등의 동사에서 이런 규칙이 성립된다. 그러나 「hope, assume, presume」 등은 뜻은 비슷하지만 옮기지 않는다.

Ex) I don't think you've met my husband.
(내남편을 만나지 않았을 거라고 생각합니다.)
I don't suppose anyone will object to my plan.
(어느 누구도 내 계획에 반대하지 않을 거라고 생각합니다.)
I don't believe he is clever.
(나는 그가 영리하지 않다고 믿고 있습니다.)
I cannot imagine who he is.
(그가 누구인지 모르겠다.)
I don't think that he is rich.
(나는 그가 부자가 아니라고 생각합니다.)

cf) I hope it won't rain.
(비가 오지 않았으면 합니다.)
I assume he didn't turn up.
(그가 나타나지 않을 것 같다.)

제14장
Essential English Grammar

형용사(Adjective)

01 be similar to~ (~와 비슷〈유사〉한)

☞ be similar to = be like = be alike = be of the same sort 「~ 와 유사한, 닮은, 비슷한」

Ex) Your watch is similar to mine in color.
(너의 시계는 색깔에 있어서 내 것과 비슷하다.)

Gold is similar in color to brass.
(금은 색깔에 있어서 황동과 비슷하다.)

It is a disease similar to infantile paralysis.
(그것은 소아마비와 비슷한 질병이다.)

I want you to get me an article similar to this.
(이와 비슷한 물건을 구해주면 좋겠다.)

Love is like the measles ; we all have to go through it.
(사랑이란 홍역 같은 것. 누구나 겪어내야만 한다.)
　　　　　　　　　　　　　　　　－Jerome.(영국의 유머 소설가 1859~1927)

A home having no child is like as the earth having no sun.
(집안에 어린아이가 없으면, 지구에 태양이 없는 거와 같다.)

These twins are very much alike.
(이 쌍둥이는 아주 꼭 닮았다.)

*주의 사항 : be similar to 또는 be like 뒤에는 목적어가 올 수 있으나 be alike 뒤에는 목적어가 올 수 없다. 이때의 alike는 전치가 아니라 형용사이기 때문이다.

02 [나이(연령) 표현 방법]

$$
\begin{bmatrix} S + be + X \text{ years old.} \\ S + be + in + \begin{bmatrix} \text{소유격} \\ \text{one's} \end{bmatrix} + \begin{bmatrix} \text{early} \\ \text{mid} \\ \text{late} \end{bmatrix} + \text{복수형} \begin{bmatrix} \text{teens} \\ \text{twenties} \\ \text{thirties} \end{bmatrix} \end{bmatrix}
$$

She's fourteen years old.(그녀는 14살이다.)
She's in her early teens.(그녀는 10대 초반이다.)

They are <u>over fifty now</u>.(그들은 지금 50이 넘었다.)
They are in their <u>fifties now</u>.(그들은 지금 50대이다.)

She's <u>almost eighty</u>.(그녀는 거의 80세가 되었다.)
She's <u>in her late seventies</u>.(그녀는 70대 후반이다.)

We shall <u>be about 35 years old</u>.(우리는 약 35세가 된다.)
We shall <u>be in our mid thirties</u>.(우리는 30대 중반이다.)

He made a great success of himself <u>when he was 28 years old</u>.
He made a great success of himself <u>(when he was) in his late twenties</u>.
(그는 20대 후반에 자수성가를 했다.)

03

S(주어)+V(동사)+ 배수사(N times)+비교급+도량형 형용사+than + 명사
S(주어)+V(동사)+ 배수사(N times)+ as + 도량형 형용사+ as + 명사
S(주어)+V(동사)+ 배수사(N times)+ the+ 도량형 명사+ of + 명사
[~의 ~배(倍)다]

Many can travel twenty times <u>longer than</u> their own bodies.
Many can travel twenty times <u>as long as</u> their own bodies.
Many can travel twenty times <u>the length of</u> their own bodies. (길이)
(많은 것들이 자기 자신의 신체 길이의 20배만큼 이동할 수 있다.)

Others are <u>bigger than</u> a football.
Others are <u>as big as</u> a football.
Others are <u>the size of</u> a football. (크기)
(다른 것들은 축구공만큼 크다.)

This is three times <u>larger than</u> that.
This is three times <u>as large as</u> that.
This is three times <u>the area of</u> that. (면적)

(이것은 저것의 세 배의 크기이다.)

This is three times <u>higher than</u> that.
This is three times <u>as high as</u> that.
This is three times <u>the height of</u> that. (높이)
(이것은 저것의 세 배 만큼 높다.)

This is three times <u>deeper than</u> that.
This is three times <u>as deep as</u> that.
This is three times <u>the depth of</u> that. (깊이)
(이것은 세 배 만큼 깊다.)

This is three times <u>wider than</u> that.
This is three times <u>as wide as</u> that.
This is three times <u>the width of</u> of that. (넓이)
(이것은 저것의 세 배 만큼 넓다.)

This is three times <u>heavier than</u> that.
This is three times <u>as heavy as</u> that.
This is three times <u>the weight of</u> that. (무게)
(이것은 저것의 세 배 만큼 무겁다.)

He has twice <u>more</u> books <u>than</u> I have.
He has twice <u>as many</u> books <u>as</u> I have.
He has twice <u>the number of</u> books that I have. (수:數)
(그는 내가 가진 책의 2배를 더 가지고 있다.)

He works three times <u>harder than</u> you.
He works three times <u>as hard as</u> you.
(그는 너보다 2배 더 열심히 일한다.)

He spends twice <u>more</u> money <u>than</u> I do every day.
He spends twice <u>as much</u> money as I do every day.

(그는 내가 매일 쓰는 돈의 2배를 더 쓴다.)

He has <u>twice more than</u> you.
He has <u>twice as many as</u> you.
He has <u>as much again as</u> you.
(그는 너의 2배를 가지고 있다.)

His house is <u>twice bigger than</u> mine.
His house is <u>twice as big as</u> mine.
His house is <u>as big again</u> as mine.
(그의 집은 내집보다 2배나 크다.)

☞ as ~ again as = twice as ~ as (~보다 2배, ~의 2배)
   half as ~ again as (~의 1.5배)
   Ex) This tower is <u>half as</u> tall <u>again as</u> that building.
       (이 탑은 저 건물의 1.5배나 키가 크다.)

prefer A(동명사) to B(동명사) : 이때 to는 「전치사」임
prefer A(to부정사) rather than B(to부정사)
(B보다는 A를 더 좋아하다)

I <u>prefer</u> staying at home <u>to</u> going out on such a rainy day.
I <u>prefer</u> to stay at home <u>rather than</u> (to) go out on such a rainy day.
I <u>would rather</u> stay at home <u>than</u> go out on such rainy day.
I <u>would sooner</u> stay at home <u>than</u> go out on such rainy day.
I <u>would as soon</u> stay at home <u>as</u> go out on such rainy day.
(그렇게 비오는 날에는 외출하는 것보다는 나는 집에 머물러 있는 것을
좋아한다.)

* 「prefer A to B」에서 A와 B는 반드시 「동명사나 명사」가 와야하며,
  「prefer A rather than B」에서 A와 B는 반드시 「to 부정사」가 와야
  한다.

05 비교급 + than ~ => 우등비교

- He is five years older than I (am).
- He is older than I <u>by five years.</u>
- I am five years younger than he.
- He <u>is five years senior to</u> me.
- He is senior to me <u>by five years.</u>
- He is five years my senior.
- (그는 나보다 다섯 살 위다.)

06 less + 원급 + than ~ => 열등비교

- He is <u>less</u> diligent <u>than</u> his brother.
- He is <u>not</u> so diligent <u>as</u> his brother.
- His brother is <u>more</u> diligent <u>than</u> he.
- (그는 형만큼 부지런하지 못하다.)

07 비례 비교급
the(관계 부사) + 비교급 ~ the(지시부사) + 비교급…
(~ 하면 할수록 그만큼 더 …하다)

☞ 접속사가 있는 종속절의 문미(文尾)에 있는 비교급을 문두(文頭)로 도치시키고 그 앞
에 the를 첨가시키며, 접속사가 탈락된다. 주절도 같은 방법으로 변형시킨다.

Ex) ┌ <u>As</u> we went up <u>higher</u>, it became <u>the colder.</u>
    └ <u>The higher</u> we went up, the colder it became.
      (위로 높이 올라가면 갈수록 그 만큼 더 추워진다.)

As she grew _older_, she became _more_ beautiful.
The _older_ she grew, _the more_ beautiful she became.
(그녀는 나이가 들면 들수록, 그만큼 더 아름다워졌다.)

As one grows _older_, one becomes _more_ forgetful.
The _older_ one grows, _the more_ forgetful one becomes.
(사람은 나이가 들면 들수록, 그만큼 더 기억력이 쇠퇴한다.)

_As_ I know him _more_, I like him _more_.
The _more_ I know him, _the more_ I like him.
(나는 그를 알면 알수록, 그를 그만큼 더 좋아하게 된다.)

If you learn more, you know less.
The more you learn, the less you know.
(배우면 배울수록 그만큼 더 아는 게 적어진다.)

If you wait _longer_, you become _more_ impatient.
The _longer_ you wait, _the more_ impatient you become.
(오래 기다리면 기다릴수록 그만큼 더 조급해진다.)

If you work _harder_, it will become _easier_.
The _harder_ you work, _the easier_ it will become.
(열심히 공부하면 할수록 그만큼 더 쉬워진다.)

If the apartment is _bigger_, the rent is _higher_.
The _bigger_ the apartment is, _the higher_ the rent is.
(아파트가 더 크면 클수록 임대료는 그만큼 더 비싸다.)

The _older_ he grow, _the more_ cautious he became.
_As_ he grew older, he became _more_ cautious.
(그는 나이가 듦에 따라서 그만큼 더 주의를 하게 되었다.)

08 양보(even)의 뜻을 가진 최상급 〈아무리 ~일지라도〉

The wisest man often makes a mistake.
Even the wisest man often makes a mistake.
Even if he is the wisest man the man makes a mistake.
Though he is the wisest man the man makes a mistake.

(아무리 현명한 사람이라도 실수를 하는 수가 있다.)

The strongest man cannot stop the stream of water.
Even the strongest man cannot stop the stream of water.
Even though he is the strongest man, the man cannot stop the stream of water.
(아무리 힘센 사람이라 할지라도 물의 흐름을 막을 수는 없다.)

The richest man in the world cannot buy everything.
Even the richest man in the world cannot buy everything.
Even if he is the richest man in the world, the man cannot buy everything.
(이 세상에서 가장 부자라 하더라도, 모든 것을 다 살 수는 없다.)

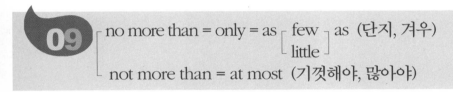

09   no more than = only = as [few / little] as (단지, 겨우)
     not more than = at most (기껏해야, 많아야)

I spent no more than ten dollars.
I spent only ten dollars.
(나는 단지 10달러 밖에 쓰지 않았다.)

cf) He is no better than fool. (~나 다를 바 없는)
He is as good as a fool.
He is a mere fool.
(그는 바보에 지나지 않는다.)

I spent not more than ten dollars.
I spent at most ten dollars.
(나는 기껏해야 10달러 밖에 쓰지 않았다.)

10
```
┌ no less than = as ┌ many ┐ as (~만큼이나)
│                   └ much  ┘
└ not less than = at least (적어도)
```

```
┌ He paid no less than ten dollars.
└ He paid as much as ten dollars.
  (그는 10달러나 지불했다. / 그는 10달러만큼이나 지불했다.)
```

```
┌ He paid not less than ten dollars.
└ He paid at least ten dollars.
  (그는 적어도 10달러는 지불했다.)
```

```
cf) ┌ He has no fewer than ten sons.
    └ He has as many as ten sons.
       (그는 아들이 10명이나 있다.)
```

11 「no more A than B」
(A 아닌 것은 B가 아닌 것과 같다)

☞ 이 구문은 「양자 부정」을 나타내므로 비록 than이하가 「긍정문」이라 하더라도 「부정」으로 해석하여야 한다.

```
┌ S + V + no more A than B
│ S + V + not A any more than B
│ S + V + as little A as B
│ A is not B what C is not D
│ A is not B (just)as C is not D
│ Neither A nor B + V
└ S + V + not ~, nor + V + S
┌ A가 아닌 것은 B아닌 것과 같다          ┐
└ A가 B 아닌 것은 C가 D 아닌 것과 같다   ┘
```

A whale is <u>no more</u> a fish than a horse is (a fish.)

A whale is <u>not</u> a fish <u>any more than</u> a horse is a fish.

A whale is <u>as little</u> a fish <u>as</u> a horse is a fish.

A whale is not a fish <u>what</u> a horse is not a fish.

A whale is not a fish (just) <u>as</u> a horse is not a fish.

<u>Neither</u> a whale <u>nor</u> a horse is a fish.

A whale is <u>not</u> a fish, <u>nor</u> is a horse.

(고래가 물고기가 아닌 것은 말이 물고기가 아닌 것과 같다.)

cf) She is <u>not more</u> beautiful <u>than</u> you are.

She is <u>not so</u> beautiful <u>as</u> you are.

(그 여자는 당신만큼 예쁘지는 않다.)

12 no less ~ than … =〉 (just) as ~ as … (… 만큼 ~ 한)

not less ~ than … =〉 perhaps more ~ than … (… 못지않게 ~한)

Ex) She is no ⌈ less ⌉ beautiful ⌈ than ⌉ her sister.
　　　　　⌊ as ⌋　　　　　⌊ as ⌋

(그녀는 그녀의 언니만큼(처럼) 예쁘다.)

She is ⌈ not less ⌉ beautiful then her sister.
　　　⌊ perhaps more ⌋

(그녀는 그녀의 언니 못지않게 예쁘다.)

13 원급으로 사용되는 관용어구

* as ~ as can be (더할 나위 없이 ~한)

⌈ not so much as A as B (A라기 보다는 B이다)

⊢ not A so much as B

⊢ B rather than A

⌊ rather B than A

* not so much as~ = not even (~조차도 않다)

* as ~ as possible = as ~ as one can (가능한 ~하게, 될 수 있는 한)

* as + 형용사(A) + as + 형용사(B) (A하기도 하고 B하기도 하다)

He is <u>as</u> poor <u>as</u> (poor) <u>can be</u>.
He is <u>as</u> poor <u>as anything</u>.
He is <u>very</u> poor.
(그는 더할 나위 없이 가난하다.)

She is <u>not so much</u> a poet as a novelist.
She is a novelist <u>rather than</u> a poet.
(그녀는 시인이라기보다는 소설가이다.)

cf) He can <u>not so much as</u> answer the question.
He can <u>not even</u> answer the question.
(그는 질문에 대답조차 못했다.)

He walked <u>as</u> fast <u>as possible</u>.
He walked <u>as</u> fast <u>he could</u>.
(그는 될 수 있는 한 빨리 걸었다.)

He was <u>as</u> brave <u>as any</u> man in the world.
(그는 이 세상의 어느 누구 못지않게 용감했다.)

He is <u>as</u> great a statesman <u>as ever</u> lived.
(그는 지금까지 살았던 어느 정치가 못지않게 위대한 정치가이다.)

She is <u>as</u> kind <u>as</u> beautiful.
(그녀는 아름답기도 하려니와 친절하기도 하다.)

14 동일인, 동일물의 비교

☞ 동일인, 동일물의 서로 다른 성질을 비교할 때는 음절에 관계없이
「more + 원급 + than + 원급」의 꼴을 사용한다.

Ex) He is <u>more</u> clever <u>than</u> honest.
(그는 정직하다기보다는 영리하다.)

cf) He is <u>cleverer than</u> she.
(그는 그녀보다 영리하다.)

It is <u>more</u> hot <u>than</u> warm.
(날씨가 포근하다기보다는 오히려 무더운 편이다.)

* 다음의 두 문장의 차이를 설명하시오.

　(1) She is <u>prouder than</u> he is.

　(2) She is <u>more</u> proud than vain.

(정답)

(1)은 she와 he를 비교하고 있다.(그녀는 그 사람보다 더 자부심이 강하다.)

(2)는 동일인인 she의 성품을 비교하고 있다. (그녀는 허영보다는 자부심이 강하다.)

15 최상급을 표시하는 원급·비교급

[1] 최상급 : the + est, most, best

[2] 원급일 때 (~ 못지 않게)

　① (긍정일 때) S + V + as ~ as any + 단수 명사

　② (부정일 때) 부정주어(No) + V + so ~ as…

[3] 비교급일 때

　① (긍정일 때) ┌ S + V + more ~ than any other + 단수명사

　　　　　　　├ S + V + more ~ than (all) the other + 복수명사

　　　　　　　├ S + V + more ~ than anything else(사물일 때)

　　　　　　　├ S + V + more ~ than anyone else (사람일 때)

　　　　　　　└ S + V + more ~ than anywhere else (장소일 때)

　② (부정일 때) 부정주어(No) + V + more ~ than…

　③ (유도부사 there를 쓸 때) There is nothing more ~ than…

　Ex) (최상급)　　Time is <u>the most</u> precious thing in the world.

　　　(원급 긍정)　Time is <u>as</u> precious <u>as any</u> thing in the world.

　　　(원급 부정)　<u>Nothing</u> in the world is <u>so</u> precious <u>as</u> time.

　　　(비교급 긍정) ┌ Time is <u>more</u> precious <u>than any other thing</u> in the world.

　　　　　　　　　├ Time is <u>more</u> precious <u>than (all) the other things</u> in the world.

　　　　　　　　　└ Time is <u>more</u> precious <u>than anything</u> else in the world.

(비교급 부정)<u>Nothing</u> in the world is <u>more</u> precious <u>than</u> time.

(유도부사 there) <u>There is nothing</u> in the world <u>more</u> precious <u>than</u> time.

(이 세상에서 시간보다 더 소중한 것은 없다 : 시간이 가장 소중하다.)

☞ 주로 비교의 대상범위가 명확하지 않거나, 광범위한 경우 위와 같이 표현하지만, 그렇지 않고 비교의 대상 범위가 명확한 경우 「no other + 명사」와 같이 other을 쓴다.

Ex) ┌ He is <u>the cleverest boy</u> in his class.
    ├ He is <u>as</u> clever <u>as any boy</u> in his class.
    ├ <u>No other boy</u> in his class is <u>so</u> clever <u>as</u> he.
    ├ He is <u>cleverer than any other boy</u> in his class.
    ├ He is <u>cleverer than (all) the other boys</u> in his class.
    ├ He is <u>cleverer than anyone else</u> in his class.
    └ <u>No other boy</u> in his class is <u>cleverer than</u> he.
    (그는 자기 학급에서 가장 영리한 학생이다.)

16

S(주어) + V(동사) + as + 형용사 원급 + as + any + 단수명사

S(주어) + V(동사) + as + 형용사 원급 + a + 명사 + as ever + P.P(과거분사)

☞ 「~ 못지않게」의 뜻으로 비교급과 최상급으로 전환시킬 수 있다.

(최상급) He is <u>the bravest</u> of all the soldiers in the world.

　　　　(그는 이 세상의 모든 군인들 가운데 가장 용감하다.)

(원 급) He is <u>as</u> brave <u>as any</u> soldier in the world.

　　　　(그는 이 세상의 어느 군인 못지않게 용감하다.)

　　　　He is <u>as</u> brave a soldier <u>as ever</u> lived.

　　　　(그는 지금까지 살았던 어느 군인 못지않게 용감하다.)

　　　　He is <u>as</u> brave a soldier <u>as ever</u> shouldered a gun.

　　　　(그는 지금까지 총을 어깨에 맨 어느 군인 못지않게 용감하다.)

　　　　<u>No other</u> soldier is <u>so</u> brave <u>as</u> he in the world.

　　　　(어느 군인도 그 사람만큼 용감하지 않다.)

(비교급) <u>No other</u> soldier is <u>braver than</u> he in the world.

　　　　(어느 군인도 그 사람보다 더 용감하지 않다.)

He is braver than ┌ any other soldier ┐ in the world.
                  ├ (all) the other soldiers ┤
                  └ anyone else ┘

(그는 이 세상의 어느 군인(모든 다른 군인들)보다 더 용감하다.)

┌ He is <u>the greatest</u> of all the dramatists in the world.
├ He is <u>as</u> great a dramatist <u>as ever</u> lived.
├ He is <u>as</u> great <u>as any</u> dramatist in the world.
├ <u>No other</u> dramatist is <u>so</u> great <u>as</u> he in the world.
├ <u>No other</u> dramatist is <u>greater than</u> he in the world.
└ He is greater than ┌ any other dramatist ┐ in the world.
                     ├ (all) the other dramatists ┤
                     └ anyone else ┘

(그는 이 세상에서 가장 위대한 극작가이다.)

┌ S + know better than to부정사 ~ (~하지 않을 만큼의 분별력은 있다)
├ S + be wise enough not to + ⓥ ~ (~하지 않을 만큼 현명하다)
├ S + be not so foolish as to + ⓥ ~ (~할만큼 어리석지 않다)
└ S + be the last to + ⓥ ~ (~결코 ~ 하지 않는다)

Ex) ┌ He <u>knows better than to trust</u> you.
    ├ He is <u>wise enough not to trust</u> you.
    ├ He is <u>not so foolish as to trust</u> you.
    ├ He is so wise <u>that</u> he <u>does not</u> trust you.
    └ He is <u>the last to trust</u> you.
      (그는 너를 믿을 만큼 어리석지 않다.)

18
much(still) more(긍정문에서) 「~은 물론」(긍정에서)
much(still) less(부정문에서) 「~은 커녕」(부정에서)

- much(still) more(긍정문에서)
- much(still) less(부정문에서)
- not to speak of
- to say nothing of （긍정문, 부정문
- not to mention 모두 사용 가능)
- without mentioning
- let alone
- as well as

「~은 물론」(긍정에서)
「~은 커녕」(부정에서)
「하물며 ~는 말할 것도 없이」
「~뿐만 아니라」

He <u>can</u> speak French, ⌈ much ⌉ more English(긍정문)
　　　　　　　　　　 ⌊ still ⌋

He <u>can't</u> speak French, ⌈ much ⌉ less English(부정문)
　　　　　　　　　　　 ⌊ still ⌋

TEST

* 다음의 두 문장의 의미가 같도록 (　)에 적당한 말을 쓰시오.

He can speak French, let alone English.
He can't speak French, (　) (　) (　) English.

(정답) not to mention

19　the + 비교급 + of the two + (명사)

☞ 둘 사이에서의 최상급을 표현할 때 사용한다. 「of the two + (명사)」가 직접 표시되지 않는 경우라도 문맥에서, 또는 사물 자체가 2개로 구분된 경우는 the를 붙인다.

Ex) <u>The elder of the two boys</u> is in college.
(큰 아이는 대학에 다닌다.)

Ranneung is <u>the taller of the two</u>.
(란능이가 그 두 명 중에서는 제일 키가 크다.)

Of gold and silver, the former is the more precious.
(금과 은 중 전자(즉, 금)가 더 귀중하다.)

About half the students were from Africa, and they were the
more industrious.
학생의 약 절반이 아프리카 출신이었는데,〈나머지 절반보다〉더 근면했다.)

His family belonged to the upper class.
(그의 가정은 상류층에 속했다.)

cf) the lower class 하류 계층

It is biological nonsense to call women the weaker sex.
(여자를 약자라고 부르는 것은 생물학적으로 말도 안된다.)

cf) the stronger sex 강자

형용사의 직유적 비유 표현
=〉 as ~ as 비유법(Simile)

1. as blind as a bat (매우 눈이 어두운) = very blind
   Ex) My grandmother is as blind as a bat.
       (나의 할머니는 눈이 매우 어둡다.)

2. as brave as a lion (매우 용감한) = very brave
   Ex) He is as brave as a lion.
       (그는 매우 용감하다.)

3. as cool as a cucumber (아주 침착한) = very cool
   Ex) The captain remained as cool as a cucumber as the passengers
       boarded the lifeboats.
       (그 선장은 승객들이 구명정에 올라탔을 때 매우 침착했다.)

4. as gentle as a dove (매우 유순한〈온순한〉) = very gentle
   Ex) The lady was as gentle as a dove.
       (그 숙녀는 매우 온순했다.)

5. as gentle as a lamb (매우 유순한) = very gentle
   Ex) The dog was as gentle as a lamb.
       (그 개는 매우 유순했다.)

6. as hungry as a hunter (몹시 배고픈) = very hungry
   Ex) The lion was as hungry as a hunter.

(그 사자는 매우 굶주렸다.)

7. as hungry as a hawk (몹시 배고픈) = very hungry
8. as light as a feather (몹시 가벼운) = very light
9. as poor as a church mouse (몹시 가난한) = very poor
   Ex) He is <u>as poor as a church mouse</u>. = He is very poor.
   (그는 매우 가난해요.)
10. as proud as a peacock (우쭐대는) = very proud
11. as red as a rose (매우 새빨간) = very red
12. as slow as a snail (매우 느린) = very slow
13. as like as two peas (꼭 닮은, 흡사한) = very like
14. as cross as two sticks (성미가 몹시 까다로운) = very cross
15. as sure as fate (반드시, 틀림없이) = surely
16. as white as snow (매우 흰) = very white
17. as greedy as a wolf (매우 탐욕스러운) = very greedy
18. as dead(deaf) as a doornail (아주 죽은/귀머거리가 되어서) = very deaf
19. as old as Adam (태고부터의) = very old
20. as strong as Hercules (매우 힘이 센) = very strong
21. as wise as Solomon (아주 현명한) = very wise
22. as cunning/sly as a fox (아주 교활한) = very cunning
23. as quickly as lightning (thought, wink) (단숨에, 즉시) = very quickly
24. as strong as an ox (매우 힘이 센) = very strong
25. as ancient as a Sphinx (매우 오래된) = very ancient
26. as old as hills (매우 오래된) = very old
27. as silent/dumb as a fish (매우 말이 없는) = very silent
28. as silent/dumb as an oyster (매우 말이 없는) = very silent
29. as deaf as a post (매우 귀가 어두운) = very deaf
30. as slippery as an eel (매우 미끈미끈한) = very slippery
31. as obstinate/stubborn as a mule (매우 완고한) = very stubborn
32. as good as gold (말썽 피우지 않고) = very good
33. as happy as a king (매우 행복한) = very happy
34. as miserable as a fish out of water (매우 비참한) = very miserable
35. as cheerful as a lark(몹시 즐거운) = very cheerful
36. as big as a whale(매우 큰) = very big

37. as busy as a bee (몹시 바쁜) = very busy

Ex) He is <u>as busy as a bee</u>. = He is <u>very busy</u>.
(그는 아주 바쁜 사람이다.)

 고유 형용사

나라명	형용사	국민 전체	국민 한 사람	복수형
Korea	Korean	the Koreans	a Korean	Koreans
America	American	the Americans	an American	Americans
Egypt	Egyptian	the Egyptians	an Egyptian	Egyptians
Germany	German	the Germans	a German	Germans
Italy	Italian	the Italians	an Italian	Italians
Russia	Russian	the Russians	a Russian	Russians
Mexic	Mexican	the Mexicans	a Mexican	Mexicans
Persia	Persian	the Persians	a Persian	Persians
England	English	the English	an Englishman	Englishmen
Ireland	Irish	the Irish	an Irishman	Irishmen
France	French	the French	a Frenchman	Frenchmen
Holland	Dutch	the Dutch	a Dutchman	Dutchmen
Japan	Japanese	the Japanese	a Japanese	Japanese
China	Chinese	the Chinese	a Chinese	Chinese
Portuga	Portuguese	the Portuguese	a Portuguese	Portuguese
Greece	Greek	he Greeks	a Greek	Greeks
Turkey	Turkish	the Turks	a Turk	Turks
Spain	Spanish	The Spaniards	a Spaniard	Spaniards

☞ 국민 한 사람은 a, an을 사용하며, 국민 전체를 나타낼 때에는 the를 붙인다.

한정사(限定詞 : Determiner)

☞ 한정사(限定詞)란 명사 앞에 놓이는 ⎡ 관사(a,an,the) ⎤ 을 말한다.
　　　　　　　　　　　　　　　　⎢ 지시 형용사(this,that,these) ⎥
　　　　　　　　　　　　　　　　⎣ 대명사의 소유격(my,you,his,etc.) ⎦

Ex) ⎡ All
　　 ⎢ Most
　　 ⎢ Many
　　 ⎢ Half　　　　　⎡ them
　　 ⎢ Some　+ of + ⎢ the students
　　 ⎢ Any　　　　　⎢ my classmates　are good swimmers.
　　 ⎢ Few　　　　　⎣ these boys
　　 ⎢ Couple
　　 ⎣ None

(Test) ⎡ Some boys (O)
　　　 ⎢ Some of the boys (O)
　　　 ⎣ Some of boys (X)
　　　 ⎡ Most students (O)
　　　 ⎢ Most of our students (O)
　　　 ⎢ Most of students (X)
　　　 ⎣ The most students (X)

23 전치한정(前置限定) 형용사가 두 개 이상일 때의 어순

한정사				형 용 사								명 사
전치한정사	한정사	서수	기수	일반 형용사 성질	대소	연령	색깔	분사	기원양식	명사	명사에서 온 형용사	명사
	the		two	typical	large					country		house
	the	first		extravagant					London	social		life
	a						gray	crumbling	Gothic	church		tower
	some			intricate		old		Chinese				design
	a				small		green	carved		jade		idol
all	his			heavy		new					filial	duties

TEST

* 다음 _____ 에 들어갈 적절한 것을 고르시오.
  The teacher got Mary to bring _____.

① five small paper boxes
② paper small five boxes
③ small five paper boxes
④ five paper small boxes
⑤ small paper five boxes

(정답) ①

☞ 형용사의 배열순서는, 「지시형용사 + 수량형용사 + 대소(大小)형용사 + 성질형용사 + 연령 + 신구(新舊)형용사…」

제15장
Essential English Grammar

부사(Adverb)

01 뜻을 구별해야 할 주요 부사

[1] ┌ I bought it <u>dear</u>.(나는 그것을 비싼 값을 치르고 샀다.)
　　└ The victory was <u>dearly</u> bought.(승리는 <u>값진 희생을 치르고</u> 얻어졌다.)

[2] ┌ The bird flew <u>high</u> in the sky.
　　│ (그 새는 하늘 <u>높이</u> 날았다.)〈고도를 나타냄〉
　　└ He was <u>highly</u> praised.(그는 <u>매우</u> 칭찬 받았다.)〈정도를 나타냄〉

[3] ┌ You must dive <u>deep</u> into the sea to get pearls.
　　│ (진주를 얻으려면 바다속 <u>깊이</u> 잠수해야 한다.)〈깊이를 나타냄〉
　　└ She was <u>deeply</u> impressed.
　　　(그녀는 매우 <u>깊은</u> 인상을 받았다.)〈정도를 나타냄〉

[4] ┌ You can eat <u>free</u> in my restaurant.
　　│ (너는 나의 음식점에서 <u>무료로</u> 먹을 수 있다.)
　　└ You can speak <u>freely</u> in this room.
　　　(너는 이 방에서 <u>자유로이</u> 이야기해도 된다.)

[5] ┌ He worked <u>hard</u> when young.(그는 젊었을 때 <u>열심히</u> 일했다.)
　　└ She could <u>hardly</u> move at the sight of the snakes.
　　　(그녀는 뱀을 보고 <u>거의</u> 움직이지도 <u>못했다</u>.)

[6] ┌ He has <u>just</u> come back.(그는 <u>방금</u> 돌아왔다.)
　　└ He was <u>justly</u> punished for his crimes.
　　　(그는 그의 죄에 대해 <u>공정하게</u> 판결 받았다.)

[7] ┌ She came <u>late</u>.(그녀는 늦게 왔다.)
　　└ I have never seen him <u>lately</u>.(나는 <u>최근에</u> 그를 못 보았다.)

　　cf) The late Mr. Brown.(고(故) 브라운씨)

[8] ┌ Which part of the concert did you like <u>most</u>?
   │   (너는 음악회의 어느 부분이 <u>가장</u> 좋았니?)
   └ My friends are <u>mostly</u> teachers.(내 친구들은 <u>대부분</u> 선생이다.)

[9] ┌ It is <u>pretty</u> warm today.(오늘은 <u>꽤</u> 따스하다.)
   └ Isn't the girl dressed <u>prettily</u>?(그 소녀는 <u>예쁘게</u> 차려입지 않았는가?)

[10] ┌ She turned up <u>right</u> after breakfast.
    │   (그녀는 아침식사후 <u>곧</u> 나타났다.)
    └ I <u>rightly</u> assumed that Henry wasn't coming.
        (헨리가 오지 않으리라고 나는 <u>옳게</u> 추측했다.)

 부사 already, yet, still

☞ already, yet은 「동작의 완료」여부를, still은 「동작, 상태의 계속」을 표시한다.

[1] Already : 긍정문에서「이미」, 의문문에서「벌써」
 ① 본동사 앞에 쓰이며
   Ex) We <u>already</u> know the answer.
      (<u>이미</u> 답을 알고 있다.)
 ② 완료형에서는 조동사와 본동사 사이에서 주로 쓰인다.
   Ex) We've <u>already</u> found the answer.
      (<u>이미</u> 답을 알아냈다.)
 ③ 의문문에서는 문미(文尾)에 놓인다.
   Ex) Has the post come <u>already</u>?
      (우편물이 <u>벌써</u> 왔는가?)

[2] Yet : yet은 보통 문미(文尾)에 놓인다.
 ① 부정문에서 ;「아직」
   Ex) He has not arrived <u>yet</u>.
 ② 의문문에서 ;「이미」「벌써」

Ex) Has he come home <u>yet</u>?
③ 긍정문에서 ; 「아직」
  Ex) They are talking <u>yet</u>.
    (= They are <u>still</u> talking.)
④ 접속사에서 ; 「그러나」 「그럼에도 불구하고」
  Ex) The story is strange, <u>yet</u> it is true.

[3] still ; 「아직」 「여전히」
① 긍정평서문에서 동사 앞에 온다.
  Ex) I <u>still</u> like her.
② 부정평서문에서 조동사 앞에 온다
  Ex) I <u>still</u> doesn't like her.
③ 의문문에서 조동사와 본동사 사이에 온다.
  Ex) Do you <u>still</u> like her?
④ be동사와 쓰일 때는 be동사 뒤에 온다.
  Ex) I am <u>still</u> studying English.

* 밑줄 친 부사의 위치가 <u>틀린</u> 것은?

① He <u>still</u> lives in the States.
② They are <u>still</u> working in the factory.
③ The man <u>still</u> doesn't like here.
④ They couldn't <u>still</u> buy so nice a house.
⑤ Has the post come <u>already</u>?

(정답) ④

03 on earth(=in the world)

[1] 지상에(서), 이 세상의(에)
  Ex) What were man's first two occupation <u>on earth</u>?
  (<u>지구상에서</u> 인간이 최초로 한 두 가지 말은?)

[2] 〈힘줌말로서〉 (도)대체 (의문사와 같이 씀)

Ex) Where <u>on earth</u> have you been?
(도대체 어디에 갔었니?)
How <u>on earth</u> can you say that?
Why <u>on earth</u> can't you go there?
Where <u>on earth</u> were you?
What <u>in the world</u> is it?

$$\left.\begin{array}{l} \text{When} \\ \text{Where} \\ \text{How} \end{array}\right\} \underline{ever}\ did\ you\ lost\ it?$$

(도대체 언제/어디서/어떻게 그것을 잃었나?)
What <u>ever</u> do you mean?
(도대체 무슨 말이냐?)

[3] 조금도, 전연(부정어의 뒤에 씀)

Ex) It is no use <u>on earth</u>.
(<u>도무지</u> 쓸모가 없다.)
There is no reason <u>on earth</u>.
(<u>조금도</u> 이유가 서지 않는다.)
There can be <u>no</u> doubt <u>whatever</u> about it.
(그것에 대해서는 의심의 여지가 <u>조금도</u> 있을 수가 없다.)
I have no intention <u>what(so)ever</u> of resigning.
(나는 <u>전혀</u> 은퇴할 생각이 없다.)

☞ not ~ at all = not ~ what(so)ever = not ~ on earth.

TEST

* 다음의 밑줄 친 부분과 의미가 같은 것은?

Why <u>on earth</u> did you do it?

① in the world ② for good ③ in particular
④ of late   ⑤ in general

(정답) ①

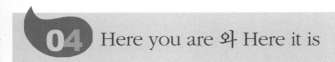
Would you please pass me the pepper, please?
(후추 좀 건네주시겠습니까?)

Here you are.

(= Here is what you want : 당신이 원하는 것이 여기 있습니다.)

☞ 「Here you are」는 「상대방에게 중점을 둔 표현」이다.

「Here it is」는 「물건에 중점을 둔 표현」으로,

즉 「Where is the pepper」와 같이 질문의 주체가 물건으로, 부탁이 아니고 단순
한 질문일 때는 「Here it is」라고 대답한다.

May I have a glass of water? (물 한잔 주시겠습니까?)

Here it is.(X) (여기 있습니다.)

Here you are.(O) => 상대방에게 중점을 두는 표현이다.

Where is my book? (내 책이 어디에 있습니까?)

Here you are.(X) (여기 있습니다.)

Here it is.(O) => 물건에 중점을 둘 때 쓰는 표현이다.

제16장
Essential English Grammar

관사(Article)

01 관사의 생략

[1] 집안 식구를 가리킬 때에는 관사를 생략한다.

☞ 「나의 아버지」를 my father로 my father로 표현할 때에는 소문자이지만, my를 생
   략하면 고유명사처럼 「대문자」로 쓴다.

Ex) Father is very generous, but Mother is stingy.
    (아버지께서는 무척 관대하시지만 어머니께서는 인색하시다.)

[2] God, Heaven, Hell, Nature, Fortune등 神, 自然 등을 고유명사화할 때 관사를 생략한다.

Ex) Heaven forbid!
    (제발 그런 일은 없기를!)

    God is almighty.
    (하느님은 전지전능하다.)

[3] 직위·신분·관직·칭호를 나타내는 명사가 고유명사 앞에서 고유명사와 동격이 되는 경우, 관사는 생략된다.

Ex) Queen Victoria died in 1901.
    (빅토리아 여왕은 1901년에 사망했다.)

    Mr. Smith is principal of the school.
    (스미스 씨는 그 학교의 교장 선생님이다.)

    They elected Kennedy president of the U.S.A in 1959.
    (그들은 케네디를 1958년 미국의 대통령으로 선출했다.)

    He became ⌈ chairman (O)   ⌉ of the meeting.
              ⌊ a chairman (X) ⌋

    They appointed me ⌈ president. (O)   ⌉
                      ⌊ a president. (X) ⌋

[4] 직책·직위를 나타내는 명사가 보어로 쓰인 경우 관사를 생략한다.

Ex) Richard was appointed <u>manager</u> of the branch.
(리챠드는 지점장으로 임명되었다.)

[5] 식사 명에도 관사를 쓰지 않는다.
Ex) He went out after <u>lunch</u>.
(그는 점심 식사 후에 외출했다.)

I'll treat you to <u>dinner</u>.
(내가 너에게 저녁을 쏘겠다.)

[6] 호칭(부르는 말)이나 chemistry, mathematics와 같은 학과 명, golf, tennis 같은 운동 경기명에도 관사를 쓰지 않는다.
Ex) <u>Waiter,</u> bring me my bill.
I like <u>mathematics</u>.
They usually play <u>tennis</u>.

[7] school, church, court 등의 공공 시설명이 본래의 목적에 쓰여 추상적인 개념을 나타낼 때 관사를 쓰지 않는 것이 보통이다.
Ex) He goes to <u>school</u>.   She goes to <u>church</u>.

[8] 병이름(病名)은 추상명사로 보기 때문에 관사를 붙이지 않는 다. 단, 「감기에 걸리다」의 뜻으로 catch (a) cold를 쓸 때는 관사를 쓸 때도 있고 안 쓸 때도 있다.
Ex) Bob is suffering from <u>influenza</u>. (밥은 유행성 독감을 앓고 있다.)
That girl has <u>measles</u>. (그녀는 홍역에 걸렸다.)
Please, take care not to <u>catch cold</u>. (감기 들지 않도록 조심하십시오.)
I am liable to <u>catch a cold</u>. (나는 감기에 잘 걸린다.)

[9] a kind of~, a sort of~ 다음에 오는 명사는 보통 관사를 생 략한다.
It is <u>a kind of</u> ⌐ plant. (O)
                    ⌐ a plant. (X)

Ex) This is a rare <u>species of</u> ⌐ lily. (O)
                                  ⌐ a lily. (X)
                                  ⌐ lilies. (X)

① ┌ of the moment = momentary = temporary
「일시적인, 순간적인, 현재의」
　Ex) He was the man of the moment.
　　(그는 당대의 인물이다.)
└ of moment = momentous = of importance = important
= of consequence 「중요한」

　　Ex) I hold that the matter is especially of moment.
　　　(나는 그 사건을 특히 중요하다고 생각한다.)

② ┌ behind the times = out of date = old-fashioned = obsolete
시대에 뒤떨어진, 구식의(≠ up to date = modern)」
　Ex) You should read newspapers not to be behind the times.
　　(시대에 뒤떨어지지 않도록 신문을 읽어야 한다.)
└ behind time = late 「(시간에) 늦은」
　Ex) You should make haste not to be behind time.
　　(지각하지 않도록 서둘러야 한다.)

③ ┌ in the course of = during 「~ 하는 동안에」
　Ex) In the course of the battle, Yi received a fatal wound.
　　(전쟁 동안에 이 장군은 치명상을 입었다.)
└ in course of = be in process of = be under 「~ 하는 중에 있는」

　　Ex) Another long bridge is in course of construction.
　　　(다른 긴 다리 하나가 건설 중이다.)

④ ┌ in the town 「그 마을에」
　Ex) He lived in the town.
　　(그는 그 마을에서 살았다.)
└ in town 「도시에」
　Ex) He lives in town.
　　(그는 도시에 살고 있다.)

⑤ ┌ out of the question = impossible = doubtful
  │ 「전혀 불가능한, 의심스러운, 생각조차 할 수 없는」
  │   Ex) To turn back was now <u>out of the question</u>.
  │   (되돌아간다는 것은 이젠 불가능이었다.)
  │   It is <u>out of the question</u> that the old man had much savings.
  │   (그 노인이 많은 저금을 하고 있으리라고는 생각지도 못한 일이다.)
  └ out of question = without doubt = beyond question = undoubtful=
    sure = easy 「의심할 여지없이, 확실히, 쉬운」
      Ex) It is <u>out of question</u> that he will be appointed chairman.
          (그가 의장으로 선출될 것은 의심의 여지가 없다.)
          This problem is <u>out of question</u>.
          (이 문제는 쉽다.)

⑥ ┌ take the place of 「~를 대신하다」
  │   Ex) He had to <u>take the place of</u> the president.
  │   (그는 대통령직을 대행해야 했다.)
  └ take place = happen = occur 「일어나다」= be held = come off 「거행되다」
      Ex) Something strange will <u>take place</u> during the night.
          (이상한 일이 밤에 일어날 것이다.)
          The graduation ceremony will <u>take place</u> tomorrow.
          (졸업식은 내일 거행된다.)   (= be held)

03

☞ 명사 앞에 형용사나 부사가 오면 관사는 이들 낱말 앞에 오는 것이 원칙이지만 다음
  의 경우에는 그 위치가 바뀐다.

[1] too(so, as, how, however) + 형용사 + 부정관사(a, an) + 명사
┌ This is <u>so heavy a box</u> that I can't carry it.
└ This is <u>too heavy a box</u> for me to carry.
  cf) This is <u>such a heavy box</u> that I can't carry it.

[2] such (quite, rather, what) + 부정관사(a, an) + 형용사 +
명사

I told him <u>what a clever girl</u> you are.
cf) I told him <u>how clever a girl</u> you are.

[3] half(double, all, both) + 정관사(the) + 명사

<u>Both the parents</u> are in good health.

TEST

* 괄호 안의 낱말의 어순을 바로 잡으시오.

1. He was as (a, as, ever, gentle, man) lived.
2. This is too (a, box, to, heavy, me, for) carry.
3. I've (never, so, kind, seen, a) lady as she.

(정답) 1. gentle a man as ever
      2. heavy a box for me to
      3. never seen so kind a

제17장
Essential English Grammar

의문 대명사
(Interrogative Pronoun)

01 Who와 Whom

[1] 의문 대명사 who는 주격 형식으로 단수에도 복수에도 쓰인다.

Ex) Who <u>is</u> that man?　Who <u>are</u> these men?

[2] Who는 또 종속의문에도 쓰인다.

Ex) Does anyone know <u>who</u> that man is?

[3] whom은 목적격으로서 전치사 뒤에 쓰인다. 이것은 주로 격식차린 문체에서 쓰인다. 격식차리지 않은 문어체(Written English)에서는 who가 잘 쓰이며, 구어체(Spoken English)에서는 who가 보통이다.

Ex) <u>Who(m)</u> do you want to see?
(누구를 만나기를 원하니?)

<u>Who(m)</u> do you think I met in the park this morning?
(오늘 아침 내가 공원에서 누구를 만났다고 생각하나?)

I don't know <u>who(m)</u> you mean.
(네가 누구 이야기를 하고 있는지 나는 모르겠다.)

[4] 전치사를 수반하는 예문

- <u>Who(m)</u> did you give it to?
- <u>To whom</u> did you give it? (형식적)

- <u>Who(m)</u> ought I to address my request to?
- <u>To whom</u> ought I to address my request? (형식적)

- A : I'm writing a letter.
- B : To <u>whom</u>?

[5] Who와 Whom의 구별 방법

☞ 예(例)를 들어 (Who, Whom) shall I say is calling의 문장이 있다고 하자.

① 주어진 문장의 <u>Shall I say</u>에서 끊어 보고
② 그 다음 어느 것이 적합한가를 알아보기 위해 her나 him을 문장에 삽입해 본다.

즉 ⌈ Shall I say <u>he</u> is calling? (O)
   ⌊ Shall I say <u>him</u> is calling? (X)

따라서 위 문장에서는 who가 옳다는 것을 알 수 있다.

⌈ (Who, <u>Whom</u>) are you visiting?
├ Are you visiting <u>him</u>? (O)
⌊ Are you visiting <u>he</u>? (X)

⌈ Is this the woman (<u>who</u>, whom) you believe has been calling me?
├ You believe <u>she</u> has been calling me. (O)
⌊ You believe <u>her</u> has been calling me. (X)

(주의) be동사 다음에 오는 대명사는 항상 <u>주격</u>(nominative case)이다.

　　Ex) It is (<u>he</u>, him)　　Was it (<u>she</u>, her)?　　This is (<u>he</u>, him)

TEST

* 다음 문장에서 <u>잘못된</u> 곳이 있으면 고치시오.

　　We believe the guilty person to be he.

(정답) he => him(여기서는 목적격 보어이다)
☞ 목적격 보어인 경우는 「목적격」으로, 주격 보어인 경우는 「주격」이 와야 한다.

Ex) ⌈ The boy is believed to be <u>he</u>.
　　├ They believe that the boy is <u>he</u>.
　　⌊ It is believed that the boy is <u>he</u>.

⌈ It is I. It was <u>he</u>.
├ It will be <u>she</u> who will meet you.
├ It was not <u>they</u>.
⌊ Is it <u>we</u> you are calling?

☞ 이러한 표현은 격식을 차린 경우이고(in formal usage) 그러나 일상생활 속에서 (in informal, colloquial usage)는 be동사 뒤에 「목적격」을 쓰기도 한다.

Ex) It's <u>me</u>. It wasn't <u>her</u>.

☞ 인칭대명사가 복합 주격의 보어(compound subject complement)인 경우는 반드시 주격으로 써야 한다.

Ex)　It was <u>she and her husband</u> at the door.
　　Is it <u>you and I</u> who are going?
　　Was it <u>Bill and I</u> they were waiting for?
　　It will <u>be he and I</u> who will have to work?

[6] A Test on Who, Whom

☞ To decide which pronoun is correct in formal writing, start reading after <u>he(she)</u> or <u>him(her)</u> wherever the personal pronoun fits and makes sense.

If <u>he(she)</u> fits, select who : if <u>him(her)</u> fits, chose <u>whom</u>.

1. (Who, Whom) do you wish to speak to?
2. (Who, Whom) are you expecting?
3. Is this the person (who, whom) you claim held up the bank?
4. Is this the person (who, whom) you saw holding up the bank?
5. (Who, Whom) is it at the door?
6. (Who, Whom) did you think it was?
7. Anyone (who, whom) you find at the desk can help you.
8. Anyone (who, whom) is at the desk can help you.
9. (Who, Whom) will you choose as the next contestant?
10. (Who ,Whom) do you suspect of taking your money?
11. (Who, Whom) shall I say wishes to talk to her?
12. This is the fugitive (who, whom) the police say escaped from San Quentin.

☞(Key)

(1) Do you wish to speak to <u>him</u>?　(2) Are you expecting <u>him</u>?
(3) You claim <u>he</u> held up the bank.
(4) You saw <u>him</u> holding up the bank.
(5) It is <u>he</u> at the door.　　　(6) Did you think it was <u>he</u>?

(7) You find <u>him</u> at the desk. (8) <u>He</u> is at the desk.

(9) You will choose <u>him</u>. (10) Do you suspect <u>him</u>?

(11) Shall I say <u>he</u> wishes to ⋯?

(12) The police say <u>he</u> escaped.

 Whoever와 Whomever의 구별

☞ The same rules apply to <u>Whoever</u> and <u>Whomever</u> that govern <u>who</u> and whom − i.e.<u>whoever</u> is nominative, <u>whomever</u> is objective. Follow the same method for determining whether to use <u>whoever</u> or <u>whomever</u> in writing that you used for who or whom.

[1] <u>Whoever</u> means <u>anyone who</u> ; <u>whomever</u> means anyone <u>whom</u>.

So : <u>talk to whomever is waiting;</u> means <u>talk to anyone who is waiting;</u>

<u>ask whomever you see</u> means <u>ask any one whom you see.</u>

[2] A Test on Whoever, Whomever

1. Give this to (whoever, whomever) is at the desk.

2. Stop (whoever, whomever) tries to come in.

3. We will sell the house to (whoever, whomever) is the highest bidder.

4. Choose (whoever, whomever) you prefer.

5. Talk to (whoever, whomever) you find at the desk.

6. Tell (whoever, whomever) is waiting to come in.

7. She gave help to (whoever, whomever) needed it.

8. Ask (whoever, whomever) is on the line to call back later.

☞ (Key)

(1) <u>He</u> is at the desk. (2) <u>He</u> tries to come in.

(3) <u>He</u> is the highest bidder.　(4) You prefer <u>him</u>.

(5) You find <u>him</u>.　(6) <u>He</u> is waiting.

(7) <u>He</u> needed it.　(8) <u>He</u> is on the line.

03 what과 how의 선택

[1] What : 대명사. 문장의 주요소가 필요한 곳에 사용한다.
즉, 주어, 보어, 목적어가 필요한 곳에 사용한다.

[2] How : 부사, 정도를 나타내어 「얼마나」, 방법의 뜻을 나타내어 「어떻게」의 뜻을 가진 수식어로 쓰인다.

① 서울의 인구가 얼마나 됩니까?

<u>What</u> is the population of Seoul? (보어)

<u>How</u> many people are there in Seoul? (수식어)

<u>How</u> large is the population of Seoul? (수식어)

② 그 결과에 대해서 어떻게 생각하십니까?

<u>What</u> do you think about the result? (think는 타동사로서 목적어가 필요하다)

<u>How</u> do you feel about the result? (feel은 자동사)

＊feel about = like

③ ┌ Korea has <u>many</u> population (X)
  └ Korea has <u>a large</u> population (O)

  cf) There <u>was</u> a large/small audience.(많은(적은) 청중이 있었다.)
     audience : 집합 명사 => 단수 취급

④ ┌ <u>How many</u> are the Korean population? (X)
  ├ <u>How large</u> is the population of Korea? (O)
  └ <u>What</u> is the population of Korea? (O)
    (한국의 인구는 얼마나 됩니까?)

  cf) How many people are there in Korea?

⑤ ┌ Korean population (X)
  ├ the population of Korea (O)
  └ Korea's population (O)

⑥ 한국은 면적에 비해 인구가 많다.
┌ Korea has <u>very large population</u> for its area.(X)
└ Korea has <u>a very large population</u> for its area.(O)
  ☞ 추상명사가 have동사와 결합될 때에는 관사 a(n)을 함께 쓴다.

⑦ large는 크기(size)에 관해 말하는 경우에 쓰이며, big보다 약간 더
   격식을 갖춘 경우에 쓰인다.
Sir Henry was feeling decidedly sleepy after <u>a large</u> lunch.
(헨리경은 점심을 많이 드시고 나서 몹시 졸리고 있다.)
Mummy, can I have <u>a big</u> lunch today?
(엄마, 오늘은 점심을 많이 먹어도 괜찮아요?)

04 What과 Which의 선택

What books have you read on this subject?
(이 문제에 관하여 지금까지 어떤 책을 읽었는가?)
Which of these books have you found most useful?
(이 책 중에서 어느 책이 가장 도움이 됐는가?)

What languages do you know?
(너는 어느 나라 말을 잘 알고 있는가?)
Which of these languages do you speak fluently?
(너는 이들 언어 중 어느 것을 유창하게 말할 수 있는가?)

What is the capital of Turkey?
(터키의 수도는 어디인가?)
Which city is larger, Ankara or Istanbul?
(앙카라와 이스탄불 중 어느 쪽이 더 큰 도시인가?)

What university did you go to?
(어느 대학에 진학했는가?)
Which university did you go to, Oxford or Cambridge?
(어느 대학에 진학했는가? 옥스포드인가 캠브리진가?)
☞ 선택의 범위가 한정되어 있어 질문자가 이 두 대학을 가장 확률이 많은 대학으로
생각하고 있음을 암시하고 있다.

05 수사(修辭) 의문문(Rhetoric Question)

☞ 「수사(修辭) 의문문(Rhetoric Question)」이란 형식은 의문문이지만, 상대방에게 어
떤 것을 묻는 것이 아니고, 말하는 자기의 뜻을 상대방에게 확신시키기 위한 것이
다. 긍정 의문문은 부정 평서문과 비슷하고, 부정 의문문은 긍정 평서문과 비슷하나,

단순한 평서문(서술문)보다 강하고 감정적이다.

Ex) ┌ Who knows? (누가 알랴?) – 수사 의문문
    ├ No one knows. (아무도 모른다.)
    └ God knows. (신은 알고 있다.)

    ┌ Who does not know? (누가 모르겠냐?) – 수사 의문문
    └ Everyone knows. (누구나 다 안다.)

    ┌ Who does not long for happiness? (누가 행복을 원치 않으랴?) – 수사 의문문
    └ Everyone longs for happiness. (누구나 다 행복을 원한다.)

    ┌ What's the use of waiting here? (여기서 기다려 봤자 무슨 소용이
    │ 있겠냐?) – 수사 의문문
    └ It is no use waiting here. (여기서 기다려 봤자 아무 소용없다.)

    ┌ Who can tell what may happen? (무슨 일이 일어날지 누가 알랴?) – 수사 의문문
    └ No one can tell what may happen. (아무도 모른다.)

    ┌ Who is there but commits errors?
    │ (잘못을 저지르지 않을 자가 누가 있겠느냐?) – 수사 의문문
    ├ There is nobody but commits errors.
    │ (잘못을 저지르지 않는 사람은 없다.)
    └ Everybody commits errors. (누구나 다 잘못을 저지른다.)

    ┌ Who does not know such a thing? (누가 그러한 것을 모르겠는가?) – 수사 의문문
    └ Everybody knows such a thing. (누구나 다 그러한 것을 안다.)

    ┌ What is the use(good) of worrying? – 수사 의문문
    │ (걱정을 해 보았자 무슨 소용이 있겠느냐?)
    └ It is no use(good) worrying. (걱정을 하는 것은 아무 소용도 없다.)

    ┌ What is the use of crying over spilt milk? – 수사 의문문
    │ (엎질러진 우유를 놓고 울어봤자 무슨 소용이 있겠는가?)
    ├ Of what use is to cry over spilt milk?
    ├ It is no use crying over spilt milk.
    ├ It is of no use to cry over spilt milk.
    └ It is useless to cry over spilt milk.
    (엎질러진 우유를 놓고 울어봤자 아무 소용없다.)

06 간접 의문문

[1] 주절 + 의문사 + 종속절

☞ 「의문문」이 know, tell, ask, hear 등 「타동사」의 「목적어」가 되어 간접 의문문으로 될 때 어순은 「평서문」의 어순이 된다.

┌ I know + Who is he?
└ I know who he is.

┌ Do you know who he is?
└ Yes, I know who he is.

┌ Do you know? + Who is he?
└ Do you know who he is?

┌ Do you know ─┐
│ Do you tell │
│ Do you ask   │ who he is?
│ Do you hear │
│ Do you believe│
└ Do you say ─┘

┌ Did you say what he wanted?
└ No, he did not.

┌ Do you believe that God will answer your prayers?
│ (하나님께서 당신의 기도에 응답하시리라 믿으십니까?)
└ No, I do not.
　(아니요, 믿지 않습니다.)

[2] 의문사 + 주절 + 종속절

☞ yes-no question이 아닌 의문문에서 「Do you think / suppose / guess / believe」 등 「자동사」가 의문사 다음에 삽입되어 「삽입절」이 된다.

┌ Do you think? + Where does he live?
└ Where do you think he live?

Do you think? + Who is he?
Who do <u>you think</u> he is?
<u>I think</u> he is Mr. Brown.

Did he say? + What did he want?
What <u>did he say</u> he wanted?
<u>He said</u> he wanted some water.

Where ⎰ do you think
⎰ do you believe
Where ⎰ do you suppose ⎰ he lives
⎰ do you imagine
⎰ do you guess
⎰ do you say

Take
A
Break!
[한국 풍속화 감상 3 – 서당(Study Room)]

글방, 즉 서당(書堂)은 지금의 초등학교와 같은 교육 장소였다. 나이가 듬직하고 근엄한 훈장과 어린 소년들이 자그마한 방에서 천자문(千字文) 등을 가르치고 배우는 곳이다. 그런데 책만 보면 머리가 멍해지고, 책만 펴 놓으면 졸음이 와 머리를 꾸벅꾸벅하는 소년도 있다.

The study room where the Chinese sentences were taught, was like a primary school of these days. The old and dignified teacher earnestly teaches the Chinese characters to young students with switch in his hand, but some students, who dislike studying, doze over a book.

제18장
Essential English Grammar

전치사(Preposition)

장소를 나타내는 전치사

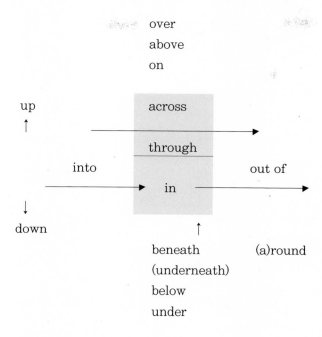

Ex) The clouds are right <u>over</u> us.
(구름이 바로 우리 위에 있다.)

The plane flew <u>over</u> the mountains.
(비행기가 날아 그 산을 지나갔다.)

Some nice people are <u>above</u> us.
(몇몇 친절한 사람들이 우리 위에 살고 있다.)

The children are lying <u>on</u> the floor.
(그 아이들은 마루 위에 누워있다.)

There was a bridge <u>across</u> the river.
(강을 가로지르는 다리가 있었다.)

The stone went <u>through</u> the window.
(그 돌은 유리창을 뚫고 지나갔다.)

She works in an office.
(그녀는 사무실에서 일한다.)

He came into the house.
(그는 집에 들어왔다.)

I sprang out of bed.
(나는 침대에서 뛰쳐나왔다.)

The boy climbed up a tree.
(그 소년이 나무위로 올라갔다.)

Santa Clause comes down the chimney.
(산타클로오즈는 굴뚝을 타고 내려온다.)

There is a ditch beneath(underneath) the church wall.
(교회 담 밑에 도랑이 있다.)

He was sitting below the branches of a tree.
(그는 나뭇가지 아래에 앉아 있었다.)

The cat is lying under the table.
(그 고양이는 식탁 아래에 누워 있다.)

The earth goes around the sun.
(지구는 태양의 주위를 돈다.)

02 제공·위탁·선사·부여를 나타내는 with

제 공	provide supply furnish present feed equip(건축에 설비물을)	A (사람) with B (사물) B (사물) for(to) A (사람) 「A에게 B를 제공하다」
위 탁	trust	A(사람) with B(사물) 「A에게 B를 위탁하다(맡기다)」

선사	present	A(사람) with B(사물) 「A에게 B를 선사(선물)하다」
부여	endow(bless gift)	A(사람) with B(사물) 「A에게 B를 부여하다」 be endowed with 「(재능·성격을) 타고나다」

[1]

$$S(주어) + \begin{bmatrix} provide \\ supply \\ furnish \\ feed \end{bmatrix} \begin{bmatrix} A(사람) \ with \ B(사물) \\ B(사물) \ for(to) \ A(사람) \end{bmatrix}$$

Ex) ┌ He provides his family with food and shelter
└ He provides food and shelter for his family.
(그는 가족들에게 음식과 살 곳을 제공하고 있다.)

┌ They supply the pupils (with) books.
└ They supply books for(또는 to) the pupils.
(그들은 학생들에게 책을 공급한다.)

cf) 요즈음 美語에서는 supply, provide, furnish에서 전치사 with를 생략하는 경향이 있다.

┌ Bees provide us (with) honey.
└ Bees provide honey for(또는 to) us.
(꿀벌들은 우리에게 꿀을 제공한다.)

The moving belt feeds the machine with raw material.
(이 이동벨트는 기계에 원료를 공급한다.)

Someone fed the patient with soup and milk.
(어떤 사람이 환자에게 수프와 우유를 주었다.)

[2] S(주어) + equip A with B (갖추게 하다, 장비하다, 준비하다)
They equipped soldiers with uniforms and weapons.
(그들은 군복과 무기로 군인들을 무장시켰다.)

[3] S(주어) + trust A with B (A에게 B를 맡기다)

You may <u>trust</u> him <u>with</u> your money. (O)
You may <u>trust</u> him <u>for</u> your money. (X)
(저 사람이라면 돈을 맡겨도 괜찮다.)

[4] S(주어) + present A with B ㄱ (A에게 B를 선물(선사)하다)
               present B to A

Ex) I <u>presented</u> him <u>with</u> a watch.
    I <u>presented</u> a watch <u>to</u> him.
    (나는 그 사람에게 손목시계를 선물했다.)

[5] S(주어) + endow(bless) A with B (A에게 B를 부여하다)
    Ex) She <u>was blessed with</u> good health. (그녀는 건강을 누렸다.)
    God <u>endowed</u> him <u>with</u> good talents.
    He <u>was endowed with</u> good talents.
    (신은 그에게 훌륭한 재능을 부여했다 : 그는 훌륭한 재능을 타고났다.)

03 유도·행동의 방향을 나타내는 into, out of

설득	persuade argue talk + 사람	into ~ing (긍정) out of ~ing (부정) 「설득하여 ~(못)하게 하다」
강요	force + 사람	
단념	dissuade + 사람	from ~ing 「단념하게 하다」

[1]
  S(주어) + persuade argue talk + 사람 + into~ing(설득하여 …하게 하다)

☞ into, out of 뒤에는 동명사 대신 명사(동사의 명사형)가 오는 경우가 더 많다.
  Ex) He <u>talked</u> his daughter <u>into</u> marriage.
      He <u>persuaded</u> his daughter <u>to marry</u>.
      (그는 자기 딸을 설득하여 결혼시켰다.)

I persuade him into staying at home.
(나는 그를 설득하여 집에 있게 했다.)

They talked him into going.
(그들은 그를 설득하여 가게 했다.)

They tried to argue him into joining them.
(그들은 그를 설득하여 자기들 편에 넣으려고 했다.)

[2] S(주어) + force + 사람 + into ~ing
(~하도록 강요하다, ~에게 억지로 ~을 시키다)

Ex) I forced the lady into complying with my proposal.
(나는 그 숙녀가 나의 제안에 따르도록 강요했다.)

[3]
S(주어) + ┌ persuade ┐
          │ argue   │ + 사람 + out of ~ing
          └ talk   ┘
S(주어) + dissuade + 사람 + from~ ~ing
(설득하여 ~못하게 하다, 단념시키다)

Ex) I managed to persuade him out of his plan.
(나는 그에게 이 계획에서 손을 떼도록 설득하는데 간신히 성공했다.)

He dissuaded a friend from marrying.
(그는 친구의 결혼을 말렸다.)

I talked the girl out of doing that.
(나는 그 소녀를 설득하여 그것을 못하게 했다.)

I talked him out of going.
(나는 그를 설득시켜 가지 못하게 했다.)

TEST

* 두 문장이 뜻이 같아지도록 (   )에 알맞은 말을 고르시오.

┌ I persuaded him not to do it.
└ I talked him (   ) doing it.

① out of   ② into   ③ from
④ not   ⑤ of   (정답) ①

04 제거를 나타내는 of

제거	deprive (~를 빼앗다)	
	rob (박탈하다)	A (사람) of B (사물)
	rid (제거하다)	
경감	clear (제거하다, 치우다)	「A에게서 B를 제거(박탈)하다」
	ease (덜어주다), cure (치료하다)	
	strip (벗기다), relieve (덜어주다)	

[1] rob A of B (A에게서 B를 강탈하다)

Ex) They <u>robbed</u> her of the handbag.
(그들은 그녀의 핸드백을 빼앗아 갔다.)

She <u>was robbed of</u> her jade ring on her way home from her work.
(그녀는 일터에서 돌아오는 길에 비취반지를 강탈당했다.)

cf) They <u>robbed</u> a portable safe.
① 그들은 휴대금고를 훔쳐갔다. (X)
② 그들은 휴대금고의 알맹이(돈)을 털어갔다. (O)

☞ 「rob a house」, 「rob a safe」는 「집을 훔치다」 「금고를 훔치다」가 아니라 「집(금고)를 털다」의 뜻이다.

〈rob과 steal의 차이점〉

☞ rob의 목적어는 「사람」 또는 「물건·돈을 넣어두는 장소나 건물」이며, steal의 목적어는 「물건」, 「돈」이다.

- rob A of B = take B by force from A   (A에게서 B를 빼앗다)
- steal B from A = take away B from A

- S(사람주어) + have + 목적어 + p.p
- S(사람주어) + steal + 목적어(사물) + from +사람
- S(사물주어) + be + stolen + from + 사람
- S(사람주어) + rob + 목적어(사람) + of + 사물
- S(사람주어) + be + robbed + of + 사물

Ex) 「나는 지갑을 도둑 맞았다」
① I had my purse stolen (O)
② He stole my purse (from me) (O)
③ My purse was stolen (from me) (O)
④ I was stolen my purse (X)
⑤ He robbed me of my purse (O)
⑥ I was robbed of my purse (O)
cf) He had his watch stolen (O)
　　His watch was stolen (from him) (O)
　　He was robbed of his watch (O)
　　He was stolen his watch (X)

TEST

1 Choose a suitable word

The post office was (stolen, robbed) last night.

(정답) robbed

2 두 문장의 뜻이 같아지게 _____에 알맞은 단어를 쓰시오.

┌ She had her purse _____.

└ She was robbed _____ her purse.

(정답) stolen / of

[2] deprive A of B (A에게서 B를 빼앗다)

Ex) The tall building <u>deprives</u> my house <u>of</u> the sunlight.
(큰 건물 때문에 우리 집에 햇빛이 들어오지 못한다.)

Astonishment <u>deprived</u> me <u>of</u> my power of speech.
(나는 놀라서 말이 안 나왔다.)

[3] rib A of B (A에게서 B를 제거하다)

Ex) We have to <u>rib</u> a house of mice.
(집에서 쥐를 제거해야 한다.)

(=> We have must <u>get rid of</u> rats in our house)

[4] strip A of B (A에게서 B를 벗기다, 빼앗다, 몰수하다)

Ex) They <u>stripped</u> a man <u>of</u> his possessions.
(그들은 어떤 사람에게서 그의 재산을 빼앗았다.)

The bandits <u>stripped</u> him of his clothes.
(강도들은 그의 옷을 벗겨버렸다.)

[5] ease A of B (A에게서 B를 덜어주다.)

Ex) I will <u>ease</u> you of your burden.
(내가 너의 짐을 덜어주겠다.)

[6] cure a of B (A에게서 B를 고치다, 제거하다)

Ex) We have to <u>cure</u> a child <u>of</u> bad habits.
(어린애의 나쁜 버릇을 고쳐야 한다.)

[7] relieve A of B (A에게서 B를 제거하다, 훔치다)

Ex) Let me <u>relieve</u> you of your suitcase.
(여행 가방을 들어줄게.)

The thief <u>relieved</u> him of his watch.
(도둑이 그의 시계를 훔쳤다.)

TEST

* of가 들어갈 수 없는 항을 찾아 그곳에 알맞은 말을 넣으시오.

① He was deprived (　　) his sight by the traffic accident.

② The man stole my watch (　　) me.

③ The doctor cured him (　　) his disease.

④ This machine will relieve you (　　) a lot of trouble.

⑤ They strip a man (　　) his money.

(정답) ②(from이 들어가야 한다)

05 수단을 나타내는 by와 with

☞ 전치사 by는 「수단」을 나타내며, 동명사는 「동작」을 나타내므로 「by + 동사 ~ing」는 「무엇을 하는데 필요한 수단이 되는 행동」을 나타내는 표현이다. 전치사 by와 with는 누가 무엇을 하는 「방법」 및 「수단」 등에 다 쓸 수 있으나, 「by」는 「동작이나 행동」에 관할 때 쓰며, 「with」는 「도구나 목적」을 지칭할 때 쓰인다.

Ex) I killed the spider <u>by hitting</u> it.
(나는 거미를 쳐서 죽였다.)

He earns his living <u>by teaching</u> English.
(그는 영어를 가르치는 일로 생계를 꾸려 나가고 있다.)

I killed the spider <u>with a newspaper</u>.
(나는 거미를 신문지로 죽였다.)

He got what he wanted <u>with flowers</u>.
(그는 원하는 것을 꽃으로 얻었다.)

06 [교통 수단을 나타내는 by
by + 무관사 + 교통에 관한 명사 (~로)]

Ex)   She came here ┌ by train (O)
                    ├ on a train (O)
                    └ by a train (X)
(그녀는 기차로 왔다.)

by ┌ air (비행기로)
   ├ plane (= on a plane) (비행기로)
   ├ streamer (기선으로)
   └ train (= on a train) (기차로)

by ┌ bicycle (= on a bicycle) (자전거로)
   ├ bus (= in a bus) (버스로)
   ├ car (= in a car) (자동차로)
   └ express (특급으로)

| Essential English Grammar | 317

by ┌ sea (해로(海路)로)
   ├ coach (마차로)
   ├ taxi (= in a taxi) (택시로)
   ├ ship (= on a ship) (배로)
   ├ land (육로(陸路)로)
   └ mail (우편으로)

cf) He came here <u>on foot</u> (걸어서, 도보로)
    He came here <u>on horseback</u> (말을 타고)

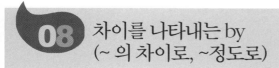

07 ┌ 통신 수단을 나타내는 by
      └ by + 무관사 + 통신에 관한 명사 (~ 로)

by ┌ word of mouth (구두로)
   ├ telegram (전보로)
   ├ letter (편지로) / air mail(항공우편으로) / surface mail(선편으로)
   ├ cable (해저 전선으로)
   ├ telephone (전화로)
   ├ wireless (무선으로)
   └ radio (무선으로)

Ex) I tried to contact her <u>by telephone</u> all day.
    (나는 온종일 그녀와 전화 연락을 하려고 애썼다.)

    Please send this letter <u>by air mail (surface mail)</u>.
    (항공 우편(선박 우편)으로 이 편지를 보내 주세요.)
    *surface mail 항공 우편이 아닌 보통 우편, 선박 우편(= sea mail,
     boat mail)

08 차이를 나타내는 by
      (~ 의 차이로, ~정도로)

Ex) I missed the bus <u>by a minute</u>.
    (1분 차이로 버스를 놓쳤다.)

318   제18장 전치사(Preposition)

The bullet missed me <u>by two feet</u>.
(총알이 2피트 정도 빗나갔다.)

09 계량의 단위를 나타내는 by
by + the + 명사 (~의 단위로, ~에 (얼마)로)

Ex) We rent a house <u>by the year</u>.
(우리는 집을 1년 단위 전세로 얻었다.)

They are paid <u>by the hour</u>.
(그들은 시급으로 돈을 받는다.)

They sell pencils <u>by the dozen</u>.
(그들은 연필을 12개 단위로 판다.)

They sell it <u>by the meter</u>.
(그들은 그것을 미터 단위로 팔았다.)

I hired a boat <u>by the hour</u>.
(나는 배 한 척을 시간 단위로 빌렸다.)

10 주어가 바뀔때 주의해야 할 표현

① A(사람) be familiar with B(사물) 「A는 B를 잘안다」
(~에 정통한, 훤히 알고 있는)
B(사물) be familiar to B(사람) 「B는 A에게 잘 알려져 있다」
(~에게 잘 알려져 있는)

Ex) Almost everyone <u>is familiar with</u> the different sounds.
The different sounds <u>are familiar</u> to almost everyone.
(거의 모든 사람들이 여러 가지 다른 소리를 잘 알고 있다.)

He <u>is familiar with</u> English.
(그는 영어에 정통하다.)

    └ Your name <u>is familiar to</u> me.
      (존함은 익히 알고 있습니다.)

② ┌ A(원인) result in B(결과)　「A는 B를 초래했다」
  └ B(결과) result from A(원인)　「B는 A의 결과였다」
  Ex) ┌ The decision <u>resulted</u> in a serious quarrel.
      └ A serious quarrel <u>resulted from</u> the decision.
      (심각한 말다툼이 그 토론에서 나온 결과였다.)

③ ┌ A(제품) be made of B(원료) 「A는 B로 만들어진다」 - 물리적 변화
  ├ A(제품) be made from B(원료) 「A는 B로 만들어진다」 - 화학적 변화
  └ B(원료) be made into A(제품) 「B로 A를 만든다 / B는 가공되어 A가 된다」
  Ex) ┌ The desk <u>is made of</u> wood. (책상은 나무로 만든다.)
      └ Wood <u>is made into</u> the desk. (나무는 가공되어서 책상이 된다.)

      ┌ Wine <u>is made from</u> grapes. (포도주는 포도로 만든다.)
      └ Grapes <u>are made into</u> wine. (포도는 가공되어서 포도주가 된다.)

④ ┌ substitute A for B ┐ 「B를(대신에) A로 대체하다」
  └ replace B with(by) A ┘
  Ex) ┌ We have to <u>substitute</u> coal <u>for</u> oil this winter.
      └ We have to <u>replace</u> oil <u>with(by)</u> coal this winter.
      (우리는 이번 겨울에는 석탄을 석유대신에 써야 한다.)

11 결과를 나타내는 to (결과의 전치사 to)
(~한 결과 ~ 했다)

☞ be crushed to death (압사하다)　　　be burnt to death (불타 죽다)
  frozen to death (얼어죽다)　　　　be starved to death (굶어 죽다)
  be suffocated to death (질식해 죽다)　be stabbed to death (찔려 죽다)
  be stricken(struck) to death (맞아 죽다)　be bitten to death (물려 죽다)
  be stoned to death (돌에 맞아 죽다)　be put to death (처형되다)

Ex) One minute later, we might <u>have been crushed to death</u>. But we
   were lucky enough.
   (1분만 더 늦었더라면 아마 우리는 압사했을지도 모른다. 그러나, 우리는
   운이 참 좋았다.)

┌ The yo<u>uth stabbed</u> <u>him to</u> death.
└ He <u>was stabbed to</u> death by the youth.
   (그 젊은이는 그를 칼로 찔러 죽였다.)

┌ They <u>put</u> him <u>to death</u> by beating.
└ They <u>beat</u> him <u>to death</u>.
(그들은 그를 때려서 죽게 했다.)

┌ stone somebody to death ┐
└ be stoned to death   ┘   아무를 돌로 쳐 죽이다.

   Ex) Christian martyrs who <u>were stoned to death</u>.
      (돌에 맞아 죽은 기독교 순교자들)

┌ put somebody to death ┐
└ be put to death   ┘   아무를 죽이다, 처형하다.

   Ex) The soldier was put to death.
      (그 병사는 처형되었다.)

be sentenced(condemned) to death 사형 선고를 받다.

   Ex) ┌ He <u>was sentenced to death</u>.
      └ He <u>was condemned to death</u>.
      (그는 사형 선고를 받았다.)

cf) ① <u>Put</u> the baby <u>to bed.</u> (아기를 재워라.)
Ex) Put me to bed after the nurse had gone.
   (보모가 간 뒤 그녀는 나를 잠재웠다.)

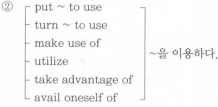

   ② ┌ put ~ to use
      ├ turn ~ to use
      ├ make use of
      ├ utilize   ┤   ~을 이용하다.
      ├ take advantage of
      └ avail oneself of
   ③ put ~ to test ~ 을 시험하다.

12 **[타동사 + 목적어 + 전치사 + the + 신체의 일부]**

S(주어) + hit(strike, beat, touch, pat) ~ on the + 신체의 일부
(툭치다, 때리다)

S(주어) + take(hold, pull. catch, seize) ~ by the + 신체의 일부
(잡다, 잡아당기다)

S(주어) + stare(look) ~ in the + 신체의 일부 (보다, 응시하다)

☞ 이때의 the는 소유격 one's 대신에 사용된 것이다. 즉 우리말처럼, He looked my face라고 하지 않고, He looked me <u>in the face</u>로 표현한다.

Ex) He $\begin{bmatrix} \text{hit} \\ \text{struck} \end{bmatrix}$ me on the head.

(그가 나의 머리를 강타했다.)

He $\begin{bmatrix} \text{patted} \\ \text{tapped} \end{bmatrix}$ me on the shoulder.

(그가 나의 어깨를 툭쳤다.)

He <u>patted</u> me lightly on the chin.
(그는 나의 턱을 가볍게 어루만졌다.)

She <u>kissed</u> him on the cheek.
(그녀는 그의 빰에 키스를 했다.)

He $\begin{bmatrix} \text{seized} \\ \text{held} \\ \text{took} \\ \text{caught} \\ \text{pulled} \end{bmatrix}$ me by $\begin{bmatrix} \text{the sleeve} \\ \text{the hand} \\ \text{he arm} \\ \text{the wrist} \\ \text{the collar} \end{bmatrix}$

He $\begin{bmatrix} \text{stared} \\ \text{looked} \end{bmatrix}$ me in $\begin{bmatrix} \text{the face} \\ \text{the eye} \end{bmatrix}$

I trod her <u>on</u> the foot by mistake.
Mother cut herself <u>in</u> the finger when cooking.
He embraced her <u>round</u> the neck.
He slapped her <u>in</u> the face.

He punched his friend ┌ <u>in</u> the nose
                               ├ <u>on</u> the chin
                               └ <u>about</u> the body

13 ┌ but ┐
├ except ├ + to 부정사
└ save ┘

☞ 여기서는 but는 「~이외에, ~밖에」(= except, save, without)란 뜻의 전치사로서 to 부정사를 목적어로 취한 것이다. 따라서 but to ~ 는 「~할 수밖에, ~하지 않고는」의 뜻이 된다. 그러나 except다음에 동사가 올 때는 대개 「to없는 부정사」가 쓰인다.

Ex) I couldn't do anything <u>except</u> just <u>sit</u> there and hope.
    (나는 단지 거기에 앉아 희망을 갖는 것 이외에는 아무것도 할 수 없었다.)
    I told him that I had no ambition <u>except to retire</u> to a quiet home.
    (너는 조용한 고향에 돌아가는 것 이외에는 아무런 야망도 없다고 대통령에게 말했다.)

☞ 단, 다음과 같은 구문은 원형 부정사가 but의 목적어가 된다.

I cannot <u>but</u> <u>agree</u> to his proposal.

(= I cannot <u>help agreeing</u> to his proposal)

(나는 그의 제의에 동의하지 않을 수 없다.)

[1] have no choice but to 부정사 (~할 수밖에 없다, ~하지 않을 수 없다)(= Nothing remains but to (do) ~)

Ex) She had no choice <u>but to blame</u> him for his rudeness.
    (그녀는 그의 무례함을 책망할 수 밖에 없었다.)

    Nothing will remain <u>but to wait</u> for him till he gets well.
    (그가 병이 나을 때까지 기다릴 수 밖에 없을 것이다.)

[2] There is nothing to do <u>but to(do)</u> (~할 수 밖에 없다)
(= There is nothing for it <u>but to (do)</u> ~)

Ex) There may be nothing to do <u>but to assist</u> him in solving it.
    (그것을 해결하는 데에 그를 도와줄 수밖에 다른 도리가 없을지도 모른다.)

There is nothing for it <u>but to do</u> the work (O)
(그 일을 할 수 밖에 없다.)

TEST

1 다음 밑줄 친 빈칸에 들어갈 알맞은 것은? (   )

1. He couldn't _____ to suffer from loss of memory.

① help disheartening   ② help having disheartened

③ but disheartening   ④ but be disheartened

⑤ but dishearten

(정답) ④

☞ 감정의 변화이므로 「수동」이 되어야 한다. 따라서 정답은 ④가 된다.

2 What are we here for _____ the matter?

① except discussing   ② unless discussing

③ but to discuss   ④ in order not to discuss

⑤ so as to discuss

(정답) ③

☞ 그 문제를 토의하지 않는다면 우리는 무엇 때문에 여기 모여 있단 말인가?

[3] cannot help ~ing (~ing하지 않을 수 없다)

Ex) ┌ I <u>cannot help doing</u> such a thing.
├ I <u>cannot but do</u> such a thing.
├ I <u>cannot help but do</u> such a thing.
├ I <u>cannot choose but do</u> such a thing.
└ I <u>have no choice but to do</u> such a thing.
(나는 그러한 일을 하지 않을 수 없다.)

＊이때의 help는 avoid의 의미를 갖는다.

[4] 부정사는 전치사의 목적어로 사용하지 못한다.
(예외 - except, but, save, about)

Ex)   The rain prevented him from ┌ to go out. (X)
└ going out. (O)

There is nothing for it <u>but to do</u> the work. (O)

He was <u>about to leave</u> when I called on him. (O)

[5] 전치사 but 다음에 원형부정사와 to 부정사가 오는 경우

Ex)
┌ I can't but obey him
├ I can do nothing but obey him
├ I can't choose but obey him
├ I have no choice but to obey him
└ There is nothing for it but to obey him
　　(나는 그의 말에 복종하지 않을 수 없다.)

TEST

* 다음의 빈 칸에 적절한 단어를 써 넣으시오.

I have no choice but obey him.
There is (　　) for (　　) (　　) to obey him

(정답) nothing, it, but.

14 to the north와 in the north

☞ 일반적으로 東西南北을 나타낼 때의 전치사 to와 in의 사용상의 구별을 설명하면 다음과 같다.

Pyongyang is to the north of Seoul. (서울의 북쪽에)
Pyongyang is in the north of Korea. (한국의 北部에)

=) 즉, to는 어느 장소에서 떨어져 있는 경우에 그 방향을 나타내고, in은 어느 장소의 범위 내에서의 위치를 나타낸다. 위의 예(例)에서 납득이 가겠지만 요컨데 to는 "방향"을, in은 어느 범위 내에서 차지하고 있는 "방위(方位)"를 나타낸다.

한편 거리를 말하자면 다음과 같다.
Pyongyang is about 400km (to the) north of Seoul.
(평양은 서울에서 약 400킬로미터 북(北)에 있다.)

cf) 접촉의 on
　　On the south of Seoul lies Anyang.
　　(서울 남쪽에 안양이 있다.)
　　Our city is on the shore of Lake Soyang.

(우리 市는 소양호 호반에 접해 있다.)
☞ 이때의 「on」은 호수에 접해있음을 나타낸다.

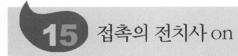

15 접촉의 전치사 on

Ex) Our city is <u>on</u> the shore of Lake Soyang.
☞ 이때의 on은 「접촉」을 나타내는 것으로 市가 호수가에 접하고 있음을 나타낸다. 춘천시의 경우와 같다.

같은 지리상의 예문을 들면 다음과 같다.
<u>On</u> the south of Seoul lies Anyang.
(서울 남쪽에 안양이 있다.)

전치사 <u>on</u>의 기본적인 관념으로서 접촉의 느낌이 내포된다. 따라서 다음과 같은 표현이 가능하다.
There is a fly <u>on</u> the ceiling.
(천정에 파리가 한 마리 있다.) [천정의 밑면에 접해서]

She has a ring <u>on</u> her finger.
(반지를 끼고 있다.)
이 접촉은 평면상의 접촉에도 적용된다. 그 대표적인 예(例)가,
Seoul is <u>on</u> the river Han.(서울은 한강변에 있다.) 이다.
이것은 서울이 한강의 양기슭에 접해서 전개되고 있음을 나타낸다.

The city is <u>on</u> the river. 라고 해도 마찬가지의 의미(혹은 한 쪽 기슭에만 접해 있는 의미)로 받아들여야 한다. 「그 市는 강위에 있다」라고 해석해서는 오역(誤譯)이 된다.

예를 더 들자면,
There were trees <u>on</u> both sides of the street.
(그 거리의 양쪽에 가로수가 있었다.)

Korea faces the East Sea on the east.
(한국은 동쪽으로 동해에 면하고 있다.)

☞ 접촉의 on은 이밖에도 용도가 넓으나, 추상적으로 확대되어 쓰이는 예를 들면 다음
과 같다.

I was on the point of telephoning you.
(막 전화를 걸려던 참이었다.)

Unfortunately he died on the eve of taking over a large business.
(그는 불행하게도 큰 사업을 계승할 참에 죽었다.)

She was on the verge of bursting into tears.
(그녀는 금시라도 울음을 터트릴 것 같았다.)

16 beyond를 이용한 관용어구

beyond belief (믿어지지 않는)
beyond comparison (비교가 되지 않는)
beyond control (힘에 겨운)
beyond comprehension (이해하기 어려운)
beyond description (말로 다 표현할 수 없는)
beyond doubt (의심할 나위 없는)
beyond dispute (논란의 여지가 없는)
beyond expectation (예상외인)
beyond question (말할 나위도 없는)
beyond one's ability (~의 능력을 넘어서는, 벗어나는)
beyond repair (수리할 수 없을 정도로)

Ex) ┌ The scenery was beautiful <u>beyond description</u>.
    ├ The scenery was <u>too</u> beautiful <u>for</u> words.
    ├ The scenery was <u>so</u> beautiful <u>that</u> no words could describe it.
    └ The beauty of the scenery there was <u>beyond description</u>.
    (그 경치는 너무 아름다워서 이루 말로 표현할 수 없었다.)
    (그곳의 풍경은 말로 표현할 수 없이 아름다웠다.)
    The bowl had been shattered <u>beyond repair</u>.
    (그 사발은 수리할 수 없을 정도로 박살났다.)

17 전치사 with

[1] 소유를 나타 낼때 (= with + 목적어 = 관계대명사 + have + 목적어 = having)

Ex) a cup <u>with</u> a broken handle (손잡이가 부서진 컵)
    a coat <u>with</u> two pockets (주머니가 둘 있는 외투)
    a girl <u>with</u> blue eyes (파란 눈의 소녀)

┌ I met a girl <u>with</u> blue eyes.
├ I met a girl <u>who</u> has blue eyes.
└ I met a girl <u>having</u> blue eyes.

┌ He lives in a house <u>with</u> a fine garden.
├ He lives in a house <u>which has</u> a fine garden.
└ He lives in a house <u>having</u> fine garden.

┌ She wears a coat <u>which has</u> two pockets.
├ She wears a coat <u>with</u> two pockets.
└ She wears a coat <u>having</u> two pockets.

* The woman <u>with</u> an angry look in her eyes was with child.
  (눈에 화난 표정을 지닌 그 여인은 임신 중이었다.)

[2] 방·수단을 나타낼 때

☞ 도구나 목적을 지칭할 때 쓰인다.

Ex) I killed the spider <u>with</u> a newspaper.

He was killed <u>with</u> a pistol.

He got what he wanted <u>with</u> flowers.

Write <u>with</u> a pen.

Cut something <u>with</u> a knife.

cf) 동작이나 행동을 나타낼 때는 by를 쓴다.

Ex) I killed the spider <u>by</u> hitting it.

He earns his living <u>by</u> teaching English.

[3] 동반·관계를 나타낼 때

Ex) He live <u>with</u> his parents.
(그는 부모님과 함께 산다.)

I went for a walk <u>with</u> a friend.
(친구와 함께 산책을 나갔다.)

Is there anyone <u>with</u> you?
(누구와 같이 있니?)

[4] 이유·원인을 나타낼 때 (= as, because, because of, owing to)

☞ with가 '이유'를 표시할 때 실제로는 'because'보다는 훨씬 약한 의미를 갖는다.

Ex) silent <u>with</u> shame (부끄러워 말을 못하는)

trembling <u>with</u> fear (공포로 떠는)

shaking <u>with</u> cold (추위에 떠는)

TEST

* 두 문장의 의미가 같아지도록 _____에 적당한 말을 쓰시오.

1. ┌ She could not speak in public with shame.
   └ She could speak in public _____ _____ shame.

2. ┌ With a good education, he can do it with ease.
   └ _____ he has got a good education, he can do it with ease.

3. 다음의 보기에서 밑줄 친 with와 그 의미가 같은 것을 고르시오.

〈보기〉 The beggar fainted <u>with</u> hunger.

① The man <u>with</u> big eyes is my English teacher.

② She has been ill in bed <u>with</u> a bad cold.

③ She went out <u>with</u> a bright smile.

④ He was killed <u>with</u> a pistol.

(정답) 1. because of 2. Because 3. ②

[5] 같은 방법 / 방향, 동시를 나타낼 때

Ex) <u>With</u> the approach of sunset it becomes chilly.
(해질녘이 되면서 싸늘해진다.)

Do you rise <u>with</u> the sun (= at dawn)?
(새벽에 일어나니?)

TEST

* 다음의 밑줄 친 부분을 절로 전환하시오.

1. <u>With the approach of night</u>, the street became hushed.

=> _____.

2. <u>With increase of wisdom</u>, our thought acquires a wider scope.

=> _____.

3. The sense of smell seems to diminish <u>with age</u>.

=> _____.

4. <u>With the coming of darkness</u>, the wind blew harder.

=> _____.

(정답) 1. <u>When(AS) night approached</u>, the street became hushed.
    * hushed = silent
  2. <u>As wisdom increase</u>, our thought acquires a wider scope.
  3. The sense of smell seems to diminish <u>as we grow older</u>.
  4. <u>As it grew darker</u>, the wind blew harder.
    (= The darker it grew, the harder the wind blew)

[6] 간호·소유·책무를 나타낼 때

Ex) Leave the child <u>with</u> its aunt.(= in the care of 간호)
(아이를 숙모에게 맡겨라.)

I have no money <u>with</u> me.(소유)
(가진 돈이 없다.)

It rests <u>with</u> you to decide.(책무)
(결정은 네가 해야 한다.)

[7] 「~에 대하여(관하여)」(= in regard to, concerning, as regards)

Ex) You must be patient <u>with</u> them.
(그들에게 대해서 인내심을 가져야 한다.)

Everybody sympathized <u>with</u> her.
(모두가 그녀를 동정했다.)

What do you want <u>with</u> me?
(나에게 볼일이 뭐냐?)

[8] 「~ 에도 불구하고」(=in spite of, notwithstanding, despite, with all, for all)

Ex) <u>With all</u> her faults he still liked her.
(그녀의 모든 결점에도 불구하고, 그는 여전히 그녀를 좋아했다.)

He failed <u>with</u> the best of intentions to win the sympathy of his pupils.
(학생들의 공감을 사려고 한 최선의 의도에도 불구하고 실패하고 말았다.)

TEST

* _____에 적당한 말을 써 넣으시오.

Though he worked hard, he failed.
Hard _____ he worked, he failed.
_____ ____ his hard work, he failed.
_____ his hard work, he failed.

(정답) As / With(For) All / Despite

제19장
Essential English Grammar

특수 구문(삽입·공통관계 부정·도치·강조·생략)

01 삽입절

Ex) This is, <u>as far as I know</u>, the whole truth.
(이것은 내가 알고 있는 한, 전체의 내막이다.)

He is, <u>as it were</u>, a sleeping lion.
(그는 말하자면 잠자는 사자이다.)

He is, <u>I think</u>, over sixty years of age.
(그는 아마 60세 이상일 것이다.)

He is, <u>I believe</u>, a reliable man.
(그는 믿을만한 사람이라고 믿는다.)

He is the man who <u>I think</u> is very honest.
(그는 내가 매우 정직하다고 생각하는 사람이다.)

02 공통 관계 =〉 [(A + B)x = Ax + Bx], [x(A + B) = xA + xB] (x가 A,B와 공통)

He <u>is not</u> and <u>cannot be</u> <u>what he was</u>.
(A + B) X

He <u>is not</u> <u>what he was</u> and <u>cannot be</u> <u>what he was</u>.
A X + B X
(그는 과거의 그가 아니며 또 그렇게 될 수도 없다.)

<u>A man</u> <u>of virtue</u> and not <u>of wealth</u>, deserves our respect.
X (A + B)

<u>A man</u> <u>of virtue</u> and not <u>a man</u> <u>of wealth</u>, deserves our respect.
X A + X B
(돈 있는 사람이 아니라 덕 있는 사람이 우리의 존경을 받을 가치가 있다.)

03 부분 부정과 전체 부정

☞ 「not. no, never」이 전체를 나타내는 말(all, every, both, always, necessarily, wholly, entirely, completely, quite 등)을 부정할 때 「반드시(모두가) ~이라고는 하지 않다」의 의미로 <u>부분부정</u>이 된다.

전체 긍정	부분 부정	전체 부정
all (셋 이상)	not ~ all (전부가 ~ 한 것은 아니다)	not ~ any (전부 ~ 아니다)
both (둘 다)	not ~ both (둘 다 ~ 는 아니다)	not ~ either ; neither (어느 쪽도 ~ 아니다)
every (전체)	not ~ every (모두가 ~ 인 것은 아니다)	no (모두가 ~ 아니다
always (항상)	not ~ always (반드시 ~ 은 아니다)	never ; not at all (결코 ~ 아니다)

He does <u>not</u> know <u>all</u> of his student.(부분 부정)
He does <u>not</u> know <u>any</u> of his student.(전체 부정)

<u>Both</u> of them are <u>not</u> married.(부분 부정)
<u>Neither</u> of them is married.(전체 부정)

He does <u>not</u> know <u>everything</u> about it.(부분 부정)
He does <u>not</u> know <u>anything</u> about it.(전체 부정)
He knows <u>nothing</u> about it.(전체 부정)

The rich are <u>not always</u> happier than the poor.(부분 부정)
The rich are <u>never</u> happier than the poor.(전체 부정)

He is <u>not altogether</u> honest.(부분 부정)
He is <u>not</u> honest <u>at all</u>.(전체 부정)

I do <u>not quite</u> agree to your plan.(부분 부정)
I do <u>not</u> agree to your plan <u>at all</u>.(전체 부정)

<u>Everybody</u> is <u>not</u> born a gentleman.(부분 부정)
<u>Nobody</u> is born a gentleman.(전체 부정)

<u>Every</u> man can <u>not</u> be a poet(부분 부정)
(= Some can be a poets, but some can not (be poets))
(누구나 다 시인이 될 수 있는 것은 아니다.)
<u>No man</u> can be a poet.(전체 부정)

<u>Both</u> of them are <u>not</u> rich.(부분 부정) => One of them is rich,
and the other is not.
<u>Neither</u> of them is rich.(전체 부정) => Both of them are poor.

<u>All</u> of the students are not present.(부분 부정)
(= Some are present, but some are absent.)
<u>None</u> of students are present.(전체 부정)
(= They are all absent.)

I couldn't understand <u>all</u> of his speech.(부분 부정)
I couldn't understand <u>any</u> of his speech.(전체 부정)

He does <u>not always</u> get up early.(부분 부정)
He <u>never</u> gets up early.(전체 부정)

TEST

* 다음 두 문장의 의미가 같도록 빈 칸에 알맞은 말을 쓰시오.
1. I always carry very little money with me.
   I (   ) carry much money with me.

(정답) seldom

2. ┌ Neither of his parents is alive.
   └ (　　) of his parents are dead.

(정답) Both

3. ┌ Some of them are absent.
   └ Not (　　) of them are present.

(정답) all

4. ┌ He is not quite himself.(그는 거의 제 정신이 아니다.)
   └ (　　) is the matter with him.(그에게 무언가 이상이 있다.)

(정답) Something

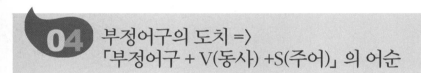

04 부정어구의 도치 =〉 「부정어구 + V(동사) +S(주어)」의 어순

┌ Not a word did he say.
└ He did not say a ward.
 (단 한마디도 그는 말하지 않았다.)

┌ Never have I seen such a sight.
└ I have never seen such a sight.
 (나는 그러한 광경을 결코 본적이 없다.)

┌ Little did I think that he would come back.
└ I little thought that he would come back
 (그가 돌아오리라고는 전혀 생각지도 않았다.)

He cannot do it, ┌ neither ┐ can I.
              └ nor　 ┘

(그도 그것을 할 줄 모르고 나도 할 줄 모른다.)

┌ Not only <u>does he read</u> English, <u>but</u> he speaks it very well.
└ He <u>not only reads</u> English, <u>but</u> he speaks it very well.
 (그는 영어를 읽을 뿐만 아니라 그것을 잘 말한다.)

┌ <u>Never was</u> he asleep.
└ He was <u>never</u> asleep.
 (조금도 그는 자고 있지 않았다.)

05 부사(구)의 도치
=> 부사(구) + V(동사) + S(주어)

┌ <u>Well do I remember</u> the scene.
└ <u>I remember</u> the scene well.
 (나는 그 광경을 잘 기억하고 있다.)

┌ <u>Down came</u> the shower.
└ The shower <u>came down</u>.
 (소나기가 쏟아지기 시작했다.)

┌ <u>Across the river</u> was sailing a boat.
└ A boat was sailing <u>across the river</u>.
 (강을 가로질러 한 척의 배가 항해하고 있었다.)

　　cf) ┌ <u>Down</u> it came.
　　　　 └ It came <u>down</u>.
　　　　　(갑자기 비가 내렸다.)

　　☞ 주어가 가벼운 뜻의 경우 어순 => 「부사(구) + 대명사 주어 + V(동사)」
┌ <u>Only slowly did he</u> understand it.
└ He understood it <u>only slowly</u>.

(간신히 그는 그것을 알았다.)

06 강조의 조동사 (동사의 강조)
=> Do + 동사원형 (실제로, 정말로, 반드시)

Ex) I do hope you will not be angry.
(화를 내지 않기를 정말로 바란다.)

cf) I hope you will not be angry.
(화를 내지 않기를 바란다.)

Do come here.
(반드시 이리 오너라.)

cf) Come here.
(이리 오너라.)

Who did break the window?
(도대체 누가 그 창문을 깨뜨렸단 말이냐?)

cf) Who broken the window?
(누가 창문을 깨뜨렸느냐?)

07 very에 의한 강조 (명사 강조)
=> very + 명사 (바로 그, ~ 조차(even))

Ex) He is the very man that I want.
(그는 내가 원하는 바로 그 사람이다.)

He came in at that very moment.
(그는 바로 그때 들어 왔다.)

The very idea of it makes me sad.
(그것을 생각만 해도 슬퍼진다.) => even의 뜻

08 의문사가 있는 의문문의 it ~ that 강조구문 (의문사 + is it that ~한다)

[
Why do other nations remain free and independent?
Why is it that other nations remain free and independent?
]

[
How did you escape from the fort?
How was it that you escaped from the fort?
]

[
When will you go abroad?
When is it that you will go abroad?
]

[
What did you do yesterday?
What was it that you did yesterday?
]

[
Where are you going?
where is it that you are going?
]

09 생략 =〉 격언, 게시, 광고, 관용적 표현

[
Good morning
I wish you a good morning.
]

[
Not for sale. (비매품)
This is not for sale.
]

[
Wet Paint. (칠 주의)
Beware of the wet paint.
]

No Parking.(주차금지)
No parking is allowed(here).

One way.(일방통행)
Drive one way.

Out of sight, out of mind.
If one is <u>out of sight</u>, one is <u>out of mind</u>.
(사람은 자주 만나지 않으면 정이 멀어진다.)

10 게시문구(揭示文句:Notices)

Watch Your Step 발밑 주의	Sold 팔렸음
Gentlemen 남자용 화장실	Ladies 부인용 화장실
Lavatory 화장실(英)	Toilet 화장실(美)
Keep Off 가까이 오지 마시오.	No Parking 주차금지
Exit ; Way Out 출구(出口)	In Operation 영업중
Business Hours: 10a.m.−6p.m.	업무시간 (10시 − 6시)
Railroad Crossing: Stop, Look,	Listen 기차길 횡단주의
Shoes Off 신발을 벗으시오.	Not for Sale 비매품
Emergency Exit 비상구	Beware of Fire 불조심
Opened Today 금일 개점	Closed Today 금일 휴업
All Sold Out Today 금일분 매진	One Way Only 일방통행
Entrance ; Way In 입구	Motor Pool 자동차 정차장
No Visitors Allowed 방문객 사절	Go Slow ; Slow Down 서행(徐行)
Beware of Pickpockets 소매치기 주의	Trash ; Waste Paper Basket 휴지통
Shut the Door after You ⎤ 개방 엄금 Not to Be Left Open ⎦	Rooms to Let (英) ⎤ 셋방 있음 Rooms for Rent (美) ⎦
House to Let 셋집 있음	One Side Only 한쪽길만 통행하시오.
Danger 위험	No Smoking 금연

Business Hours 근무 시간
Out of Order 고장
Call Box (英)
Telephone Booth (美)] 공중 전화
Fit for Drinking 음료수
Admission Free 입장 무료
Wet Paint 페인트(칠)주의
Not in Use 사용 정지
Under Repair 수리중
Off Limits 출입 금지, 접근 금지
No U Turn 회전 금지
For Sale 매물(賣物)
Handle With Care 조심히 다루시오.
Inquiry ; Information Office 안내소, 접수구
Keep Off the Grass 잔디밭에 들어가지 마시오.
Kindly Refrain from Smoking 흡연을 삼가시오.
No Admittance Except on Business 무용자 출입금지
Keep Out From Driver's Seat 운전대에 들어오지 마시오.

Under Construction 공사중
Fragile 깨지기 쉬운 물건
Don't Disturb 면회 사절
Keep to the Left 좌측통행
Unfit for Drinking 마시지 마시오.
Main Entrance 앞 현관
No Left Turn 좌측으로 돌아가지 마시오.
No Nuisance 소변 엄금
Speed Limit 속도 제한
No Upside Down 뒤집어엎지 마시오.
Hands Off 손대지 마시오.
Don't Spit 침을 뱉지 마시오.
No Thoroughfare 길이 막힘, 통행 금지
No Right Turn 우측으로 돌지 마시오.

〈Reading Signs in English〉

제20장
Essential English Grammar

무생물 주어
(物主構文)

01 생물 주어(人主構文)와 무생물 주어(物主構文)

☞ 우리 말은 사람이나 생물을 주어로 하는데, 영어에서는 흔히 무생물을 주어로 하는 수가 있다. 이것을 「무생물 주어(物主 構文)」이라고 하며, 「조건, 양보, 이유, 방법, 시간」을 나타내는 「부사어구」만이 「무생물 주어」로 사용 가능하다.

[1] 생물(사람) 주어 + come / reach ~ 부사어구
     무생물 주어 + bring + 목적격(사람) ~

He <u>has come</u> here on business.
Business <u>has brought</u> him here.

☞ 명사나 대명사 앞에 전치사가 붙으면 주어, 목적어, 보어가 될 수 없으므로 전치사는 생략한다.

When she heard the cry, she <u>came to</u> the spot.
The cry <u>brought</u> her to the spot.

We walked ten minutes, and <u>came to</u> the station.
After ten minutes' walk, we <u>came to</u> the station.
Ten minutes' walk <u>brought</u> us to the station.

[2] 생물(사람) 주어 + go / get to ~ 부사어구
     무생물 주어 + take + 목적격(사람) ~

<u>I went</u> to Seoul on commercial business.
Commercial business <u>took</u> me to Seoul.

We rode in a bus for an hour, and <u>got to</u> the park.
After an hour's bus ride, we <u>got to</u> the park.
An hour's bus ride <u>took</u> us to the park.
It took us an hour to get to the park.
It took an hour for us to get to the park.

[3] ┌ 생물(사람) 주어 + have / get / derive ~ 부사어구 ┐
    └ 무생물 주어 + give + 목적격(사람) ~   ┘

┌ I <u>have</u> a good appetite after a short walk.
└ A short walk <u>gives</u> me a good appetite.

┌ We <u>get</u> wisdom from books.
└ Books <u>gives</u> us wisdom.

┌ We can <u>derive</u> great pleasure from books.
└ Books <u>gives</u> us great pleasure.

[4] ┌ 생물(사람) 주어 + can / be able to + V(동사)~ 부사어구 ┐
    └ 무생물 주어 + enable / make it possible for + 목적격(사람) + to부정사 ~ ┘

┌ People <u>can</u> travel through the air <u>by airplanes</u>.
│ Airplanes <u>enable</u> people <u>to travel</u> through the air.
└ Airplanes <u>make it possible for</u> people <u>to travel</u> through the air.
(사람들은 비행기를 타고 하늘을 여행할 수 있다.)

┌ People <u>can</u> travel fast <u>thanks to airplanes</u>.
│ Airplanes <u>enable</u> people <u>to travel</u> fast.
└ Airplanes <u>make it possible for</u> people <u>to travel</u> fast.
(사람들은 비행기 덕택에 빠르게 여행할 수 있다.)

┌ We <u>can</u> observe the stars <u>by means of the telescope</u>.
│ The telescope <u>enables</u> us <u>to observe</u> the stars.
└ The telescope <u>makes it possible for</u> us <u>to observe</u> the stars.
(우리는 망원경 덕택에 별을 관찰할 수 있다.)

[5]┌ 생물(사람) 주어 + cannot + V(동사) ~ 부사어구
 │   ┌ disable ┐
 │   ├ prevent │
 │   ├ keep   │
 ├ 무생물 주어 + ├ stop   │ + 목적격(사람) + from ~ ing
 │   ├ prohibit │
 │   ├ hinder │
 │   └ restrain ┘
 ├ 무생물 주어 + make it impossible for + 목적격(사람) + to부정사
 └ 무생물 주어 + forbid + 목적격(사람) + to부정사

┌ He couldn't continue his study due to(owing to) his poverty.
├ His poverty disabled him from continuing his study.
└ His poverty made it impossible for him to continue his study.
(그는 가난 때문에 공부를 계속할 수 없었다.)

┌ She couldn't go out because of(owing to) her illness.
├ Her illness has disabled her from going out.
├ Her illness has made it impossible for her to go out.
└ Her illness has forbidden her to go out.
(그녀는 병 때문에 나갈 수가 없었다.)

┌ Her marriage did not keep her from taking part in politics.
└ She could take part in politics in spite of her marriage.
(그녀는 결혼에도 불구하고 정치에 참여할 수 있었다.)

[6]┌ 생물(사람) 주어 + must / have to + V(동사) ~ 부사어구
  └ 무생물 주어 + force / compel / oblige + 목적격(사람) + to부정사~

┌ He had to put off his departure because of(owing to) rain.
└ The rain forced him to put off his departure.
(그는 비 때문에 출발을 연기해야만 했다.)

[7] ┌ Why + 조동사 + 주어 + 동사~
   ├ What + 사역동사(make / let) + 목적격(사람) + V(동사) ~
   └ What + 사역동사(cause) + 목적격(사람) + to 부정사 ~

┌ Why do you think so?
└ What makes you think so?

┌ Why did he get so angry?
└ What made him get so angry?

┌ How did he become so popular?
└ What made him become so popular?

┌ Why did you come to Seoul?
└ What brought you to Seoul?

┌ Why couldn't he go to school?
└ What prevented him (from) going to school?

┌ Why did you wait so long?
└ What kept you waiting so long?

┌ How could you have done that much work?
└ What enabled you to have done that much work?

[8] ┌ 이유 부사구 또는 이유 부사절
   └ 무생물 주어 + make / cause / drive + 목적격(사람) + to부정사/형용사/P.P.

┌ He got so angry because they laughed.
└ The laughter made him get angry.

┌ As his son died, he went almost mad.
├ Because of his son's dead, he went almost mad.
└ His son's death made(drove) him almost mad.

[9] 무생물 주어가 조건을 나타낼 때

A closer examination of it will reveal the fact.
If you examine it more closely, it will reveal the fact.
(그것을 좀 더 세밀히 조사하면 사실이 드러날 것이다.)

A glance at the map will show you the way to the airport.
If you glanced at the map, you will find(see) the way to the airport.
(그 지도를 힐끗 본다면, 공항으로 가는 길을 알 수 있을 것이다.)

If he had attended the party, it would have encouraged them.
His attendance at the party would have encouraged them.
(만약 그가 그 파티에 참석했다면, 그들에게는 큰 격려가 되었을 것이다.)

This medicine will make you feel better.
If you take this medicine, you will feel better.
(만약 이 약을 먹는다면, 좀 나아질 것이다.)

This path will lead you to the house.
If you go along this path, you will get to the house.
(이 길을 따라간다면, 그 집에 도달할 것이다.)

A moment's thought will make it clear.
If you think for a moment, it will be clear.
(잠깐만 생각한다면, 분명해 질 것이다.)

[10] 무생물 주어가 양보를 나타낼 때

No amount of wealth can satisfy him.
However wealthy he may be, he cannot be satisfied.
(그가 아무리 부자라고 해도, 만족할 수는 없다.)

His hard work has brought him little money.
He has got little money in spite of his hard work.
He has got little money even though he had worked hard.
(그는 열심히 일했음에도 불구하고, 돈을 별로 받지 못했다.)

TEST

* 다음의 두 문장의 의미가 같아지도록 빈 칸에 적당한 말을 쓰시오.

Even a superficial glance at the history of science and invention during the past two centuries makes it difficult for us to doubt that progress is one of the laws of human life.

=> _____ _____ we _____ a glance at the history of science and invention during the past two centuries, it is _____ _____ _____ to doubt that progress is one of the laws of human life.

(정답) Even if(Though), have, difficult, for, us.
[전문 해석] 비록 지난 2세기 동안의 과학과 발명의 역사를 일견한다할지라도, 진보가 인간 삶의 법칙중 하나라는 사실을 의심하기 어렵다.

[11] 생물(사람) + see / know + ~ 부사어구
무생물 주어 + show / tell / find / reveal + 목적격(사람) ~

The fact shows (us) that he is innocent.
From this fact we know that he is innocent.
According to the fact, we know that he is innocent.
(그 사실에 따르면, 그는 무죄다.)

제21장
Essential English Grammar

병렬(평행) 구조
(Parallel Structure or Parallelism)

01 병렬(평행) 구조(Parallel Structure or Parallelism)

☞ 「병렬 구조」란 접속사나 comma에 의하여 단어(word), 구(句:phrase), 절(節:sentence)이 병렬로 연결될 때 그 문법적 구조나 형태를 같게 하는 문장 기법을 말한다. 즉 A and B, A but B, A or B, either A or B, neither A nor B, A nor B, not A but B, both A and B 일 때 「A와 B」는 동일한 품사나 동일한 문법적인 구조로 이루어 져야 한다. 즉 A가 명사면 B도 명사, A가 형용사면 B도 형용사, A가 부정사 면 B도 부정사, A가 절이면 B도 절이어야 한다.

Ex) Jennifer raised her hand <u>and</u> asked a question.
　　(제니퍼는 손을 들어 질문을 했다.)

　　She is beautiful <u>but</u> foolish.
　　(그녀는 아름답지만 어리석다.)

　　Shall I call you, <u>or</u> will you call me?
　　(제가 전화를 걸까요, 그렇지 않으면 전화를 해주시겠습니까?)

　　You are <u>either</u> guilty or innocent.
　　(너는 유죄이거나 무죄이다.)

　　He <u>nor</u> I was there.
　　(그도 나도 거기 없었다.)

　　<u>Neither</u> Father <u>nor</u> Mother is at home.
　　(아버지도 집에 안 계시고 어머니도 집에 안 계십니다.)

1 다음 밑줄 친 부분 중 어색한 것이 있다면 그 부분은?

<u>When</u> free at home, my sister <u>likes</u> <u>to read</u>, to sing, and <u>cooking</u>.
　(A)　　　　　　　　　　　　　　(B)　(C)　　　　　　　　　(D)

① 어색한 부분 없음 ② (A) ③ (B) ④ (C) ⑤ (D)

(정답) ⑤

☞ 윗글에서 (A)는 when (she is) free at home 이므로 맞는 문장이며, like 의 목적어는 「to read, to sing, and cooking」이나 이 세가지의 문법적인 성분이 같은

것이라야 하므로, 즉 같은 「to 부정사」이어야 하므로 (D)의 「cooking」은 「to cook」으로 고쳐써야 한다. 따라서 정답은 ⑤가 된다.

(전문 해석)

내 누이는 집에서 시간이 있을 때면 독서를 하고, 노래 부르고, 요리하는 것을 좋아한다.

2 다음 밑줄 친 부분 중 어색한 것이 있다면 그 부분은?

On New Year's Day, most Korean go to a temple or Church,
    (A)   (B)

visiting friends, or relax around the house.
    (C)   (D)

① 어색한 부분 없음 ② (A) ③ (B) ④ (C) ⑤ (D)

(정답) ④

☞ 윗글의 주어는 「most Korean」이며 술어 동사는 「go, visit, relax」이며, 이들은 등위 접속사(and, or)로 연결되어 있으므로 문법적인 성분이 같아야 한다. 따라서 (C)의 「visiting」은 「visit」로 고쳐 써야 한다.

◀ NOTES ▶

＊New Year's Day 설날 ＊Korean 한국인 ＊temple 사원, 절 ＊relax 편히 쉬다 ＊around ~주변에

(전문 해석)

새해 첫날 대부분의 한국인들은 절이나 교회에 가거나 친구들을 만나고, 또는 집 주변에서 편안히 쉰다.

3 다음 밑줄 친 부분 중 어색한 것이 있다면 그 부분은?

If we finish all of our business as planned, Jennifer and me
    (A)   (B)   (C)

will leave for New York on Monday morning.
    (D)

① 어색한 부분 없음 ② (A) ③ (B) ④ (C) ⑤ (D)

(정답) ④

☞ 밑줄 친 (C)의 「Jennifer and me」는 「will leave…」의 주어이면서 등위 접속사 「and」로 연결되어 있으므로 목적격 「me」가 아니라 주격 「I」가 되어야 한다. 따라서 정답은 ④가 된다.

◀ NOTES ▶

∗business 일, 사업 ∗as (we) planned 계획한대로 ∗leave for ~를 향해 떠나다

(전문 해석)
만일 우리가 우리의 일을 계획대로 끝낸다면, 제니퍼와 나는 월요일 아침 뉴욕으로 떠날 것이다.

4 다음 밑줄 친 부분 중 어색한 것이 있다면 그 부분은?

> Venus <u>approaches</u> the Earth <u>more closely</u> <u>than</u> any other
>   (A)   (B)   (C)
> <u>planet is</u>.
> (D)

① 어색한 부분 없음 ② (A) ③ (B) ④ (C) ⑤ (D)

(정답) ⑤

☞ 윗글은 「more than」으로 연결되는 2개의 문장구조가 같아야 하므로, 앞의 주어, 동사 「Venus approaches」처럼 (D)의 「planet is」는 「planet (does)」(이 때의 does는 approaches를 받음)로 고쳐 써야 한다.

◀ NOTES ▶

∗Venus 금성 ∗approach 다가오다, 접근하다 ∗Earth 지구 ∗closely 가까이, 밀접하게 ∗planet 행성, 혹성

(전문 해석)
금성은 그 어떤 행성보다 지구에 가장 가까이 접근해 있다.

5 다음 밑줄 친 부분 중 어색한 것이 있다면 그 부분은?

> Swimming is a <u>more strenuous</u> <u>daily exercise</u> <u>than</u> <u>to walk</u>.
>   (A)   (B)   (C) (D)

① 어색한 부분 없음 ② (A) ③ (B) ④ (C) ⑤ (D)

(정답) ⑤

☞ 윗글은 「more than」으로 연결되어 있으므로, 비교되는 것끼리는 서로 문장구조가 같아야 하므로 앞의 주어 「swimming」 처럼 (D)의 「to walk」도 「walking」으로 고쳐 써야 한다.

◀ NOTES ▶

＊a more = very ＊strenuous 활발한, 격렬한, 격심한 ＊daily 일상적인
＊exercise 운동

(전문 해석)
수영은 걷는 것보다 매우 격렬한 일상적인 운동이다.

6 다음 밑줄 친 부분 중 어색한 것이 있다면 그 부분은?

Jack likes all sports, tennis, basketball, football, and etc.
　　 (A) 　　 (B) 　　　　　　　 (C) 　　 (D)

① 어색한 부분 없음 ② (A) ③ (B) ④ (C) ⑤ (D)

(정답) ⑤

☞ 「따위」의 뜻으로 「등등(等等)」의 영문 표현으로는 「and the like; and so forth (on); and what not; and all that; and all the like (the rest); and such like (things); etc.」등이 있다. 따라서 위의 밑줄 친 (D)의 etc.(=et cetera)는 and와 함께 쓰이지 않으므로 즉 「et cetera」에서 「et」는 「and」의 의미이므로 「and」를 없애야 한다.

◀ NOTES ▶

＊etc 기타 등등(=and so forth, and so on, and the like, and what not)

(전문 해석)
잭은 테니스, 농구, 축구 등등 모든 스포츠를 좋아 한다.

제22장
Essential English Grammar

기타
(Miscellany) - (1)

방향 표시법 (영어에서는 南, 北이 앞에 오며, 東, 西가 뒤에 온다)

[1] northeast 「北東」 northwest 「北西」 southeast 「南東」
southwest 「南西」

cf) eastnorth (X) westnorth (X) eastsouth (X) westsouth (X)

[2] east-north-east 「東北東」 west-north-west 「西北西」
east-south-east 「東南東」 west-south-west 「西南西」

☞ 이 경우에는 east, west가 앞에 올 수 있으며 그 뒤에 연결되는 것은 [1]항에 준해야
한다. 따라서 「east – east – north」나 「west – west – south」등으로 쓰지 못한다.

[3] north-north-east (O) south-south-east (O)
north-east-north (X) south-east-south (X)

 인칭 대명사의 배열법

[1] 단수인 경우 : 「2인칭 + 3인칭 + 1인칭」의 순서
Ex) You and I He and I You and he You, he and I You, John,
and I / me

☞ 인칭대명사가 겹칠 때는 관례적으로 politeness(공손함)를 나타내기 위해 제1요소
로 'you'가 놓이며, 'I'는 마지막 요소로 쓰인다.

[2] 복수인 경우 : 「1인칭 + 2인칭 + 3인칭」의 순서
Ex) You and they We and you We and they We, you, and they

[3] he와 she를 같이 쓸 때에는 he를 앞에 둔다.
Ex) He and she
cf) 실제에 있어서는 복수형을 쓰는 경우가 많다.
Ex) You and I = we He and I = we You and he = you He and she = they

[4] 소유격일 때의 제1요소 : 소유격의 경우에는 his가 제1요소인 것이 관례이다.

Her or his friends(X) / His or her friends(O)

Our and my work(X) / His and my work(O)

☞ 구어체의 경우에도 역시 politeness(공손함)를 위해 다음과 같은 표현을 하는 것이 관례이다.

Your, his, and my reports are all here.

Those are your and my books.

[5] 주어가 아닌 경우의 어순 : 주어가 아닌 경우에는 me and ~ 의 형을 쓰기도 한다.

It is easy to please me and my wife.

① This(book) and that book; these (chairs) and those chairs; etc.

② This book and those; that method and the other; his friends and mine; your proposals and other; your work and his; many guests or few; her idea and John's; much satisfaction or little; etc.

③ This and several other arguments were presented.

④ These and many other men have managed it.

TEST

* 다음의 빈 칸에 가장 적절한 것은?

1. Whom do you know better, _____?

① her or his friends   ② his or her friends

③ his friends of her   ④ her or his

(정답) ②

☞ 소유격의 경우, 제1요소는 his다.

따라서 ③은 his friends or hers로 고쳐 써야 한다.

cf) 영국 영어에서는 선택 의문문의 경우, which를 쓰지만 미국 영어에서는 who/whom을 씀.

(전문해석)

당신은 그의 친구들과 그녀의 친구들 중에 어느 쪽을 더 잘 압니까?

2. She'd like _____ reports printed immediately.

 ① his, yours and mine   ② your, his and my

 ③ his, your and my   ④ my, your and his

(정답) ②

☞ 주어진 글에 reports가 있으므로 소유격을 필요로 한다.

   그리고 1, 2, 3인칭이 동시에 나올 경우, 제1요소는 you/your, 마지막 요소는
   I/my/me이다.

(전문 해석)

그녀는 당신의 리포트와 그의 리포트 그리고 나의 리포트가 즉각
프린트되기를 바란다.

03 Story와 Floor

☞ story와 floor는 같은 뜻의 단어로 건물의 「층(層)」수(數)를 나타내는데 쓴다. floor
가 영국·미국 양쪽에 두루 쓰이는 데 비해, story의 경우 미국에서는 story라고 쓰
고, 영국에서는 storey라 쓴다. 층계를 따질 때 floor를 쓰면 영국과 미국의 경우가
좀 다르다. 즉, 영국에서는 1층을 「ground floor」라 하고 2층을 「1st floor」라고 하
는 반면, 미국에서는 1층이 바로 「1st floor」부터 시작된다. 그러나 「story」를 쓰면
「ground story」는 없으므로 영국과 미국이 일치한다.

England & America	England	America
3rd story	2nd floor (3층)	3rd floor (3층)
2nd story	1st floor (2층)	2nd floor (2층)
1st story	ground floor (1층)	1st floor (1층)
(지하실)	basement (지하실)	basement (지하실)

☞ 「means」는 복수일 때 「수단, 방법, 재산, 수입」의 의미를 갖는다.

[1] He used every <u>means</u> imaginable.
(그는 모든 상상할 수 있는 수단을 다 썼다.)

[2] English is the <u>means</u> of communication.
(영어는 의사소통의 수단이다.)

[3] He is a man of <u>means</u>.
(그는 재산가이다.)

[4] He lives on his own <u>means</u>.
(그는 자신의 수입으로 생활한다.)

[5] as far as one's <u>means</u> allow.
(~의 재력이 허용하는 한)

[6] by any <u>means</u>
(아무리 해도, 도무지)

[7] by fair <u>means</u> or foul
(무슨 일이 있어도, 꼭)

[8] by <u>means</u> of
(~에 의하여, ~으로 (= through = with the help of))

[9] by no (manner of) <u>means</u> = not by any (manner of) means
(결코 ~하지 않다(= never, anything but, not at all))

[10] by some means or other
(이러저러해서)

[11] live within [beyond, above] one's means
(분수에 맞게 [넘치게/지나치게] 살다)

Ex) Let us all be happy and <u>live within our means</u>, even if we have
to borrow the money to do it with. – Artemus Ward –
(모두 행복하고 신분에 맞는 생활을 하자. 비록 그러기 위해서 돈을 꿔야만 하
더라도.)

05 Yes, No의 응답에서 주의할 사항

☞ 부정의문문 및 부정명령문의 응답에서 Yes와 No의 해석이 우리말과 다르므로 주의해
야 한다. 부정의문이든 긍정의문이든 상관없이 그 답의 내용이 긍정이면 Yes,로 부정이
면 No로 답하면 된다. 즉 「Are you hungry?」에 대한 답이든 「Aren't you hungry?」
에 대한 답이든 배가 고프면 「Yes, I am」이 되고 배가 고프지 않으면 「No, I am not」
이 되는 것이다. 그러므로 누가 「Aren't you hungry?」라고 물으면 그것은 「Are you
hungry?」로 물은거나 다름없다고 생각하고 답하면 아무런 착오가 없게 된다.

〈Yes와 No〉
⌈ Aren't you hungry? (배가 안 고프십니까?)
⌊ Yes, I am. (아니오, 배가 고픕니다.)

⌈ Don't forget to lock the room.
│ (문 잠그는 것을 잊지 마세요.)
⌊ No, I won't. (네, 잊지 않겠습니다.)

    cf) ⌈ Do you think it will stop raining? (비가 멎을 거라고 생각합니까?)
        ├ I hope so. (그렇게 되길 바랍니다.)
        ⌊ I'm afraid not. (안됐지만 그렇지 못할 것 같습니다.)

* (1~2) 빈 칸에 들어갈 알맞은 것을 고르시오.

1. A : Don't forget to mail the letter on your way.

   B : _____.

① No, I'm not   ② Yes, I could

③ No, I won't   ④ Yes, I would

(정답) ③

2. A : Don't you know where the Baltic Sea is?

   B : _____.

① Yes, I don't know. Could you tell me where it is?

② No, I know very well where it is.

③ Yes, but not exactly. Isn't it somewhere in the south?

④ No, I sailed on it five years ago.

(정답) ③

3. 응답으로 적당하지 <u>못한</u> 것은?

   Doesn't he like to have a rest?

① No, he likes to.   ② Yes, he likes to.

③ Yes, he likes to.   ④ No, he doesn't.

(정답) ①

4. 밑줄 친 부분과 뜻이 같은 것은?

   "Can you come next week?"

   "I am afraid <u>not</u>."

① I am afraid that I cannot come.

② I am not afraid that I cannot come.

③ I am afraid that I can come.

④ I am not afraid whether I can come or not.

(정답) ①

5. 다음 밑줄 친 우리말을 영어로 바르게 옮긴 것은?

A : Don't forget to post the letter on your way to school.

B : <u>예, 잊지 않겠습니다.</u>

① No, I won't   ② Yes, I will

③ No, I forget   ④ Yes, I won't

(정답) ①

06 실수하기 쉬운 표현

[1] 가격은 <u>얼마입니까?</u>

- <u>How much</u> is the price? (X)
- <u>What</u> is the price? (O)
- <u>How much</u> is it? (O)
- <u>How much</u> do I owe you? (O)

[2] 그는 <u>하루에</u> 2시간 공부한다.

- He studies two hours <u>in a day</u>. (X)
- He studies two hours <u>a day</u>. (O)

     cf) There are 24 hours in a day.

☞ 부정 관사(a, an)가 per(~에 대해)의 의미로 사용될 때 그 앞에 전치사 in을 붙여서는 안된다.

[3] 그녀는 <u>시골에서</u> 살고 있다.

- She lives in <u>a country</u>. (X)
- She lives in <u>the country</u>. (O)

     ☞ country는 「시골」의 의미로 사용될 때는 정관사를 붙인다.

[4] 당신으로부터 편지를 받고 기뻤다.

- <u>It was happy</u> to hear from you. (X)
- <u>I was happy</u> to hear from you. (O)

☞ 「happy, glad, pleases, sorry, afraid」 등의 형용사는 「사람」을 주어로 해서 사용해야 하는 형용사이다.

 ## 07 수사(數詞)와 관련된 but

[1] first but one (two, three)
  하나(둘, 셋)건너 첫째.

[2] next but one (two, three)
  하나(둘,셋)건너 다음.

[3] last but one (two, three)
  끝에서 둘(셋, 넷)째. (or 끝에서 두 번째, 세 번째, 네 번째)

Take <u>the next turning but one</u> on your left
  (= the second turning)
(왼쪽에서 두 번째 모퉁이를 돌아라.)

I live in <u>the last house but two</u> in this street.
    (= the third house from the end)
(이 거리의 끝에서 세 번째 집에서 살고 있다.)

Smith <u>was the last but one</u> to arrive.
    (= second to last)
(스미스는 꼴찌에서 두 번째로 도착했다.)

I was <u>next but one</u> in the <u>queue</u> [kjuː] to see the doctor.
    (= not the next one, but the one after)
(나는 의사의 진찰을 받기 위해서 서 있는 줄에서 한 사람 건너 다음 차례에 있다.)

☞ 다음 차례가 아니라 다음 다음 차례였다는 뜻임.

My friend Jackie lives <u>next door but one</u>.
(= two house from me)
(내 친구 재키는 한 집 건너 다음 집에 산다.)
☞ 내 집에서 두 집째라는 뜻임.

I was <u>last but one</u> in the race yesterday.
(= the one before the last)
(나는 어제 경주에서 거꾸로 두 번째였다.)
☞ 맨 마지막 바로 앞, 꼴찌에서 두 번째라는 뜻임.

[4] second to none 최고의(= the best)
I want to be <u>second to none</u> in English.(= the best)
(영어에서 제 1인자가 되고 싶다.)
 I am <u>second to none</u> as far as the computer is concerned.(= the best)
(나는 컴퓨터에 관한 한 누구에게도 뒤지지 않는다.)

TEST

* (1~9) 다음 영어를 우리말로 옮기시오.

1. America is <u>second to none</u> in natural resources.
   (   )

2. Don't give it <u>a second thought</u>.
   (   )

3. I met him <u>a second time</u>.
   (   )

4. <u>Ten to one</u> he will win.
   (   )

5. Saudi Arabia's oil reserves are <u>second only to</u> those of Kuwait.
   (   )

6. Smith was <u>the last but one</u> to arrive.
   (   )

7. Take <u>the next turning but one</u> on your left.

(   )

8. I live in <u>the last house but two</u> in the street.

(   )

9. _____ 의 부분과 의미가 같은 것은?

I planned to go to Pusan by car.

But, <u>on second thoughts</u>, I went there by bus.

① changing my mind   ② at second hand   ③ by no means

(정답) 1. 미국은 천연 자원에 있어서 첫째이다.

    2. 그것을 다시는 생각하지 마라.

    3. 나는 그를 또다시 만났다.(=again)

    4. 십중 팔구 그가 이길 것이다.(=In nine cases out of ten)

    5. 사우디 아라비아의 석유 매장량은 쿠웨이트 다음으로 첫째다.

    6. Smith는 꼴찌에서 두번째로 도착했다.(=second to last)

    7. 왼쪽에서 두번째 모퉁이를 돌아라.(=the second turning)

    8. 이 거리의 끝에서 세번째 집에 살고 있다.

      (=the third house from the end)

    9. ① (= after further consideration : 더 생각한 후에)

08 숫자가 들어가는 관용 표현

Let's take ten. (10분간 휴식하자)

Give me five. (악수하자)

by halves (불완전하게 = incompletely)

ten to one(십중팔구, 거의 틀림없이 = In nine cases out of ten)

by twos and threes (삼삼오오)

a thousand to one (거의 절대적인 일, 틀림없이)

on the double (구보로, 속히)

go fifty-fifty (반반씩 나누다)

take the fifth (질문에 대답하지 않다)

six of one and half a dozen of the other (오십보 백보)

Give him an inch, and he'll take a mile. (그의 욕심은 끝이 없다.)

count to ten (신중을 기하다)

give a second thought (다시 생각하다)

by the thousands (무수히)

a second time (다시 = again)

by the hundreds (몇 백이나, 수많이)

second to none (첫째이다 = the best)

09 미국의 돈(American Money)

[1] 동전(銅錢) 및 은전(銀錢) : coin

⌐ penny – 1 cent (구리의 합금)

├ nickel – 5 cent (니켈과 구리의 합금)

├ dime – 10 cents (구리, 니켈의 합금)

├ quarter – 25 cents (구리와 니켈의 합금) 1/4弗로서 팁(tip)의 기본
  단위로 되어 있다.

├ half-dollar – 50 cents (구리와 니켈의 합금)

└ one-dollar – 100 cents. 보통「silver dollar」라고 한다.(주로 기념
  주화)

[2] 지폐(bank note / bill)

☞ 지폐(note = bill)는「bank note」혹은 뒷면이 green 색깔이라고 해서「green back」이라고도 하나 정확히 말하여「Federal Reserve Note」라고 부른다. 미국의 달러지폐는 금액의 대소(大小)에 관계없이 다 크기와 색깔이 똑같기 때문에 돈을 주고받을 때는 혼동하지 않도록 주의해야 한다.

10 시간을 묻는 표현

[1] 시간을 물을 때 흔히「What time is it?」로 묻는다.「지금 몇 시입니까?」의 뜻이다.

「What time is it?」대신에「What is the time?」도 쓰인다.

시간을 묻고 응답할 때의 요령은 다음과 같다.

① 「O분」까지를 말하지 않고「X시」만을 말할 때는 시간을 나타내는 기수(숫자)를 말하고 o' clock을 붙이면 된다.

What time is it? 혹은 What is the time? (몇 시입니까?)

- It is <u>just</u> eight o' clock. (정각 8시입니다.)
- It is <u>about</u> eleven o' clock. (약 11시쯤 됩니다.)

「지금 몇 시입니까?」

- Excuse me, would you please tell me <u>the time</u>?
- Could you tell me <u>the time</u>?
- May I ask you <u>the time</u>?
- What time do you have now?
- What time is it now?
- What time do you make it?
- Do you have <u>the time</u>?
- What time have you got?
- What time does your watch say?
- What time is it by your watch?
- Do you have any idea what time it is now?

「정각 10시 입니다?」

It's <u>just</u> ten (o' clock).

It's ten (o' clock) <u>sharp</u>.

It's ten (o' clock) <u>on the dot</u>.

It's <u>exactly</u> ten (o' clock).

It's <u>precisely</u> ten (o' clock).

② 「X시 O분」 즉, 「O분이 지났다」를 말할 때는 「past + 시간」 앞에 「O 분」을 앞에 써서 나타낸다. past는 「지난」의 뜻이다.

「What time is it?」

It is ten <u>past</u> two. (2시 10분이다.)

It is twenty <u>past</u> three. (3시 20분이다.)

It's ten (minutes) <u>past</u> seven.

It's ten (minutes) <u>after</u> seven.

It's seven ten.

(지금 시각은 7시 10분 입니다.)

③ 「X시 O분전」 즉 「X시까지는 O분이 남았다」의 뜻으로 나타낼 때는 「O분 + to + 시간」의 표현을 빌어 말한다.

「What time is it?」

It is ten <u>to</u> twelve. (12시 10분 전이다.)

It is five <u>to</u> two. (2시 5분 전이다.)

It's ten (minutes) <u>to</u> seven.

It's ten (minutes) <u>before</u> seven.

It's ten (minutes) <u>of</u> seven. (가끔 사용)

It's ten (minutes) <u>till</u> seven. (가끔 사용)

(지금 시각은 7시 10분 전(前) 입니다.)

④ 우리말과 다르게 영어는 15분을 a quarter(1/4을 뜻함 : 60분이 한 시간이므로 15분은 1/4임), 30분은 half(1/2로 나타냄 : 30분은 60 분의 1/2)를 써서 나타낸다.

It is a quarter <u>past</u> two.(2시 15분이다.)

It is a quarter <u>to</u> two. (2시 15분 전이다.)

It is a half <u>past</u> two. (2시 30분이다.)

It's (a) quarter <u>after</u> seven. (7시 15분이다.)

It's (a) quarter <u>to</u> ten. (10시 15분 전이다.)

└ It's half <u>past</u> eight. (8시 30분이다.)

⑤ 그러나 15분, 30분을 꼭 a quarter, half로 하거나, past(지난), to 전(前)를 꼭 쓰지 않아도 좋다. 우리말과 같이 간단히 나타내어도 된다.

┌ It is two-fifteen. (2시 15분이다.)
├ It is two-thirty. (2시 30분이다.)
└ It is twelve-forty-five. (12시 45분이다.)

즉, 시간을 말하고 경과된 분(分)을 말하면 된다.

⑥ 다음과 같이 「몇 시 몇 분이 지났다.」「몇 시 몇 분이다.」와 같은 시간의 경과를 나타내지 않는 경우는 「시간 + 분」의 꼴이 자연스럽다.

My lunchtime is twelve thirty.
(나의 점심 시간은 12시 30분이다.)

[2] this day week 내주(또는 지난주의) 오늘 [시제로 판단한다.]

this day month 내달(또는 지난달의)오늘

this time yesterday 어제 이맘 때

this time tomorrow 내일 이맘 때

every other(= every second) 하나 걸러서

every fourth day = every four days 나흘에 한번

Ex) milk deliveries <u>every other</u> day
(하루걸러의 우유 배달)

I go to the dentist's <u>every other</u> day.
(나는 하루걸러 치과에 간다.)

Write on <u>every other</u> line of the paper.
= Leave a line blank between two lines of writing.
(시험지에서 한 줄씩 떼어 쓰세요.)

TEST

1. _____에 알맞은 것을 고르시오.

If he is not in, I'll come _____ day week.

① this ② that ③ next ④ same

2. _____ 에 적당한 말을 써 넣으시오.

If today is March 4, this day _____ will be March 11.

제22장 기타(Miscellany) - (1)

3. 다음 중 밑줄 친 부분과 그 의미가 같은 것을 고르시오.

The doctor visited her every second day.

① two ② other ③ another ④ each

[전문 해석] 그 의사는 이틀에 한 번씩(하루걸러) 그녀를 방문했다.

(정답) 1. ① 2. week 3. ②

[3] 기타 시간에 관계되는 표현들

It must be getting near eleven thirty.
(지금 시각은 틀림없이 11시 30분이 다 되어 갈 겁니다.)

It's getting close to midnight.
(지금 시각은 자정이 가까와져 가고 있습니다.)

It's close to six.
(지금 시각은 6시가 다되어 갑니다.)

Now is exactly thirteen minutes and thirty three seconds past
three o'clock.
(지금 시각은 정확히 3시 13분 33초입니다.)

My watch loses a minute every day.
(제 시계는 매일 1분씩 늦습니다.)

This clock gains a minute every day.
(제 시계는 매일 1분씩 빨라집니다.)

My watch is behind time.
(제 시계는 느립니다.)

cf) behind the times = out of date = old-fashioned = obsolete
(구식의, 시대에 뒤떨어진)

My watch is five minutes slow.

(제 시계는 5분 늦습니다.)

This clock is five minutes <u>fast</u>.
(이 시계는 5분 **빠릅니다**.)

I've set my watch five minutes <u>back [ahead]</u>.
(제 시계를 6분 느리게[더 가게] 맞췄습니다.)

I forgot to <u>bring</u> my watch today.
(오늘은 깜박 잊고 시계를 안차고 왔습니다.)

My watch just has <u>stopped</u>.
(제 시계는 멈췄습니다.)

I <u>set</u> my alarm.
(시계를 지정된 시간에 울리도록 맞춰놓았습니다.)

The alarm went <u>off</u> at 7.
(시계의 경종은 7시에 울렸습니다.)

This clock <u>keeps</u> good time.
(이 시계는 시간이 잘 맞습니다.)

I want to have my watch <u>repaired</u>.
(제 시계를 수리하려고 합니다.)

How much time do we <u>have</u> until one o'clock.
(1시까지는 몇 분이나 남았습니까?)

11 돈을 세는 법

[1] 금액을 나타내는 숫자 읽는 법

$ 25.00 – (정식) twenty five dollars (약식) twenty five

$ 0.25 – (정식) a quarter 혹은 twenty five cents (약식) twenty five

$ 1.25 – (정식) one(a) dollar (and) twenty five cents (약식) one twenty five

$ 125.00 – (정식) one hundreds and twenty five dollars (약식) one twenty five

$ 125.25 – (정식) one hundreds and twenty five dollars and twenty five cents (약식) one twenty five twenty five

☞ 따라서 「twenty five」는 상황에 따라 「25센트」일 수도 있고 「25달러」일 수도 있지만 문맥을 통하여 구분이 가능하다.

[2] 거스름돈(change)을 세는 법

☞ 우리는 보통 거스름돈을 내어줄 때 언제나 [amount received] – [purchase price] = [change:거스름 돈]의 공식을 쓰지만 이때는 customer가 이 암산에 따라서 못하는 경우도 있고 때로는 당돌한 느낌까지 주기 때문에 미국에서는 보통, [purchase price] + [change] = [amount received] 의 공식을 쓴다. 즉, 우선 판 물건을 내놓고 그것에다 거스름돈을 가산해 나간다. 예를 들어 6불 50센트짜리 물건을 사는데 10불짜리를 내놨을 경우, 점원은 우선 "Six-fifty" 하고 그 값을 미리 부른 다음, 거스름 돈 50센트를 놓고 "seven" 그리고 1불짜리를 내놓으며, "eight", 또 1불짜리를 놓고 "nine", 그리고 최후의 1불짜리를 놓고 "ten" 하고 나간다.

12 규격을 말하는 법

[1] 세로 3인치, 가로 5인치의 카드

a card 3 <u>by</u> 5 inches

a card 3 inches <u>in length</u> and 5 inches <u>in width</u>.

[2] 그 책상은 가로가 5피트다.

The desk is five feet in width.

The desk is five feet wide.

[3] 세로 2피트, 가로 1피트

two feet by one(foot)

two feet long and one foot wide.

2 by 1

[4] 그 방은 세로 6미터, 가로 5미터 높이 4미터였다.

The room measured six (meters) by five by four (high).

[5] 그것은 길이 20m, 폭 15m 입니다.

It's 20 meters long (and) 15 meters wide.

It's 15 by 20 (meters).

[6] 그의 키는 5피트 6인치이다.

He's five feet [foot] six.

He's five feet [foot] six inches.

☞ 구어(口語:Spoken English)에서는 feet대신 foot을 쓸 때도 있다. 그러나 「5피트의 나무 (a five-foot tree)」나 「폭 8피트의 길이(an eight-foot wide path)」처럼 foot가 수사와 함께 복합어를 이룰 때는 항상 foot가 된다.

13 소수(Decimal) 읽는 법

① 2.5 : two point [decimal] one five
② 15.15 : fifteen point [decimal] one five
③ 0.24 : nought [zero] point [decimal] two four

  cf) Decimal System 10진법

    Binary System 2진법

14 분수(Fraction) 읽는 법

☞ 분수(分數:Fraction)는 보통 위의 분자(分子)를 기수(基數)로, 아래의 분모(分母)를 서수(序數)로 읽는다.

① 분자가 2이상일 때는 분모의 서수에 −s를 붙인다.
② 분자 . 분모의 단위가 높은 것은 over나 by를 사용한다.
③ 대분수는 and를 넣어서 읽는다.

Ex) 1/2 = a(or one) half. 5/2-five halves.
  1/3 = a(or one) third. 2/3 = two-thirds.
  1/4 = a(or one) quarter(fourth).
  3/4 = three-fourths or three-quarters.
  $9\frac{3}{8}$ = nine and three-eighths.
  123/789 = one hundred (and) twenty-three over(or by) seven hundred (and) eight-nine.

15 가감승제(加減乘除)

① 1 + 2 = 3
One plus two <u>equals</u> three.
One and two <u>is [are]</u> three.
One and two <u>makes [make]</u> three.

② 5 − 2 = 3
Five minus two <u>is equal to</u> three.
Two from five <u>leaves</u> three.

③ 2 × 4 = 8
Two times four <u>is [are]</u> eight.
Two (multiplied) <u>by</u> four <u>is [are]</u> eight.

④ 2 × 0 = 0

| Essential English Grammar | 373

Two multiplied <u>by</u> nought <u>is</u> nought.

⑤ 8 ÷ 2 = 4

Eight <u>divided</u> by two <u>makes</u> four.

Two <u>into</u> eight <u>goes</u> four times.

⑥ (3 + 2$\frac{1}{4}$ − 2.36 × 2) ÷ 5$\frac{1}{3}$

Three plus two and a quarter minus two point three six.

multiplied by two, all divided by five and a third.

 비율(Ratio)

① 7 : 3

the ratio of seven to three

② 3 : 6 = 4 : 8

⌐ Three is to six as four is to eight.
├ The ratio of three to six equals the ratio of four to eight.
└ Three divided by six is equal to four divided by eight.

 온도 읽는 법

① 영상 – above zero ; above freezing ; plus
   영도 – just freezing
   영하 – below zero; below freezing ;minus ;negative(가끔 사용)

   Ex) It's above [just, below] freezing in Seoul.
        (서울의 기온은 영상[영도, 영하]이다.)

② −14° : fourteen degrees below zero⟨freezing⟩
    40° : forty above (zero⟨freezing⟩)
   −17° : seventeen below (zero⟨freezing⟩)

5° : five above (zero〈freezing〉)

③ 섭씨 : C = Centigrade = Celsius

Ex) 영상 10°C : Ten degrees above zero Centigrade
영상 10°F : Ten degrees above zero Fahrenheit
화씨 : F = Fahrenheit
F = 9/5 C + 32
C = 5/9 (F−32)

* 다음 글을 읽고 _____에 들어 갈 말을 고르시오.

The Fahrenheit degree is smaller, being only 5/9 the size of the Centigrade degree. This is the same as saying that the Centigrade degree is larger, being 9/5 the size of the Fahrenheit degree. Thus, readings will show a change of 9 degrees on the Fahrenheit thermometer for every 5 degrees on the Centigrade thermometer. So, to convert from Centigrade to Fahrenheit, first of all, multiply the degrees centigrade by 9/5 to obtain the corresponding span in Fahrenheit degrees. Second, add 32 degrees to obtain the corresponding temperature on the Fahrenheit thermometer. In mathematical language this is _____.

① F = 5/9 C + 32   ② F = 9/5 C + 32
③ C = (F − 32) × 5/9   ④ C = (F + 32) × 9/5

(정답) ②

18 번지수, 빌딩 번호, 호실 번호 읽는 법

① 호실번호

Room 205 : Room two oh five
Room 1035 : room ten thirty-five

② 2012번지 ：twenty twelve

☞ 앞에 number를 붙이지 않으며 2자리씩 끊어 읽는 것이 가장 일반적인 방법이다.

③ 현대 아파트 21동 1403호

Hyundai Apartments building twenty-one,

apartment fourteen oh three.

☞ 이때 「room NO. 1403」이라고는 하지 않는다.

19 전화번호 읽는 법

① 582 - 5311

- five, eight two, five three, double one
- five, eight two, five three, one one

② 633 - 1040

- six three three, one oh, four oh
- six double three, one zero, four zero

③ 633 - 0800

- six, three three, oh, eight hundred
- six, three three, oh eight, double oh

④ 633 - 5000

 six, three three, five thousand

⑤ 777 - 3668

- seven seven seven, three, six, six, eight
- triple seven, three, six, six eight

☞ 이렇게 중간에 끼여 있을 때는 「double six」라고는 잘 읽지 않는다.

⑥ (051) - 72 - 2400

- The area code, zero, five one, (the exchange number) seven two, (the local office number), twenty four hundred
- The area code, zero, five one, telephone number seven two, twenty four hundred

⑦ 대대표 전화 453 – 5311/81, 교환 153번
대대표 전화를 굳이 영어로 옮긴다면 「main switchboard」가 되겠으나
회화를 할 때는 그냥 「Telephones are from 453-5311 to 81, and
extension number is 153」라고 하면 된다.

20 전화와 관련된 표현

[1] May I speak / talk to ~? (~씨 부탁합니다)
☞ 전화로 호출을 부탁할 때의 상투어로서 「I'd like to speak / talk to~」도 잘 사용된다.
더욱 formal한 표현은 「Is this Mr.A's home / residence?(그쪽은 A씨의 댁입니까?)」
인데 이 경우 한국에서는「그쪽」이라고 해도 영어에서는 「Is that~」이라고 하지 않는다.

[2] Who's calling, please? (누구십니까?)
☞ please는 어미를 올려 발음한다. 비서 등이 전화를 받는 경우는 「May I have
your name, please」나 「Who shall I say is calling, please」가 사용된다.

[3] This is ~ speaking. (예, ~입니다만)
☞ 보통 회화에서는 「This is ~」도 생략되어 간단히 「Speaking.」이라고 한다. 「This
is I.」라고는 하지 않고 「This is he [she]」라고 대답한다.

A : Hello.
B : Hello. This is Myung-Hee Park speaking.
A : Oh, hello. Myung-Hee. This is Ranneung.
B : Fine, thank you. How about you?
A : Fine, thanks. I'm calling to ask if you can go to the
    movies with me tonight.
B : Oh, how wonderful ! I'd happy to.

[4] ~ is out. (~는 외출 중입니다)
☞ 이밖에 회사에 걸려 온 전화에 대해 자리에 없는 경우는 「~is not in. (~는 부재중
입니다)」, 「~has just stepped out.(~는 방금 나갔습니다)」, 「~is away from

his desk.(~는 자리에 없습니다)」, 「~hasn't come back yet. (~는 아직 돌아오지 않았습니다)」등이 상황에 따라 사용될 수 있다. 자택의 경우라면 「~is not at home.(~는 부재중입니다)」이 가장 일반적인 표현이다. 각각의 앞에 「I'm sorry」를 붙이면 정중한 표현이 된다.

[5] You have the wrong number. (전화번호가 틀립니다.)

☞ 잘못 걸린 전화에 대한 대답이다. 앞에 「I'm afraid」를 붙이면 좋다.
또한 「You're wrong」「You're mistaken」「Your number is wrong」이라고 말하지 않는 점에 주의해야 한다.
자기가 틀리게 걸었을 때는 I'm sorry.
I think I have the wrong number.
(죄송합니다. 전화가 잘못 걸린 것 같군요)라고 사과한다.

[6] I'd like to place a person-to-person call to Seoul.
(서울에 개인 지정의 전화를 걸고 싶습니다.)

☞ 「A person-to-person call to Seoul, please」라고 해도 통한다. 이것은 특정인하고만 통화하고 싶을 때에 「operator」에게 신청하는 것으로 그 특정인이 부재중일 때는 요금을 지불하지 않는다. 또 번호만 지정한 전화는 「station-to-station call」이고, 요금을 상대가 지불할 전화는 「collect call」이라고 한다.

[7] Please, hold on. (끊지말고 그대로 기다려 주세요.)

☞ hold on (전화를) 끊지 않고 기다리다.
　「Will you hold the line?」도 같이 사용된다.
　반대로 「일단 전화를 끊어 주세요.」는 「Please, hang up.」이라고 한다.
　Ex) Could you <u>hold on</u> a moment and I'll get a pen.
　　　(잠깐만 기다리세요, 펜을 좀 가져올께요.)

　　　Will you <u>hold the line</u>, please. I'll go get him.
　　　(전화 끊지 말고 기다리세요. 제가 가서 그분을 데려 올게요.)

[8] The line's busy. (통화중입니다.)

☞ 큰 회사에 전화를 걸었을 때 「operator」가 이렇게 대답하면 「I'll hold on.(이대로 기다리겠습니다)」이나, 「I'll call (back) later.(다시 걸겠습니다)」라고 말하면 된다.

[9] hang up (전화를 끊다)

  Ex) Excuse me. I have to <u>hang up</u> now.
     (송합니다만, 이제 전화를 끊어야겠습니다.)

[10] Would you care to leave a message?
    (무언가 전할 말이 있습니까?)
    May I take a message?
    (전할 말씀이라도 있습니까?)
    May I leave a message?
    (메모 좀 해주시겠습니까?)
    Would you take a message?
    (전갈 좀 받아주시겠습니까?)

A : May I speak to Miss. Kim please?
B : I'm sorry. She's out on business.
A : May I ask when she's coming back?
B : She won't be back in the office today, I'm afraid.
    <u>May I take a message?</u>
A : Yes, will you tell her to call me first thing in the morning
    tomorrow?
B : Certainly, I will. Thank you for calling.

[11] ⌜ I'm calling from a pay phone.
    ⊢ I'm at a pay phone.
    ⌞ This is a public phone.
    (지금 공중전화에서 거는 겁니다.)

    Is there a pay phone near here?
    (이 근처에 공중전화가 있습니까?)

[12] ⌜ I guess the line are crossed.
    ⌞ Maybe we're connected with another line.
    (전화가 혼선이 됐나 봅니다.)

[13] <u>Your party</u> is on the line. Go ahead please.
   (상대방이 나왔으니 말씀하세요.)
☞ 이때의 「party」는 「사교적인 모임」이란 뜻이 아니고 「(신청자가 통화를 하고자 하는) 상대방」을 의미한다.

[14] Miss Kim, you are wanted on the phone.
   (김양, 전화왔습니다.)
☞ 위 예문은 직역하면 「전화에서 당신이 원해지고 있다.」의 의미이므로 곧 「당신에게 전화가 왔다.」는 뜻이 된다. 만약 전화를 건 사람이 「Miss Lee」라면 「Miss Lee wants you on the phone. (김양으로부터 전화왔습니다.)」가 된다.

[15] ┌ He's taking on another phone.
    └ He's on another line.
     (그분은 지금 다른 전화를 받고 계십니다.)

제23장
Essential English Grammar

기타
(Miscellany) - (2)

01 기식군(氣息群:Breath-Group)

☞ 다음의 경우는 띄어 읽는다.(띄어 읽기)

[1] 주절과 종속절 사이에 끊어 읽는다. (명사절, 형용사절, 부사절)

Ex) I don't know / whether she is dead or not.(명사절)

That he is lazy / is clear.(명사절)

This is the girl / whom I met yesterday.(형용사절)

If it rains tomorrow, / I shall be very glad.(부사절)

[2] 긴 주부(主部)와 동사 사이에 끊어 읽는다.

Ex) The house on the hill / is mine.

[3] 동사와 긴 목적어 사이에 끊어 읽는다.

Ex) The worst thing is / that he never answers our letter.

[4] 동사와 긴 목적어 사이에 끊어 읽는다.

Ex) He visited / some old friends of his.

[5] 부사(부사구) 앞.뒤에서 끊어 읽는다.

Ex) In spite of rain / I went there.

Where did he go / yesterday?

[6] 명사와 동격의 명사절 사이에 끊어 읽는다.

Ex) The news / that she intended to come / gave me much pleasure.

[7] 가주어, 진주어 사이 및 가목적어, 진목적어 사이에 끊어 읽는다.

Ex) It is strange / that he should fail.

I found it hard / to master English in a year or two.

It is difficult for us / to read this book.

[8] 강조어구 뒤에서 끊어 읽는다.

Ex) It is you / who are wrong.

[9] 부르는 말(呼格) 뒤에서 끊어 읽는다.

Ex) John, / where are you going?

[10] 생략된 곳에서 끊어 읽는다.

Ex) To err is human; to forgive / divine.(is가 생략됨)

[11] 인용문 앞.뒤에서 끊어 읽는다. (인용어구가 짧으면 주문으로
계속된다)

Ex) "I know him," / said the boy, / "He is Tom's father,"
They said, "Yes," / and went away.

[12] 인용문 또는 보통문 중간에 있는 said he 혹은 I think와 같
은 것은 앞으로 계속되고 그 다음에 끊어 읽는다.

Ex) "Alas, sir," said the boy, / "my father is dead!"
This letter, I think, / is for you.

[13] 삽입어구는 앞 어구를 붙여 읽는다. (앞 어구가 길 때는 앞.뒤
에 끊어 읽는다)

Ex) London is, as you know, / the capital of England.

※ 위의 형식은 보편적인 형이며 절대성은 없다.

02 구두점 (Punctuation)

[1] 마침표(Period or Full stop / .)

 1. 서술문 · 명령문 끝에 Honesty is the policy. Open the box. Don't
 open the door.
 2. 약자의 끝에 C.O.D. (= the Concise Oxford Dictionary)

[주의] 1. TV처럼 (.) 찍지 않는 경우도 있음.
    2. 영국에서는 Dr (Doctor)처럼 본딧말의 끝자가 있으면 종지부(.)를 생략하
      기도 한다.

3. 서술문의 끝에 약자가 있으면 종지부는 한개만 취한다.

☞ The word plural is abbreviated into pl. (plural이라는 낱말은 pl.이라는 약자로 단축된다)

3. 표제·서명·날짜·주소 등의 끝에

　The story of Hamlet. (햄릿 이야기)　November 1. (11월 1일)

　20 Nakwon-dong, Chongno-gu, Seoul.

4. 로마 숫자의 뒤 . 여러 종류의 소수점으로

　Elizabeth II.　8.30 A.M (오전 8시 30분)

[2] 콤마(Comma / ,)

1. 호격어 : John, tell me the truth. Come in, John.

2. 문법상 같은 관계를 가진 세 개 이상의 어구가 결합 될 때 :

　She showed it to Frank, Tom, and Dick.

☞ and, or 앞에 comma(,)는 생략할 수도 있지만 생략되면 오해되기 쉬운 경우에는 생략하지 않는 것이 좋다.

　She showed it to Frank, Tom and Dick.

3. 동격어 : Milton, the great poet, was blind.

[주의] 1. 동격의 낱말이 서로 밀접하게 결합되어 한 낱말처럼 쓰일 때는 comma를 찍지 않는다. We Koreans (우리 한국 사람들), Alexander the Great(알렉산더 대왕)

　　　2. that로 이끄는 동격절 앞에는 comma를 찍지 않는다.

　　　I know the fact that she is unkind.

4. 공통 관계에 : She has been, and will be, beautiful.

5. 계속적 용법의 관계사 앞에 : I met a boy, who gave me this book.

6. 분사구에 : Night coming on, we started for home.

7. 절이나 however, therefore, moreover, indeed, namely, in short, in fact, too 등이 삽입된 경우 : They haven't arrived. They will, however, come soon.

8. 인용문 앞 또는 뒤에서 : He said, "I like spring."

9. 생략된 곳에 : London is the capital of England ; Paris, of France.

10. 조건 명령의 and나 or앞에 : Study hard, and you will succeed.

11. 문장의 뜻을 명백하게 하기 위해서 (주어가 되는 명사절이 동사로 끝나거나 주어가 길 때) : Who he is, is not known to me.
12. 어순이 바뀐 경우에 : Why he came here, I don't know
13. Yes나 No 또는 감탄사 well, why, oh뒤에
    Can you swim? Yes, I can. No I can't.
    Well, here is your pen. Oh, what shall I do?
14. 이름을 반대 어순으로 쓸 때 또는 이름 다음에 경칭을 쓸 때
    Mill, John Stuart.(존 스튜어트 밀) J. Smith, Esq. (J. 스미드 귀하)
15. 대조적 어구를 들 때에 : It is not a dog, but a cat.
16. 독립구문이나 부사절이 앞에 오는 경우에
    To tell the truth, I don't like her. : If I am allowed, I will
    stay here.
17. 주소 · 날짜에 : 2F, 447-57, Bulkwang-Dong, Eunpyung-
    Gu, Seoul.
18. 천(千) 이상의 숫자는 셋째 자리마다 콤머로 끝난다 : 1,325,566,281
    (단, 연호에는 콤머를 사용하지 않는다 : 1950)
19. 동격의 or 앞에 : botany, or the science of plants

[3] 의문 부호(Question Mark or Interrogation Mark / ?)

1. 직접 의문문 뒤에 : Do you like apples?
   [주의] 의문문 둘 이상이 and로 연결되어 있으면 맨끝에 하나만 붙는다 : Who is he,
   and where does he live?
2. 형식적으로는 평서문이지만 내용상 의문문인 경우
   And then? (그 다음엔?) You are wrong, then? (그러면 당신이 틀렸지?)
3. 문중어구에 의문 · 불확실을 나타낼 때 (괄호에 넣어서 사용) :
   He died in the year of 1959 (?)
4. 한 낱말이라도 의문문이 성립될 때 : What? (무어라고?)
                                    What? (왜 그래?)

[4] 감탄부호(Exclamation Mark / !)

1. 감탄문에 : How happy he looks !
2. 감탄사 다음에 : "Oh !" was all I could say then.

3. 주의를 환기시키는 문장이나 강한 감정을 표시하는 어구나 문장에

[5] 세미콜론(Semicolon / ;)

☞ 세미콜론은 종지부(.)와 콤마(,) 중간 정도의 구둣점 역할을 한다.

1. 중문에서 접속사 대신에 두 절 사이에서 사용한다.

   Ex) Art is long; life is short.(예술은 길고 인생은 짧다.)

2. however, therefore, so, yet 등 접속 부사 앞에 쓴다.

   Ex) It rained hard; therefore he did not go there.

3. Yes(예), 또는 No(아니오) 다음에 오는 대답이 직접적인 것이 아닐 때 쓴다.

   Ex) Did you go to America? (미국에 갔었니?)

       No, I did not go America. (아니, 가지 않았어.)

       No; I went to Africa. (아니, 아프리카에 갔었어.)

4. 중문 다음의 절이 but, as, moreover, thus, therefore, and 등으로 인도될 때에 앞절의 끝에 사용한다.

   Ex) Make the best use of time; for the loss of it can never be regained.

       (시간을 잘 활용하라. 왜냐하면 잃어버린 시간은 결코 되찾을 수 없기 때문이다.)

[6] 콜론 (Colon / :)

1. 세목 또는 보기를 들 때에 (dash(-)와 함께 쓸 때가 많다.)

   I need the following articles; - a pen, a pencil and a knife.

2. 원인·이유·결과·대조 등 나타내는 절 앞에 접속사 대신에

   It is growing dark.: the sun has set.

   (어두워진다. : 왜냐하면 해가 졌기 때문에.)

   Tom likes English: Mary likes French.

3. 대화문에서 발언자와 내용 사이에

   Mary : Do you like coffee? -- Judy: No, I don't

4. 시간을 숫자로 나타내는 경우에 「시간」과 「분」 사이에 (주로 미국에서)

   He missed the 6 : 30 A.M. train. (미국식)

   He missed the 6.30 A.M. train. (영국식)

5. 연설·상업용 편지의 호칭 뒤에 Ladies and Gentlemen: Dear Sir:

6. 격식을 갖춘 동격어구 앞에

He spoke on the subject: "International Trade and the World Market"

7. 저자와 저서 사이에

　　Shakespeare: Caesar (셰익스피어작 시저)

[7] 대쉬 (Dash / −)

1. 이야기의 내용을 갑자기 바꿀 때

　　I will tell you why. − what are you laughing at?

　　(너에게 이유를 말할게. − 무엇이 그렇게 우스우냐?)

2. 삽입 어귀의 전후에 괄호와 같은 뜻으로

　　Tom − your brother − was very kind.

　　(톰은 − 네 동생이지만 − 매우 친절했어.)

3. 주저함이나 문의 중단을 표할 때

　　I−I−won't−shouldn't−die now.

　　(나는−나는−지금 죽지는−아니야 죽어서는 안돼.)

4. 뜻을 강조하기 위하여 앞에 온 같은 어구를 반복할 때

　　I shall never forget you. − never, never!

　　(나는 결코 너를 잊지 않겠어. − 결코, 결단코 !)

5. 총체적인 어구의 앞에

　　Health, friends, position, − all are gone.

　　(건강도, 친구도, 지위도 − 모두 다 사라져 버렸다.)

6. 인용문 뒤에 저자 이름을 나타낼 때

　　The pen is mightier than the sword. − Lytton.

　　(문은 무보다 강하다. − 릿턴경.)

7. 다른 사람의 말을 같은 줄에 쓸 경우에

　　Can you swim well? − No, I can't.

　　(수영 잘 합니까? − 아니오, 못합니다.)

8. 어구·문자·숫자를 생략했을 때, 사람·장소를 말하지 않을 때

　　G−d(=good)　D−m(=demn)

　　In the year 19 −, I went to the city of K −.

　　(19−년에 나는 K−시에 갔다.)

9. 앞에 말한 것을 정정할 때

She is – or was – very kind.
(그녀는 매우 친절하다–아니면 매우 친절했다.)

[8] 하이픈 (Hyphen / –)

1. 복합어 : mother-in-law (장모), well-to-do (부유한)
2. 단어 음절 구별에 : re-turn, foun-da-tion, sit-u-ate
3. 철자는 같아도 뜻이 다른 두 낱말 이상을 구별 할 때
   proverb (속담)   recreation (오락)
   pro-verb (대동사)   re-creation (개조)
4. 연속된 두 개의 모음 철자가 따로 발음될 때 :
   re-exchange (재교환), co-operation (협동)
5. 21에서 99까지 수의 10자리와 1자리 사이에 또 분수에 :
   twenty-one, ninety-nine, two-thirds (2/3)

[9] 어포스트로피 (Apostrophe / ')

1. 명사의 소유격에 : Tom's pen, today's newspaper
2. 문자·숫자·약자의 복수형에 : 3R's, 5's, M.P's
3. 글자나 숫자(연호)를 생략할 때 : I'm(=I am), '77(=1977)

[10] 괄호 (Parenthese, Brackets, and Braces / ( ) [ ] { })

☞ (   ) – Brackets,   [   ] – Parentheses,   {   } – Braces

1. Brackets–(   )
 (1) 삽입문 및 설명절 어구에 : He (My brother) went alone.
 (2) 생략해도 좋은 것에 : Which do you like better, spring or summer?
    I like spring better (than summer).
 (3) 인용문의 출처 표시에 : To be, or not to be: that is the question.
    (Shakespeare: Hamlet III)

2. Parentheses–[   ]
 (1) 생략·정오·비평 따위 삽입에 : She is the girl [whom] I met in
    the park.
 (2) 문장 가운데 주석이나 설명 삽입에 : Who [Tom and I] seldom

go there.

  (3) 발음이나 어원 표시에 : literally [literərli], literary [litəreri]

3. Braces-{   }

  항목을 가로 또는 세로로 묶을 경우에 쓰인다.

       you, your, you

       thou, thy, thee

[11] 인용 부호 (Quotation Mark / " ", ' ')

☞ Donble Quotation Marks " ", Single Quotation Marks ' '

1. 직접화법의 인용 내용 앞 뒤에 : He said, "I am happy."
2. 특히 주의를 환기시키는 부분에 : He calls himself a "hero."
  (그는 자기를 "영웅"이라고 말한다.)
3. 신문·서적·잡지·선박·비행기 이름에, 노래·연설·강의의 제목 등에
    사용 : "Hamlet" was written by Shakespeare.
4. 인용문 속에 다른 인용문이 있으면 Single Quotation Marks(' ')를
    사용 : She exclaimed, "You said, 'Time is money!' "
    ("'시간은 돈이다' 라고 당신이 말했어요"라고 그녀는 외쳤다.)

[요점] 의문 인용문이 문미(文尾)에 올 때 인용부호와 의문부호의 관계
① 주절이 평서문이면 인용부호는 뒤에 온다.

  He said, "Do you like English?"

② 주절이 의문문이면 인용부호는 앞 또는 뒤에 온다.

  ┌ Did she say, "Do you like me"?
  └ Did she say, "Do you like me?"

③ 의문문 가운데 감탄문이 인용되고 문미에 올 때, 감탄부호, 인용부호,
  의문부호 순서이다

  Do you know who it was that said "Death, or Victory!"?
  ("죽음 아니면 승리를"라고 말한 사람이 누구였는지 당신은 아십니까?)

03 부가의문문(Tag-question)

☞ 「부가의문문(Tag-question)」은 단축형을 쓰며, 주어진 글에 부정어가 있다면 「부가의문문」은 긍정문으로, 긍정문은 부정문으로 하고 반드시 시제를 일치시킨다.

[1] 서술문의 부가의문문

Ex) He cannot go, <u>can he</u>? (그가 갈 수 없지요?)

He seldom came here, <u>did he</u>? (그는 여기에 좀처럼 오지 않았지요?)

He rarely used to oversleep, <u>did he</u>? (그는 과거에 좀처럼 자곤 하지는 않았지요?)

☞ 서술문이 There로 시작했을 경우의 부가 의문문에서도 「there」를 쓴다.

There's something to do, <u>isn't there</u>? (할 일이 좀 있지요?)

[2] 명령문의 부가의문문

Ex) Do it at once, <u>will you</u>? (그것을 즉각 하시겠어요?) 〈의뢰〉

Don't open the door, <u>will you</u>?

cf) Have a cup of coffee, <u>won't you</u>? 〈권유〉

[3] Let로 시작하는 간접 명령문인 경우

Ex) Let's go now, <u>shall we</u>?

cf) Let's not go to the party, <u>Ok</u>? / <u>all right</u>?

[4] 부가의문문에서의 부정형

☞ 부가의문문에서의 부정형은 단축형(n't)을 쓰지만, 〈조동사 + 주어 + not〉의 어순을 취하기도 한다.

Ex) He saw this last night, <u>did he not</u>?

cf) ┌ I'm doing it,   <u>ain't I</u>? 〈구어체〉 / <u>am I not</u>?
   └ I'm kind,

[5] Have가 일반 동사인 경우의 부가의문문

☞ Have가 일반동사인 경우의 부가의문문에서는 조동사 「do, does, did」를 이용한다.

Ex) You have two children, <u>don't you</u>?

cf) You have two children, <u>haven't you</u>? 〈영국 영어〉

[6] Have to, used to; had better, would rather가 있을 경우 의 부가의문문

☞ 「Have to, used to; had better, would rather」가 있을 경우의 부가의문문에서

① 「Have to, used to」는 「do」를 이용하며, 「used to」는 「use(d)n' t」 로 할 수도 있다.

② 「had better」는 「hadn' t」로,

③ 「would rather」는 「wouldn' t」로 한다.

Ex) She has to stay home, <u>doesn' t she</u>?

His mother used to visit here, <u>didn' t / use(d)n' t she</u>?

We' d better lock the door, <u>hadn' t we</u>?

You' d rather buy this, <u>wouldn' t you</u>?

[7] 부가의문문을 쓰지 못하는 문장

(1) some, several 등 「긍정의 뜻을 지닌 수량형용사」가 「부정문」에 있을 경우

Ex) Several students didn' t laugh, <u>did they</u>? (X)

John didn' t answer several / some questions, <u>did they</u>? (X)

cf) John hasn' t read <u>any</u> of the books on phrenology, <u>has he</u>? (O)

(존은 골상학에 관한 책을 한 권도 읽지 않았지요?)

(2) 수행동사(Performative Verb)가 포함된 문장의 경우

Ex) I <u>name</u> this ship the 'Hercules,' <u>don' t I</u>? (X)

(나는 이 배를 「헤라클레스 호(號)」라고 명명한다.)

I <u>pronounce</u> you man and wife, <u>don' t I</u>? (X)

(그대들을 부부로 선언하는 바이다.)

☞ 기타 수행동사 : advise, answer, appoint, authorize(인정하다) beg, claim(주
장하다) command, declare(선언하다) demand, grant, implore(애원(탄원)하다)
offer, order, propose, request, say, vow, warn, etc.

(3) 「That-절」이 있을 경우의 부가의문문

「That-절」이 있을 경우의 부가의문문의 주어는 「that-절」속의 주어와 일치시킨다.

① 주절의 주어가 「1인칭」이고 시제가 「현재」가 아니거나, 또는 「It seems to / like ~ that ~, It looks to / like~ that~ 구문」에서의 「to/like 의 목적어」가 「1인칭」이 아니거나 시제가 「현재」가 아니면 「부가의문

문」은 쓰이지 않는다.

Ex) ┌ He doesn't suppose the Yankees will win, <u>will they</u>? (X)
    ├ I didn't suppose the Yankees would win, <u>would they</u>? (X)
    └ I <u>don't</u> suppose the Yankees will win, <u>will they</u>? (O)
      (양키즈가 이길 것 같지 않지요?)

    ┌ It doesn't seem/look to Sally that it's gonna rain, <u>is it</u>? (X)
    └ It doesn't seem/look to me that it's gonna rain, <u>is it</u>? (O)
      (비가 올 것 같지 않지요?) *gonna = going to

② 화자(話者:speaker)가 자기의 주장에 대해 확신을 가질 때는 부가의
   문문을 쓰지 않는다.

   I know that it isn't very important, <u>is it</u>? (X)

cf) ┌ I don't know that it's very important, <u>is it</u>? (O)
    ├ I'm not sure that's sure, <u>is it</u>? (O)
    ├ I can't see that it matters, <u>does it</u>? (O)
    └ I'm not certain that it's the same as the previous one, <u>is it</u>? (O)

[8] 기타 부가 의문문

① Think, believe, suppose, expect, imagine, guess, seem, appear,
   figure(=think) 등의 경우는 that-절의 내용을 강하게 하기 위하여 부
   가의문문을 쓸 수 있다.

   Ex) I think this car needs tune-up, <u>doesn't it</u>?
       (이 차는 엔진 조정을 할 필요가 있을 것 같지요?)
       I suppose the Yankees will lose again this year, <u>won't they</u>?
       (금년에도 다시 양키즈가 질 것 같지요?)

I guess it's a waste of time to read so many comic books, isn't it?
(그렇게 많은 만화책을 읽는 것은 시간낭비인 것 같구나.)

② 장문(長文)일 경우에는 부가의문문은 삽입된다.

   Ex) It's true, <u>isn't it</u>, that you're thinking of giving up your job?
       (직장을 그만둘 생각이라는 것이 사실인가?)

* (1~9) 다음 글을 읽고 빈 칸에 적절한 말을 고르시오.

1. It isn't as nice as it was yesterday, _____?

  ① isn't it   ② doesn't it   ③ does it   ④ is it   ⑤ will it

(정답) ④

2. We've finished this section. Let's read the next, _____?

  ① shall we   ② will we   ③ are we   ④ don't we   ⑤ do we

(정답) ①

3. Let me see the photographs you took last next, _____?

  ① dont' you   ② will you   ③ didn't you   ④ let me   ⑤ do we

(정답) ②

☞ Let~ 로 시작하는 명령문일지라도 「Let's (= Let us)」가 아니고 「Let me」일 경우에는 상대방의 의사를 묻기 때문에 부가의문문은 「will you?」로 한다.

4. "Frank is up late working again."

  "This is the third time week he's had to study late, _____?"

  ① isn't it   ② hasn't he   ③ isn't he   ④ hasn't it   ⑤ is it

(정답) ①

5. "We had to read the first chapter, _____?"

  ① didn't we   ② shouldn't we   ③ don't we

  ④ weren't we   ⑤ won't we

(정답) ①

☞ 「have to」는 조동사 「do」를, 「has to」는 「does」를, 「had to」는 「did」를 사용한다.

6. "You seem to be dissatisfied with your present post. I don't think you judged your ability objectively when you applied for it, _____?"

  ① do I   ② did you   ③ don't I   ④ don't you   ⑤ do you

(정답) ②

☞ 「think」류의 동사의 목적어로 「that절」이 있을 경우, 부가의문문의 주어는
「that절」속의 주어에 일치시킨다.

7. We'd decided to go there with him, _____?
   ① wouldn't we   ② would he   ③ hadn't we   ④ didn't we
   ⑤ did we

(정답) ③

☞ 「had + p.p」에 대한 부가의문문은 조동사 「have」를 사용한다.

8. _____ living in the town now, is there?
   ① There's nobody   ② There're no men
   ③ Isn't there anybody   ④ Aren't there any citizens
   ⑤ Is there anybody

(정답) ①

☞ [전문해석] 이제 읍에는 아무도 살지 않죠?
   부가의문문이 「is there」이므로 「There isn't ~」 문장이 시작된다.
   ①주어(nobody)에 부정어가 포함되어 있다. ② ⇒ There is no man.

(9 - 10) 다음 밑줄 친 곳 중 잘못된 곳을 고르시오?

9. At first sight I can easily imagine that the girl will become a good
       ①   ②   ③   ④

actress, can't I?
    ⑤

(정답) ⑤

☞ that절에서의 주어는 the girl이므로 ⑤의 「can't I?」는 「won't she」로 고쳐 써야
한다.

10. If there were nothing unusual to forward to, one wouldn't want
      ①   ②   ③

to get up in the morning, would they?
  ④   ⑤

04 부가 의문문에 대한 응답으로 안성맞춤인 「That's right」

☞ 「네, 맞았습니다」라고 말하고 싶으면 「That's right」이라고 응답한다. 「That's right」 또는 더 간단하게 「Right」는 한국어의 「맞았습니다」, 「그렇습니다」에 해당하는 말이다. 상당히 광범위하게 사용되는 표현인데, 「All right」가 「좋다」, 「괜찮다」하는 「허가를 포함하는 의미」를 갖고 있는데 반하여, 「That's right」는 「그렇다」, 「맞았다」하고 「상대방말을 그대로 긍정」하는데 쓰여진다. 비슷한 뜻의 「That's correct」보다 폭이 넓으며, 따라서 정식의 장면은 물론 허물없는 사이에서도 사용할 수 있는 편리한 표현이라 하겠다. 이것은 특히 「…이죠?」하는 형식의 「부가의문(附加疑問)에 대한 응답」으로 자주 쓰여진다. 즉 무엇인가를 확인하기 위한 질문에 대한 응수로 적절한 표현이라 하겠다. 예를 들어서, 여행자에게 가장 필수적인 호텔 예약을 확인하는 장면인 다음의 회화를 살펴보자.

Front desk : Good afternoon. May I help you?
Mr. Jones : Yes, my name is Robert Jones, I have a reservation.
Front desk : Mr. Robert Jones. Here we are. That's through
　　　　　　　the 16th, isn't it?
Mr. Jones : <u>That's right.</u>
프론트 : 어서오십시오. 무슨 용건이시죠?
존슨씨 : 내 이름은 로버트 존스인데, 예약을 했는데요.
프론트 : 로버트 존스씨, 네 예약이 되어 있습니다. 16일까지죠?
존스씨 : <u>맞습니다.</u>

☞ 위와 같은 경우 「네」하고 「Yes」를 써도 무방하겠지만, 「Yes」하고 한마디로 끝나는 것 보다는「That's right」하는 것이 상대방 말을 확인하는 기분을 전해준다. 「(That's) right」는 또한 말 맞장구에도 쓰여 진다. 이런 경우에는 「맞았다」, 「옳다」하는 딱딱한 뉘앙스는 없고 다만 대화를 부드럽게 진행시키는 역할만을 하는 것이다.「Uhhuh」나 「Right」를 적당히 섞어서 쓰면 회화는 훨씬 부드럽게 된다.

05   cloth / clothe / clothes / clothing

[1] cloth [klɔ(:)θ, klɑθ] ⓝ 천, 헝겊 (복수형의 발음은 cloths
[klɔðz])
  ① cut one's coat according to one's (분수에 맞는 생활을 하다)
  ② lay the cloth (식탁 준비를 하다)
  ③ remove [draw] the cloth (식사의 뒤를 치우다)

[2] clothe [klouð] ⓥ ~에게 옷을 주다
  ① be clothed in (~을 입고 있다)
  ② clothed in (~에게 의식(衣食)을 대어 주다)
    work to clothe and feed one's wife and family
    (처자에게 의식을 대기 위해 일하다)

[3] clothes [kouz] ⓝ 옷, 의복
  ① a suit of clothes (옷 한 벌)
  ② put on [take off] one's clothes (옷을 입다[벗다])
  ③ Clothes do not make the man.
    (옷이 사람을 만들지 않는다) [옷으로 인품이 바뀌지 않는다]
  ④ Fine clothes make the man. (옷의 날개)

[4] clothing [klouðiŋ] ⓝ 의복, 의류

06   Word Stress(어강세)

☞ 같은 단어라도 액센트의 위치가 달라짐으로서 품사가 달라지는 경우와, 품사가 달라
  지면서 spelling, 발음 및 액센트의 위치가 동시에 변하는 경우에 유의해야 한다. 2
  음절 이상의 영어 단어의 대부분이 제1음절에 강세가 있다. 접두사(Prefix), 접미사
  (Suffix)에는 보통 강세가 없다.(예외도 있음)

[1] Stress 의 이동에 따라 의미가 달라지는 경우

다음의 2음절들은 전강세(前强勢)를 받았을 때는 명사 또는 형용사가
되고 후강세(後强勢)를 받았을 때는 동사가 된다. (명전동후(名前動後))

conflict[kánflikt](충돌; 상충) =⟩ [kənflíkt](모순되다)

content[kántent](내용)   =⟩ [kəntént](만족[시키다])

contract[kántræt](계약)   =⟩ [kəntrǽkt](계약하다)

convert[kánvəːrt](개심자)   =⟩ [kənvəːrt](전환하다)

object[ábdʒikt](물건; 목적)   =⟩ [əbdʒékt](반대하다)

present[préznt](현재의; 선물)   =⟩ [prizént](선사하다)

progress[prágres](전진)   =⟩ [prəgrés](전진하다)

record[rékərd](기록)   =⟩ [rikɔ́ːrd](기록하다)

[2] 주의해야할 파생어(派生語)의 Stress

parent[pɛ́ərənt](어버이)   =⟩ parental[pérentl](어버이의)

satire[sǽtaiər](풍자)   =⟩ satirical[sətirikəl](풍자적인)

compare[kəmpɛ́ər](비교하다)   =⟩ comparable[kampərəbl](비교되는)

photograph[foutəgrǽːf](사진)   =⟩ photography[fətagrɑ́fi](사진술)

photographer[fətágrəfər](사진사)   =⟩ photogenic[fóutədʒénik](사진촬영에 적합한)

habit[hǽbit](습관)   =⟩ habitual[həbitjuəl](습관적인)

memory[méməri](기억)   =⟩ memorial[mimɔ́ːríəl](기념의)

history[hístəri](역사)   =⟩ historical[histərikəl](역사적인)

labor[leíbər](노동)   =⟩ laborious[ləbɔ́ːriəs](힘드는)

luxury[lʌ́kʃəri](호화)   =⟩ luxurious[lʌgʒjuériəs](사치스러운)

miracle[miríəkl] (기적)   =⟩ miraculous[mirǽkjulə́s](기적적인)

error[erər](실수)   =⟩ erroneous[iróunjəs](잘못된)

specify[spésifái](상술(詳述)하다)   =⟩ specific[spisifíc](특유한)

Asia[éiʒə](아시아)   =⟩ Asiatic[áiʒiǽtik](아시아의)

botany[bátəni](식물학)   =⟩ botanical[bətǽnikəl](식물학의)

[3] 강세가 있는 접두사(Prefix)

any - anybody[énibádi], anything[éniθiŋ]

by - bygone[báigón], byname [báineim]

down - downpour[dáunpɔ́ːr], downward[daunwərd]

every - everyone[évriwʌ́n], everything[évriθi]

fore – forefront[fɔ́ːrfrʌ̀nt], forehead[fɔ́ːrid]

mono – monoplane[mɑ́nəplèin], monogram[mɑ́nəgræ̀m]

no – nobody[nóubɑ̀di], nowhere[nóuhwɛ̀ər]

some – omeone[sʌ́mwʌ̀n], sometimes[sʌ́mtáimz]

para – paradise[pǽrədàis], parallel[pǽrəlél]

[4] 강세가 있는 접미사(Suffix)

-ade	parade	lemonade
-ee	examinee	guarantee
-eer	pioneer	engineer
-ese	Chinese	Portuguese
-esque	grotesque	picturesque
-ette	cigarette	gazette
-ere	sincere	revere
-ever	whoever	however
-ier	cavalier	
-ine	machine	routine
-self	himself	ourselves
-oo	bamboo	kangaroo
-oon	balloon	typhoon

[5] 직전에 강세가 있는 어미

(1) -cian, -cial, -geon, -gion, -tial, -tian, -tion 등

　　musician, official, surgeon, region, essential, station

(2) -cient, -iant, -tient, -ety, -ify, -tory, -ity 등

　　efficient, brilliant, patient, society, classify, victory, ability

(3) -ia, -iar, -io, -ior, -ic, -ical, -ics 등

　　Asia, familiar, curio, superior, economic, musical, phonetics

(4) -ican, -itan, -isan, -sor, -tor, -eter, -ular 등

　　American, puritan, artisan, scissor, actor, barometer, popular

(5) -ious, -sive, -tive, -ible, -ish, -ury 등

　　curious, extensive, active, audible, publish, century

(6) -graphy, -logy, -meter, -metry, -omy, -pathy 등

biography, zoology, thermo<u>meter</u>, geo<u>metry</u>, eco<u>nomy</u>, sym<u>pathy</u>
예외) pólitic, Lúnatic, cátholic, aríthmetic, Árabic, rhétoric

[6] 끝에서 세째 음절에 강세가 있는 어미(-ate, -tude, -tute, -ize, -fy, -y 등)

Ex) stlmul<u>ate</u>, atti<u>tude</u>, substi<u>tute</u>, organ<u>ize</u>, satis<u>fy</u>, philos<u>ophy</u>

[7] 첫 음절에 강세가 있는 어미(-ism, -ary, ery, -at 등)

Ex) commun<u>ism</u>, contr<u>ary</u>, dormi<u>tory</u>, rob<u>bery</u>, demo<u>crat</u>
예외) contémporary, recóvery, eleméntary

[8] 강세에 영향을 받지 않는 접두사 (a-, dis-, en-, mis-, re-, un-, with- 등)

Ex) <u>a</u>sleep, <u>dis</u>cover, <u>en</u>able, <u>mis</u>deed, <u>re</u>gard, <u>un</u>happy, <u>with</u>in

[9] 강세에 영향을 받지 않는 접미사(-ed, -er, -est, -ful, -ing, -ly, -ment, -ness, -y 등)

Ex) visit<u>ed</u>, pretti<u>er</u>, prett<u>est</u>, hand<u>ful</u>, begin<u>ning</u>, certain<u>ly</u>, amuse<u>ment</u>, kind<u>ness</u>, beaut<u>y</u>.

[10] 동사·명사가 같은 음절에 강세가 있는 경우(즉 품사 전환에 관계없이 항상 같은 음절에 Accent가 있는 경우)

Ex) benefit, balance, comment, comfort, consent, concern, control, demand, dispute, express, interest, influence, lament, offer, order, quarrel, regret, report, resque, support, suprise, ect.

Phrase Stress(구강세)

1. 「명사 + 명사」: _/_ + ___ school bus, book store
2. 「형용사 + 명사」: ___ + _/_ green house(푸른집), kind girls
3. 「부사 + 형용사」: ___ + _/_ very honest, much better

4. 「부사 + 부사」 : ___ + / just now, very much, too soon
5. 「동사 + 부사」 : ___ + / stand up, come down, come in
6. 「동사 + 전치사」 : / + ___ look at, get to, arrive at
7. 「동사 + 형용사」 : ___ + / look happy, sound good, grow dark
8. 「동사 + 목적어」 : ___ + / buy a car, count chickens
9. 「동명사 + 명사」 : / + ___ smoking room(끽연실), sleeping car(침대차)
10. 「분사 + 명사」 : ___ + / smoking room(연기 나는 방)

08 Sentence Stress(문장 강세)

☞ 문강세(文强勢:Sentence Stress)란 구(句), 절(節), 문장(文章)을 이루고 있는 두개 이상
의 낱말 중에서 어느 한쪽을 더 강하게 발음해야 하는 부분을 말한다. 낱말 자체가 뜻이
있는 것들을 「내용어(內容語:Content Word)」라 하고 낱말 그 자체 하나로서는 특별한
뜻이 없고 문법적인 기능만을 표기하는 것들을 「기능어(機能語:Function Word)」라 한
다. 대체로 「내용어」에는 강세가 있고 「기능어」에는 강세가 없다.

1. 보통 강세가 있는 낱말(Content Word) : 내용어(內容語)
 (1) 명사 : pencil, box, book, car 등
 (2) 형용사 : nice, good, interesting 등
 (3) 부사 : very, much, well 등
 (4) 동사 : grow, go, break, enter, return 등
 (5) 지시대명사 : this, that, these, those 등
 (6) 의문사 : who, which, how, when, why 등

2. 보통 강세가 없는 낱말(Function Word) : 기능어(機能語)
 (1) 관사 : a, an, the 등
 (2) 전치사 : to, in, at, into 등
 (3) 인칭대명사 : I, he, she, it, we, you, they 등
 (4) 소유형용사 : my, his, their 등
 (5) 관계사 : who, which, that 등
 (6) 접속사 : and, or, but, as, if 등

(7) 대명사로 쓰인 one : the red dress and the blue one.

(8) 조동사 : be, have, do, will, shall, can, may, must 등

(9) be 동사

☞ 위의 내용은 대체적인 것을 말할 뿐 절대적인 것은 아니며 강조의
  대상에 따라 강세의 위치가 달라지기도 한다.

 ## 주의해야 할 강세(Stress)

[1] be, have 동사 : 문장에서는 강세가 없지만 문미(文尾)에서는
  강세가 있다.
  He is a soldier. Is he a soldier? Yes, he is.
  He has a nice car. Has he a nice car? Yes, he has.

[2] 도치된 문장의 동사에는 강세가 없다.
  Down came the boy.

[3] 전치사라도 강세를 두는 경우
  ① 문미(文尾)에 올 때 : Where are you from?
  ②「전치사 + 대명사 목적어」가 문미(文尾)에 올 때 : He came with her.
  ③ 대조적으로 쓰일 때 : Is the book on the desk or under the desk?

[4] 반복되는 말에는 강세가 없다.
  Tall boys went there with short boys.

[5]「의문사 + be + 인칭대명사」일 때 be 동사가 강세가 있다.
  How are you? cf) What is this?

[6] 재귀대명사는 강조용법에서만 강세가 있다.
  I went there myself.

[7] 감탄문의 what, such 다음의 형용사에 강세가 있다.

What a <u>pretty</u> doll he has!

I have never seen such a <u>kind</u> man!

[8] 비교급, 최상급의 more, most에는 강세가 없다.

It is more interesting. It is the most interesting of all.

[9] do (동사 강조), very (명사 강조)는 강세가 있다.

I <u>did</u> go there. He is the <u>very</u> man.

[10] 강세의 이동 단독인 경우 뒤에 온 강세가 있는 단어가
부가적 용법의 형용사로 쓰이면 강세가 앞으로 이동한다.

He is a Japańese. ⎯⎯⎯→ He is Jápanese boy.

He is fiftéen. ⎯⎯⎯→ He is fífteen years old.

10 그리스·로마 神과 그 地位

Greek	Roman	Position
1) Zeus	Jupiter	모든 神의 지배자
2) Aphrodite	Venus	美의 女神
3) Apollo	Apollo	태양의 神
4) Ares	Mars	전쟁의 神
5) Artemis	Diana	달의 女神, 出産.사냥의 神
6) Athena	Minerva	지혜.공예.전술의 神
7) Eros	Cupid	사랑의 神
8) Dionysus	Bacchus	술의 神
9) Hermes	Mercury	神들의 사자(死者)
10) Hades	Pluto	저승의 神
11) Poseidon	Neptune	바다의 神

〈태양계 명칭〉

1) 수성 Mercury

2) 금성 Venus

3) 지구 Earth

4) 화성 Mars

5) 소혹성 Asteroid

6) 목성 Jupiter

7) 토성 Saturn

8) 천왕성 Uranus

9) 해왕성 Neptune

10) 명왕성 Pluto

Western Superstion(서양의 미신)

과학 문명이 고도로 발달한 구미 사회에서는 아직도 미신이 남아 있다. 서양의 미신을 살펴보면 다음과 같다.

[1] 말굽 쇠(horseshoe)는 행운의 표시다. 대문 위에 편자를 붙이면 액운을 물리친다는 것이다. 영국에서는 옛부터 말이 행운의 상징으로 여겨져 왔다. 따라서 말굽 쇠를 환자 이불 밑에 깔아 두면 병이 완쾌된다고 믿어 왔다. 말굽 쇠를 주으면 재수가 있다고 생각한다.

[2] 금요일(Friday)은 여러 가지 의미에서 불행한 날로 여기고 있다. 금요일에는 바다에 나가는 것을 꺼리고, 결혼하는 것도 피한다. 그러나 묘한 일은 금요일이 행운의 날이라고 하여 결혼식을 올리는 지방도 있기는 하지만, 시인 Byron이 불길하다고는 생각하면서도 금요일에 그리스를 향하여 항해에 나섰다가 드디어 병으로 사망한 예도 있다. Christ가 처형당한 날이 금요일이며, Adam과 Eve가 하나님의 말씀을 어기고 금단의 열매를, 따먹은 것도 금요일이었다. 그러나 경우에 따라서는 반드시 금요일이 불길한 날만은 아니었다는 예도 있다. 즉 Columbus가 Spain의 Palcos을 출항한 것이 1492년 8월 3일 금요일이요, 미대륙을 발견한 것이 같은 해 10월 12일 금요일이었다. Mayflower호가 최초의 미국 이민들을 태우고 Provincetown항에 도착한 날짜가 1620년 11월 10일로, 역시 금요일, George Washington의 생일이 1732년 2월 22일 금요일이라는 등, 이와 같이 미국에서는 금요일에 오히려 경사스러운 일이 많았다.

[3] 13(thirteen)이라는 숫자가 대개 불행한 것으로 알려져 있는데, 즉 13명이 같이 식사를 하면 그중 한사람이 반드시 죽는다고 믿었다. 따라서 13명이 합석했을 때는 한 사람이 물러나던가, 한 사람이 더 참가하여 14명이 되어야 한다. 미국의 Hotel에서 13호실이 없는 예는 우리나라에서 4호실이 없는 것과 비슷하다. 이러한 미신의 근본은 아마도 Christ가 최후의 만찬을 제자들과 함께 하실 때에, 그 수효가 13명이

였다는 데에서 유래한 것으로 짐작이 간다.

[4] 소금(salt)에 관한 미신은 많다. 식사를 할 때에 소금 그릇을 엎는다던가 소금을 흘리는 것은 불길한 징조로 믿었으며, 또 소금이 쏟아지는 방향에 앉아 있는 사람에게는 불행이 온다고 생각했다. (포도주가 엎질러지는 것도 마찬가지). 이러한 경우 소금 한 줌을 집어 왼쪽 어깨 너머로 던지면 액운을 모면한다는 미신이 있다. 지금도 Roman Catholic에서는 영세할 때 소금을 사용한다. 소금은 sanctify(순결하게 하다)에서, emblem of purity(순결의 상징)로 여기고 있으며 「마태복음」 5장 13절에는 「salt of the earth(이 세상의 소금)」라는 귀절이 있다.

[5] mirror(거울)이 깨지면, 곧 죽음을 알리거나 앞으로 7년간 불행이 닥친다는 것.

[6] 물에 빠진 사람을 건져 주면 불행이 온다. 즉 물귀신에게 사람을 제물로 바치는 것이나 마찬가지인데, 이것을 막으면 액운이 닥친다는 것.

[7] 네잎 클로버(four-leaf clover)를 왼쪽 구두 속에 넣어 두면, 자기의 소원을 성취한다는 것이다. 그러나 다섯 잎 clover는 악운(惡運)의 표시.

[8] 여자의 머리 핀(hair-pin)이 떨어져 있는데, 그 끝이 자기를 향하고 있지 않는 경우에는 그것을 줏어서, 왼쪽 주머니에 넣고 다니면 좋은 친구를 벗으로 삼는다는 미신이 있다.

[9] 개구리를 죽이면 사흘 동안 큰 비가 온다.

[10] 왼쪽 손바닥이 가려우면 선물을 받을 징조.

[11] 갈매기는 선원의 죽은 혼이 따라 다닌다고 하여, 해를 끼치지 않는다.

[12] 배가 항해할 때 바스켓(basket - a shallow wooden box used especially, to carry fuel or ashes)을 잃는다든가, 고양이를 바다에 던

지면 불길하다.

[13] 닭이 밤중에는 물론 오후에 우는 것도 불길한 징조.

[14] 고양이는 액운을 쫓는 동물로 사랑을 받는다. 특히 비행기 조종사는 비행기안에 고양이를 데리고 가면 추락을 방지한다고 믿고 있다.

[15] Zeus(Jupiter)神의 사랑을 받았던 여신 가운데 천벌의 여신 Nemesis 가 있는데, 이 여신은 거만한 자를 꺾고, 불행한 사람을 도와주는 중용 을 지키는 신이기 때문에, 그리스 사람들은 지나친 장담을 한 뒤에, 이 여신의 보복이 두려워 나무로 만든 가구를 만진다거나, 두세 번 두들 기는 미신이 있었다.

Take A Break!   [한국 풍속화 감상 4 – 고드름(Icicle)]

"고드름, 고드름, 수정 고드름, 고드름 따다가 발을 엮어서 각시방 영창에……" 이 동요는 한국의 어린이들에게 인기 있었던 노래의 일부이다. 처마에 길게 얼어붙은 얼음은 추운 겨울철에나 볼 수 있는 즐거운 광경이다.

"Icicle, icicle, chrystal icicle / Picking it, make a blind / Then, hang it on the door of bride's room……." This is part of a song popular among Korean children. A fringe of ice on the eaves is one of the impressive scene to be seen during the cold winter season.

제24장
Essential English Grammar

종합 평가 문제

* (1 - 3) 다음의 긍정문을 <u>부정문</u>으로 고쳐 쓰시오.

1. I want some money.
   (⇒   )

2. He had already come.
   (⇒   )

3. I know, too.
   (⇒   )

* (4 - 8) 다음의 긍정문은 <u>부정문</u>으로, 부정문은 <u>긍정문</u>으로 고쳐 쓰시오.

4. You may swim in this pond.
   (⇒   )

5. You must do your homework.
   (⇒   )

6. He ought to have said so.
   (⇒   )

7. He cannot have arrived there by this time.
   (⇒   )

8. I never see you without thinking of my brother.
   (⇒   )

* (9 - 14) 다음의 전체 부정을 <u>부분 부정</u>으로 바꿀 때 _____에 들어갈
  적당한 말을 쓰시오.

9. ┌ None of us can be a poet.
   └ (   ) of us can not be a poet.

10. ┌ He never tells a lie.
    └ He does (   ) (   ) tell a lie.

11. ┌ I know neither of them.
    └ I don't know (   ) of them.

12. ┌ They are not at all happy.
    └ They are (   ) (   ) happy.

13. ┌ This book is nowhere to be had.
    └ This book is not to be had (   ).

14. ┌ I don't understand any of his speech.

└ don't understand (　) of his speech.

* (15 - 19) 다음 본문을 <u>부정사</u>를 써서 단문으로 전환하시오.

15. They expect that they will succeed.
(⇒ 　　　　　　　　　　　)

16. They expected that he would go.
(⇒ 　　　　　　　　　　　)

17. The teacher ordered that they should not go out of the room.
(⇒ 　　　　　　　　　　　　　　　　)

18. It is requested that visitors should keep off the grass.
(⇒ 　　　　　　　　　　　　　　)

19. It is generally believed that he was honest.
(⇒ 　　　　　　　　　　　　)

* (20 - 26) 다음 복문을 <u>(동)명사</u>를 써서 단문으로 전환하시오.

20. I know that she stays in Seoul.
(⇒ 　　　　　　　　　)

21. He insisted that I should pay the money.
(⇒ 　　　　　　　　　　　　)

22. You may rely upon what I say.
(⇒ 　　　　　　　　　)

23. His success depends upon whether he is diligent.
(⇒ 　　　　　　　　　　　　　)

24. No one can tell when he will arrive.
(⇒ 　　　　　　　　　　　)

25. There is no adequate reason why he should refuse to do it.
(⇒ 　　　　　　　　　　　　　　　)

26. He showed us a picture which he had painted himself.
(⇒ 　　　　　　　　　　　　　　)

* (27 - 32) 다음 복문을 <u>단문</u>으로 고쳐 쓰시오.

27. A man who values his honor will not do such a thing.
(⇒ 　　　　　　　　　　　　　　)

28. The explanation they gave cannot be true.

(⇒   )

29. I should have been glad, if I had met him.

(⇒   )

30. I was very glad when I heard of your success.

(⇒   )

31. She could not see far because her sight was weak.

(⇒   )

32. He has failed though I assisted him.

(⇒   )

* (33 - 55) 다음 글을 지시에 따라 고쳐 쓰시오.

33. It goes without saying that knowledge is power. (to부정사로)

(⇒   )

34. If you take this medicine, you will feel all right. (This medicine을 주어로)

(⇒   )

35. We all consider it wrong to cheat in examinations. (복문으로)

(⇒   )

36. I know him to be an able man. (복문으로)

(⇒   )

37. The problem was too difficult for him to solve. (복문으로)

(⇒   )

38. I should be happy to be of service to you. (복문으로)

(⇒   )

39. It would have done you good to have been there. (복문으로)

(⇒   )

40. I made a promise to assist her. (복문으로)

(⇒   )

41. He denied that he was guilty. (단문으로)

(⇒   )

42. Though it rained, we went on an excursion. (단문으로)

(⇒   )

43. If it had not been for your help, he would have failed in the examination. (단문으로)

  (⇨   )

44. As wisdom increases, our thought acquires a wider scope. (단문으로)

  (⇨   )

45. I do not know the day when he will depart. (단문으로)

  (⇨   )

46. Are you going out when it is raining so heavily? (단문으로)

  (⇨   )

47. He made several efforts, but failed. (부정사를 써서)

  (⇨   )

48. I worked hard but could not carry out my plan. (부정사를 써서)

  (⇨   )

49. Tom did not try to hit me, but threw aside the stick. (단문으로)

  (⇨   )

50. I walked many mules but I did not get tired. (단문으로)

  (⇨   )

51. He not only holds an important office but often writes good novels.
  (단문으로)

  (⇨   )

52. I lost a book, but I have found it. (단문으로)

  (⇨   )

53. She searched for the book, but could not find it. (단문으로)

  (⇨   )

54. We are disappointed, for he has failed in the examination. (단문으로)

  (⇨   )

55. He is strong and he can lift a boy with one arm. (동사 enable을 써서)

  (⇨   )

∗ (56 – 85) 다음 두 문장의 의미가 같아지도록 _____에 적당한 단어를 쓰시오.

56. ┌ He worked hard so that he might not fail.
  └ He worked hard _____ he _____ fail.

57. ┌ It is natural that he should be proud of his son.

  ⌐ He _____ _____ be proud of his son.

58. ⌐ He is very rich, but he is not contented.
  L _____ he is very rich, he is not contented.

59. ⌐ The higher you go up, the rarer becomes the air.
  L _____ you go up, the air becomes rare.

60. ⌐ This is twice as large as that.
  L This is twice the _____ of that.

61. ⌐ He was trusted by his friends as he was honest.
  L _____ _____ made his friends trust him.

62. ⌐ She got angry because they laughed.
  L _____ _____ made her angry.

63. ⌐ He was dismissed because he was idle.
  L _____ _____ caused him to be dismissed.

64. ⌐ Why are you so angry?
  L _____ makes you so angry?

65. ⌐ He derives much pleasure from books.
  L Books _____ him much pleasure.

66. ⌐ I have a good appetite after a short walk.
  L A short walk _____ me a good appetite.

67. ⌐ After half an hour's walk he got to the station.
  L Half an hour's walk _____ him to the station.

68. ⌐ He went to London on business last year.
  L Business _____ him to London last year.

69. ⌐ People can travel through the air by airplane.
  L Airplanes _____ people to travel thorough the air.

70. ⌐ It is likely that he will consent.
  L He is _____ to consent.

71. ⌐ There is no accounting for tastes.
  L It is _____ to account for tastes.

72. ⌐ When I see this picture, I think of my brother's death.
  L This picture _____ me _____ my dead brother.

73. ⌐ I have had my purse stolen.
  L Somebody _____ _____ my purse.

74.
- I was robbed of my purse by the man.
- The man _____ me _____ my purse.

75.
- He took hold of my hand.
- He took me ___ the hand.

76.
- I am familiar with the voice.
- The voice is _____ _____ me.

77.
- Your assistance is the cause of his success.
- He _____ his success ____ your assistance.

78.
- He plays tennis well.
- He is a _____ tennis player.

79.
- He answered me politely.
- He gave me a _____ answer.

80.
- He was so kind as to help me.
- He _____ helped me.

81.
- The question is of great importance.
- The question is _____ _____.

82.
- They live in comfort.
- They live _____.

83.
- He is nothing but a scholar.
- He is _____ a scholar.

84.
- She always complains of her husband's shortcomings.
- She does _____ _____ complain of her husband's shortcomings.

85.
- Would that my son were as wise as you.
- _____ _____ my son were wise as you.

* (86 – 157) 두 문장의 의미가 같아지도록 빈 칸에 적당한 말을 쓰시오.

86. a) Who knows what will happen tomorrow?

   (   ) knows what will happen tomorrow.

   b) Who does not know that the earth is round?

   (   ) knows that the earth is round.

87. a) He is not idle at all.

   He is (   ) (   ) being idle.

   b) There is no rule but has exceptions.

(   ) rule has exceptions.

88. a) Work hard, and you will succeed.

    (   ) you work hard, you will succeed.

  b) Work hard, or you will fail.

    (   ) you do (   ) work hard, you will fail.

89. a) He was ill, and could not attend the meeting.

    (   ) he was ill, and could not attend the meeting.

  b) He went out, but I stayed at home.

    (   ) he went out, but I stayed at home.

90. a) I saw the picture and found it valuable.

    I saw the picture (   ) (   ) it valuable.

  b) He tried, but failed.

    He tried (   ) (   ) fail.

  c) He went abroad, and never returned home.

    He went (   ) (   ) return home.

91. a) He did not go out, but stayed at home.

    He stayed at home (   ) (   ) going out.

  b) He not only wrote a play, but acted a drama himself.

    (   ) writing a play, he acted a drama himself.

92. a) It seems that he is ill.

    He (   ) (   ) be ill.

  b) It seems that he was ill.

    He seems to (   ) (   ) ill.

  c) It was believed that there lived a ghost in the woods.

    A ghost (   ) (   ) (   ) live in the woods.

93. a) It is impossible that she should jump over the fence.

    It is impossible (   ) (   ) (   ) jump over the fence.

  b) It is necessary that the students should attend school.

    It is necessary (   ) the students (   ) should attend school.

94. a) I think that he is honest.

    I think (   ) (   ).

  b) I found that he was sleeping on the sofa.

    I found (   ) (   ) on the sofa.

c) I think that he was seriously ill.

I think ( ) ( ) ( ) ( ) seriously ill.

95. a) I believe that he knows the truth.

I believe ( )( )( ) the truth.

b) I expect that she will come.

I expect ( ) ( ) ( ).

c) All the neighbors supposed that she was a widow.

All the neighbors supposed ( ) ( ) ( ) a widow.

96. a) Tell me what I should do next.

Tell me ( ) ( ) ( ) next.

b) I don't know how I should do it.

I don't know ( ) ( ) ( ) it.

c) Where did he tell you should wait?

Did he tell you ( ) ( ) wait?

97. a) Do you know where he was born?

Do you know the ( ) of his ( )?

b) Tell me how much this watch costs.

Tell me the ( ) of this watch.

c) He is glad that I have succeeded.

He is glad ( ) ( ) ( ).

98. a) The news that he had lived in the jungle for twenty-eight years gave a great shock to the world.

The news ( ) ( ) ( ) lived in the jungle for twenty-eight years gave a great shock to the world.

b) There is no possibility that he will win the prize.

There is no possibility ( ) ( ) ( ) the prize.

c) The report advised him that they had attacked the South.

The report advised him ( ) ( ) attack of the South.

d) They warn us that the task would be difficult.

They warn us ( ) ( ) ( ) of the task.

99. a) He insists that I should do so.

He insists ( ) ( ) ( ) said so.

b) He is sorry that he has said so.

He is sorry (　　) (　　) said so.

c) I am ashamed that I made a mistake.

I am ashamed (　　) (　　) made a mistake.

100. a) He denied that he knew anything about the plan.

He denied (　　　　　　) anything about the plan.

b) Do you mind if I open the window?

Do you mind (　　) (　　) the window?

101. a) That is the way it should be done.

That is the way to (　　) (　　).

b) He was the first man that came.

He was the first man to (　　).

c) It is time the children went to bed.

It is time (　　) (　　) (　　) to go to bed.

102. a) A man who values his honor will not lie.

A man (　　　　　) his honor will not lie.

b) I received letter which was written in French.

I received letter (　　　　　　　) in French.

c) A stone that rolls gathers no moss.

A (　　　) stone gathers no moss.

103. a) This is a question that cannot be answered.

This is an (　　　　　　) question.

b) I wish to secure a prosperity that will last forever.

I wish to secure a (　　　　　) prosperity.

c) This is evidence that cannot be disputed.

This is (　　　) evidence.

104. a) Look at the woman who is holding her baby in her arms.

Look at the woman (　　　　　) her baby in her arms.

b) I did all that I could.

I did all (　　) (　　) power.

c) A student I know has won the prize.

A student (　　) (　　) acquaintance has won the prize.

105. a) This is a composition which he wrote himself.

This is a composition (　　) (　　) (　　) writing.

b) He died in the cave which he had dug himself.

He died in the cave (   ) (   ) (   ) digging.

c) Is this a cabin which they built for themselves.

Is this a cabin (   ) (   ) (   ) building.

106. a) He is working hard so that he may pass the examination.

He is working hard (   ) (   ) to pass the examination.

b) He went to bed early lest he should be taken worse.

He went to bed early (   ) (   ) (   ) to be taken worse.

107. a) This book is so difficult that I cannot understand it.

This book is (   ) difficult for me (   ) understand.

b) He is so tall that he can reach the ceiling.

He is (   ) tall (   ) (   ) reach the ceiling.

He is tall (   ) (   ) reach the ceiling.

108. a) He looked surprised when he saw me dance.

He looked surprised (   ) (   ) me dance.

He looked surprised at (   ) (   ) (   ) my dancing.

b) He was sad when he thought of his future.

He was sad (   ) (   ) of his future.

He was sad at (   ) (   ) of his future.

109. a) If he should heard the news, he would be surprised.

(   ) (   ) would surprise him.

b) As I was ill, I could not go with them.

(   ) prevented me from going with them.

110. a) When he found me by the window, he approached me.

(   ) me by the window, he approached me.

b) As it had rained during the night, the river rose.

(   ) (   ) rained during the night, the river rose.

111. a) As soon as he saw me, he ran away.

(   ) (   ) me, he ran away.

b) No sooner she read the letter than she began to laugh.

(   ) (   ) the letter than she began to laugh.

112. a) When I got to the city, I visited me mayor.

(   ) (   ) to the city, I visited the mayor.

b) Don't be afraid of making mistakes when you speak English.

Don't be afraid of making mistakes (   ) (   ) English.

113. a) Whenever we meet, we quarrel with each other.

We (   ) meet (   ) quarreling with each other.

b) When he comes to up to Seoul, he always call on me.

He (   ) comes to up to Seoul (   ) calling on me.

114. a) Though it rained heavily, he had to go out.

(   ) (   ) (   ) heavy rain, he had to go out.

b) Although he is rich, he is never contented.

(   ) (   ) his riches, he is never contented.

115. a) As the earthquake was severe, a lot of houses were destroyed.

A lot of houses were destroyed (   )(   ) of the severe earthquake.

b) He was punished because he did not tell the truth.

He was punished (   ) not telling the truth.

116. a) If you agree, I should like to do it.

(   ) your agreement I should like to do it.

b) He always gets up when the sun rises.

He always gets up (   ) the sun .

c) As wines become older, they get better.

Wines get better (   ) age.

117. a) Such an idea, fully developed, will result in a great invention.

(   ) (   ) (   ) (   ) developed, such an idea will result in a great invention.

b) Left to himself, he would go his own way.

(   ) he (   ) (   ) (   ) to himself, he would go his own way.

c) The book, written in haste, has only a few mistakes.

(   )(   )(   )(   ) written in haste, the book has only a few mistakes.

118. a) He would be glad to see you.

He would be glad (   ) (   ) (   ) see you.

b) It would have been better for you not to go with them.

It would have been better (   ) (   ) (   ) gone with them.

119. a) A Korean would not so.

( ) he ( ) a Korean, he would not so.

b) A poet could have expressed better.

( ) he ( ) ( ) a poet, he could have expressed better.

120. a) With your help I could finished the work.

( ) ( ) ( ) your help, I could finished the work.

b) With a little more effort he could have passed the examination.

( ) he ( ) ( ) a little more effort he could have passed the examination.

121. a) Without the sun, the earth always be dark.

( ) ( ) ( ) ( ) for the sun, the earth would always be dark.

b) But for your help, he would have been drowned.

( ) ( ) ( ) ( ) ( ) for your help, he would have been drowned.

122. a) I shall have to pay the money.

The money will have to ( ) ( ) by me.

b) They ( ) my money.

My money was stolen.

I ( ) my money ( ).

123. a) They say that he is a great novelist.

It ( ) ( ) ( ) he is a great novelist.

He ( ) ( ) ( ) be a great novelist.

b) People used to think that the earth was flat.

It used to ( ) ( ) that the earth was flat.

( ) ( ) used to ( ) ( ) to be flat.

124. a) Two years have passed since he went to America.

It is two years ( ) he went to America.

b) It has ( ) ( ) ten days.

It is ten days since it began to rain.

125. a) Two months have passed since he fell ill.

( ) has been ill ( ) two months.

b) Ten years have passed since he went aborad.

(   ) has been abroad (   ) ten years.

126. a) She went to Hawaii two years ago.

        Two years (   ) (   ) since she went to Hawaii.

    b) She was sent to hospital two weeks ago.

        She (   ) (   ) in hospital these two weeks.

127. a) He is as clever as any boy in his class.

        He is (   ) (   ) boy in his class.

    b) I had never read such an interesting book as this.

        This is (   ) (   ) interesting book that I have ever read.

128. a) Nothing is more precious than time.

        Nothing is so precious (   ) time.

        Time is (   ) (   ) precious thing of all.

    b) (   ) (   ) boy in the class is $\left[\begin{array}{l}(\ \ ) \text{ than} \\ (\ \ ) \text{ clever as}\end{array}\right]$ Tom.

        Tom is the cleverest boy in the class.

129. a) He is taller than (   ) (   ) boy in the class.

        He is the tallest boy in the class.

        He is the tallest of all the (   ) in the class.

    b) The Nagdong river is longer than any other river in Korea.

        The Nagdong river is (   ) (   ) river in Korea.

        The Nagdong river is the longest of (   ) (   ) (   ) in Korea.

130. a) I have never read a more interesting book than this.

        This is (   ) (   ) interesting book that I have ever read.

    b) I never climbed a higher mountain than this.

        This is (   ) (   ) mountain that I ever climbed.

131. a) This elephant is four times the size of a horse.

        This elephant is four times (   ) large (   ) a horse.

        This elephant is four times (   ) (   ) a horse.

    b) The Han river is five times the length of this river.

        The Han river is five times (   ) long (   ) this river.

        The Han river is five times (   ) (   ) this river.

132. a) He tried, but he failed.

        He tried (   ) (   ) fail.

b) The car was very expensive. I could not buy it.

The car was (　　) expensive for me (　　) buy.

133. a) May I smoke here? Do you mind?

Do you mind (　　　) (　　　) here?

b) His father is famous a painter. He is very proud of it.

He is very proud (　　) his father (　　) a famous painter.

134. a) She was ill. She could not go out.

(　　　　　) ill, she could not go out.

b) We stopped searching. The sun had set.

The sun (　　) (　　) we stopped searching.

c) He was reading a book. I found him.

I found him (　　　　) a book.

135. a) The news cannot be true.

It is (　　) that the news is true.

b) She may succeed.

It is (　　) that she will succeed.

c) She must have been ill.

It is (　　) that she was ill.

d) He need not have hurried.

It was not (　　) for him to hurry, but he did.

136. a) She cooks well.

She is a (　　) (　　).

b) She speaks English very well.

She is a (　　) (　　) of English.

c) She swims well.

She is a (　　) (　　).

d) She has progressed remarkably in learning.

She has made a (　　　) (　　　) in learning.

137. a) It is certain that she said so.

(　　　　　　　) she said so.

b) If we speak briefly, the facts are these.

(　　　) (　　　　　), the facts are these.

138. a) To my great surprise, I found myself lying on the bench.

I was greatly ( ) ( ) find myself lying on the bench.

b) She has failed to my disappointment.

I am ( ) that she has failed.

139. a) Child as he was, he was brave.

( ) he was a child, he was brave.

b) Rich ( ) he is, he works hard.

Though he is rich, he works hard.

c) Hard as he works, he makes little progress in his English.

( ) he works hard, he makes little progress in his English.

140. a) I cannot but admire her.

I cannot help ( ) her.

b) I could not but punish her.

I could not help ( ) her.

141. a) He had the kindness to tell me which was the better of the two.

b) He was kind ( ) to tell me which was the better of the two.

c) He was so kind ( ) ( ) tell me which was the better of the two.

d) He ( ) told me which was the better of the two.

142. a) He is not so much a novelist as a historian.

He is an historian ( ) than a novelist.

He is ( ) of a historian than a novelist.

b) The question is not so much what it is as how it looks.

The question is how it looks ( ) that what it is.

143. a) It is very kind of you to say so.

( ) are very kind ( ) say so.

b) It was stupid of her to do such a thing.

( ) was stupid ( ) do such a thing.

144. a) Let's go swimming, shall we?

( ) about going swimming?

What ( ) going swimming?

What do you say to ( ) swimming?

b) Let's sit down and take a rest, ( ) we?

How ( ) sitting down and taking a rest?

What ( ) sitting down and taking a rest?

What do you ( ) to sitting down and taking a rest?

145. a) He is so honest that he cannot tell a lie.

His ( ) does not allow him to tell a lie.

b) I was disappointed that he refused to help.

His ( ) to help was a disappointment to me.

146. a) There is no knowing what may happen.

It is ( ) to know what may happen.

b) There was no telling how many people would be present.

It was ( ) to tell how many people would be present.

147. This is a picture which she has painted herself.

This is a picture of ( ) ( ) ( ) .

148. a) It is possible that he was rich.

He ( ) ( ) ( ) rich.

b) It is possible that he is rich.

He ( ) ( ) rich.

c) I am sure that he was ill.

He ( ) ( ) ( ) ill.

d) I am sure that he is not rich.

He ( ) ( ) rich.

e) I am sure that he was not rich.

He ( ) ( ) ( ) rich.

f) I am sorry that you did not study hard.

You ( ) ( ) ( ) hard.

g) You paid the money, but it was not necessary.

You ( ) ( ) ( ) ( ) the money.

h) We could buy the car, but we did not.

We ( ) ( ) ( ) the car.

149. He played me a trick.

He played a trick ( ) me.

150. a) I will buy you a watch.

I will buy a watch ( ) you.

b) I asked him a question.

I asked a question ( ) him.

151. a) She is fourteen years old.

 She is ( ) her ( ) teens.

 b) They are over fifty now.

 They are ( ) their ( ) now.

152. a) These shoes are so small that I can't put them on.

 These shoes are ( ) small ( ) me.

 b) The scenery was so beautiful that no words could.

 The scenery was ( ) beautiful ( ) words.

153. He is such an honest man that he can't deceive anybody.

 He is ( ) honest ( ) man that he can't deceive anybody.

154. It takes me two hours to go to Seoul by bus.

 It takes two hours ( ) ( ) to go to Seoul by bus.

155. a) She absented herself from school.

 She was ( ) ( ) school.

 b) The boy lost himself in the wood.

 The boy was ( ) in the wood.

156. a) He was never to see his wife again.

 He was ( ) never to see his wife again.

 b) Not a star was to be seen.

 Not a star ( ) ( ) seen.

 We ( ) ( ) no star.

 c) To hear him talk, you would taken him for an America.

 ( ) you ( ) him talk, you would taken him for an America.

157. a) I hoped to have seen the show.

 I ( ) ( ) to see the show.

 I hoped to see the show, ( ) I couldn't.

 b) He intended to have done so.

 He ( ) ( ) to do so.

 He intended to do so, ( ) he did not.

158. a) They paid no attention to my words.

 ( ) ( ) was paid to my words by them.

 b) We know a man by the company he keeps.

 A man is known ( ) the company he keeps.

c) Do it at once.

(　　) it (　　) done at once.

Take
A
Break!
　[한국 풍속화 감상 5 – 공기놀이(Playing Jackstones)]

아이들이 장난감으로 가지고 노는 다섯 개의 작은 돌이나, 계집아이들이 가지고 노는 콩 따위를 헝겊으로 싼 작은 장난감을 공기라고 한다. 마당에서 시간 가는 줄 모르고 공기놀이를 하는 소녀들, 아기에게 젖을 먹이는 엄마, 빨랫줄에 앉아 짹짹거리는 한 쌍의 제비 등이 농촌의 한가로운 한때를 보여주고 있다. 공기놀이는 한국의 어린 아이들이 가장 좋아한 놀이였다.

A group of young girls is playing jackstones on the ground. The mother nursing her baby and a pair of swallows singing on the clothesline show a scene of leisure time in the countryside. Playing jackstones was a favorite game of Korean children.

[정 답]

1. I don't want any money.

 ☞ not any = no를 쓰면 I want no money.

2. He has not come yet.

3. I do not know, either.

4. You must not swim in this pond.

5. You need not do your home work.

 =You don't have to do your home work.

6. He ought not to have said so.

7. He must have arrived there by this time.

8. Whenever I see you, I think of my brother.

 =When I see you, I always think of my brother.

9. All

10. not always

11. both

12. not always

13. everywhere

14. any

15. They expected to succeed.

16. They expected him to go

17. The teacher ordered them not to go out of the room.

18. Visitors are requested to keep off the grass.

19. He is generally believed to have been honest.

20. I know of her staying in Seoul

21. He insisted on my paying the money.

22. You may rely upon my words.

23. His success depends upon his diligence.

24. No one can tell the time of his arrival

25. There is no adequate reason for his refusing to do it.

26. He showed us a picture of his own painting.

27. An honorable man [혹은 A man of honor] will not do such a thing.

28. Their explanation cannot be true.

29. I should have been glad, if I had met him.

30. I was very glad to hear of your success.

31. She could not see far because her sight was weak.

32. He has failed in spite of my assistance.

33. It is needless to say that knowledge is power.

34. This medicine will make you feel all right.

35. We all consider that it is wrong to cheat in examinations.

36. I know that he is an able man.

37. The problem was so difficult that he could not solve it.

38. I should be happy if I could be of service to you.

39. It would have done you good if you had been there.

40. I made a promise that I would assist her.

41. He denied his guilty.

42. In spite of the rain, we went on an excursion.

43. But for your help, he would have failed in the examination.

44. With increase of wisdom, our thought acquires a wider scope.

45. I do not know the day of his departure.

46. Are you going out in such a heavy rain?

47. He made several efforts only to fail.

48. I worked hard <u>only to fail to carry</u> out my plan.

☞ not의 뜻을 나타내기 위해 fail을 쓴다.

또는 I worked hard <u>never to carry</u> out my plan.

49. Instead of[또는 Without] trying to hit me, Tom threw aside the stick.

50. I walked many miles without getting tired.

51. Besides [또는 In addition to] holding an important office, he often writes good novels.

52. I have found the lost book.

53. She searched for the book in vain.

54. To our disappointment, he had failed in the examination.

55. His strength enables him to lift a boy with one arm.

56. lest, should 57. may, well 58. Though 59. As 60. size

61. His, honesty 62. Their, laughter 63. His idleness 64. What

65. give 66. give 67. brought 68. took 69. enable 70. likely

71. impossible 72. reminds, of 73. has, stolen 74. robbed, of

75. by 76. familiar, to 77. owes, to 78. good 79. polite

80. kindly 81. very, important 82. comfortably 83. only

84. nothing, but 85. I, wish

86.(a) Nobody (b) Everybody 87.(a) far from (b) Every 88. (a) If (b) If, not

89.(a) As (b) Though 90.(a) to find (b) only to (c) never to 91.(a) instead of (b) Besides

92.(a) seems to (b) have been (c) was believed to 93.(a) for her to (b) for, to

94.(a) him honest (b) him sleeping (c) him to have been

95.(a) him to know (b) her to come (c) her to be 96.(a) what to do (b) how to do (c) where to

97.(a) place, birth (b) price (c) of my success

98.(a) of his having (b) of his winning (c) of their (d) of the difficulty

99.(a) on my doing (b) for having (c) of having 100.(a) knowing (b) my opening

101.(a) do it (b) come (c) for the children 102.(a) valuing (b) written (c) rolling

103.(a) unanswerable (b) perpetual(permanent) (c) indisputable 104.(a) holding(with) (b) in my (c) of my 105.(a) of his own (b) of his own (c) of their own 106.(a) in order (so as) (b) so as not (in order not) 107.(a) too, to (b) so, as to, enough to 108.(a) to see, the sight of (b) to think, the thought

109.(a) The news (b) Illness 110.(a) Finding (b) It having 111.(a) On seeing (b) On reading

112.(a) In getting (b) in speaking 113.(a) never, without (b) never, without

114.(a) In spite of (b) With all 115.(a) on account (b) for 116.(a) With (b) with (c) with

117.(a) If it is fully (b) If, should be left (c) Though it has been

118.(a) if he could(should) (b) if you had not 119.(a) If, were (b) If, had been

120.(a) If I had (b) If, had made 121.(a) If it were not (b) If it had not been

122.(a) be paid (b) stole, had, stolen 123.(a) is said that , is said to (b) be thought, The earth, be thought 124.(a) since (b) been raining 125.(a) He, these(for) (b) He, these(for) 126.(a) have passed (b) has been 127.(a) the cleverest (b) the most 128.(a) as, the most (b) No other, cleverer, so

129.(a) any other , boys (b) the longest, all the rivers 130.(a) the most (b) the highest

131.(a) as, as, larger than (b) as, as, longer than 132.(a) only to (b) too, to

133.(a) my smoking (b) of, being 134.(a) Being (b) having set (c) reading

135.(a) impossible (b) probable(possible) (c) certain(sure) (d) necessary

136.(a) good cook (b) good speaker (c) good swimmer (d) remarkable progress

137.(a) Certainly (b) Briefly speaking 138.(a) surprised to (b) disappointed

139.(a) Though (b) as (c) Though 140.(a) admiring (b) punishing 141. enough, as to, kindly

142.(a) rather, more (b) rather 143.(a) You, to (b) She, to

144.(a) How, about, going (b) shall, about, about, say 145.(a) honesty (b) refusal

146.(a) impossible (b) impossible 147. her own painting

148.(a) may have been (b) may be (c) must have been (d) cannot be (e) cannot have been

(f) should have studied (g) need not have paid (h) could have bought

149. on 150.(a) for (b) of

151. (a) in, early (b) in, fifties 152.(a) too, for (b) too, for 153. so, a 154. for me

155. (a) absent from (b) lost 156. (a) destined(doomed) (b) could be, could see (c) If, heard

157.(a) had hoped, but (b) had intended, but 158. (a) No attention (b) by (c) let, be

◆ 21세기 영어교육연구회 지도 교수 및 연구 책임 집필위원 ◆

■ 지도교수 ■

고연희 교수님 (한국관광대학교)
김경보 교수님 (University of Kentucky)
문경환 교수님 (연세대학교)
박순옥 교수님 (고려대학교)
박주은 교수님 (신구대학교)
양윤국 교수님 (상명대학교)
이후지 교수님 (상명대학교)
전은실 교수님 (서울시립대학교)
조순정 교수님 (서울시립대학교)
채서영 교수님 (서강대학교 / 美 피츠버그대 연구 교수)

■ 연구 책임 집필위원 ■

Maria V. Sun (필리핀 University of the Philippines)
Rebecca Bishopp (호주 Griffith University)
David S. Ingels (영국 University of Surrey)
Lyrma R. Ingels (영국 University of Surrey)
Kathryn W. Sulloway (미국 University of Georgia)
Jonathan NG (말레이시아 Jonathan NG Publishers Agency)
Winnie Sammy(홍콩 香港中文大學校)

강기석 선생님 (중앙학원)
강보배 선생님 (영훈중학교)
강영회 선생님 (인천 광성고등학교)
강원희 선생님 (수도여자고등학교)
강정숙 선생님 (부천도당고등학교)
계성환 선생님 (경복여자고등학교)
고광만 선생님 (대광고등학교)
고금석 교수님 (그리스도 신학대학교)
고연희 교수님 (한국관광대학교)
권용경 선생님 (신용산초등학교)
길현주 선생님 (선일여자고등학교)

428

김규선 선생님 (숙명여자고등학교)
김기수 선생님 (경희고등학교)
김남희 선생님 (서울시립대학교)
김대수 선생님 (스탬포드 칼리지)
김병국 선생님 (대일외국어고등학교)
김병호 선생님 (선덕고등학교)
김봉기 선생님 (안산 단원고등학교)
김성범 선생님 (의왕 우성고등학교)
김성환 선생님 (개포고등학교)
김숙애 선생님 (숭례초등학교)
김영돈 선생님 (선일여자상업고등학교)
김재규 선생님 (아산고등학교)
김정겸 선생님 (교연학원)
김정대 선생님 (용인 남사초등학교)
김정운 교수님 (인하대학교)
김정희 선생님 (서울 대성고등학교)
김제옥 선생님 (신용산초등학교)
김종수 선생님 (부산여자고등학교)
김주애 선생님 (서울 대성고등학교)
김지미 선생님 (원당중학교)
김창환 선생님 (인천 동산고등학교)
김태호 선생님 (스탬포드 칼리지)
김향숙 선생님 (광영여자고등학교)
김현숙 선생님 (시사학원)
김현진 선생님 (진명여자고등학교)
김현희 선생님 (아세아고등학교)
김향숙 선생님 (광영여고등학교)
김형석 선생님(서울 서정초등학교)
나경원 선생님 (민병철 어학원)
남헌기 선생님 (한서전문학교 학장)
노강우 선생님 (성동고등학교)
노경희 선생님 (화원중학교)
노순남 선생님 (홍파초등학교)
노재석 선생님 (서울여자고등학교)
도남희 선생님 (일산정보산업고등학교)
류창열 선생님 (대구 계성고등학교)
류혜경 선생님 (신용산초등학교)

박경순 선생님 (상현중학교)
박경희 선생님 (봉림중학교)
박광노 선생님 (인천 계산초등학교)
박명희 선생님 (스탬포드 칼리지)
박석순 선생님 (문산중학교)
박은경 선생님 (미국 콜럼비아대학교)
박차랑 선생님 (오류여자중학교)
배영식 선생님 (스탬포드 칼리지)
배중현 선생님 (낙생고등학교)
변마섭 선생님 (인천 송도여자고등학교)
서연임 선생님 (서울 구일초등학교)
서연화 선생님 (충암고등학교)
송상현 선생님 (주한 호주대사관)
송영신 선생님 (예일여자고등학교)
송정선 선생님 (혜화여자고등학교)
신영자 선생님 (화곡중학교)
신춘남 선생님 (관악고등학교)
신현숙 선생님 (삼성고등학교)
심미라 선생님 (스탬포드 칼리지)
안경옥 선생님 (영동여자고등학교)
안광언 선생님 (인천 문일고등학교)
안순철 선생님 (일산공업고등학교)
안용균 선생님 (인천 숭덕여자고등학교)
연남수 선생님 (숭실고등학교)
오병갑 선생님 (오산고등학교)
오세종 선생님 (인천 작전여자고등학교)
오은주 선생님 (덕수종합상업고등학교)
유경희 선생님 (동일여자전산디자인고등학교)
유선종 선생님 (양동중학교)
윤선애 선생님 (양동중학교)
윤의선 선생님 (예일여자고등학교)
윤종은 선생님 (예일여자고등학교)
윤현주 선생님 (동일여자고등학교)
이광식 선생님 (충암초등학교)
이달수 선생님 (충주 봉명중학교)
이명선 선생님 (부천 원미고등학교)
이미애 선생님 (진선여자고등학교)

이상규 선생님 (명덕고등학교)
이상칠 선생님 (광양고등학교)
이선희 선생님 (광신고등학교)
이예진 선생님 (진선여자고등학교)
이웅한 선생님 (경북 문경시 화령고등학교)
이은재 선생님 (정상외국어학원)
이인숙 선생님 (서울 문창초등학교)
이재운 선생님 (서초고등학교)
이정화 선생님 (종로외국어학원)
이제원 선생님 (충북 청원군 청석고등학교)
이종혜 선생님 (동일여자고등학교)
이지선 선생님 (前 대성중학교)
이진영 선생님 (대구 달성고등학교)
이현용 선생님 (충암초등학교)
이현정 선생님 (스탬포드 칼리지)
이혜진 선생님 (동서대학교)
이화정 선생님 (한국정신문화연구원)
임병기 선생님 (숭실고등학교)
임정열 선생님 (여의도초등학교)
임혜란 선생님 (강남중학교)
임호수란 선생님 (선일여자상업고등학교)
장경원 선생님 (광문고등학교)
장계화 선생님 (불곡고등학교)
장영배 선생님 (서울 법성고등학교)
장용환 선생님 ((주)플러스원)
장현용 선생님 (양정고등학교)
전성호 선생님 (영락고등학교)
전수진 선생님 (서울 신중초등학교)
정광연 선생님 (군포중학교)
정승남 선생님 (서울 대성고등학교)
정운철 선생님 (낙생고등학교)
정 윤 선생님 (삼성고등학교)
정재은 선생님 (명성여자고등학교)
조선영 선생님 (장성중학교)
조순정 교수님 (서울시립대학교)
조영순 선생님 (온수고등학교)
조영준 선생님 (경문고등학교)

조현왕 선생님 (충남 서산 서령고등학교)

조혜숙 선생님 (여의도고등학교)

진명희 선생님 (이수중학교)

최경희 선생님 (염리초등학교)

최경희 선생님 (서울 우신초등학교)

최규섭 선생님 (대일고등학교)

최도현 선생님 (몬테소리교육원원장)

최등자 선생님 (상현중학교)

최영중 선생님 (충암고등학교)

최장용 선생님 (신일중학교)

최철순 선생님 (경동고등학교)

최치범 선생님 (인천 정석고등학교)

최혜정 선생님 (건대부속고등학교)

하진호 선생님 (세화여자고등학교)

한기남 선생님 (역삼초등학교)

한문희 선생님 (장평중학교)

한보형 선생님 (상명여자중학교)

한봉현 선생님 (울산 무거초등학교)

한주상 선생님 (대일고등학교)

허예진 선생님 (인헌중학교)

홍경옥 선생님 (숙명여자대학교)

홍성건 선생님 (수원 수원공업고등학교)

홍연실 선생님 (서울 대성고등학교)

홍주희 선생님 (주한 호주대사관)

황윤식 선생님 (휘여자고등학교)

황인경 교수님 (부천대학교)